Herb Gardening
FOR
DUMMIES®
2ND EDITION

by Karan Davis Cutler, Kathleen Fisher, Suzanne DeJohn, & the Editors of the National Gardening Association

WILEY

Wiley Publishing, Inc.

Herb Gardening For Dummies® 2nd Edition
Published by
Wiley Publishing, Inc.
111 River St.
Hoboken, NJ 07030-5774
www.wiley.com

WILEY

About the Authors

Karan Davis Cutler: A former magazine editor and newspaper columnist, Karan Davis Cutler is the author of seven other garden books. She publishes regularly in horticultural magazines and is an eight-time winner of the Quill & Trowel Award from the Garden Writers Association of America.

Kathleen Fisher: Kathleen Fisher was an editor of *The American Gardener,* published by the American Horticultural Society, and a longtime newspaper reporter and magazine editor. The author of several books and many articles, she died in May 2005.

Suzanne DeJohn: A writer and horticulturist at the National Gardening Association for 14 years, Suzanne now writes, gardens, and runs a pet-friendly B&B in northern Vermont.

The National Gardening Association (NGA) is committed to sustaining and renewing the fundamental links between people, plants, and the Earth. Founded in 1972 (as "Gardens for All") to spearhead the community garden movement, today's NGA promotes environmental responsibility, advances multidisciplinary learning and scientific literacy, and creates partnerships that restore and enhance communities.

NGA is best known for its garden-based curricula, educational journals, international initiatives, and several youth garden grant programs. Together these reach more than 300,000 children nationwide each year. NGA's Web sites, one for home gardeners and another for those who garden with kids, build community and offer a wealth of custom content.

For more information about the National Gardening Association, write to 1100 Dorset St., South Burlington, VT 05403, or visit the Web site at www. garden.org or www.kidsgardening.org.

Dedication

To Kathy Fisher, who was bright, capable, and enormous fun — and who died far too young. And to our mothers and fathers, who encouraged our interests in plants and in words.

Authors' Acknowledgments

We've depended greatly on the kindness of many (herb-growing) strangers — and friends. For specific help, we are indebted to Gwen Barclay, Hank Becker, Kathy Bond Borie, Rosalind Creasy, Barbara Ellis, David Ellis, Donald M. Maynard, Patsy Jamieson, Susan Romanoff, and Holly Shimizu.

Publisher's Acknowledgments

We're proud of this book; please send us your comments at http://dummies.custhelp.com. For other comments, please contact our Customer Care Department within the U.S. at 877-762-2974, outside the U.S. at 317-572-3993, or fax 317-572-4002.

Some of the people who helped bring this book to market include the following:

Acquisitions, Editorial, and Media Development

Project Editors: Kelly Ewing, Natalie Harris

Acquisitions Editor: Stacy Kennedy

Copy Editors: Christine Pingleton, Susan Hobbs

Assistant Editor: David Lutton

General Reviewer: Cathy Wilkinson Barash

Senior Editorial Manager: Jennifer Ehrlich

Editorial Supervisor and Reprint Editor: Carmen Krikorian

Editorial Assistant: Jennette ElNaggar

Art Coordinator: Alicia B. South

Cover Photos: © iStockphoto.com / kkgas

Cartoons: Rich Tennant (www.the5thwave.com)

Composition Services

Project Coordinator: Kristie Rees

Layout and Graphics: Claudia Bell, Carl Byers

Proofreader: Laura Bowman

Indexer: Dakota Indexing

Illustrator: D.D. Dowden

Special Art: Color photos by Cathy Wilkinson-Barash

Publishing and Editorial for Consumer Dummies

Diane Graves Steele, Vice President and Publisher, Consumer Dummies

Kristin Ferguson-Wagstaffe, Product Development Director, Consumer Dummies

Ensley Eikenburg, Associate Publisher, Travel

Kelly Regan, Editorial Director, Travel

Publishing for Technology Dummies

Andy Cummings, Vice President and Publisher, Dummies Technology/General User

Composition Services

Debbie Stailey, Director of Composition Services

Contents at a Glance

Table of Contents

Introduction

You've probably already decided that you want to grow herbs, so we'll keep this introduction short and sweet so that you can dive right into the more important and exciting stuff. But just in case you need a little more convincing, here are a few compelling reasons to try your hand at growing herbs:

- ✔ **Herbs are versatile.** As a group, herbs are both ornamental and practical, beautiful and useful. Most are fragrant, many taste good, and some are highly nutritious. Plus, they're just plain interesting — many have colorful names and equally colorful lore associated with them.

- ✔ **You get the freshest harvest.** There's a big difference between herbs plucked fresh from the garden and the dried herbs sitting for who knows how long on the grocery store shelf.

- ✔ **You can control how they're grown and stored.** If you want herbs that haven't been sprayed with synthetic pesticides or irradiated after they're dried, then you have two choices: Buy expensive organic herbs (if you can find them) or grow them yourself.

- ✔ **The variety is almost endless.** You've seen peppermint and thyme in the dried herb section of the supermarket, and perhaps you've even seen them fresh in the produce aisle. But have you ever seen chocolate mint or lemon thyme? Or horehound, hyssop, or lemon balm? Probably not. For anything out of the ordinary, you'll have to grow it yourself.

About This Book

We cover a lot of ground in this book, from preparing soil to choosing herbs to using the harvest in a variety of ways. You can access the information in whatever way suits you — you can read the book from cover to cover, refer to selected chapters as you need them, flip through pages to browse the contents, or use the detailed table of contents and index to home in on specific information. Because you may not read the book straight through, each chapter includes the background information you need to understand the topic at hand.

Conventions Used in This Book

Although we keep garden jargon to a minimum in this book, we do use some garden shorthand. To help you navigate, here's a list of some of the conventions we use:

- When we refer to a plant's hardiness — a plant's ability to survive extreme winter weather — we're using the U.S. Department of Agriculture's Plant Hardiness Zone Map. You can view the zone map in Chapter 3.

- All temperatures are given in degrees Fahrenheit.

- In general, when we refer to a plant we use the most common of the common names, followed by the botanical name in italics.

- All Web addresses appear in monofont, as in www.dummies.com.

What You're Not to Read

We understand that readers are in a hurry and just want the nuts and bolts on a subject. If you find yourself in that boat, feel free to skip over sections in sidebars. We think this information is interesting or useful (or it wouldn't be in the book), but it's not critical to the topic at hand.

Foolish Assumptions

We've crammed much of what we know about growing herbs between these yellow covers. We wrote each chapter primarily for beginners. At the same time, we hope that what we have to say also interests intermediate and even experienced herb gardeners.

How This Book Is Organized

This book is divided into five parts, starting with background information, and then leading you step-by-step through the process of growing, harvesting, and using herbs. You can also find an encyclopedia of herbs in the appendix.

Part 1: Herb Basics

This part covers some background information on growing herbs, how herbs have been used throughout history, and some basic botany principles.

Part II: Deciding How and What to Grow

Before you sow your first seed or set out your first transplant, you'll want to evaluate the growing conditions in your garden. This part shows you how to do so. And even the most spontaneous gardener benefits from have a basic garden plan, so we get you started on that aspect, too.

Part III: Getting Down to Earth

It's time for the nitty-gritty of herb gardening. In this part, we demystify soil so that you know what you're digging in and how to improve it. Then we look at techniques for planting and caring for herbs, as well as dealing with pest problems.

Part IV: Cut and Dried: Handling the Herbal Bounty

For some gardeners, gathering and using herbs are the fun parts. (It's _all_ fun for us — yes, even the weeding.) This part is all about harvesting herbs, preserving them, and using them in all sorts of ways, in the kitchen, home, medicine chest, and more.

Part V: The Part of Tens

A side benefit of herb growing (or perhaps the main benefit for some people) is the array of gifts you can make from what you've grown. In this part, we suggest ten great gift ideas. And if you can't decide which of the dozens of herbs to try, you can find lists for different garden situations, culinary uses, and other ways to help you choose.

Appendix: An Encyclopedia of Herbs

If you have a question about a particular herb, turn to this appendix. Arranged alphabetically by common name, the encyclopedia includes specific information about how to plant, grow, preserve, and use individual herbs.

Icons Used in This Book

This book uses a variety of icons to highlight really helpful tips, common pitfalls, and other useful information. Here's what they mean:

This icon flags special techniques and helpful shortcuts.

This icon warns you of potential trouble — be it herbs that are dangerous to you or things that are dangerous to your herbs.

This icon highlights important pieces of information that you'll want to keep in mind as you garden.

You don't have to read this information to understand the topic at hand. But if you're interested in the more technical side of herbs or simply want extra detail, you may want to.

Where to Go from Here

This book is organized so that you can jump into any chapter that grabs your attention. If you're an experienced gardener who wants to add herbs to your plantings, consider skipping over some of the introductory material in Part I and go right to Part II. Because healthy soil plays such an important role in successful gardening, we hope you'll find time to read through Chapter 7. If your garden is up and growing and you're looking for ways to manage pests, refer to Chapter 10. You can read the other parts of the book after your pest problems are under control.

One of the great things about growing herbs — and about gardening in general — is that there's always more to discover and new plants and techniques to try. We hope this book is helpful to you as you explore the wonderful world of herbs.

Part I
Herb Basics

The 5th Wave By Rich Tennant

"It's an herb garden I started just after Ted and I were married. There's some Listenup, Errandthyme, and Lightmyfire."

In this part . . .

Whether you're hoping to grow a basil plant or two to spice up your frozen pizza or you envision yourself tending row after row of medicinal and culinary herbs (or your herb-growing goals fall somewhere in between), you'll be more successful if you understand some of the basics of herb gardening before you get started.

In Part I, we open the door to the fascinating and sometimes zany realm of herbs. We touch on some of the reasons gardeners choose to grow herbs and survey the variety of roles herbs can play in the kitchen, medicine chest, and elsewhere in daily life. We delve into a bit of botany, including some must-have information on common and botanical names. And finally, we offer some thoughts about herbs you may want to avoid.

Along the way, you discover some of the magical powers attributed to specific herbs. For example, did you know that you should drink horehound tea, hot from the fire, if you're poisoned by your stepmother? And if you place a sprig of rosemary under your bed, "Thou shalt be delivered of all evil dreams."

Chapter 1

Why Grow Herbs?

Gardeners love kindred souls, and if you decide to grow herbs, you'll be in the company of plenty of kindred souls, both in the present and from times past.

Even before recorded history, herbs were the sources of countless culinary, medicinal, and craft materials. Historically, growing herbs wasn't a hobby; it was necessary for survival. Then, during the last half century or so, chemists began developing synthetic forms of aromas, flavors, medicines, and dyes that formerly had been extracted from herbs. (Notice how often artificial flavors and colors appear in the ingredients lists on packaged foods.) Because it was cheaper to make these imitations in a lab than it was to grow and extract the real thing, herb gardening fell out of favor to some degree. Now that the "better living through chemistry" heyday is over, there's renewed interest in getting back to natural sources of the stuff we ingest and otherwise use in our daily lives. And herb gardening is experiencing a renaissance.

This chapter is a potpourri of herb information — our effort to introduce you to the subject, including some of its historical and entertaining aspects, and to inspire you to join the legions of herb gardeners, past, present, and future.

What Makes an Herb an Herb?

Before we talk about growing herbs, it's only fitting to define the meaning of the word *herb*. (We pronounce it "erb" with a silent "h." If you want to sound British, pronounce the "h," as in the name Herb.) What, exactly, is an herb? Different resources define the word in different ways, depending upon their frame of reference.

A biologist might use the term *herb* as shorthand for *herbaceous plant* — a plant that forms a soft, tender stem rather than a woody stem. However, that definition leaves out many plants that are typically considered herbs, including rosemary, a charter member of the culinary herb hall of fame. And it includes plants like daffodils, which aren't on anyone's herb list.

Some *ethnobotanists* (people who study plants in the context of how they're used by different social groups) might define herbs as "useful plants," but hundreds of plants are useful, such as corn and oats, that few of us would call herbs. Others define herbs as "plants grown for medicinal qualities and for seasoning foods," but that definition leaves out dye plants, plants used in rituals, and those used for making cosmetics, crafts, and more.

The Herb Society of America (HSA) follows the "big-tent" philosophy and defines herbs as plants valued for their "flavor, fragrance, medicinal and healthful qualities, economic and industrial uses, pesticide properties, and coloring materials." If it's good enough for the HSA, it's good enough — and broad enough — for us. So if you've planted something that tastes or smells good (or bad), cures what ails you, or can be used in some way, feel free to call it an herb. You won't get an argument from us.

As for this book, we focus on some of the most common herbs that are popular for their flavor, their medicinal qualities, and other purposes. Most of their names will be familiar, even if you haven't sown a single seed.

Seeing Why and Where to Grow Herbs

If you garden at all, you've probably grown some herbs, even if you weren't aware of it. If you have bee balm, lavender, roses, or sage in your ornamental beds, you're growing herbs. Ditto if you tuck in some basil, fennel, or garlic among your edibles. But if you need more convincing to add herbs to your garden plant palette, here are a few reasons to give them a try:

- **Herbs are versatile.** They're pretty, smell nice, are useful, or all of the above.
- **Many herbs are easy to grow.** Annual herbs like basil, cilantro, and nasturtium are among the most reliable plants, even for beginner gardeners.
- **They benefit other plants.** Even if you don't plan to harvest and use the herbs directly, you'll enjoy the way some herbs repel pests and attract beneficial insects.
- **Herbs are great conversation starters.** Once you know a bit of lore about the plants you're growing, you can entertain garden visitors with their historical significance or fun factoids.
- **They'll kick up the flavor of your culinary creations.** Fresh rosemary, thyme, or tarragon can turn an everyday dish into a gourmet delight.

> ✔ **You'll save money.** If you've ever looked at herbs in the supermarket, you've probably noticed two things about them: They usually appear wilted or shriveled, and they're very expensive. If you grow your own herbs, you'll have access to the freshest herbs possible — clipped right before you need them — for a fraction of the price.

Herbs in your garden

You don't need a special herb garden to grow herbs. Most herbs are very companionable and happily share garden space with more flamboyant ornamentals or more familiar edibles. (A notable few, described in Chapter 2, are decidedly invasive and should be avoided or grown in a confined area.) For ideas on designing your herb garden, as well as incorporating herbs into your existing beds, flip to Chapter 4.

Herbs in containers

Even if you don't have a backyard garden, you can still grow herbs. Most herbs readily adapt to growing in containers, and some can even be grown on a sunny windowsill. And even if you have a big yard, you may want to grow some of your favorite culinary herbs in pots just steps away from the kitchen for easy harvesting. Find out more about growing herbs in containers in Chapter 6.

Considering Culinary Herbs

Before the advent of refrigeration, herbs with antibacterial properties, including garlic, oregano, and thyme, were enlisted to help preserve foods that had to be stored for use during times of scarcity, such as in midwinter when fresh foods were hard to come by. These and other herbs and spices with strong flavors and aromas were also used to mask the tastes and smells of foods that were beginning to go rancid, making them more palatable.

Now that we can control the temperature in our refrigerator with the turn of a dial, most of us enjoy herbs for the way they enhance the flavor and coloring of food and drink. Most recipes contain one or more ingredients purely for aesthetics — better taste, more attractive presentation. What would pickles be without dill, or pesto without basil?

Purists use the word *herb* to refer to plants grown for their leaves and stems; *spices* are those cultivated for their flowers, seeds, bark, wood, resin, and roots. You also may come across the word *potherb*. That's an old term that refers to vegetables and herbs used in salads, soups, and stews. For our purposes, *spices* are culinary herbs.

Upping your nutrition quota

If aesthetics aren't a good enough reason to grow herbs, consider the fact that many herbs are good for you, too. According to the U.S. Department of Agriculture (USDA), a teaspoon of dill seed contains 32 milligrams of calcium; a teaspoon of ground basil contains 6 milligrams of magnesium.

But when it comes to nutrients, the herbal champ is the chili pepper: One teaspoon of chili powder contains potassium, sodium, ascorbic acid (vitamin C), niacin, and vitamin A. (However, if you decide to substitute chili powder for your multivitamin, we recommend taking each teaspoon with a gallon of milk to offset the heat of the chili.)

A few culinary herbs have recently made the news because of their antioxidant levels. *Antioxidants* are chemicals contained in plants that are thought to play a role in preventing some forms of cancer, as well as in helping to slow the aging process. In one study researchers tested the antioxidant levels of a variety of herbs and found the highest levels in oregano, sage, peppermint, and thyme. They concluded that herbs are an important source of dietary antioxidants, right up there with red wine and green tea.

Finding ways to cook with herbs

There's nothing like freshly harvested rosemary tossed in with roasted potatoes or chopped basil topping a bowl of pasta. Scan any cookbook worth its salt, and you'll find inspiring ways to incorporate herbs into your meals. If you have a particular herb in mind, flip to its entry in the appendix for tips on using it. When you start growing herbs, you'll be inspired to try things you might never have considered. (We've all tasted mint-flavored ice cream, but how about making your own using bee balm or lavender?)

Adding flavor to oils, vinegars, dressings, and marinades

Browse supermarket shelves and you'll find a growing array of herb-flavored oils and vinegars, usually at premium prices. The same goes for salad dressings and marinades. But there's no need to break the bank to enjoy the flavors provided by these products. You can easily create homemade versions using fresh ingredients right from your garden. (And you can feel safe without the artificial colors, flavors, and preservatives that give store-bought products an extended shelf life.) In Chapter 12 you'll find recipes galore.

Brewing herbal teas

Your choice in the tea section at the grocery store used to be simple: Lipton or Tetley? Now there are dozens, if not hundreds, of variations on the tea theme, some that are combined with traditional tea *(Camellia sinensis)* and others that are completely herbal: from hibiscus to blueberry to chai to acai, with many teas touted for their health-boosting properties as well as their taste. Certainly some of these teas contain exotic ingredients grown in some far-off land, but many are made from herbs you can easily grow yourself. Flip to Chapter 12 for suggestions on flavorful herb combinations, as well as a few recipes to try.

Exploring Medicinal Herbs

Plants and medicines have been partners as far back as history reaches, and the partnership continues today. In the last few decades, both echinacea and St. John's wort have become popular herbal remedies, both readily found on supermarket and pharmacy shelves. More recently, supplements containing ginkgo, ginseng, goji berry, acai, goldenseal, and licorice root have invaded store shelves.

Historically, different cultures have taken a variety of approaches to herbal remedies. Many Eastern cultures, for example, traditionally view illness as a sign of cosmic disharmony. Herbal cures are calculated to restore balance — to create peace between the opposing principles of yin and yang — rather than treat specific problems. The European herbal medicine tradition has been less holistic, and is usually focused on treating symptoms rather than preventing problems. The ancient Greeks, for example, viewed life in terms of four universal elements — earth, air, fire, and water — and the four bodily humors — sanguine, phlegmatic, choleric, and melancholic (hot, cold, moist, and dry, respectively). "Hot" and "dry" herbs were prescribed for "cold" and "moist" ailments, and vice versa. Astronomy, too, has played a role in herbal medicine, and old herbals are filled with references to herbs "owned by Venus" or "under the dominion of the moon."

People have prescribed herbs for every condition known to humankind: boils and burns, coughs and constipation, drunkenness and dog bites, fevers and fits, giddiness and gout, heartaches and hiccups, impotence and indigestion, nightmares and nerves, snoring and sneezing, and worms and wounds. Chapter 13 is the place to find information and recipes for herbal remedies you can make from your own homegrown herbs.

You may be skeptical about the power of fennel to cure "every kind of poison in a man's body" — the claim in one 13th-century herbal — but plants are unquestionably rich with substances that can ease, cure, and even prevent diseases. Early physicians called herbs *simples,* meaning that each herb was a simple, or single, medicine, not a compound medicine. In fact, most herbs contain more than one chemical compound — nearly 1,500 have been isolated to date.

Making history

More than a few herbs deserve a place on everyone's plants-that-changed-the-world list. Willow bark (*Salix* species) from which acetylsalicylic acid, or aspirin, was derived in 1899, comes near the top of that enumeration. Other candidates? Quinine (*Cinchona* species), the original drug to cure malaria; opium poppy (*Papaver somniferum*), the world's most important painkiller; foxglove (*Digitalis lanata*), one of the first heart medicines; and hemp (*Cannabis sativa*), which has kept people tied up in knots — or, when smoked, has freed them from time and space.

Herbal remedies aren't just quaint relics of days gone by; in fact, we've only begun to discover the power of plants to enrich and improve our lives. The bark of the neem tree (*Azadirachta indica*), which has been used for centuries in India as a cure for all sorts of ailments from acne to malaria, is now being investigated for its antiviral properties. And common cinnamon, which comes from the inner bark of the cinnamon tree (*Cinnamomum* species), is being used to lower blood sugar in Type 2 diabetics.

Going mainstream

Herbal remedies have moved from the hippie/back-to-the-land fringe and are now mainstream. To wit: On her Web site (www.marthastewart.com), Martha Stewart gives detailed instructions on how to make your own herbal remedies along with tips on how to fold fitted sheets. And the magazine section of the Sunday newspaper regularly features snippets about the latest research results regarding the medicinal qualities of this or that herb, right alongside news about the most recent celebrity scandal.

Food or drug . . . or neither?

Before herbal remedies became big business, most were homemade or made in small batches, with the grower/producer selling directly to the end user. Because the government didn't regulate or oversee these transactions, consumers had to trust that the herbal concoctions contained what their makers said they did. However, over the last few decades, interest in "natural" remedies has grown, and bigger and bigger players — including large pharmaceutical companies — have entered the market, driving the stakes higher. Talk began to circulate about the possibility of the government stepping in to regulate herbal remedies. The reaction was swift and strong. Manufacturers feared that government regulations would prevent them from selling their wares; consumers rebelled against government control over what they could put into their bodies. A grassroots campaign to limit government regulation was successful, and the result was the Dietary Supplement Health and Education Act of 1994 (DSHEA).

You may have noticed that the medicinal claims of herbal products are couched in vague terms and that the products are described as supplements, not remedies. There's a good reason for this. The DSHEA defines a dietary supplement as a product that's intended to supplement the diet rather than cure a disease. The result is that the makers of dietary supplements are permitted to make broad claims that the product can support this or that structure or function. For example, vendors can say that echinacea supplements "support a healthy immune system" or that chamomile "calms the digestive tract." They can't claim that the product cures an ailment; doing so would change the product classification from supplement to drug, and thus require the clinical trials and rigorous testing pharmaceutical companies must do before introducing a medicine to the market.

Under DSHEA, a manufacturer is responsible for determining that the dietary supplements it makes are safe and that claims made about them are substantiated by adequate evidence to show that they aren't false or misleading. However, dietary supplements don't need FDA approval before they're marketed.

Creating Herbal Body Care Products: Beauty or Bust?

From rosemary shampoo to calendula salve, herbal body care products command top dollar. A close look at the ingredients (which are listed in order of the relative amounts of each ingredient, from most to least) often reveals just how little of the touted herb is actually in the product. For example, to make shampoos sound like they contain lots of herbs, some labels start their ingredient list with "an aqueous solution of herbs," which sounds fancier than the translation: "water with some herbs in it." Because water is a main ingredient in shampoo anyway, this is a clever way to make it sound like the shampoo contains a high concentration of herbs when, in reality, it gives no indication of the actual amount of herbs. That's not to say that herbs can't play a role in body care products, but rather that the premium price you're paying may be going toward marketing or fancy labels rather than expensive ingredients. In many cases, you can grow your own herbs and make your own products for a fraction of the cost, using the ingredients that you want and leaving out those that you don't. Chapter 14 delves into the art of making your own herbal body care products and includes recipes for hair care, skin care, and fragrances.

Using Herbs for Hearth and Home

The usefulness of herbs extends beyond their culinary, medicinal, and body care properties and into the realm of hearth and home. Perhaps as many, if not more, herbs are now grown for decorative uses — potpourris, sachets, pressed flower art, and the like. Some herbs are utilized to dye paper, fabric, yarn, and other craft materials. In Chapter 15, we introduce these and some of the other ways herbs are used, such as to create wreaths and bouquets, and to make bug repellants, cleaning compounds, and more.

Looking at Herb Folklore

In addition to their ties to the kitchen and medicine chest, herbs have an ancient connection to rites and myths. The lotus *(Nelumbo nucifera)* was sacred to Isis, the Egyptian goddess of fertility; white roses *(Rosa* species) and Madonna lilies *(Lilium candidum)* represent the Virgin Mary; victorious Greek athletes were awarded wreaths of bay *(Laurus nobilis)*. The following sections describe some of the tall tales that herbs have inspired and the superpowers that have been ascribed to herbs through the ages.

Sage renders men immortal, and other tall tales

As the saying goes, "Never let the facts get in the way of a good story." Herbs come bearing as many stories as they do names — and many of the tales have nothing to do with the facts. But they're wonderful fun, evocative connections with people and events in other places and other times. Knowing about them makes growing and using herbs a richer experience.

Absolutely every herb is laden with reputed associations and powers. Yarrow, for example, has been cultivated for at least 5,000 years. Most plant-name scholars believe it gets its genus name *Achillea* from Achilles, the warrior hero of *The Iliad.* Achilles, according to one version of the Greek myth, used yarrow during the Trojan War to treat the wounds of Telephus, the son of Heracles, as well as his own soldiers — leading to one of the other common names, staunchweed.

Yarrow is also associated with seeing into the future. According to British folklore, a woman could discover who her husband would be if she picked yarrow leaves in a churchyard and recited this verse:

Yarrow, sweet yarrow, the first that I have found,

In the name of sweet Jesus, I pluck thee from the ground;

As Joseph loved Mary, and took her for his dear,

So in a dream this night, my love will appear.

Following are some other examples of the folklore surrounding herbs:

- Sorrel turns red in autumn (and its leaves turn toward graveyards) in honor of the blood spilled by Irish soldiers more than 1,000 years ago.

- Prometheus used a fennel stalk as the torch when he stole fire from the gods and brought it to earth.

- Diana, goddess of the hunt, was so enraged that one of her nymphs didn't come to her defense that she turned her nymph into a violet.

- Rosemary, according to Christian legends, never grows taller than 6 feet, which was Christ's height.

- In a Peruvian legend, the nasturtium sprang up from a sack of gold ripped from the hands of thieving Spaniards by the god of the mountains.

- Garlic sprang from Satan's left footprint when he left the Garden of Eden.

- The white rose was born of Venus's tears, crying over the slain Adonis. Red roses are the result of Cupid's spilling a cup of wine.

Virtues of delight

If the legends and tales about herbs are numerous, their reputed virtues, or powers, are super-numerous — and often supernatural. Herbs can protect against devils and witches, predict the future, make people fall in love, take away sadness, and instill bravery. Herbs can also bring good luck, as anyone who finds a four-leaf clover knows.

Take a look at these other "virtuous" examples:

- Placing rosemary leaves under your pillow prevents nightmares.

- To see ghosts, wear lavender.

- Pick wild chervil and you'll break your mother's heart.

- A sprig of bay protects against being struck by lightning.

- Sniffing basil breeds scorpions in the brain.

- A hedge of rue keeps out witches, but rue left at the church will curse a marriage.

Mulling over mullein

The woolly leaved mullein (see the accompanying figure) has been prescribed for scores of ailments — everything from toothaches, coughs, and "fluxes of the body" to warts, colic, and "stiff sinews."

Mullein *(Verbascum thapsus)* is a good example of a multi-purpose herb. For example, people first coated mullein stalks with suet or pitch and used them as torches more than 2,000 years ago. Mullein has been used in sorcery to light midnight covens (and to guard against witches). American colonists made dyes from its roots and flowers, and stuffed its leaves in their mattresses (and in their shoes to keep their feet warm). Children have turned its leaves into doll blankets, and adults (and more than a few adolescents) have smoked them in place of tobacco — even as a treatment for coughs and lung ailments.

Women once rubbed mullein leaves on their cheeks to stimulate a fresh blush instead of using rouge. Mullein decoctions were used to kill worms in livestock, and the herb's honey-scented flowers have flavored drinks and perfumed rooms. Plants were also used as weather predictors: If the blooms clustered at the top of the stalk, a late winter with heavy snow was said to be certain. Flowers thrown into the hearth fire were thought to protect a house against storms.

Read All About It

This book focuses on the nuts and bolts of growing and using herbs, with some folklore thrown in because it's just so much fun. If you want to delve further into herb folklore and traditional cures, turn to *herbals,* books containing descriptions and uses of plants. The oldest surviving herbals date back 2,000 years. Most were written by physicians (but also by astrologers and alchemists) and combined botany, natural history, horticulture, cooking, medicine, myth, magic — and mistakes. These are some of the names you'll encounter when reading about herbs:

- **Dioscorides:** The Greek physician (first century A.D.) whose writing (*De Materia Medica*) was influential into the 1700s

- **Galen:** The second-century Greek physician who codified existing medical knowledge and popularized the theory of humors

- **William Turner:** The 16th-century author of the first "scientific" English herbal, *New Herball*

- **John Gerard:** Herbalist-gardener author of the most famous and important of all herbals, *Herball or General Historie of Plants* (1597)

✔ **John Parkinson:** English gardener and author of the enormous *Theatrum Botanicum* (1640), which describes more than 4,000 plants

✔ **Nicholas Culpeper:** An English astrologer/physician and author of the influential *English Physician*, an early version of the home medical reference that has been a strong seller ever since it was published in 1652

You don't need to live near the British Museum or the Vatican to have access to ancient herbals. Most have been reprinted in inexpensive editions and are available at bookstores, online, or in libraries.

You must take the information with a proverbial grain of salt when you delve into their pages. These are the texts, after all, that include illustrated descriptions of the fanciful goose tree. (John Gerard was among those who insisted it was real: "I have seene with mine eies, and handled with mine hands.") In case you haven't seen one with your "eies," the goose tree is covered with shells in which, Gerard wrote, "are contained little living creatures." If the creatures fell into water, they became birds, "bigger than a Mallard, and lesser than a Goose." If all this weren't zany enough, 16th-century clerics argued over whether or not tree geese were fowl or vegetable, which affected whether or not they could be eaten during Lent, a period of penance and fasting for some Christians.

You can't read about herbs without running into a reference to the Doctrine of Signatures. It was a theory popularized in the 16th century by a Swiss alchemist, physician, and herbalist who wrote under the name Paracelsus. The Doctrine of Signatures claimed that plants had signatures, or visible qualities, that indicated which ailments they could cure.

Because lettuce contained a milky sap, for example, it was recommended for mothers who were having problems nursing their babies. Herbs with heart-shaped leaves were prescribed for heart ailments (including those that were romantic in nature). Garlic, which has a hollow stem, was said to cure obstructions of the windpipe, and hanging mosses were believed to be antidotes to baldness. Herbs with spotted leaves were prescribed for lung diseases, while those with thorns were recommended for removing splinters. Herbs with yellow flowers were remedies for jaundice. Presumably, herbs with multi-colored leaves or flowers can cure aging surfers still addicted to Hawaiian shirts.

Chapter 2

Herbs 101

*I*n this chapter we cover some of the basics of herb gardening — and gardening in general. Like all hobbies, gardening has its own set of terminology, and getting a handle on the terms makes communicating easier. So we start with how plants are named, and then move on to life cycles and anatomy. It's not the most exciting part of herb gardening, but this information forms a foundation from which you can begin to build your herbal oasis. Later in the chapter are some important words of caution.

What's a Wort? Plant Name

Plant names are one of the special pleasures of gardening. Who wouldn't want to grow a marmalade bush, maybe next to a bread-tree and just down from a chocolate vine? Herbs, among the first plants to be cultivated, have some of the most evocative common names: liverwort, adder's tongue, heartsease, lamb's ear, monkshood, corn cockle, toothache plant, lady's bedstraw, lady's mantle, love-lies-bleeding, queen-of-the-meadow, boneset, star of Bethlehem, scullcap, lungwort. The list goes on and on. . . .

Speaking of lungwort and all the other worts you've probably come across in your gardening travels . . . just what is a *wort?* It's an archaic word for "plant." You see it attached to other words, usually nouns that tell something about what people believed the plant did or how it looked. Lungwort cured lung ailments, spiderwort healed the bites of spiders, and feverwort brought down fevers. Bellwort has bell-shaped flowers, ragwort has ragged foliage, and we don't have to tell you how spoonwort's leaves are shaped.

Another word you'll come across is *bane,* as in leopard's-bane and wolf's-bane (which are reputed to repel leopards and werewolves, respectively). If something is the bane of your existence, maybe there's a plant to repel it. Just remember that if something has *bane* in its name, it may well be toxic to you, too.

Clearing up common name confusion

As fun as they are, the problem with common names is that they're not unique; the same name can be used for more than one plant. Starflower, for example, is one name for borage, but it's also the informal name for a native California wildflower and 60 of its cousins, a large clan of perennials that grow from corms, and any number of other plants that at one time or another conjured up the image of a star in someone's mind.

What's more, one plant may have many common names. Take southernwood: It's a shrubby perennial that repels flies, fleas, and moths (and once was prescribed as a cure for pimples, worms, baldness, cramps, and convulsions, and as "an antidote against all poisons"). It's also called lord's wood, maid's ruin, lover's plant, lad's love, lemon plant, boy's love, old man, old man's tree, mugwort, garden sagebrush, and wormwood.

The common names of herbs are great fun, and each has a story — even the ubiquitous dandelion. Its name comes from both Latin *(dens leonis)* and French *(dent de lion)*. Each alludes to the plant's serrated leaves, which supposedly resemble the teeth in a lion's mouth — giving rise to another common name for the plant, lion's tooth. But there's more. The dandelion is called earth nail in China because of its long root. In France, the dandelion is known as *pissenlit,* which highlights its diuretic effect. Tradition holds that anyone who even picks dandelions will wet the bed. Hence, another common English name for the dandelion, pissabed. Other names? Blowball and pull-ball, after its fluffy seed head; and priest's crown and monk's head, allusions to the flower head after its seeds have blown away. Even if you have no intention of growing herbs, finding out about them gives insight into times past.

Getting scientific with names

Over the centuries, a string of prominent scientists has tried to clear up all the naming confusion, but it took Swedish naturalist Carolus Linnaeus (1707–1778) to get everyone using the same two-word (or *binomial*) system to group and name plants. Achieving agreement wasn't easy, especially because some conservatives were scandalized by Linnaeus's views on plant sexuality, but the general rules were established in 1753. (Linnaeus exacted his revenge by naming several noxious weeds after his critics.) Here's how botanic nomenclature, or scientific naming, works.

Genus and species

Every plant has at least two names, a *genus* name and a *species* name, that together make up its scientific name (also referred to as its Latin name, botanical name, and Latin binomial). A genus is a collection of similar plants; *genera* is the plural. A species name, sometimes called a *specific epithet,* is a descriptive name for a distinct group within the genus. (The word *species* is both singular and plural; there's no such thing as *specie,* unless you're talking money.) When written, scientific names (both the genus and species names) are set in italics, and the genus name is capitalized. For example, *Viola* is the genus name for all the violet-like plants, of which there are more than 500. The common violet is one type, or species, within the genus *Viola;* its species name is *odorata.* So the common violet's scientific name is *Viola odorata.*

Sometimes the term *species* is abbreviated as "sp." (singular) or "spp." (plural). A genus name followed by "spp." refers to more than one species within that genus, but not necessarily *all* the species within that genus. For example, you might say, "Mints *(Mentha* spp.) are popular herb garden plants," without specifically naming spearmint *(Mentha spicata)* and apple mint *(Mentha suaveolens)* as examples, or specifically excluding Australian mint *(Mentha australis),* which may be common down under but is relatively unknown elsewhere. In a list of botanical names, the genus name is sometimes abbreviated after the first mention. For example, in a list of different mints, such as *Mentha spicata, M. suaveolens,* and *M. australis, Mentha* is abbreviated as *M.* The species name is never abbreviated.

The species name often reveals something about the plant, and different plants can have the same species name. For example, *odorata* means "sweet" or "fragrant," so any plant with a form of *odorata* in its species name — such as sweet woodruff, or *Galium odoratum* — is fragrant. The species name *officinalis* means "has medicinal uses." Now you know something about *Althaea officinalis, Borago officinalis,* and *Rosmarinus officinalis* — marsh mallow, borage, and rosemary — they all have medicinal uses. Once you become familiar with some of these terms, you'll be able to tell something about the herb just from its name.

Cultivar and variety

In addition to their genus and species names, many herbs have a third, or *cultivar,* name (the word derives from "cultivated variety"). The cultivar name is neither italicized nor underlined but is capitalized and placed in single quotation marks (for example, *Viola odorata* 'Royal Robe'). A cultivar is a plant produced not by Mother Nature but by plant breeders and gardeners through cultivation. A cultivar is different from the species and from other cultivars in one or more respects and is often touted as better. 'Royal Robe,' for the record, has gorgeous, deep violet blooms and flowers in spring and again in autumn.

You often see the word *variety* used interchangeably with *cultivar*. In fact, the two are different things: A cultivar is intentionally bred or selected, whereas a variety is a naturally occurring form that is different from the species. Varieties are designated by the abbreviation "var." followed by the variety in italics. For example, rosemary, which has blue flowers, is *Rosmarinus officinalis;* the naturally occurring white-flowered rosemary is *Rosmarinus officinalis* var. *albiflorus.*

Pronunciation

We admit that all these distinctions are pretty picky, and that scientific names are a mouthful. Pronouncing them doesn't come easily. We'll let you in on two secrets: First, plant names are horticultural Latin, not classical Latin. And second, no one really knows how the Romans sounded when they spoke. Whether you pronounce *Petroselinum* (the botanical name for parsley) petroh-seh-LINE-um or petroh-seh-LEEN-um isn't all that important. Knowing exactly what plant you're seeing or buying is all that matters.

Remembering scientific names is no walk in the park either. Don't despair. The longer you garden, the more names you'll recognize and remember. And sometimes, just when you've got a name committed to memory, the name will change because scientists have discovered something new about the plant. However, the two-word (or binomial) system is always the rule.

Following is a table of some Latin words that are commonly used in species and variety names.

Latin Term	English Translation
alba, albus	White
angustifolia, angustifolius	Narrow-leaved
annuua or annuus	Annual
argentea-, argenteo-	Silvery
aurea-, aureo-	Golden or yellow
biennis	Biennial
caerulea, caeruleus	Blue
coccinea, coccineus	Scarlet red
cordata, cordatus	Heart-shaped
dioica, dioicus	Having male and female flowers on separate plants
floribunda, floribundus, floridus	Having showy and/or abundant flowers
-flora, -florus	Referring to the flowers of a plant
-folia, -folius	Referring to the leaves of a plant
fragrans	Fragrant or sweet-smelling

Latin Term	*English Translation*
frutescens, fruticans, fruticosus	Shrubby or bushy
glabra	Smooth or hairless
glauca, glaucus	Covered with a waxy coating, or *bloom*
hirtus, hirta, hirsutus	Covered with stiff, bristly hairs
humilis	Low-growing or dwarf
lact-	Milky (can describe color or sap)
leuc-	White
lutea, luteo-	Yellow
macro-	Very large
maculatus	Spotted
micro-	Very small
mollis	Soft or covered with soft hairs
montana, montanus	Native to mountain habitats
nana, nanus	Small or dwarf
nigra, niger,	Black or very dark
officinalis	Referring to plants with medicinal properties
pallida, pallidus	Pale
palmatum, palmatus	Having palmate (handlike) leaves
perennis	Perennial
-phylla, -phyllus	Referring to the leaves of a plant
pumila, pumilus	Small or dwarf
purpurea, purpureus	Purple
repens, reptans	Creeping
rosea, roseus	Pink
rubra	Red
rugosa, rugosus	Wrinkled
sativa, sativus	Cultivated
sempervirens	Evergreen
tomentosa, tomentosum, tomentosus	Densely covered with wooly hairs
tuberosa, tuberosus	Producing tubers
veris, vernalis	Flowering in early spring
-virens, virida-	Green
vulgaris	Common
xanth-	Yellow

The terms in the following table usually indicate a plant's native region.

Latin Term	Native Region
boralis	Northern
canadense, canadensis	Canada
chinensis	China
indicus	India
japonica, japonicus	Japan
koreana, koreanus	Korea
nipponicus, nipponicum	Japan
occidentalis	Western Hemisphere
orientalis	Far East
persica, persicus	Persia (Iran)
sinensis	China

Looking at the Herbal Cycle of Life

Like other garden plants, herbs have different life cycles. Herbs can fall into any of the following categories:

- **Annuals:** These plants burn the candle at both ends: They germinate, flower, set seeds, and die in one growing season. No matter where you live, you have to plant basil, borage, calendula, summer savory, and other annuals every year.

- **Biennials:** Biennials live for two growing seasons — germinating and forming leaves in the first year, then flowering, setting seeds, and dying in the second. Some biennial herbs, such as parsley, are treated as if they were annuals and are harvested in their first year. Biennials grown for their flowers or seeds, such as angelica and caraway, need a second season in your garden.

- **Perennials:** Perennials, such as anise hyssop, mint, purple coneflower, and sweet woodruff, are plants that live for at least three seasons. Horseradish and a few others may outlive you.

Perennials are either *herbaceous* — plants such as lovage, whose stems and leaves die back in winter, then resprout from the roots in spring — or woody. All woody plants, including shrubs, vines, and trees, are perennial. However, if a gardener tells you she grows perennials, she invariably means the herbaceous kind.

Just because a plant is a perennial doesn't mean that you can stick it in your garden and forget it. *Tender perennials,* such as bay, can't stand prolonged freezing temperatures; if you live in a cold-winter area and leave them outdoors in autumn, come spring you'll have a bare spot where they once grew. In contrast, *hardy perennials,* tough guys like comfrey and sage, will be there in spring. USDA Hardiness Zone ratings are an attempt to give gardeners a fair idea of how much cold a plant can tolerate without dying. See Chapter 3 for more information about hardiness zones.

Don't try to memorize all this now — just keep in mind that herbs don't grow the same way in all locations. Herbs that are hardy in southern Texas may not survive in northern Montana, and those that thrive in Southern California are likely to freeze in the cold winters of the Northeast or Midwest. Knowing the difference between a tender and a hardy perennial can save you from some expensive and time-consuming mistakes. End of lesson.

Surveying Herb Anatomy

In this section, we explore roots, stems, leaves, and flowers. When you have all four — and a little luck — you also have a living plant.

The root of the matter

Forgetting about the bottom portion of a plant is easy — out of sight, out of mind. Yet roots are as important as the plant parts you see aboveground. Roots anchor the plant in the soil. They take in water and nutrients, and move them to the herb's aboveground parts.

Most herbs have either fibrous roots, which are fine and highly branched, or a taproot, which is long and tapering with a few small side roots (think of a carrot). Some herbs are grown for their roots, including ginger and horseradish.

Stem dandy

Stems not only hold up the leaves and flowers, they carry water and nutrients from the roots. Only a few herbs — flax is one — are grown primarily for their stems, although the stems of many species are used in cooking and medicines.

When gardening books, including this one, tell you to cut below or above a *node,* they're referring to the places along a stem where leaves are attached. The clear spaces between nodes are called *internodes;* without enough light, the internodes stretch more than usual, producing tall, spindly plants that gardeners term *leggy.*

Leaf it be

The leaf, as science teachers like to say, is like a factory. This part of the plant captures light, and through the process called *photosynthesis,* uses the energy of the sun to produce food. Anyone with an herb garden becomes keen about leaves, as these are often the most useful parts of the plant. Leaves come in all sorts of sizes, colors, textures, and shapes. (See Chapter 4 for ways to highlight these features when designing your garden.)

Understanding leaf descriptions

Each leaf variation (and the variations are numerous) has its own technical description, but you can garden successfully for a lifetime without having to know that bee balm leaves are "simple, usually serrate," or that geraniums' leaves are "alternate, palmate or pinnate, simple or compound, usually lobed." However, knowing some of these terms will help you make sense of entries in plant encyclopedias. You'll also be better able to identify herbs whose labels you've lost, and understand other gardeners' descriptions.

Following are a few of the most general leaf terms — ones you'll encounter so often that you'll want to remember them:

- ✔ **Deciduous:** Refers to plants with leaves that die and fall off in autumn and are replaced by new leaves in spring.

- ✔ **Evergreen:** A plant that retains its leaves throughout the year.

- ✔ **Simple:** Comprised of a single leaf, like mint (see Figure 2-1).

- ✔ **Compound:** Describes a leaf that's made of several leaves, or leaflets, like those of chervil, which is also shown in Figure 2-1.

- ✔ **Blade:** The flat part of the leaf.

- ✔ **Margin:** The edge of the leaf.

- ✔ **Lobed:** Refers to a leaf that has rounded sections, like the leaves of most geraniums.

- ✔ **Serration:** A leaf margin that's jagged like a saw blade, as in most mints. A leaf without serration, such as that of orrisroot, has *entire* margins.

Seeing how leaves and stems go together

The way the stems and leaves are put together on a plant accounts for its *growth habit.* Knowing an herb's growth habit is necessary in order to pick the right plant for the location you have in mind. If you're looking for herbs to cover that steep, unmowable strip on one side of your backyard, look for the words *mat-forming, prostrate, cushion-forming, groundcover,* and *mound-forming.*

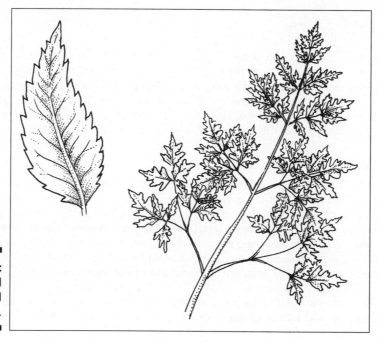

Figure 2-1:
Simple and
compound
leaves.

Erect plants grow upward. Some shoot straight up, rigidly vertical and often with few side stems, like bee balm. Others with more branched stems tend to *sprawl. Climbing* (or *scandent*) plants want to grow even farther upward and need some type of structure to support them.

Factoring in flowers

Some herbs are grown simply for the beauty of their flowers, but some flowers are useful in other ways, too. Chamomile flowers make a calming tea; lavender flowers have a soothing fragrance, making them popular in sachets and aromatherapy. However, a plant's perspective on the purpose of its flowers differs from that of the people who grow it.

Seeing flowers from a plant's point of view

Botanically speaking, flowers serve one purpose for the plant — reproduction. The function of flowers, at least from a plant's point of view, is to produce the next generation. To do that, the pollen on the male stamen has to get to the pistil, the female part of a blossom. Many flowers use colors, markings, fragrance, form, and the promise of nectar to entice insects to do their bidding. In most cases, insects like bees visit flowers for the nectar, inadvertently collecting pollen on their bodies and passing it along to another flower. The male pollen fertilizes the female egg, resulting in the production of seeds.

Looking at flowers from the human perspective

The ancient Greeks were talking about atoms when they wrote about "the symmetry of their shapes and sizes and positions and order," but they could just as easily have been describing the wonderful shapes, sizes, and arrangements of flowers — the characteristics of flowers that are most important from a human perspective.

It's logical that a single, or solitary, is one flower on one stalk, yet flowers also come in clusters, or *inflorescences.* In fact, most herbs produce flower clusters rather than singles.

Gardeners describe clusters both in terms of the individual blooms and the way those blooms are arranged. Knowing the basic terms for these inflorescences helps you choose the flower shape you want — and, as with leaf shapes, helps you identify plants. So when other gardeners start talking blossoms, it won't be all Greek to you.

- ✔ **Composite:** A daisylike flower, such as the sunflower or purple coneflower, that looks like a single but actually consists of a center made up of scores of tiny, tightly packed disc flowers surrounded by a ring of ray flowers (*rays* are the flower parts we pick off while reciting, "He loves me, he loves me not").

- ✔ **Panicle:** An open, loosely branched cluster of flowers on a branched stem. Southernwood and sweet woodruff bear panicles of flowers.

- ✔ **Raceme:** A cluster of flowers attached to a single, upright stem with short, individual stalks. Sage and comfrey serve as examples.

- ✔ **Spike:** An upright stem of flowers, like those of agrimony and hyssop, that have little or no stalk and attach directly or almost directly to the stem.

- ✔ **Umbel:** An umbrella-like structure, with each flower stalk emerging from the same place at the top of the stem. Dill and lovage have umbel inflorescences (see Figure 2-2).

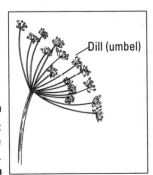
Dill (umbel)

Figure 2-2:
An example
of umbel.

The seed stops here

You can usually dig or pull invasive herbs that multiply by seeds more successfully than perennial climbers and crawlers. Just don't give the seeds time to get the upper hand.

Lay down a thick layer of mulch to discourage seeds from sprouting and to smother young plants. Pouring boiling water on seedlings is a lethal treatment; you can also kill some plants by repeatedly cutting off their tops.

Tilling is supposed to bury seeds, blocking the light they need to sprout. Not so! Churning the soil usually brings more seeds to the surface — where they will sprout — than it buries.

If you do nothing else, stop invasive plants from reseeding by picking their flowers as soon as they wilt. This tedious activity is known as dead-heading. Get into the proper mood by wearing a tie-dyed shirt and playing a Jerry Garcia CD.

A last note on flowers: You're likely to come across the word *bract* (that's botany talk for the modified leaves that circle the base of a blossom). In most flowers, they're small, green or brown, and pretty nondescript. In a few plants, such as bee balm, they're large, colorful, and look like flower petals.

Caution: Invasive Herbs Ahead

Although we're card-carrying, unrepentant herb appreciators, we need to tell you that all herbs aren't created equal, or equally nice, as you'll find out if you choose invasive herbs as companions for your genteel basil and lady-like rosemary. As the term suggests, an invasive plant is a botanical Attila the Hun. Draw a line in the sand and these bullies hop over it. When a garden seed catalog says a plant is "vigorous and grows anywhere," be prepared for something that can scale a telephone pole faster than you can get rid of a telephone solicitor.

Plants that will make you rue the day

Climbing and clambering plants are especially notorious for exterminating everything in their path. There's a good reason why kudzu *(Pueraria lobata)*, which the Chinese use to treat alcoholism, is known as "the vine that ate the South." It's shown in Figure 2-3. English ivy *(Hedera helix)* and wild grape *(Vitis* spp.) are two more vigorous vines that are used medicinally — ivy for controlling skin problems, grape as a diuretic — but both may be prescriptions for trouble in your garden.

Figure 2-3:
Stay away
from kudzu.

Most non-vining herbs make congenial neighbors for the other occupants of your garden, but not all. Turn your back on any mint, and it will overwhelm the lettuce and lay siege to the parsley. Despite their sweet scent, mints are thugs. Even when you pull them, you leave broken runners behind that will sprout new stems.

Set out a tidy clump of garlic chives, famous for its pungent flavor and power to ward off disease, and you'll discover that even two or three unpicked flower heads will give birth to hundreds of new plants. Come spring, your well-tended garden will look like scruffy lawn. Hoe down the grasslike stalks and they reappear, as dependable as the swallows that arrive each year at the San Juan Capistrano mission.

Location is everything

Once an invasive takes hold in your yard, you might feel that a nationwide alert should go out; but, like politics, all gardening is local. Sweet marjoram is a weed in Southern California, but it must be grown as an annual in areas where the mercury dips below 35 degrees Fahrenheit. English ivy is a steroid case in the Southeast, but it must be pampered to survive in northern Vermont.

While the master list of universally incorrigible herbs is short, a list for your region may be much longer. To avoid catastrophe — years of swearing at yourself for planting that ~#@*! thing — find out which herbs may turn traitor. If you yearn to make a concoction that calls for an unabashed bully, don't plant more of it. Do the world a favor and harvest some from a friend's lawn. Consult other gardeners, local nurseries, and your local Cooperative Extension Service about invasives. And if your neighbor brings you kudzu seedlings, find a nice way to say, "In a pig's eye."

Solitary confinement

No self-respecting herb garden is complete without spearmint or yarrow, but pulling, digging, or tilling these ground-spreaders may mean more plants, not fewer. To keep them from crowding out the carrots and zinnias, grow them in containers, either aboveground or sunk in the garden. If you plan to bury a container (which should be at least 18 inches deep), cut away the bottom, and then set it so its lip is 2 inches above the soil surface. Refer to Chapter 6 for more on gardening in containers.

Underground travelers

Some herbs, such as the aforementioned mint, travel by sending out root-like stems, or *rhizomes,* that scoot just under the soil surface, sprouting new plants as they go. Other herbs overrun their neighbors by scattering seeds that sprout in the most awful conditions — such as the spaces between your patio stones — and without any help from you. Toss 100 basil seeds on the ground and you'll still be buying, not making, pesto. But let one dandelion flower go to seed and you'll have enough plants to make wine for the Bowery Boys.

Be wary of the following, and be prepared to arm yourself as an "herban" guerilla if you plant any of them:

- ✔ **Artemisia** *(Artemisia* spp.): Gardening books advise dividing this herb to create more. But artemisia, famous for thriving in poor soil, multiplies so rapidly on its own that you'll need a calculator to add it up.

- ✔ **Comfrey** *(Symphytum officinale):* Notice that *Symphytum* has the same word root as the word "sympathy." Trust us; you'll get neither sympathy nor comfort from comfrey when your plants multiply.

- ✔ **Costmary** *(Chrysanthemum balsamita):* Costmary leaves traditionally were used as bookmarks, thus the herb's other common name, Bible leaf. The plant is rarely found in the wild, but in the garden it increases fast enough to supply bookmarks for the Library of Congress.

- ✔ **Fennel** *(Foeniculum vulgare):* The seeds taste like anise, the leaves like dill. But watch out! Fennel has invaded farm fields in California and Virginia, where it's now officially *herbus non grata.*

- ✔ **German, or annual, chamomile** *(Matricaria recutita):* This herb self-sows almost anywhere. In Boulder, Colorado, where Celestial Seasonings teas get poked into those little bags, chamomile sprouts in sidewalk cracks, a pleasant alternative to crab grass.

✔ **Herb-Robert** *(Geranium robertianum):* Long associated with snakes, this plant slithers through the garden with ease, popping up where you least expect — or want — it.

✔ **Horseradish** *(Armoracia rusticana):* You're likely to leave behind a few bits of root when you dig horseradish, and every bit will turn into a new plant. Once you have it, you have it.

✔ **St. John's wort** *(Hypericum perforatum):* St. John's wort is an herbal mood-lifter with a reputation for getting wildly out of hand in the garden. Keep an eye on it, or you could end up depressed.

✔ **Tansy** *(Tanacetum vulgare):* Tansy can repel flies, ants, and other insects, and it can be a pest in its own right.

✔ **Violet** *(Viola odorata):* Shrinking violets? Don't believe it. One day you have a demure clump of violets, the next week you have enough plants to open a flower shop.

✔ **Yarrow** *(Achillea* spp.): Multiplying without help may be okay for a plant that reputedly heals bruises, burns, wounds, and sores; conditions oily hair; and looks great in dried arrangements. Just choose a spot where it won't overtake everything else.

Avoiding Dangerous Herbs

Herbs have been associated with curses every bit as long as they've been associated with cures. The 16th-century English poet Edmund Spenser wrote about the power of herbs, pointing out that they could "worke eternal sleepe."

If you have small children — or big children, or even no children — you need to be aware that a good number of herbs are toxic. Their effects range from irritating skin to causing death. When Socrates drank hemlock, he wasn't kidding around. The same precautions apply if you have pets; puppies in particular are fond of chewing on anything, including toxic plants.

Know the risks before planting the following; use them with care, or avoid them altogether:

✔ **Aconite** *(Aconitum* spp.): This herb, also known as monkshood and wolf's-bane, deserves a skull and crossbones; it's highly poisonous.

✔ **Comfrey** *(Symphytum officinale):* Laboratory research indicates comfrey, even ingested in low concentrations, is carcinogenic in rats.

✔ **Deadly nightshade** *(Atropa belladonna):* In folklore, this is a favorite ingredient of witches' brews. The common name says it all.

- **Foxglove** *(Digitalis purpurea):* A common biennial flower (shown in Figure 2-4), it's also the source of digitalis, a powerful heart medication. Foxglove can cause convulsions and even death if used improperly.

- **Hellebore:** Both American false hellebore *(Veratrum viride)* and the popular black hellebore *(Helleborus niger)* are dangerous characters; they're major-league skin irritants and can be fatal if ingested.

- **Pennyroyal** *(Mentha pulegium, Hedeoma pulegioides):* Found in some herbal insect repellent sprays and lotions, pennyroyal can cause severe illness if ingested. Because it can induce abortions, products containing pennyroyal should never be used by pregnant women.

- **Pokeweed** *(Phytolacca* spp.): All parts of mature pokeweed plants, including their pretty purple berries, are toxic.

- **Rue** *(Ruta graveolens):* Rue is a pretty plant, but its bad attributes make it best to avoid altogether. Touch the foliage and you may end up with severe, burnlike welts and blisters; ingest it and be prepared for cramps and hallucinations.

- **Water hemlock** *(Contium maculatum):* Think nausea, paralysis, and death.

Some herbs, like comfrey, are fine to use externally, such as in a poultice, but should never be consumed. Refer to the entries in the appendix for details.

Figure 2-4:
Danger!
Foxglove.

Just because a plant is called an herb doesn't mean it's nontoxic! With herbs, it's downright stupid to imbibe first and ask questions later. Don't put any herb in your mouth without knowing what it is and what it does. And don't go rolling around in your herb garden, especially if you have sensitive skin. If you choose to plant any dangerous herbs, label them clearly and fence them in to protect those who can't read.

Herbs from the Wild

Wildcrafting is the term for gathering herbs and other plants from the outdoors. This activity is so popular that many species are being threatened by over-collection. Irresponsible collectors who take plants for profit are only part of the problem. The other part is that familiar feeling everyone gets upon seeing a stand of goldenseal or bloodroot: "Oh, it won't matter if I take just a few." Multiply "take a few" by 100 or 1,000 collectors, and you see the problem.

Many herbs are highly sensitive and need particular conditions to thrive, making it unlikely that the plants you dig up will survive anyway. Nearly all herbs are available for sale from nurseries. Make sure that the firm you patronize *propagates* its plants — grows them from seeds or cuttings — rather than dig them in the wild and putting them in pots. Seeds also are available for most endangered herbs.

Another reason to avoid wildcrafting: Unless you're truly an expert at identifying herbs, you risk mistaking highly toxic herbs like water hemlock for their benign look-alikes.

Part II
Deciding How and What to Grow

The 5th Wave   By Rich Tennant

"I never meant it to be a planter. It just hadn't been washed in so long that stuff started growing out of it."

In this part . . .

Before planting herbs — or anything else — it's important to know a little bit about the conditions in your garden. In this part, we look at some of the factors that influence whether or not a plant will thrive, starting with the big picture — climate — and then narrowing down the focus to the different growing conditions in your particular landscape.

Because designing an herb garden can be daunting, we walk you through the basics and offer some sample gardens. And if you're short on garden space, don't despair; herbs grow well in containers, too.

Chapter 3

Getting to Know Your Home Ground

*L*ocation, location, location — words as important to gardeners as to real-estate agents looking for a quick sale. Gardeners in Honolulu never fear having a frost, while gardeners in Barrow, Alaska, can expect less than a week of frost-free days each year. It's a big world out there — and where you live affects what herbs you can grow, how you grow them, when you grow them, and how successful you're likely to be.

In addition to looking at the big picture — factors such as climate and topography — this chapter helps you assess your property and make sensible decisions about where your herbs will grow best.

Climate Is Key

Climate has a lot to do with growing herbs successfully. You don't have to be a seasoned gardener to know that the back yards of Minneapolis, Minnesota, aren't filled with 50-foot coconut palms and lush banana trees — tropical plants can't survive winter in the far north. But do you know that sugar maples and birch trees won't survive in San Diego, Miami, or Houston? Heat limits what you can grow just as much as cold does.

Most of us are pretty casual about the words *climate* and *weather,* but they're not the same thing. Climate refers to prevailing, or average, conditions. Weather is what's happening right now in your back yard. New Hampshire has a cold climate, but the weather today in Nashua may be hot and humid.

Factors that influence what you can grow

Many factors influence your region's climate. Some of the most important are latitude, elevation, wind, and proximity to large bodies of water. Collectively, these factors determine to some extent what you can grow and when you can grow it. There are ways to work with what nature has given you (see the later section "Making the most of microclimates"), but overall, your climate has a big influence on how you garden.

Here's what you need to know about the factors that influence your region's climate:

- **Latitude:** In general, the farther north of the equator you live, the colder and longer winter will be — and the shorter your growing season. The latitude for Dallas is about 10 degrees south of Boston's. On average, gardeners in Dallas have about 60 more frost-free gardening days each year than people in Boston do. That may not sound like much, but 60 days is long enough to grow all the basil you'd need to make a winter's worth of pesto.

- **Elevation:** Latitude is only part of the story. The higher up you live, the colder it will be in both winter and summer, and the shorter the growing season. A good rule of thumb is that for every 300 feet of elevation, ten garden days are lost. In fall and spring, those who live at low elevations get rain while those perched in the clouds get snow. These differences can occur only a few miles apart. It can be raining on the shores of Lake Champlain in Burlington, Vermont (elevation 100 feet), but snowing like crazy at the top of the ski lift in Stowe, 35 miles southeast of Burlington at an elevation of 3,700 feet.

- **Wind:** As a rule, winds in the United States blow from west to east. Mountain ranges can block the wind currents that push weather (or send it in unexpected directions). Live on the west side of the Cascade Mountains, for example, and you'll get all the rain you need and then some. Move to the other side of that range, where rain is as rare as a cat that comes when called, and you'll need extra watering cans in your toolshed. Weather fronts moving over large bodies of water usually pick up lots of moisture; those coming from inland tend to bring little or no precipitation.

- **Water:** Large bodies of water typically affect weather by moderating it. If you're lucky enough to have an oceanfront address or live on the shore of a good-sized lake, your garden season is probably two or three weeks longer than that of someone who lives a couple hundred miles inland. And while your daytime temperatures in spring may be cooler, your chance of having nighttime frosts is reduced. Even small lakes can have these effects, albeit to a lesser degree. You can usually expect more precipitation if you live near a large body of water, too.

Far northern and high elevation gardeners may have brief growing seasons, but most have the advantage of a winter-long snow cover. Snow is a great insulator, making it possible for some perennial herbs to survive in conditions far colder than they can without snow to protect them. Plus, a deep, insulating cover of snow protects plants from alternating freeze/thaw cycles that can damage roots.

Weather matters

Climate dictates what's likely to grow in your locale; weather dictates what will grow right now. For example, statistics show that rainfall in Asheville, North Carolina, averages between 3 and 5 inches per month year-round, perfect for growing many herbs with little or no supplemental watering. However, in the last few years that region has experienced extended droughts, during which plants have withered without regular watering. Climate statistics are interesting and useful for planning, but keep in mind that your current weather conditions and the short-term weather forecast are what really matter to the plants in your garden, and they dictate what garden tasks you'll need to perform on a day-to-day basis.

Using Climate and Zone Maps

Some scientists study climate full time, and there's data aplenty about the high and low temperatures, precipitation, and other climate factors for most of the country. This information can go a long way toward helping you decide what to plant and determine what type of care your gardens will need. To make the information easier to access, scientists have compiled this data into various maps.

The USDA Hardiness Zone Map

The Hardiness Zone Map developed by the U.S. Department of Agriculture (USDA) divides North America into 11 zones based on the average annual minimum temperature (see Figure 3-1). Zone 1 is the coldest; the mercury dips below –50 degrees Fahrenheit in an average year. Zone 11 is the warmest; the average low is above 40 degrees Fahrenheit — 90 degrees warmer than Zone 1. Each zone (except zones 1 and 11) is further divided into two subzones (the *a* subzone is, on average, 5 degrees colder than the *b* subzone). For a full-color version of the map, check out the Web site for the U.S. National Arboretum at www.usna.usda.gov/Hardzone/ushzmap.html.

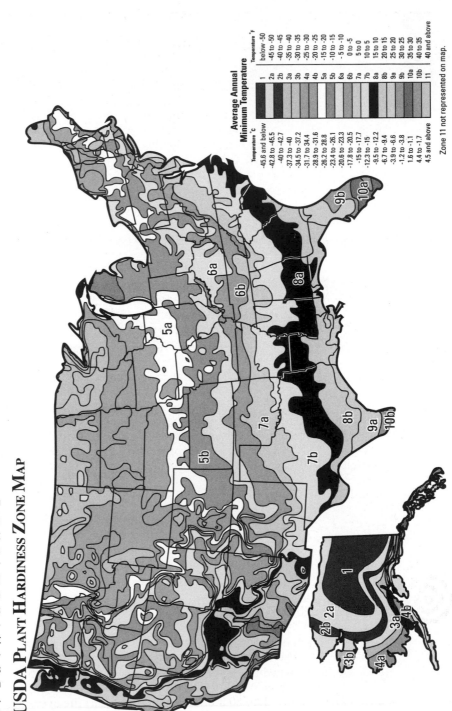

Figure 3-1:
USDA plant hardiness zones for the United States. The map shows the average lowest winter temperatures that you can expect.

USDA PLANT HARDINESS ZONE MAP

Strictly by the numbers

We know that our weather memories are notoriously bad, and we suspect yours are too. To a gardener, every dry summer seems like the driest ever, every early frost the earliest ever. Although climate and weather records are available for the major cities throughout North America, National Weather Service data may not exist for your location. Your local Cooperative Extension Service or a nearby airport may have some records, but the best weather records are those that you keep.

One of the most useful garden tools is a weather diary, a daily record of high and low temperatures and precipitation in your garden. You'll need several years of records before you can begin to draw conclusions — for example, that the last frost of spring usually comes in the second week of May. Comparing your records with those of your closest weather station can help you make predictions, too. For example,

if your data show temperatures consistently 5 to10 degrees cooler than those predicted in the weather forecast, you'll know to protect plants from frost when the forecast calls for temperatures in the high 30s or low 40s. Keeping records will make you weather-savvy, and being weather-savvy means making fewer mistakes in the garden.

If you ignore our advice about keeping a weather diary and still want to know how much rain fell last year or when the first frost came, visit the National Weather Service Web site at `www.nws.noaa.gov`. For long-time climate records and trends, see whether a nearby library has a copy of *Climates of the United States*. Scientists at the National Oceanic and Atmospheric Administration (NOAA) compiled this two-volume gold mine of facts from every state.

Garden authors cite zone ratings when they write about perennial plants. (You don't have to worry about hardiness zones with annuals, because they live only for one growing season.) You also see zone ratings given for perennials at nurseries and in plant catalogs. For example, rosemary usually is designated as a Zone 8 plant, which means you can grow it in your garden 12 months a year in Zones 8 and warmer, but it's unlikely to survive in Zones 7 and colder. If you want to keep your rosemary alive in Zones 2 through 7, you'll have to bring it inside in winter. Few folks even live in Zone 1, so the listings you see generally don't go below Zone 2.

We say rosemary is "usually designated" Zone 8 because books, catalogs, and plant tags may differ on the zone ratings of individual plants. That difference of opinion is one reason why buying locally grown perennial herbs is a good idea — you know they'll be hardy.

Keep in mind that the hardiness zone map is based on just one statistic: the *average* minimum temperature. And this is only part of the story when it comes to deciding what plants will thrive in your garden. Consider Mobile, Alabama and Tucson, Arizona. They're both in Zone 8, but Mobile receives an average of more than 60 inches of rain each year; the average rainfall in Tucson is a measly 12 inches.

Determining your growing season

Except for gardeners living where the mercury never dips below freezing, most of us have a *growing season* — the time between the last spring and first fall frosts — that is far shorter than 365 days. As you might expect, gardeners who live in the North or at high elevations have the fewest days for growing herbs. The growing season in Fairbanks, Alaska, for example, averages 88 days, while gardeners in Tampa, Florida, often have more than 300 days between the last spring frost and first fall frost.

The last- and first-frost dates aren't guaranteed. Those dates are based on 50 percent probability, which means there's a 50 percent chance that frost will come after the spring date and before the autumn date. Put another way, if you set out basil seedlings on the frost-free date of March 19 in Birmingham, Alabama, you have a 50 percent chance that they'll be killed by a late frost. Still, the dates are a useful planning tool; you just have to be prepared to protect tender plants. Visit the National Climatic Data Center Web site at www.ncdc.noaa.gov/oa/climate/freezefrost/frostfreemaps.html to peruse the frost/freeze maps for your region.

The length of your growing season affects how well some herbs will do for you — and how you should grow them. Even if your weather seems as hot as Hades, you may not be able to produce mature plants if you have a season shorter than 100 days. Most large-leaf basils, for example, take about three months to reach full size. If your growing season is very short, you should start seeds indoors several weeks before the average last spring frost. Even warm-weather gardeners may want to begin indoors: Anyone can get a head start this way.

The Heat Zone Map

The average temperatures during your growing season also influence your herb garden. You have only 119 days between the last and first frosts if you live in Green Bay, Wisconsin, but your mean, or average, temperature in July and August is a relatively balmy 70 degrees Fahrenheit. In contrast, gardeners in San Francisco have at least 307 growing days (in fact, they only have a killing frost one year out of ten), but in July and August the mean temperature is about 60 degrees. Many herbs grow slowly or cease growth altogether in temperatures lower than 50 degrees. Plants that require heat to fully mature, such as chili peppers, may have plenty of *time* to turn red in San Francisco, but they may not have enough *heat.*

Likewise, at very high temperatures many herbs slow or cease growth and go into survival mode. Rather than risk losing too much moisture, they close their pores and shut down photosynthesis. For example, in the Deep South, basil will die out in summer from the heat. Most plants prefer moderate conditions — not too hot, not too cold.

When the dogwood flowers appear

Long before the NOAA (National Oceanic and Atmospheric Administration) became our weather guru, gardeners relied on natural signals, or phenological signs, to know when to plant and harvest. The term *phenology* comes from the Greek word *phaino*, meaning "to show or appear"; phenological signs are recurring events in the life cycles of plants and animals.

Natural signs adjust for variations in day length, temperature, rainfall, and more, which make them more reliable predictors than a single indicator like an average frost-free date. The first blooms of the pink lady slipper, which appear a week after the black flies arrive and just as the volunteer apple trees flower, are Karan's most trustworthy sign that all danger of frost has passed, and it's safe to set out basil and other tender herbs.

A worldwide phenological network of gardeners and scientists exists, but the best phenological data are those you collect in your garden, your microclimate. Record any natural event you like: the date that the bluebirds return, the first appearance of fireflies or mosquitoes, or the first chamomile flowers. After you have several years of observations, the correlations jump out.

By the way, according to lore, flowering dogwoods are a useful frost indicator: "When the dogwood flowers appear, Frost will not again be here."

To help gardeners factor heat into their gardening equation, the American Horticultural Society developed the Heat Zone Map. The 12 zones of the map indicate the average number of days each year that the thermometer hits 86 degrees Fahrenheit (30 degrees Celsius). A day during which the temperature rises above that level is called a *heat day*. Zone 1 averages less than one heat day per year, and Zone 12 averages more than 210 heat days.

You won't find heat-zone ratings on plant tags, but if you live in a region with scorching summers, you may see or hear references to the map. You can find out more about heat-zone ratings and view the map at the following Web site: www.ahs.org/publications/heat_zone_map.htm.

In the Southeast, heat partners up with humidity, creating ideal conditions for many plant diseases to strike. If you live in an area where every day is a scorcher, check with local gardeners about herbs that do, and don't, grow well for them.

Don't despair if you feel that all this information seems to be getting way too complicated. Keep in mind that most people live in a temperate climate — a climate that has distinct seasons and average temperatures above 60 degrees Fahrenheit in summer and gets at least 30 inches of precipitation each year. That means that in summer, they can grow most herbs outdoors — in their gardens and on their decks, patios, or rooftops.

Native versus Exotic Plants

The study of what naturally grows in any given region is called plant geography. North America's plant geography is amazingly diverse. Scientists have identified more than a dozen different floristic (from flora, or plant) regions. You can find everything from the arctic tundra of Alaska and northern Canada, with its grasses, lichens, and sedges, to the hot, arid deserts of the Southwest and the steamy, tropical conditions of southern Florida and Hawaii. Plants in gardens there shudder at the very thought of frost.

Natives or *indigenous plants* are those that grew in North America before people from other parts of the world arrived on the continent. In contrast, *exotic* species (also called exotics, non-natives, and introduced plants) are floral immigrants, species brought to a location from other continents or regions. Which plants are here on green cards may surprise you. Dandelions are as common as flies at a picnic, but the dandelion isn't a native plant. It came to New England with the first settlers, who used its leaves in the stewpot and its roots to treat liver diseases. Like the colonists, it liked it here and made itself at home, or naturalized. Chicory, another familiar roadside flower, is also an exotic.

Some exotics have become invasive, which means they've made themselves too much at home: They're crowding out important and desirable native plants, changing the natural ecological balance on which other living things depend, and making general pests of themselves. (For more on invasives, see Chapter 2.)

However, most exotics are welcome guests — and among them are some of our most popular herbs. (See the sidebar "Your address, please.") Finding out where herbs come from is fun for its own sake, but the geographical origin of an herb also tells much about the garden conditions that will best suit its cultural needs (what a plant needs to succeed in cultivation, such as highly acid soil or great amounts of water). Herbs from hot, arid regions are used to sandy soil and prepared for drought. Planting them in heavy soil and watering them frequently is a prescription for disaster.

Don't worry too much if the herbs you want to grow come from the Himalayas and you live on the prairie, or if they come from the tropics of Africa and you're gardening in northern Idaho. Herbs don't have to be natives to do well in your garden — they just have to be able to cope with the conditions in your garden. The good news is that most herbs are remarkably flexible: They survive — even thrive — in conditions as broad as the proverbial barn door.

Your address, please

Many herbs, such as members of the onion family, are native to more than one region, but here's a short list of herbal home addresses:

✔ **Africa:** *Aloe vera* (aloe), *Artemisia afra* (wild wormwood), *Coffea arabica* (coffee), *Gloriosa superba* (glory lily), *Ocimum* spp. (basil), *Pelargonium* spp. (scented geraniums), *Ricinus communis* (castor bean)

✔ **Australia:** *Colocasia esculenta* (taro), *Eucalyptus* spp., *Melaleuca alternifolia* (tea tree), *Pandanus odoratissiums* (screw pine)

✔ **China:** *Artemisia annua* (sweet Annie), *Cinnamomum camphora* (camphor), *Ginkgo biloba, Panax ginseng*

✔ **Europe:** *Artemisia absinthium* (wormwood), *Borago officinalis* (borage), *Calendula officinalis* (pot marigold), *Chamaemelum nobile* (Roman chamomile), *Crocus sativus* (saffron), *Digitalis* spp. (foxglove), *Foeniculum vulgare* (fennel), *Humulus lupulus* (hops), *Laurus nobilis* (bay), *Lavandula* spp. (lavender), *Mentha* spp. (mint), *Origanum* spp. (oregano), *Petroselinum crispum* (parsley), *Rosmarinus* spp. (rosemary), *Salvia officinalis* (sage), *Silybum marianum* (milk thistle), *Thymus* spp. (thyme), *Valeriana officinalis* (valerian)

✔ **Indian Subcontinent:** *Allium sativum* (garlic), *Berberis* spp. (barberry), *Cinnamomum zeylanicum* (cinnamon), *Elettaria cardamomum* (cardamom), *Piper nigrum* (pepper)

✔ **Middle East:** *Allium* spp. (onion, garlic), *Anethum graveolens* (dill), *Brassica* spp. (mustard), *Cannabis sativa* (hemp), *Carum carvi* (caraway), *Coriandum sativum* (coriander), *Cuminum cyminum* (cumin), *Papaver somniferum* (opium poppy), *Rosa damascena* (damask rose), *Trigonelia foenum-graecum* (fenugreek)

✔ **North America:** *Echinacea* spp. (coneflower), *Eschscholzia californica* (California poppy), *Hamamelis virginiana* (witch hazel), *Helianthus* spp. (sunflower), *Hydrastis canadensis* (goldenseal), *Monarda* spp. (bee balm), *Panax quinquefolius* (American ginseng), *Passiflora* spp. (passion flower), *Sassafras albidum* (sassafras)

✔ **South and Central America:** *Capsium* spp. (chili peppers), *Cephaelis ipecacuanha* (ipecac), *Erythroxylum coca* (coca), *Pimenta dioica* (allspice), *Tropaeolum* spp. (nasturtium), *Vanilla planiflolia* (vanilla)

✔ **Southeast Asia:** *Myristica fragrans* (nutmeg, mace), *Syzygium aromaticum* (clove)

Giving Herbs What They Want

In a perfect world, we would all have Garden of Eden conditions. Put another way, each of us would have a sunny, sheltered, well-drained, southwest-facing plot with organically rich loam and plenty of rainfall — ideal conditions for many popular herbs. But even if you don't have ideal conditions (and few gardeners do), you can make the most of your yard by getting to know its *microclimates* — places that are warmer, cooler, or otherwise different from the prevailing conditions elsewhere in your yard.

Making the most of microclimates

As you look at your site, begin with the big picture. Are you located in the bottom of a small valley — which often means cold nighttime temperatures as cool air drains down the hillsides? Or are you located on a north-facing slope — where your plants will receive less direct sun? Then look more closely. Does the wind come roaring through one part of your property? Is there an area that stays wet for three days after it rains?

As you're assessing your site, remember that different herbs have different requirements and there's an herb for nearly any garden locale. Here are some of the variables, starting with light.

Letting the sunshine in

Light is the most critical consideration when locating any garden — it's the one element that you, the gardener, can't supply. Most herbs are devoted sunbathers. To them, sun is as essential as fast food is to a teenager. At a minimum — and it really is a minimum — herbs need six hours of full sun daily (full sun is unobstructed sunlight). Eight hours of full sun are better than six. (Herbs labeled "full sun" do best if they have an entire day of unobstructed sunlight.)

Not only do sun-starved gardens warm slowly in the spring and cool quickly in the fall, but their residents tend to be spindly, weak, and susceptible to diseases. In most regions, the best location for herbs is a southern exposure. In hot areas, you may need to site your garden so that it receives some protection from the afternoon sun. (If the choice is between morning and afternoon sun, choose morning sun, which will warm things up early in the day yet give plants relief during the hot afternoon hours.)

If you're reading this in the middle of winter and looking out on a sunny area, don't forget that come springtime deciduous trees will leaf out and cast shadows. Of course, evergreens, shrubs, and tall plants, as well as fences, buildings, and other vertical structures, offer shade year-round. Midsummer is the best time to measure what's shading what — trees are in full leaf and the sun (in the Northern Hemisphere) is high in the sky. (See Figure 3-2.)

Finally, if you're planting in rows, run them from east to west, and plant tall herbs or vines on the north side of the garden. Both these techniques help plants get the best possible sun exposure and keep taller plants from shading their smaller neighbors.

Figure 3-2:
Take note
of where
deciduous
trees cast
shadows in
midsummer.

Shady characters

A few herbs — angelica, chervil, ginger, sweet woodruff, and violets come to mind — actually prefer a semi-shady site. Others do moderately well in partial shade.

If your garden doesn't get full sun, try some of these herbs:

- Bee balm
- Betony
- Catnip
- Chamomile
- Chives
- Cilantro
- Comfrey
- Costmary
- Dill
- Fennel
- Feverfew

- Horseradish
- Lemon balm
- Lovage
- Mint
- Mustard
- Pennyroyal
- Tansy
- Tarragon
- Valerian
- Watercress
- Wormwood

When the wind blows

Thomas Hill, who wrote *The Gardener's Labyrinth,* the first English-language how-to garden book in 1577, was quick to point out that both gardens and their gardeners need fresh air: "Evil aire . . . doth not only annoy and currupt the plants . . . but choke and dul the spirits of men."

To keep your herbs — and yourself — from being annoyed, corrupted, choked, or dulled, keep your garden away from low spots, where air can pool. (See Figure 3-3.) Cold air is heavier than warm air; that's why low areas are susceptible to frost. Pick a mountain town with "Hollow" in its name, and you've probably picked a place that holds some kind of record for a late spring frost.

Figure 3-3:
Cold air likes to settle in low-lying areas.

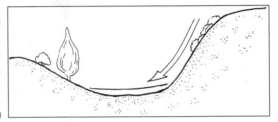

Poor air circulation also provides the stagnant conditions that encourage plant diseases, especially in humid climates. Do everything you can to ensure good air circulation. If you must fence your garden to ward off wild-life, don't make it a solid wall that will keep your herbs from getting the fresh air they need.

On the other hand, if your property is near the ocean — or regularly in the path of prevailing winds — your herbs may need protection. Any garden site that regularly gets winds in the 15-mph range needs a *windbreak,* or wind barrier.

Anything that obstructs wind does more than keep your herbs from being tattered and torn, or toppling over — it also safeguards the soil from erosion and helps keep it from drying out. If it's cold, wind can annihilate a row of young basil plants in a matter of hours (or, if you're lucky, just slow their growth for weeks to come). In contrast, hot winds *desiccate,* or dehydrate, plants, and that, too, can be lethal.

If the wind that roars through your garden is constant, you'll probably want a permanent windbreak, such as trees, shrubs, vines, fences, and walls. Temporary barriers can tame winds that come and go — mostly in early spring, for example. You can choose from dozens of possibilities, including floating row covers (secured), wire cages wrapped with plastic, cloches, and more.

Before you erect a permanent barrier, make absolutely sure you know the direction of the prevailing winds. Put your windbreak on the wrong side and you could have cold winds pooling on your angelica and rosemary. By the way, you don't have to build the Great Wall of China. Semi-open structures do a better job than solid ones (plus they don't blow over in gales).

Living windbreaks are one of the most attractive solutions, but they're also like kids' appetites: They get bigger and bigger. Plant them — especially trees — at a distance (from your garden) of four times their mature height.

Water, water everywhere

You only have to watch the news to know that some regions get a lot more rain than others. If it doesn't rain at your house during the growing season, you'll have to water. It's as simple as that. (For instructions on when and how, skip to Chapter 9.)

But if it does rain, especially if it rains often and long, make sure you don't pick the wettest spot on your property to grow herbs. Does a river run through it? Is the turf spongy? These are dead giveaways, Mother Nature's way of saying, "Not a good place for herbs."

Waterlogged ground is air-poor, and your herbs' roots need air as well as moisture. A large number of common herbs not only don't like wet ground, they prefer moderately arid conditions.

Herbs that tolerate damp soil

Some herbs are willing to put up with ground that tends to stay damp — not soppy wet, or heavy, or compacted.

- ✓ Bee balm
- ✓ Borage
- ✓ Cardamom
- ✓ Chervil
- ✓ Dill
- ✓ Elecampane

- ✓ Ginger
- ✓ Horseradish
- ✓ Lemon verbena
- ✓ Marsh mallow
- ✓ Sorrel
- ✓ Valerian

You can do one of two tests to measure your soil's *porosity* — how fast or slow it drains:

- ✔ **If you suspect your soil drains poorly,** dig a hole 1-foot deep and 1-foot square, and fill it with water. Refill it 24 hours later, and then keep track of how quickly the water drains. If the hole doesn't empty in 12 hours, drainage is poor.

- ✔ **If you suspect your soil drains too rapidly,** water your garden area thoroughly — at least to a depth of 6 inches. After 48 hours, check the soil. If the top 6 inches are dry, your soil dries faster than it should to support most plants.

You can do a number of things to your soil to make it drain better or retain water better. (Those details are in Chapter 7.) Raised beds, which you find out about in Chapter 5, are one solution for moderately wet spots. But if the ground is excessively wet, it may require draining. Think backhoe, drainage tiles, French drains, dry wells, and money. Then consider putting the garden somewhere else.

Location, Location, Location

Creating a garden is hard work. It takes time and energy. But a garden is made in soil, not stone. If in three years — or even one year — you decide that your first location was a mistake, you're allowed a do-over. Even so, it makes sense to carefully consider the placement of your herb garden. Take into account how you treat and use the plants you'll be growing. For example, if you use pesticides on your rose bushes, keep herbs away from them unless you're growing the herbs purely for their ornamental value. (Better yet, find out how to manage pests without resorting to sprays. Flip to Chapter 10 for nontoxic ways to control pests.)

Here are a few thoughts about where to locate your garden:

- ✔ **Near, but off, the beaten path.** You want family and friends to walk near your herbs but not on them.

- ✔ **Close to a water supply.** Being near a faucet will keep you from having to buy a 1,000-foot hose.

- ✔ **Away from the street and other sources of possible contamination.** Contaminated soil is commonplace alongside roads and driveways and surrounding old buildings, so avoid gardening in these locations if you can. If you must use a problematic site, have your soil tested for its lead content. (Lead contamination comes from leaching paint and paint chips, and from years of auto exhausts when lead-based gasoline was the norm.) Your county health department can point you to a lab in your area that can test for different contaminates. Remember, you'll be eating, smelling, or otherwise getting up close and personal with your herbs.

✔ **Close to your tools and supplies.** If you want to work on your biceps, however, place your garden far away from the toolshed.

✔ **In clear view.** We get pleasure in just looking at our gardens. You will, too.

Chapter 4

Designing Your Herb Garden

When people think of an herb garden, they often imagine a formal garden laid out in a knot shape or another precise geometric pattern, but this is just one way to grow herbs. You can also grow herbs in informal beds or mix them in among ornamentals and vegetables — after all, many herb plants are beautiful in their own right, and many are edible, too.

Ideally, you'll have a design in mind before you buy or sow your first herb plant. But if you're like most gardeners, herbs are at least occasionally an impulse buy: You see a plant you like and buy it — but when you get it home, you wonder where to plant it. Although it pays to have a general design in mind, flexibility is also important — that is, unless you're that one-in-a-million gardener who can actually walk past an herb display without buying at least one plant.

In this chapter, you discover the basics of designing an herb garden. Once you have the fundamentals down, you'll be ready to create your own herbal nirvana. Or, you can flip to Chapter 5 for specific herb garden plans. And because most herbs are ideal for containers, too, Chapter 6 is devoted to that subject.

Getting Started

As you consider how and where to grow your herbs, keep in mind that the definition of herbs assumes that you want to use them in a practical way. So before you make that trip to the nursery or dig your first hole, ask yourself a few questions:

- ✔ **Why am I growing herbs?** Primarily for their beauty? Or for use in the kitchen, or to make tinctures or salves?
- ✔ **How often will I harvest?** Will I snip a few sprigs every day, or do one big harvest each year?
- ✔ **Do I want a separate herb garden?** Or would it make more sense to incorporate herbs into existing vegetable and ornamental gardens?

Catering to convenience

If you'll be harvesting oregano, dill, and rosemary daily to season gourmet meals, you'll want the plants just seconds away from your chopping block. Consider mixing herbs into the ornamental beds around your house — most are attractive as well as tasty. Or, if you have the room and enough sunlight, make a small kitchen garden just outside the door, and fill it with culinary herbs (along with a few tomato and pepper plants and maybe some lettuce). At the very least, you can plant a large container of your favorite herbs outside the kitchen door. You'll be that much closer to having dinner ready in a jiffy.

Deliberating one-shot deals

Are you planning to make tinctures for a good night's sleep, dry lots of herbs to cook with in winter, or create arrangements and wreaths of dried herbs? In that case, you might harvest the entire herb crop once a year. If so, proximity to your kitchen is less important. Instead of starting a new herb garden, consider expanding your vegetable garden and growing your chamomile, rosemary, or yarrow the way you grow your other crops, in easy-to-maintain rows.

Creating an herbal oasis

Are you looking for an herbal retreat? Maybe all this talk of crops and harvests smacks too much of menial labor. Instead of being like Ma Joad toiling in the fields, *Grapes-of-Wrath* style, you picture yourself as Greta Garbo pining, "I vant to be alone." If so, your garden needs to be a place where you can escape workaday cares and revel in the pure pleasure of herbs' textures, scents, and colors. Put your herbs in a secluded spot and, if necessary, create a sense of privacy with a screen of conifers or vine-clad trellises. And don't forget to include a comfy chair or hammock.

An Herbal Nod to History

The first step in designing a garden is to consider the overall "feel" you're trying to achieve. Do you like symmetry and order? Or is a free-form look more your style? History is filled with gardens at both extremes. Of course, you may want to go for something in between.

Formal designs — tux optional

You may have formed your impressions of herb-garden design through woodcuts of medieval monasteries. These images usually show large, walled gardens with raised, rectangular beds. Everything growing in them had a use: Even the flowers weren't frivolous; they were used to decorate the altar.

Meanwhile, outside the monastery walls, wealthy Europeans were creating knot gardens, probably the most impractical garden design ever devised. Intended to be admired from upper stories, knot gardens required boxwood or various herbs to be planted in squares, circles, triangles, fleurs-de-lis, and loop-de-loops, and then meticulously pruned so they seemed to be growing over and under each other. Those swirls could contain the equivalent of a healthy, 20-foot row of rosemary, but a gardener couldn't gather much more than a leaf or two from such an arrangement without spoiling its appearance.

The tradition of geometric designs for kitchen gardens came to American shores in the 1600s, and was eventually translated in Pennsylvania by no-nonsense German settlers. Theirs was the so-called foursquare garden: four perfectly square blocks separated by 2-foot walkways. These gardeners eventually modified the look with more beds and rectangles, but still with nary a hint of a curved line.

Formal design is first and foremost geometric, with straight paths and symmetrical plant placements. Some plants are more formal than others as well, forming tidy mounds with not a leaf out of place, and these are obvious choices for a traditional herb garden. Statuary and heavy urns containing topiary also look at home in a formal garden, usually set at the center as a focal point.

Informal designs — the laid-back look

Ironically, the stiff-upper-lipped English gave us the relaxed cottage garden in which plants grown for household use were mingled in a seemingly haphazard fashion, usually in a small front yard. Favorite herbs included flowery calendula, chive, monarda (bee balm), artemisia, and damask roses alongside fragrant lilacs, lily-of-the-valley, mock orange, and dame's rocket.

But in fact, the layout underlying these cottage gardens was often as geometric as those of the monasteries. What made these gardens seem informal was the lavishness with which plants were crammed together, often climbing up the side of the dwelling and around the door, and flopping onto the walkway so that hard surfaces seemed softer.

Today, the trend in American gardens is toward a more natural look in garden design. Beds and paths are shaped with flowing curves, emulating those you see in a woodland, meadow, or on a hillside. Garden ornaments, too, may look as though they were left casually behind — wooden wheelbarrows, antique tools, or perhaps a thatched birdhouse.

Incorporating Design Basics

Beginning gardeners invariably think first about flower color, and the more boisterous the better. Some never tire of the unrelenting yellow of marigolds or the magenta of petunias. But usually, like a Lothario ready to settle down, a seasoned gardener begins to look beyond superficial flashiness to more lasting qualities: foliage color and texture, the shape of the entire plant, and fragrance. In all of these attributes, herbs are champions.

Before you go on to plant selection, though, you need to understand some of the "hard" stuff.

Garden bones: Hardscapes

Winter is the best time to see the structure of your landscape, or what the experts call its *bones*. What does your garden look like after annual herbs have given up the ghost and all but the evergreen perennial herbs are dormant below ground? In a well-designed landscape your eye should discern rhythmic lines in your paths and the edges of your beds. You should see some strong vertical lines — tree trunks or an arbor, perhaps with the bonus of a snow-shrouded garden ornament such as a statue.

Landscape designers use the word *hardscape* to refer to the permanent, nonliving parts of your garden. These include natural elements, such as boulders, as well as everything made of rock, concrete, wood, or plastic.

Paths

Every landscape needs paths, both for visual reasons (to create a sense of movement and boundaries) and for practical reasons (to get you from one area to another without tromping through the growing beds). Formal herb garden designs often have intersecting paths with an ornament placed in the center, which also serves as a focal point to draw the eye in. You can widen the path to create a terrace, giving you room to kneel or stoop when you want to harvest a sprig of mint for tea, cilantro for salsa, or sweet Annie for a dried bouquet. Widen the path a bit more and you have a spot for a bench where you can kick back and relax.

In a formal herb garden, the paths are generally straight, except when surrounding a circular knot garden. In a cottage-style or mixed garden, you have the freedom to include sinuous curves, perhaps winding under an arched trellis of passionflower (*Passiflora* spp.) or hops *(Humulus lupulus)*. You can create a path with turf, gravel or other small stones, bark mulch, or flagstones. Think about adding in some low-growing herbs between stepping-stones. Traditionally, the material of choice for paths in herb gardens is aged brick, which speaks to the plants' history. Permanent and solid, the texture of brick is a perfect foil for feathery leaves, and the mellow color of brick — varying from red through yellow — is a lovely counterpoint to the many shades of green you find in herbs.

Edging

You can edge your herb bed with one of the shrubby or low-growing herbs popular for that purpose (read more about them in the section "Developing good habits," later in this chapter), but most gardeners find it easier to employ non-living materials: landscape timber, stone, or the aged brick used for the paths. Even informal gardens benefit from having some type of border to define the beds and keep the lawn from infiltrating them.

Structures

Arbors, pergolas, and trellises provide focal points and add interest to gardens year-round. The same goes for walls and fences. Patios, decks, and terraces — any flat spot with a few pieces of comfortable outdoor furniture — invite visitors to relax and should be included in a garden design.

Color considerations

When it comes to their flowers, the best-known culinary and medicinal herbs are shrinking violets. Basil and mint have relatively insignificant flower spikes that, while capable of driving bees into passionate frenzies, should be removed if you want to keep the fresh flavor of the herb and avoid lessening its health-giving components.

Many herbs have blue, purple, or pink flowers, so if you're partial to this cool combination you can reap great satisfaction by combining thyme, chives, oregano, rosemary, and sage, perhaps with a border of lavender.

Bee balm, or monarda, offers you a choice of intense, deep pink ('Marshall's Delight') and red ('Cambridge Scarlet'). You can add yellow to the palette with elecampane, evening primrose *(Oenothera biennis),* goldenrod *(Solidago* spp.), and tansy. Calendula takes you from yellow into sunny oranges.

Garden ornaments

Because herb gardens are both historic and homey, they cry out for decoration. Yet you don't have to spend a lot of money. Browse roadside shops; check out auctions, estate sales, architectural salvage yards, and yard sales for recycled, weather-beaten treasures. And don't forget Habitat for Humanity's ReStores, where you can find unique ornamentation as well as materials you can use in construction. Or make a scarecrow with last year's fashions! Here are just a few of the ornaments often associated with herb gardens:

✔ Armillary

✔ Birdbaths

✔ Birdhouses and feeders

✔ Gates (wooden or metal)

✔ Old wagon wheels

✔ Old well pumps

✔ Small fountains

✔ Stone urns

✔ Sundials

✔ Whirligigs

✔ Wooden wheelbarrows

You can create a more lasting tapestry of color, however, by collecting herbs with an eye to their foliage:

✔ **Gray, white, and silver:** Herbs are famous for pale foliage that helps tone down or blend bright colors that might otherwise clash. Choose from catmint *(Nepeta* spp.), curry plant *(Helichrysum italicum),* lamb's ear *(Stachys byzantina),* virtually any lavender, sage, lavender cotton *(Santolina chamaecyparissus),* or woolly thyme *(Thymus pseudolanuginosis).* Among the artemisias, in addition to southernwood and wormwood, look for *Artemisia alba* 'Canescens'. Or how about one of the gray-green dianthus cultivars, such as 'Miss Sinkins'?

✔ **Purple and red:** You can bring deep burgundy red into the garden by planting perilla, purple sage ('Purpurea'), or the basil cultivars 'Rubin' and 'Osmin'. Orange mint gets its name from its smell, but its leaves have a subtle purple color.

✔ **Yellow:** Just look for some form of *aureum,* the Latin word for "gold," in a species or cultivar name. Some of these plants range from yellow to chartreuse. You can buy golden varieties of feverfew, pot marjoram *(Origanum onites),* oregano, hops, sage, thyme, and valerian.

✔ **Blue:** Color is often in the eye of the beholder, but to most, rue has the bluest foliage among herbs, especially the cultivar plant called 'Jackman's Blue'. (Refer to Chapter 2 for cautions about growing rue.) The foliage of some varieties of rosemary tends toward blue-green, and is a safer bet.

✔ **Bronze:** Bronze fennel is in a color class by itself with its distinctive, shimmery, reddish brown foliage.

✔ **Variegation:** You don't want to overdo variegated leaves — those that are tinged with white, yellow, pink, or some combination — if you don't want your garden looking like a three-ring circus. But a few variegated plants scattered here and there provide a lively counterpoint to solid green, and can brighten up a dark corner. Tri-colored sage, which has swirls of pink and white on the usual green, and variegated thymes are among the most popular variegated herbs. You'll also find subtle colors among the scented geraniums. Look for 'Fair Ellen', 'Chocolate Mint', and 'Skies of Italy'.

Fuzzy, frilly, shiny, lacy

As you grow and study herbs, you'll notice that the texture of their leaves is even more varied than their color. Deciding which plants contrast most strikingly when planted next to each other is one of the endless pleasures of herb gardening. For soft fuzziness, nature hasn't come up with anything that begs to be petted more than lamb's ear, an ornamental perennial. Its herbal cousin, betony, has greener but still hairy leaves (and contains tannins that can soothe a sore throat or treat diarrhea). A scented geranium collection is a menagerie of tactile thrills: velvety, sandpapery, and crinkly. Here are some of the herbal textures you can play with in your garden:

✔ **Fernlike:** Herbs with leaves that are divided or toothed like fern leaves include chamomile, chervil, feverfew, parsley, and tansy. The leaves of valerian are deeply divided, too, but the effect is quite different on this 5-foot-tall plant.

✔ **Feathery:** Dill, fennel, southernwood, wormwood, and yarrow are among the herbs with leaves so finely divided as to approach hairlike. Anise has fine leaves at the top of the plant, while those near its base are more like parsley.

✔ **Smooth 'n' shiny:** The smooth leaves of bay and eucalyptus reflect light and brighten a garden.

✔ **Tiny:** When you visit a well-stocked herb nursery, you may think the thyme breeders are having a contest to see who can produce the tiniest leaves. Ground-huggers such as 'Minus' thyme have the smallest — pinpoints that would do pointillist painter Georges Seurat proud.

✔ **Prickly:** What's the point? Spiny leaves give your domain a bit of drama. Try cardoon *(Cynara cardunculus)*, or its cousin globe artichoke *(Cynara scolymus)*, liver-rejuvenating milk thistle, or a thicket of the prickle-surfeited eglantine rose *(Rosa eglantina)*. Of course, keep these away from paths — unless you *want* to deter visitors.

✔ **Rough:** Running your finger across a sunflower leaf will send shivers down your spine, but for true grit, grow sage. Rub a leaf over your teeth to clean them after dinner — it's good for your gums, too!

✔ **Succulent:** These plants have their own botanical category because of the way their thick, fleshy leaves store water. Aloe is the most common herb among them. Purslane *(Portulaca oleracea),* a nutritious weed that's rich in anti-aging anti-oxidants, looks a bit like a jade plant that has been stomped on.

✔ **Pleated:** The leaves of lady's mantle *(Alchemilla mollis)* and nasturtium are round and puckery, while those of silver sage *(Salvia argentea)* add white fuzz to the garden mix.

Developing good habits

You may not be able to distinguish the sandpapery look of sage leaves or the satiny sheen of basil from a distance. But in a well-designed garden, your eye will be drawn to the overall effect of the different shapes and sizes of the plants. Informal gardens combine plants with a wide variety of shapes and sizes; formal gardens rely on a more symmetrical arrangement and some-times incorporate plants that have been carefully pruned to specific shapes. Even in informal gardens, repeating a shape gives rhythm to the design.

The shape and growth pattern of a plant is called its *habit.* Basil and sage have shrubby habits — their branching stems form more or less rounded mounds. Creeping thyme crawls flat along the ground like a living carpet. Some plants have a strongly vertical habit — mullein, with its tall flower stalks reaching skyward, is a good example. Still others are climbers, such as passionflower and hops. The following list of plant habits, along with exam-ples of herbs that fit the bill, gives you an idea of the range of shapes you have to work with when you're planning your garden.

✔ **Tall spires:** Angelica *(Angelica archangelica),* black cohosh *(Actaea racemosa),* evening primrose, Joe-Pye weed *(Eupatorium purpureum),* mullein, and other vertical herbs have an air of stateliness and drama. These plants command attention, so use them sparingly. Mullein also has a basal rosette (a circle of foliage near the stem) of big felty leaves, so you'll get a habit and texture bonus.

✔ **Big 'n' bushy:** Lovage, marsh mallow, meadowsweet *(Filipendula ulmaria),* and Jerusalem artichoke *(Helianthus tuberosus)* look more like the Capitol Building than the Washington Monument. Tall, yes, but they also gobble up lots of ground.

✔ **Grasslike:** The fanlike foliage of orris root *(Iris florentina),* like that of all irises, is handsome long after the flowers are gone. For a similar grass-like shape, lusty lemongrass *(Cymbopogon citratus)* and chipper chives are the long and short of it, respectively.

✔ **Monster leaves:** Grow cardoon, which reaches a height of 6 to 8 feet, for pure mass. Plant it where you won't inadvertently brush up against the spines of this thistle relative. Or surround your house with a living fence of closely spaced cardoon plants and ditch your home security system.

✔ **Mound:** Some herbs form such perfect mounds that you want to reach down and pet them like a sleeping cat. These make good edging plants, or you can use them for contrast with floppy or spiky plants. Good mounders include chamomile, feverfew, many types of lavender, and some of the artemisia clan such as 'Silver Mound' and 'Powis Castle'.

✔ **Groundcovers:** Creepy crawly herbs, such as sweet woodruff, cover ground and suppress weeds between other plants. An herb gardener's trick is to tuck chamomile and the low-growing thymes between stepping-stones, where they release their fragrance when you step on or brush against them.

✔ **Hanging:** Herbs with limp stems look lush dangling from a hanging basket or draped across the side of a raised bed or window box. A few good candidates are borage, catmint, lemon balm, prostrate rosemary, thyme, nasturtium, oregano (especially dittany of Crete, *Origanum dictamnus*), and some scented geraniums.

✔ **Vines:** Use climbing herbs such as hops, honeysuckle (*Lonicera* spp.), Carolina jasmine *(Gelsemium sempervirens)*, climbing nasturtium, or passionflower on a trellis for privacy or to give other herbs a windbreak.

In a border (a planting area that backs to a wall or fence), put tall plants toward the back; in a bed (a planting area exposed on all sides), set tall plants in the center. Floppy plants work best along the edges, while groundcovers will blanket bare earth between other herbs. (Make sure that taller neighbors don't steal all their sun.)

Aroma wasn't built in a day

Look up the word "fragrance" in a thesaurus, and what do you see? A list of herbs, from allspice to vanilla. In fact, fragrance so characterizes herbs that coming up with a list of herbs that don't smell wonderful might be the easiest way to deal with this category. Nonetheless, we plunge daringly ahead, suggesting a few of our favorites. Crush a few leaves of the following plants and see whether you agree:

✔ **Scented geraniums:** These olfactory superstars deserve billing above the title, as they say in the marquee biz. You can choose from scents such as rose, apricot, almond, mint, cinnamon, nutmeg, chocolate mint, coconut, eucalyptus, lemon, orange, camphor, pine, strawberry, and apple.

✔ **Mints:** If geraniums get the gold medal, mint and thyme tie for silver. There are mints that smell of apple laced with menthol, or lime, chocolate (think York Peppermint Patties), banana, ginger, grapefruit, orange, and more.

- ✔ **Thymes:** Go straight for lemon thyme, which actually does smell like citrus. Then try orange, caraway, lavender, mint, and nutmeg. You can even find thyme that smells like oregano.

- ✔ **Lavenders:** The discerning nose will find some varieties sweeter and others more medicinal. English lavender *(Lavandula angustifolia)* has the clean scent of lace handkerchiefs, while French (also known as Spanish) lavender *(L. stoechas)* smells more like something used for treating sports injuries and battling bugs.

- ✔ **Catmint:** Said not to attract cats the way catnip does, catmint also has a stronger and more appealing scent for the human nose. Some compare it to mint jelly; we think it has undertones of pine or cedar.

- ✔ **Curry:** It's a marvel how nature stuffed the aroma of curry, an East Indian concoction made up of as many as 20 different herbs and spices, into a single plant. Ironically, curry is not a culinary herb, but the silvery 12- to 18-inch plants make a great edging, and you can pluck the leaves for potpourri.

Chapter 5

Herb Garden Plans

We think the designs in this chapter are pretty magnificent, and we had fun with them in our own gardens. But feel free to do with them as you please. Make the designs bigger or smaller, rounder or squarer. Mix 'em or match 'em. Put medicinal herbs in the Shakespeare beds or bee herbs in the culinary stair steps. We're here to encourage and inspire, not to make home visits to see whether you stayed between the lines.

Raising 'em Right: A Beginner's Garden

Our first few herb gardens were variations on the design shown in Figure 5-1. You can give yours a new cast of characters every year. The sage will get too big; transplant it and use the space for more parsley. If the dianthus rebels against your hot summers, trade it out for a licorice plant.

Figure 5-1 shows a raised bed made by raking soil into a mound. If you're more ambitious, build a raised bed with a naturally rot-resistant wood, such as cedar, and top one edge with a wide board so that you can sit and admire your lavender. You can keep plants neatly trimmed or let them spill over the edges. Located just outside the kitchen door, this garden gives you quick access to ingredients when tarragon chicken is on the menu.

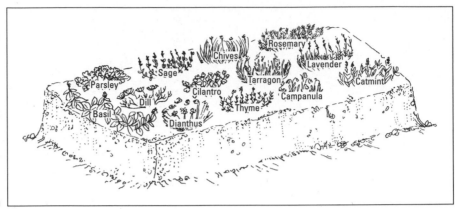

Figure 5-1:
This simple
raised bed
allows flexi-
bility in plant
choices and
easy access
to frequently
harvested
herbs.

Flying High: A Garden for Bees and Butterflies

If you enjoy watching butterflies float and bees industriously gather pollen, consider planting a garden of their favorite herbs. (Check out Figure 5-2.) Back-yard pollinator gardens are especially in vogue because of the sharp decline in the populations of many pollinating insects over the last few years. By planting herbs that attract honeybees (along with the many native bee species), you'll ensure their presence when the squash and pumpkin flowers need pollinating.

Because most people enjoy butterflies even more than bees — their seemingly effortless gliding and floating make a nice counterpoint to the frenzied vibrations of the honey-producers — we've created a garden that also includes a few of their favorite plants, as well as plants that supply food for their larvae. (As with second marriages, attracting butterflies is a case of "love me, love my children.")

Keep in mind that caterpillars are butterfly and moth larvae, so use pesticides judiciously, or you may kill the very butterflies you're trying to attract. Get a good insect field guide to help you distinguish friend from foe.

Our butterfly site is an old well that needed gussying up to keep it from looking like a wart on the landscape. This central feature could just as well (forgive the pun) be an old tree stump or a rock too big to move. The garden butts up against the edge of a deck, so viewers can look down on it.

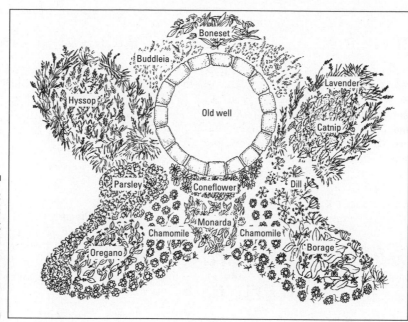

Figure 5-2:
Most herbs attract bees, and some are the favorite foods of butterfly larvae.

We also added a trio of *skeps*, straw or wicker beehives that are available in various sizes at nurseries and garden centers. If you have only a tree stump or small rock, one skep will do nicely. (Prolong the life of a skep by bringing it indoors for the winter and during prolonged periods of rain.)

The butterfly shape may be way too cute for a lot of gardeners, but if children are frequent visitors to the garden, cute is in order. At the butterfly's nether end, we've included a little puddle pub. Some male butterflies congregate in mud puddles, because during mating season they need the sodium and other minerals that leach from the soil. Here, poorly draining soil, otherwise cursed by gardeners, is ideal. (You'll need to make mud with the garden hose on days that it doesn't rain.) To one side of this area, set out a shallow dish of water for the butterflies that don't patronize mud baths, such as hackberries, commas, and question marks. (Yes, these are butterflies, but don't expect to attract any semicolons.)

Although you should normally harvest herbs on a sunny day, you may want to break that rule if you create a bee garden or if you find that your herbs attract unruly throngs of them. Collect herbs in the cool of the morning or on an overcast day, when the bees will be more laid back.

Bee and butterfly garden: More about the plants

Butterfly bush: Our garden includes this shrub, *Buddleja davidii*, to provide height behind the well — and because you can't be a self-respecting butterfly gardener without it. It smells just like the bees' honey, too! Cultivars range from pink ('Pink Delight') to magenta and pale blue, to the dark purple 'Black Knight'. Be careful, though, because butterfly bush can self-sow shamelessly in some climates; check your state's invasive species lists before planting one. To be on the safe side, choose varieties described as producing fewer viable seeds, such as 'Summer Rose' and 'Orchid Beauty', and deadhead religiously to keep the plants from producing mature seeds.

Butterfly weed: Most butterfly gardens also include pink-flowered milkweed *(Asclepias syriaca)* or orange butterfly weed *(A. tuberosa)*, an environmentally important group of plants because they're the only ones on which monarch butterflies lay their eggs.

Monarchs undergo metamorphosis in a *chrysalis* (a cocoon providing a protective covering for a moth or caterpillar) that appears to have a necklace of 24-carat gold. Another name for butterfly weed is pleurisy root. Native Americans used it to treat respiratory ailments, but the root is toxic in high doses, so don't make it part of your herbal medicine chest.

If you don't have a well or similar feature, you could plant the tall boneset in the center and plant 2-foot-tall butterfly weed on the outside. If you grow milkweed, plant it in the center, because it grows to 6 feet.

Boneset: All members of the *Eupatorium* genus attract butterflies. The best known is probably towering Joe-Pye weed *(E. purpureum)*, the purple-headed 7-footer named after an 18th-century snake-oil salesman who traveled the country promoting Native American culture and medicine.

For something only half as tall, use white-flowered boneset *(E. perfoliatum)*. Its common name has nothing to do with setting bones. Instead, it refers to the infectious disease dengue, called "bone break fever" because victims feel as though their bones are being broken. While 19th-century doctors used boneset frequently to induce sweating and vomiting, it's another herb you'll want to avoid ingesting — leave it to the bees and butterflies.

Will's Way: A Shakespearean Conceit

"Uppity" isn't the only definition of the word *conceit*. It can also mean an elaborate metaphor — an extended comparison like those that gave Shakespeare so much pleasure — or it can mean a fanciful idea, the likes of which herb gardeners are quite fond. We're kind of uppity about our Shakespearean garden design (shown in Figure 5-3), created for those who might picture themselves strolling along their garden path with an old college chum, quoting lines from Ophelia's death scene, or perusing sonnets at dusk. Shakespeare's plays and poems are full of more plants than anyone could cram into a single garden, so the list of substitutions is limited only to the time you have to spend hunkered down with his greatest works.

Figure 5-3: Many public gardens have a Shakespearean corner where you can get more ideas for this literary theme.

To make this a soothing place to read or meditate, all the plants' flowers are in restful shades of blue and pink, and the design is formal, which is less distracting than the random patterns of an informal garden.

Bay and rosemary are both handsome, aromatic plants, but they aren't cold-hardy in most of the country. Thus, we imagine them planted in ornate containers, set in the four corners, so that they can easily be brought inside to overwinter.

If you see a Shakespearean area in a botanic garden or grand private landscape, it will often have a bust of Will as a focal point. But ours is a cozy retreat, not a library, and let's face it, the man is extremely dead. To bring life and music to this haven, how about a place for avian friends to splash? To stick to the theme, you can dub it your Bard Bath.

Shakespeare garden: More about the plants

Honeysuckle: Europeans once used common honeysuckle (or more poetically, woodbine, *Lonicera periclymenum*) to treat infected skin. Don't confuse it with Japanese honeysuckle *(L. japonica),* an out-of-control weed in much of the country. Common honeysuckle is just as fragrant, but its flowers are more often tinged with red.

We picture honeysuckle clambering over an arbor, a support made of three sections of simple latticework — one on each side and another across the top. (Latticework is available at lumberyards and large garden stores.) Locate the arbor against a fence or hedge, or create a back for this bower with additional pieces of lattice.

Chamomile bench: Herbal benches planted with low-growing plants such as Roman chamomile are an appealing idea — until it rains. Here's a simple solution: Flank a seating area made from planks with two planters of chamomile. This way, you can sit on the fragrant herb when the weather is dry, and drag your fingers through the pungent foliage when it's not.

Rose: The sweetbriar or eglantine rose, is the "official" rose of Shakespeare. Its single pink flowers appear only in spring. Forget flowers. The leaves of this shrub waft the scent of green apples on a breeze, especially after a rain. But sweetbriar isn't happy until it's 6 feet tall and almost as wide. You can find some hybrids of old-fashioned musk roses *(Rosa moschata)* — such as apricot-colored 'Felicia' — that are slightly smaller.

Dianthus: If your site is right — full sun and soil that drains well and has near-neutral pH — you can try growing one of these romantic and usually fragrant annuals and perennials. Rand Lee, long-time chairman of the American Dianthus Society, says that the cheddar pink *(Dianthus gratianopolitanus)* is his favorite for the front of a border. They're intensely fragrant and have gray-green leaves.

Bayberry: Lists of Shakespearean plants often include the common myrtle, *Myrtus communis.* We suggest substituting bayberries, cold-hardy native plants from the same family. In the North, use *Myrica pensylvanica*, which grows from 5 to 12 feet high and spreads equally wide. In the South, choose the evergreen bayberry, *M. cerifera,* which grows even bigger. You can prune it or choose from many compact cultivars that will give you privacy without swallowing your whole property — and thrill you with their bayberry candle scent when you brush against them. (Zone 7 gardeners are on the borderline and can generally grow either of these species.)

Something's Cooking: A Culinary Garden

If you love to cook, grow your herbs where you can harvest a handful easily in all kinds of weather. We've designed our culinary herb garden (shown in Figure 5-4) for a house with steps that descend from the kitchen door toward the west, giving most of the garden a warm, sunny exposure. This hot site, combined with the overhang from the house, may mean watering more often (the overhang will block much of your rain).

To either side of the stairs, we've built stair-step raised beds for this cook's most frequently used herbs. Like automobile mileage, yours may differ. The raised bed to the right of the stairs gets a bit less sun, so here's where we've planted the more shade-tolerant mints, parsley, and chervil.

The garden ornament that inspired the U-shaped bed was an old metal wash-tub on which we mounted a whirligig of a washerwoman. (In some parts of the country, whirligigs get about as much respect as pink flamingos. Check your own neighborhood taste-makers for prevailing attitudes — then feel free to ignore them.)

We've used the tub as a place to sink a pot of rosemary, which can be lifted out and brought inside during the winter in cold-winter areas. Because the tub is so large, we had room to tuck other herbs around the edges, and we chose nasturtiums to add bright colors to the garden.

Figure 5-4:
This garden puts cooking herbs right outside your door.

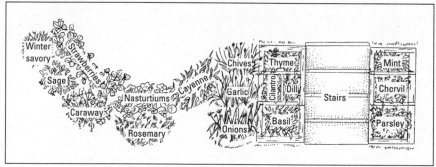

Patio Pleasures: A Garden for the Senses

Herbs are some of the most sensuous plants ever created, but gardeners don't always situate them where all their qualities can be savored. Most of them don't release their delectable fragrances into the air by themselves, as lilacs or rugosa roses do. Instead, they must be crushed or at least brushed against, so we urge you to plant them where you can stroke them or even dance on them.

The area to the north of the patio shown in Figure 5-5 is shady and damp, providing ideal conditions to grow tall valerian and sweet woodruff as a groundcover.

Fragrant, feathery-foliaged fennel (say that fast 20 times) and the fragrant double soapwort cultivar *Saponaria officinalis* 'Rosea Plena' are containerized (both species are invasive in a friendly climate). Next to our chaise we have a wrought-iron shelf for herbs that we like to caress: scented geraniums are a great choice. So are rosemary, thyme, lemon balm, and lavender.

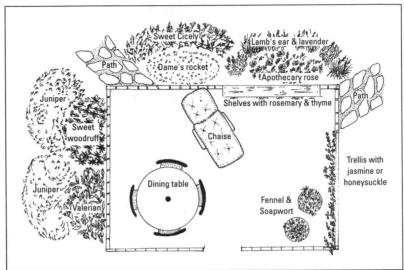

Figure 5-5:
This patio is full of herbs to smell and touch.

Patio gardens: More about the plants

Lamb's ear: If you're an herbal purist, you'll grow betony *(Stachys officinalis),* at the base of your apothecary rose *(Rosa gallica officinalis).* You can use betony to make a tea that may treat a headache or sore throat. But no garden for the senses is complete without lamb's ear *(Stachys byzantina),* betony's second cousin. It likes full sun and makes a fine edging plant, and its fuzzy gray leaves are endless fun to pet. It self-sows unless you get a non-flowering cultivar, such as 'Silver Carpet'. Both Stachys tolerate a little shade, and will be perfectly happy on the north side of your big rose.

Dame's rocket: Also called sweet rocket and dame's violet, *Hesperis matronalis* will perfume an entire garden when it produces its magenta (or occasionally white or lavender) flowers in early summer. This plant lives only a couple of years, but self-sows eagerly. Europeans use the new leaves of dames rocket to spice up salads, plus, they're rich in vitamin C.

Carolina jasmine: A southeastern native, *Gelsemium sempervirens* is an evergreen vine with fragrant yellow flowers that open in early spring. Not a true jasmine, it's also known as false jasmine and Carolina jessamine. Herbalists use it externally for facial pain, but it's extremely poisonous if ingested; gardeners in areas where the average minimum temperature is zero (Zone 7) and south should plant it for its scent and year-round screening. Gardeners in colder regions can plant woodbine, a honeysuckle we also recommend for the Shakespeare garden.

Juniper: The common juniper, *Juniperus communis,* is the plant whose berries are used medicinally and to flavor gin. If you just want a pretty, low hedge, you can plant golden yellow 'Depressa Aurea'. For privacy, choose three or four 'Hibernica', plants that grow 15 feet high but only a foot wide. If you expand your search to Chinese juniper, *J. chinensis,* you can still have pungent foliage and find shrubs that grow both relatively tall and broad. 'Sea Green', which grows 6 feet high and across, is a good choice.

We've also designed this patio to give you some privacy, with a trellis to the north and an evergreen shrub to the south, so neighbors can't catch you as you wallow around in the thyme or rub leaves of lamb's ear over your face.

Tied Up in Knots: A Garden for Teas and Medicines

If you look at drawings of old knot gardens, you can see that they weren't intended for growing herbs for harvest so much as for showing off the wealth (or leisure time) of their owners. Often, the areas between the "knots" were filled not with plants but with pebbles or turf, or earth that was colored with crushed minerals. A closed knot had no paths between blocks to allow access for picking the herbs.

But even if you have both space and time to spare, you may want to put it to a more productive purpose than impressing the neighbors with your pruning skills. So in the interest of efficiency, we've designed an intensively planted but relatively simple knot design (shown in Figure 5-6) that gives you an ample variety of herbs useful for medicine and tea. The traditional knot in the center, based on an equilateral triangle, is a *triquetra* (also known as a shamrock design). By surrounding it with an outer edging, we've provided divisions for six additional herbs. See the sidebar "Tying a triquetra knot" for how-to info.

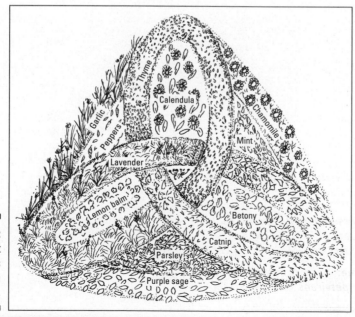

Figure 5-6: This knot design is easier than it looks.

The germander of an idea

Germander *(Teucrium chamaedrys)* has fallen by the wayside. At some point in history, people thought it could treat almost every ailment under the sun — quaint things like dropsy, quinsy, melancholy, and palsy, which sound like four of Peter Rabbit's siblings. It was a long-standing favorite remedy for gout.

But mostly, germander was so popular for making knot gardens that some people called it poor man's box, because not every Elizabethan could afford boxwood. (Gardeners have been clipping various forms of common boxwood, *Buxus sempervirens,* into hedges and edges for about 6,000 years.) With or without a knot garden, you can enjoy germander's chivelike aroma in potpourri, wreaths, and similar crafts.

Consider how much of each herb you'll be cutting before you plant, because some sections are bigger than others. (And if you harvest too much of a knot, you'll "untie" it!) Although knot garden plants are usually low-growing, we broke the rules by allowing taller plants, such as anise and fennel, in the center. Because this area is the hardest to reach, you may want to use the space for an herb that you won't be consuming — you may not harvest your own echinacea root, for instance, since echinacea capsules for cold prevention are so readily available. Or, you can follow another tradition and set an ornament, such as a sundial, in the center.

Keep the whole design to 5 feet across or less if you want to have any hope of reaching plants near the center without treading on the bed.

Because you want your herbs to knit together quickly, plant them — annuals in particular — close together. You can make your plants appear to grow under and over each other by pruning one plant on the underside of its growth and pulling the long top growth over the adjacent plant — exactly like a balding man combing what hair he has left over a bald spot.

The next list contains good candidates for tying a knot. If, like most of us, you find knots too quaint and time-consuming, use several of these plants along the edge of a less contrived herb bed to add punch to the picture you've painted:

- ✔ **Boxwood** (*Buxus sempervirens* 'Suffruticosa', 'Vardar Valley', 'Newport Blue')
- ✔ **Bush basil** (*Ocimum minimum* 'Purple Bush', 'Green Globe', 'Green Bouquet')
- ✔ **Dwarf common sage** (*Salvia officinalis* 'Minimus'*)*
- ✔ **English lavender** (*Lavandula angustifolia* 'Hidcote', 'Jean Davis', 'Lady', 'Munstead')
- ✔ **Hyssop** (*Hyssopus officinalis* 'Pink Sprite')
- ✔ **Santolina** (*Santolina chamaecyparissus* 'Nana')

> ✔ **Southernwood** *(Artemisia abrotanum)*
> ✔ **Winter savory** *(Satureia montana)*

Fine Friends: A Mixed Garden

Mixing herbs with vegetables or flowers isn't a radical technique. English cottage gardeners were doing it centuries ago. Today, the most upscale "life-style" magazines show tidy country gardens filled with edibles and cutting flowers, surrounded by gravel paths and protected from predators by fences that mix the rustic (saplings with the bark still attached) and the necessary (chicken wire to keep out predators).

The garden in Figure 5-7 combines the stylish, the practical, and the historical. You can choose your own style of fencing, from highbrow English wattle to common, yet practical, chain-link. White picket is never passé. The four beds are a rectangular version of the traditional German four-square garden. The ground around them should be easy to care for, perhaps just a mower's width of lawn. A thick layer of mulch or gravel is better still — minimal maintenance.

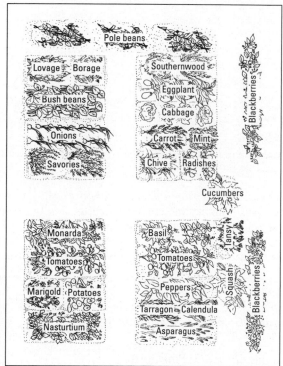

Figure 5-7: Herbs and vegetables are famously good chums.

Tying a triquetra knot

Try your hand at creating the knot garden shown in the accompanying figure. Choose a sunny, level site that can be seen from above, even if the vantage point is only a low porch or deck — a second-story window is even better.

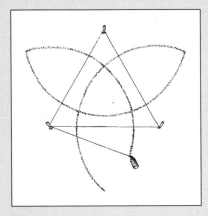

1. **Remove all turf grass and weeds, and generously amend the soil with organic matter.**

   For details on amending soil, see Chapter 7.

2. **Using stakes and string, draw the outline of the equilateral triangle that serves as the basis for the triquetra.**

A carpentry device called a *combination square* can help you figure the three 45-degree angles, but if you know how big you want your design to be (say 4 feet on a side), just triple this measurement to get a total length for your string (in this case, 12 feet). Then have a friend help you move the pegs around.

To check an angle, measure an equal distance from each peg — 1 foot, say — and mark the string at this point. If you connect those two points, the distance between them will also be 1 foot, and you have a 45 degree angle.

3. **Draw the inside arcs.**

   Tie a string to the peg, and with a stick tied to the other end, pull the string taut as you draw the arc in the earth. Mark the arc with ground limestone or flour.

4. **Make the outside arcs freehand, again using limestone or flour.**

   If you give the arc less curve, the garden will require fewer plants. Just remember to make the midpoint of each outer arc at a similar distance from the rest of your design.

Raised beds edged with boards or landscape timbers make the garden easier to weed and harvest. More important, raised beds provide better drainage. In arranging these plants, we kept these two important considerations in mind:

✔ **Choose boon companions:** We suggest placing the plants based on companion planting, which holds that some plants fare better or worse depending on their neighbors (a concept we all can relate to).

The scientific jury is still out on a lot of these relationships, but we do know that diversity — growing a variety of plants rather than a *monoculture* (a single species) — is healthier, whether you're trying to grow food crops or restore a rain forest. Basil, which may repel tomato hornworms, has long been paired with tomatoes, and fragrant yarrow may scare away insects that plague the squash family, such as pumpkins, zucchini, and cucumbers. Southernwood supposedly strikes terror into flea beetles, a scourge of eggplant.

✔ **Let a swag be their umbrella:** You can also use plants to create microclimates for others. (See Chapter 3 for more about microclimates.) Some companion plants may work their magic simply because they shade the roots of their chums. You can create even more shade with tall plants, such as the tansy and berries we planted on the west side, or a tall swag of pole beans or other climbers, which we put on the south side of the garden.

A *swag* is a rope that hangs in a curve between two poles (you may be familiar with the term as it relates to window drapes). In gardens, you can make a swag with a vine, such as English ivy. In Figure 5-7, we've hung a length of trellis netting between two bean tepees for pole beans to climb. A row of giant sunflowers is another popular and cheery approach to create shade in the garden.

Themes and Variations

An herb garden is its own theme, but you can specialize by choosing only herbs from the Bible, herbs used by Native Americans, herbs for teas, or herbs for dyes. Children love to grow "pizza" and "salsa" gardens, filled with vegetables and herbs necessary for these favorite foods. Or you can tuck herbs into other specialized gardens, such as rock gardens or even water gardens.

Rock gardens

Many of our most popular culinary herbs are native to the Mediterranean, where summers are warm and dry, winters are mild, and soil is poor and rocky. These plants are happy when snuggled against a warm rock, which retains heat at night but keeps roots cool by day. If you have a rock wall or retaining wall, you may be able to plant herbs in some of its crevices. The best herbs for planting in the crevices in rock walls are small plants that cling, creep, or droop. Good candidates include

✔ **Corsican mint** (*Mentha requienii*)

✔ **Creeping rosemary** (*Rosmarinus prostratus*)

✔ **Creeping sage** (*Salvia repens*)

✔ **Creeping thyme** (*Thymus praecox* subsp. *articus,* 'Minus', 'Elfin')

✔ **Dwarf artemisia** (*Artemisia pontica A. stellerina* 'Silver Brocade')

- **Dwarf lavender** (*Lavandula angustifolia* 'Jean Davis', 'Rosea')
- **Feverfew** (*Tanacetum parthenium* 'Aureum', 'Golden Moss', 'Golden Ball', 'White Stars')
- **Oregano** (*Origanum vulgare* 'Compacta', 'Aureum Crispum')
- **Pinks** (*Dianthus gratianopolitanus* 'Tiny Rubies'; D. chinensis)
- **Santolina** (*Santolina chamaecyparissus* 'Nana')
- **Violets** (*Viola* spp.)

Or perhaps you'll decide to give herbs a rock home of their own. An alternative is to create a *scree* bed, in which you use coarse gravel to mimic a sunny hillside. Either build it on a natural incline or create a slope with large rocks and a mix of gravel and well-draining soil. The scree bed should be at least a foot deep. When planting the herbs, remove any potting soil from their roots. Then mulch the herbs with gravel and water generously for the first few weeks. Before long, the plants will take care of themselves.

Under the big topiary

Topiary is the ancient art of clipping woody plants into shapes: spirals, pompons, wreaths, geometric patterns, even birds and animals. Most topiaries are appropriate only in formal gardens, although whimsical topiaries like cowboy boots and giraffes have a place in informal gardens. Topiaries are often grown in containers and make an especially nice feature as the centerpiece where paths intersect.

When choosing a plan for topiary, look for evergreens with small, dense leaves that grow back rapidly after shearing (which makes them bushy). Among herbs, the most popular choices are bay, rosemary, and myrtle (*Myrtus communis*).

You may be able to create some simple topiaries — cone shapes for instance — by working freehand, but you'll find the job easier if you buy a wire frame or shape your own with chicken wire. After fitting the frame over the plant (or beside it, if you're creating a wreath or working with a vine), tie the plant's new, pliable stems to the frame with green twist ties or other soft material. Check frequently as your plant grows to make sure the old ties aren't too tight; retie them if necessary. After the plant covers its frame, you need to give the plant frequent haircuts.

A specialized topiary that's easy to create with woody plants is called a *standard* — sort of a botanical lollipop with a single stem and a round head. Herbs that work well for standards include curry plant, lavender, lemon verbena, sage, and santolina.

To make a standard, remove the plant's lower stems or branches (usually about one-half to two-thirds of the way up the stem), and then pinch back new growth on the rest of the plant to encourage bushiness. When the foliage at the top of the plant is large and dense enough, clip it into a ball shape.

Gone fishin' — moisture-loving herbs

If you already have a water garden, you may want to include some herbs in it. The following plants need standing water to flourish but don't need a big pond. In fact, you can even grow these herbs in a plastic-lined whiskey barrel or similar-sized container.

- **Lotus** (*Nelumbo* spp.): Asians cook and pickle both the roots and seeds of the lotus, and drink rice wine through its stem. For a smaller pond, look for the American lotus, *Nelumbo lutea,* sometimes called "pond nuts." It has yellow flowers and grows 2½ to 5 feet tall.

- **Sweet flag** (*Acorus calamus*): Native Americans chewed the root of this iris for toothaches and boiled the root to treat burns (the Food and Drug Administration banned it as medicine after studies linked it to cancer). The variegated form is especially striking with its white-bordered foliage.

- **Water chestnut** (*Trapa natans*): This floating annual is the source of those crunchy white vegetables you get in Asian dishes. The plant is an annual with white flowers; the "nuts" are inside spiny black pods.

- **Watercress** (*Nasturtium officinale*): One of the few water plants that loves running water, watercress is happy alongside a stream or waterfall and yields peppery leaves for salads or sandwiches.

Herb gardeners often spend a good deal of time trying to make their soil drain better. (See Chapter 7 for details on soil drainage.) Fortunately, some herbs are happy in damp soil. Just remember that there's a difference between damp and soggy. These plants need plenty of moisture but won't put up with having their feet in standing water:

- **Black cohosh** (formerly *Cimicifuga racemosa,* renamed *Actaea racemosa*): This native perennial grows more than 6 feet tall and bears long spikes of off-white flower clusters. The roots are used to treat symptoms of menopause.

- **Elderberry** (*Sambucus nigra*): You may be familiar with elderberry wine, which is made from berries of this shrub. It has white umbels — flat-topped, umbrella-shaped clusters of tiny flowers — and its leaves are used to treat the flu.

✔ **Horsetail** *(Equisetum spp.):* This grasslike perennial contains silica and can be used to scrub and polish metal. Grow it in a container or it will romp all over your garden.

✔ **Male fern** *(Dryopteris filix-mas):* The ancient Greeks used the fronds of this 3- to 4-foot fern to expel worms. The male fern is a good-looking guy, too.

✔ **Marsh mallow** *(Althaea officinalis):* A 6-foot perennial with pale lilac flowers like those of a hibiscus, marsh mallow has roots known for their power to sooth sore throats (and they were traditionally the main ingredient in the confection we roast over bonfires).

✔ **Swamp sunflower** *(Helianthus angustifolia):* This moisture-loving perennial has 3-inch-wide flowers similar to those of other wild sunflowers and grows 7 feet tall. Its seeds are not only rich in vitamin E but contain substances that relieve pain and inflammation.

✔ **Water mint** *(Mentha aquatica):* This herbs smells like its landlubber kin. It will spread like them, too, if you don't keep it contained.

✔ **Willow** *(Salix spp.):* The white willow *(S. alba),* whose bark is used as a painkiller, is too big for most gardens. Choose rosegold pussy willow *(S. gracilistyla)* or the black catkin willow *(S. melanostachys).* Both have interesting catkins but stay under 10 feet tall.

Chapter 6

Herbs in Containers, Indoors and Out

Growing herbs in containers isn't just for gardeners with limited space. Picture a half-barrel planter overflowing with rosemary, thyme, sage, and tarragon right outside your kitchen door. Wouldn't you be more inclined to harvest a few sprigs for dinner there than if you had to trudge out to the back yard? (Besides, can you go out to the garden without stopping to pull a few weeds and deadhead a few flowers — forgetting the food that's burning on the stove?) When you grow herbs in containers, you can play musical plants: Try the potted rosemary in the perennial border for its visual pizzazz, then scoot the container close to the barbecue for smoking bluefish, and finally, whisk it inside when winter's chill descends.

Herbs adapt so well to containers that you can grow an impressive collection even if you have nowhere to garden but on a balcony or in a window box. Most annual herbs can thrive in pots for their brief span on earth, and many perennials also cotton to these cozy confines.

Why Containers?

Even if you have a sprawling estate, consider containerizing some of your herbs for several good reasons. If you have heavy clay soil, pots provide better drainage. You can readily move tender plants (like basil) and tropicals (like ginger) indoors. If your herbs seem unhappy, you can instantly put them in shadier, sunnier, wetter, or drier conditions.

When you grow herbs in containers, you can have plants that have different soil and water requirements next to one another — in separate pots. And if you simply don't like the way your herbs are arranged, you can create new combinations in minutes, rather than hours, weeks, or months. By setting potted herbs on pedestals, stairs, concrete blocks, or old milk crates, you can bring them closer to your nose for sniffing, to your fingers for stroking, and to your pruners for harvesting.

Container culture requires some new skills but also offers fun and new opportunities.

Choosing and Using Containers

Just about anything that can hold soil can be used to grow herbs. We've all seen plants growing in unlikely "pots" — old boots, discarded watering cans, and the like. Whether you use purchased containers or create your own, keep the following four factors in mind:

- **Drainage:** Plant roots need oxygen, and that means they can't tolerate saturated soil. Many common herbs are especially sensitive to overly moist soil, including Mediterranean herbs like lavender, sage, and thyme. Make sure excess water can drain from containers via holes at the bottom of the pot. If you use saucers to catch excess water, drain them after watering.

- **Porosity:** Porous materials allow moisture and air to pass through them. Porous pots, such as wood and unglazed terra cotta, are good choices for herbs that need good drainage; however, these containers also tend to dry out more quickly than nonporous ones. This is especially true if the pot is small or the plant is root-bound.

- **Weight:** Moist potting soil can be surprisingly heavy; add in the weight of a heavy pot, and you end up with a container that's difficult to move. If you're planting large containers, look for lightweight pots made of plastic or resin. On the other hand, if you place lightweight pots filled with top-heavy plants in a windy site, you'll spend a lot of time picking up toppled plants. Consider placing large, heavy pots on plant dollies — low platforms on heavy-duty casters — to make them easier to move.

- **Size:** For single plants of most culinary herbs, you need a pot 8 to 10 inches in diameter. A container 18 inches in diameter can hold three or four plants. Pots, unlike garden beds, restrict root growth. A too-small pot is like a too-small shoe: It cramps an herb's style. A too-large pot, on the other hand, holds extra water that your plant won't use. Just as in an overstocked refrigerator, the excess can turn ugly and even make your plant sick.

There used to be two basic choices in pots: clay or plastic. These days, garden centers devote almost as much display space to containers as they do to plants. Here's a rundown of some of the most popular types, along with their pros and cons.

Clay pots

If you have heavy clay soil, you know what raw clay looks like. You can mold it into a shape and it becomes hard when it dries, and even harder if it's fired in a kiln. Clay pots are attractive, but fragile. If you happen to drop one — while wrestling a potted 'Meyer' lemon onto the sun porch in fall, for instance — it will break. They're heavy, so you don't have to worry about them tipping over in wind. Clay pots can be unglazed or glazed:

✔ **Unglazed:** Unglazed clay, especially the familiar orangey-red terra cotta, has a natural, earthy look that blends with any decor. Because the material is porous, it "breathes," so herbs growing in clay pots are less likely to get waterlogged, making them ideal for herbs that need relatively dry soil, like rosemary and lavender. On the flip side, the soil in unglazed clay pots dries out quickly, so plants need more frequent tending than those growing in nonporous containers.

Bring these pots indoors in cold-winter climates; any water in the porous pots expands when it freezes, breaking the containers. If the pots are too large to move, protect them with a waterproof cover. (Ditto concrete and stone pots.)

✔ **Glazed:** To add color and sheen and make containers waterproof, potters apply *glazes* — silica-based coatings that, upon firing at high temperatures in a kiln, harden and adhere to the surface. Glazed pots are nonporous and available in a rainbow of colors. Although they don't absorb water like unglazed clay, it's still a good idea to bring glazed pots indoors or cover them in winter because soil left in the pot can freeze and expand, cracking the pot.

Wood

Window boxes made of wood are charming — until you try to grow something in them. The relatively small soil mass plus wood's porosity means these window boxes dry out very quickly. Save wood for large containers like half-barrels. Use a waterproof liner (with a few drainage holes) in small wooden containers to conserve moisture.

Plastic

Plastic pots are no longer synonymous with tacky. You can find a range of inoffensive colors, including some that look a lot like terra cotta. Plastic weighs less than clay, so moving these pots is easier. Plastic isn't porous, so any plants growing in plastic pots need watering less often. Make sure that excess water can drain freely.

Resin, fiberglass, and polypropylene

Often made to look like terra cotta or glazed clay, containers made from these synthetic materials have certain advantages over the real deal. They're lightweight and won't break if you drop them. Some are soft and dent easily; others have a hard shell that can take a reasonable amount of abuse.

Self-watering containers

Small pots dry out quickly and may need daily watering. That means no weekend trips to the beach unless you hire plant-sitters . . . or you use self-watering pots like the one shown in Figure 6-1. These pots contain a reservoir and a delivery system that brings the water to the plant — usually some type of wicking material. You may need to fill the reservoir every few days, but it's better than having to water several times a day. Experiment with different types of soil mixes, because their ability to draw water from the reservoir can vary depending upon the ingredients in the mix. You can purchase self-watering pots or buy kits to convert regular pots into self-watering ones.

Figure 6-1:
Self-watering pots contain a hidden reservoir.

Creative containers

Before you plunk down hard-earned cash for new containers, take a look around your home and neighborhood. You'll see potential containers when you start looking outside the box. Check out your attic, flea markets, and yard sales. Herbs, in particular, look wonderful in anything that spells "old."

Use your imagination when choosing a growing pot. The following list is incomplete, but it shows that you can use almost anything to grow herbs. Just make sure the pot has drainage holes in the bottom. If not, use it as a cachepot (see the next section).

- **Old coffee cans or tins from olive oil or other foods:** Imported brands have the most panache.

- **Decorative metal cookie and popcorn containers.** Those without lids are almost free at flea markets. You can easily punch holes in the bottom of these containers, but they'll rust out eventually.

- **Pottery, such as cookie jars:** Pottery is more expensive than tins but longer-lasting. Make drainage holes with an electric drill equipped with a masonry bit. (Practice first on that chipped casserole dish from your ex-mother-in-law.)

- **Flue tiles:** Used to line chimneys, these rectangular clay tubes can be cut to lengths of 12 or 18 inches to make instant raised beds for individual herbs.

- **Children's toys, such as sand buckets and trucks:** Metal toys look more charming but are now valuable collector's items. Plastic can be quirky.

- **Work boots:** Like baby shoes, these boots get their appeal from the creases of hard wear. If they come from a beloved's foot, even better.

- **Watering cans:** Glossy garden magazines with "Country" in the title show these cans sprouting herbs and other plants. Pretty nifty, but the spout and handle take up extra room if your space is tight.

- **Seashells:** Unless you go beachcombing in more exotic places than we do, you won't often pick up conches and other shells roomy enough for anything bigger than a seedling. Fortunately, such natural treasures often become yard-sale bargains when the neighbors' kids head for college.

- **Hollow logs:** These items rarely last longer than a season (and drainage is a problem), but if it's the rustic look you seek, the price is right.

- **Old galvanized metal buckets and tubs:** A few dents and dings only give these metal objects more personality, and they last virtually forever.

- **Whiskey barrels:** These oak containers are probably used for plants more than they're used for bourbon. Rugged, handsome, and big enough for small trees, they rot eventually. Extend their lives by placing them on bricks and lining them with an old trash bag — but remember to include enough holes for drainage.

Cachepots

A fancy word for a simple idea, a *cachepot* is a decorative outer container. If that black nursery pot is exactly the right size, leave the rosemary plant in it and hide the plastic in one of the growing pots suggested in the preceding list or in one of the following. Use sphagnum moss to obscure the top of the growing pot.

Consider these decorative containers:

- ✔ **Wood crates and boxes:** Herbs look down-home and funky arranged in recycled wooden containers, such as fruit crates, packing crates, or antique toolboxes. Lengthen their lives by giving them a coat of polyurethane.

- ✔ **Baskets:** Every garage sale has a surfeit of old baskets in endless shapes and sizes. You can employ deeper baskets as a surround for larger herbs or group small pots in a shallower one.

- ✔ **Wheelbarrows:** Often serving as centerpieces in herb gardens, these small vehicles can do double duty as planters or plant holders.

- ✔ **Window boxes:** You can put your herbs right in your window box (see Figure 6-2), of course, but their roots won't get tangled if you leave them in separate pots. This planting approach also makes it easier to pull out spent herbs and replace them with new ones.

Figure 6-2: Window boxes are great places for herbs.

Cleanliness is next to . . .

To avoid spreading soil diseases, always plant herbs in clean containers. Wash previously used pots with dish detergent, and then dip them in a 10 percent bleach-water solution (1 part bleach, 9 parts water). Rinse the containers and let them dry completely before using.

Choosing Soil Mixes and Fertilizers

When you grow herbs in containers, you need to handle the essentials — soil, water, and fertilizer — a bit differently than you would if you were growing the same plants in the ground.

The unreal dirt

Potting mix is a lot like pesto: Such a simple affair with so few basic ingredients, yet all gardeners have their favorite recipe.

Today, almost everyone starts with a soilless mix, whether straight from the bag, amended slightly, or homemade from raw ingredients. Never use soil straight from the garden for growing plants in containers. Garden soil is too heavy, compacts readily, and often contains weed seeds or disease organisms.

The easiest approach to filling containers with a healthy planting medium is to buy a bagged, high-quality potting mix. A good mix has a balance of water-holding capacity and drainage. Here's a rundown of materials you might see on the label and why they're used.

These materials help hold water:

✔ **Sphagnum peat:** Partly decomposed organic material harvested from ancient bogs in Canada and the United States, peat is difficult to wet initially, but once it's moist, it helps bind other ingredients together. Peat is also acidic, so soil mixes containing peat usually contain limestone or dolomitic limestone to neutralize the acidity.

- **Coir:** Coir is residue from coconut shells. Because coir is a renewable resource, it's becoming popular as a substitute for peat.

- **Compost:** Compost is decomposed vegetable matter. Leaf mold (another name for composted leaves) and composted bark are two common ingredients in potting mixes.

- **Water-retaining polymer:** These crystals absorb many times their weight in water and slowly release it back to plants as the soil mix dries. Soil mixes that contain these crystals remain too wet for some herbs (like the Mediterranean herbs), so experiment before using them in all your containers.

These materials provide drainage:

- **Perlite:** These tiny white pellets come from crushed volcanic rock that has been heated.

- **Vermiculite:** These silvery flakes are derived from expanding mica. Vermiculite is great for starting seeds, but it compacts more quickly than perlite in long-term plantings.

- **Sand:** Sand was once a standard ingredient in most potting mixes, but experts now debate whether or not sand belongs in a container. Sand is heavy; mix some into potting soil to weigh down a container that's top-heavy.

Pre-moisten dry soil mixes by stirring in some warm water an hour or so before you plan to use them, so the water has time to be absorbed through the mix.

Mixing it up

You can look for specialty mixes or doctor up a standard mix to suit different herbs. A basic, soilless potting mix consists of one part each of peat, vermiculite, and perlite with a little limestone thrown in. For succulents, such as aloe (an essential herb for your kitchen windowsill, where you can grab a stem for treating minor burns), look for soil mixes formulated for cactuses or add some extra perlite into a basic mix. A tropical plant like ginger, on the other hand, likes a more humus-rich soil, so you might add some compost to the basic mix. You can also add fertilizer to the mix. Slow-release formulas, such as Osmocote, break down slowly, releasing nutrients to plants over the course of a few months. Organic slow-release blends often include kelp, alfalfa, and fish meals.

Chuck those shards

Like the urban legend of the alligator in the sewer, some gardening myths refuse to go away.

No matter what you hear, or who you hear it from, do not put a layer of broken pieces of crockery, pebbles, or Styrofoam peanuts at the bottom of your container to improve its drainage. You'll actually make the drainage worse by giving plants a shallower column of soil and creating a place for water to accumulate and rot roots.

An exception is when using cachepots. If you set a growing pot with drainage holes inside a cachepot without drainage holes, you can become blithely unaware of overwatering and drown your herb in the resulting bathtub. Setting some pebbles on the bottom of the cachepot can lessen this possibility, but you still have to pay attention: Don't let excess water creep up past the bottom of the inside pot. (If you've hidden the inside pot with Spanish or sphagnum moss, peel it back and check occasionally.)

A final reminder: Potting mix is like bath water. You need to toss it after it has been used. If you're raising annual herbs, recycle the contents of your containers at the end of the growing season. As long as the plant wasn't diseased, add it and the soil mix to the compost pile. (If you're growing perennial herbs in containers, repot them, or at least refresh the potting mix they're growing in, every two or three years.)

A no-drainer

It's crucial that your pots have drainage holes. But make sure they don't allow too much drainage so that water gushes out and takes soil with it. To help hold soil in, put a piece of old window screen or a scrap of landscape fabric in the bottom of the pot.

Drainage holes located on the bottom of a pot are useless if the pot is on a surface that impedes water flow, such as a concrete walkway. Prop up the pot with bricks, wood blocks, or decorative "pot feet" to allow water to drain freely. If your pot sits on a wood deck or any other surface that can stain or rot, place a saucer under the pot to catch runoff water; just remember to empty it regularly.

Make sure the saucer is at least as wide as the pot's rim in case there's any overflow when you're watering. (And remember that terra-cotta saucers are porous and become damp — they'll ruin wood, carpet, and other surfaces unless you place a nonporous material under them or coat them with polyurethane.)

Beware of plastic hanging baskets that come with attached saucers. The saucers are invariably too small, and water will quickly stream out onto whatever is below. If you can strategically locate your hanging basket over a big planter and you don't mind a bit of splash, it's a nice water-saving trick.

Now, the Easy Pot: Putting It All Together

You have a container. You have a bucket of pre-moistened planting mix. You have a plant. Now what?

1. **Lift the herb out of its seed tray or tap it out of its nursery container, and examine the roots.**

   If the roots are coiled, badly tangled, or crowded, the plant is *root-bound* — it's been growing in a too-small container for too long. Try to loosen and spread the roots before repotting the plant. If the plant isn't root-bound, don't disturb the root ball.

2. **Add a base layer of potting mix to the new container, firming it gently.**

   Adjust the depth of this base layer by placing the plant's root ball on the soil surface; add or remove soil until the top of the root ball sits an inch or so below the rim of the pot.

3. **Holding the plant upright, add potting mix all around the plant.** Fill in around the root ball, firming it gently as you go, until it's level with the surface of the root ball.

4. **Set the pot in a tray of room-temperature water for several hours or water it gently from above.**

   This will settle the potting mix so it makes good contact with the root ball.

5. **Let any excess water drain.**

   If necessary add more potting mix to reach a level of 1 inch below the top of the pot and water again. Figure 6-3 shows a properly planted herb.

How dry I am

Most plants that fail in containers placed outdoors do so for lack of water. Heavy spring rains can lure gardeners into complacency. This tendency is especially true with easy-going, low-water plants like herbs. The sun will come up tomorrow, and it will rain a couple times this week, right? Then comes August, a week at the beach, and an adolescent house sitter. . . .

Figure 6-3:
A properly planted herb.

Plan on watering outdoor containers every day from mid- to late summer, more often and for a longer period of time if you live in an arid climate or if the weather is windy. (Gardeners in hot regions also should avoid planting in small containers, which dry out too quickly.) You may not need to water daily, but set aside the time so you get into the habit of doing it.

Take a look at these tricks to cut down on watering:

✔ **Mulch:** Organic mulches (bark, compost, or shredded leaves) on the surface of the potting mix slow evaporation, retaining moisture. Because you can't see whether the soil is dry, poke under the mulch with your finger to test whether it's time to water. Pebbles or gravel, on the other hand, tend to absorb heat and may dry out the mix faster.

✔ **Polymers:** These absorbent crystals swell up like gelatin when wet and then release the water gradually. Follow directions carefully; if you use too much, your herb roots will suffocate in a mass of goo.

✔ **Drip systems:** If you have many valuable herbs, you can invest in a drip-irrigation system with timers and little tubes that drip water into individual containers, like the one in Figure 6-4.

✔ **Watering wands:** These extension devices attach to a hose for watering hanging baskets. A great tool, but because you can water the basket without lowering it (and without seeing or feeling the soil), using a wand can encourage overwatering.

Figure 6-4:
A drip
irrigation
system on a
timer is a
convenient
way to
water.

Fertilizer: A strict diet

Herbs are, by and large, strict dieters. Like supermodels, they become soft
and vulnerable when overfed. But because most soilless mixes are the equivalent of bread and water (that's white bread), you need to feed them some
chicken and broccoli periodically.

We didn't raise our children on potato chips, and we don't give our container
plants junk food either. Give the potted plants the same healthy, organic stuff
that you would the herbs in your planting beds. Many different formulations
are available, including fast-release for quick pick-me-ups and slow-release
for long-lasting results. For herbs growing in containers, we use half the recommended amount in monthly doses.

Surviving the big chill

When it comes to enduring cold winters, growing herbs in containers has its
challenges and benefits. Plants growing in containers aren't as cold-hardy
as those growing in the ground. In the garden, soil temperatures may dip
into the 20s and 30s, but the sheer mass of the soil keeps it from getting any

colder. However, when air temperatures dip below zero, the soil in containers, having less mass, may get nearly as cold as air temperatures. Roots of even the hardiest plants can't take that extreme cold. If you're growing annual herbs like basil, you can just toss plants at the end of the season (or bring them inside in late summer). Perennial herbs require some special care.

One big plus to growing plants in containers is that you can move them around. If an early cold snap threatens, move the containers into a sheltered place until the weather warms up again. Then, when winter really starts to dig in its heels, you can move the containers to a sheltered place to spend the winter — a cool porch, for example.

As a rule, you can leave perennial herbs outdoors in containers all winter if they're hardy to one or two zones farther north than your home. If you live in USDA Zone 6, for example, choose perennial herbs that are hardy to Zones 4 or 5 if you want to winter them outdoors.

Another way to overwinter perennial herbs is to bury them. In fall, dig holes for the containers of your perennial herbs and tuck them in for their winter sleep, backfilling around the containers with soil and covering the tops with a comforter of leaves. A cold frame is handy for this, as is a *nursery bed* (a small tilled garden that you use in spring for starting seeds and in summer for heeling in, or temporarily planting, new perennials and other plants).

One caveat: If you live in the far north, you may be growing herbs that won't survive even with this coddling. The section titled "Gimme shelter" in this chapter has more on bringing herbs indoors.

Ideas for Outdoor Container Combos

To whet your container appetite, we're sharing a few of our favorite outdoor container plantings. Once you get started, we're sure you'll come up with your own favorite combinations.

The whiskey sour barrel

The half-barrel in Figure 6-5 may make you pucker up — not because it's lovable, but because all the herbs in it are lemon-scented or lemon-flavored. The figure also illustrates principles that apply to planting any large container with a group of herbs. For example:

- ✔ **Choose plants that require similar cultural conditions** — the same amounts of light and water, the same kind of soil.

✔ **Put a vertical or spiky plant in the center** (or at the back if the container will be against a wall). In this case, we've used the old-fashioned lemon daylily *(Hemerocallis lilioasphodelus)*. If you prefer something you can use in the kitchen, substitute lemongrass.

✔ **Save room around the rim for at least one plant that flops becomingly over the side.** Lemon thyme *(Thymus* x *citriodorus)* is usually described as upright, but you can persuade it to droop earthward. Or look for 'Doone Valley', a creeping cultivar with gold variegation.

Figure 6-5:
A tall plant at the center of a barrel planting provides a focal point.

You can grow many other "lemon" plants, including lemon balm, a hardy 2-foot member of the mint family, lemon catnip *(Nepeta cataria* var. *citriodora),* and even a lemon marigold *(Tagetes tenuifolia* 'Lemon Gem').

For you die-hard lemon lovers, here are a few more:

✔ **Lemon geraniums:** Look for *Pelargonium limoneum; P.* 'Frensham Lemon', which is unmistakably citrus; *P. crispum* 'Fingerbowl Lemon', which boasts tiny crinkled leaves; and *P. crispum* 'Variegatum' with handsome green and white leaves.

✔ **Lemon bee balm:** *Monarda citriodora* grows 1–2 feet high and has pink-purple flowers. The Hopis used it to flavor game; you can use it for tea.

✔ **Lemon basil:** Look for two cultivars of *Ocimum basilicum* var. *citriodorum* — 'Mrs. Burns' or 'Sweet Dani', which won the respected All-America Selection award in 1998.

✔ **Lemon trees:** Like lemon verbena, lemon eucalyptus *(Eucalyptus citriodora)* and 'Meyer' lemon *(Citrus* x *meyeri)* trees have to come indoors in winter. Try one or the other in the center of your arrangement, with pots of smaller lemon herbs at its feet.

Strawberry jars forever

Strawberry jars, those tall terra-cotta pots with side holes at different levels, are a space-efficient way to grow small herbs such as sweet marjoram, thyme, dwarf scented geraniums, or bushy basils. A word of advice: Go plant shopping early; the root ball of each herb you grow needs to be smaller than the hole in your jar.

To plant your strawberry jar, fill it up with potting mix to the level of the first holes. Remove your first herbs from their pots and soak their roots briefly in clean water; cut away any long, stringy roots that will be hard to work with. Slide the roots and stem into the hole, angling them slightly downward (if necessary, use a pencil to push and guide them) until the plant's *crown* (the place where the stem and roots meet) is even with the edge of the hole. Add about an inch of potting mix (to cover the roots), and water gently to settle the plant in.

Add more potting mix, up to the next level of holes, and repeat the process. When you near the top of the jar, center an upright or slightly larger plant — chives, lavender, parsley, and basil are good choices — and fill the jar to within an inch of the lip. Water gently, and remember to rotate the container frequently so that all the herbs get an equal amount of sun.

All in a row

A trio or quartet (or nonet . . . or more) of identical pots filled with different herbs creates a unified display, as in Figure 6-6. You can create your own pizza herb container garden by planting basil, marjoram, oregano, parsley, and thyme in different pots. Or combine the basil and parsley in one pot (they like moist soil) and marjoram, oregano, and thyme in a different pot (they prefer soil on the drier side). Create your own Simon and Garfunkel garden with parsley, sage, rosemary, and thyme. Or maybe a salsa garden, with cilantro and a few hot and sweet pepper plants.

Hang 'em high

Hanging baskets are another striking way to display herbs — if you have a good place to hang them, as shown in Figure 6-7. While Victorian porches are a great place for hanging ferns (all that cool shade), and smack under the eaves of a house is a great place for baskets of succulents (all that protection from rain), most herbs need a sunny home where they can benefit from an occasional shower.

An ideal place for hanging baskets is a *pergola,* an arborlike structure that consists of a series of upright supports topped by horizontal beams. You can hang baskets not only from the overheads, but on hooks attached to the uprights, as well.

Figure 6-6:
Similar pots give an herb display a sense of unity.

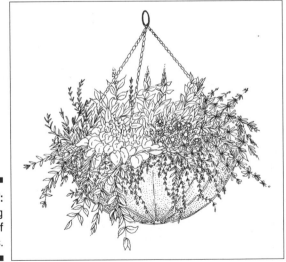

Figure 6-7:
A hanging basket of herbs.

Don't hang your baskets so high that you can't reach them to water, pinch off dead flowers and stems, or harvest occasionally. And don't hang them so low that tall friends have to duck under them.

As for the containers themselves, ceramic pots are too heavy to hang, and unglazed terra-cotta pots dry out even faster in the air than they do on the ground. Wire baskets lined with sheets of sphagnum moss dry out quickly, too. Plastic, fiberglass, polypropylene, and resin pots are lightweight and waterproof, making them good choices. Look for self-watering baskets to make watering chores easier. As tenants for your hanging basket, choose herbs that don't grow too tall. Look especially for plants that dangle gracefully — ones with words like "creeping" and "prostrate" in their names.

Some good candidates for hanging baskets are

- **Catmint** (*Nepeta* spp.)
- **Creeping golden oregano** (*Origanum vulgare* 'Aureum')
- **Creeping rosemary** (*Rosmarinus officinalis* 'Prostratus', 'Lockwood de Forest', 'Huntington Carpet', 'Ken Taylor')
- **Creeping savory** (*Satureja repandra*)
- **Creeping thyme** (especially *Thymus citriodorus* 'Doone Valley' and 'Silver Needle' thyme [*T. cherlerioides*])
- **Curly parsley** (*Petroselinum crispum* 'Triple Curled')
- **Dittany of Crete** (*Origanum dictamnus*)
- **Trailing nasturtium** (*Tropaeolum majus* Gleam and Whirlybird series)

If plants don't hang down enough initially, you can train woody stems, such as thymes, by tying fishing weights to them.

Growing Herbs Indoors

Several years ago, coauthor Kathy asked a nationally known herb expert which herbs grow best indoors. It was a brief chat. "You can't grow herbs indoors," he responded. Later, we learned that he is notoriously cranky on many subjects. We also learned that he wasn't far off the mark.

Don't get us wrong. You can grow herbs indoors. In fact, you can grow many beautiful tropical herbs that you can't grow outdoors unless you live just a short swim from Central America. And you can keep others alive, hanging in there for a few weeks of hard winter until you can safely move them back outside again.

But herbs are not philodendrons or even African violets. In other words, they aren't a snap to grow inside. This section shows you which ones will feel at home in the family room and how to increase your chances of success with some of the more finicky types.

How sweet it is!

An unusual tender herb you might want to try in a hanging basket indoors is Aztec sweet herb (*Phyla dulcis,* formerly *Lippia dulcis*). Garden writer Elvin McDonald says it reminds him of a trailing lantana, "except the blossoms are greenish and conelike." The camphor aroma would seem to contradict its common name, but the leaves are so sweet — 1,000 times sweeter than sugar — you can mince them up for tea time. You can also use the herb to treat colds and colic, as the Aztecs did. Aztec sweet herb likes somewhat moist, rich soil but tolerates average house temperatures.

What really works

Of course you can try growing herbs indoors, especially if you live in a climate where the growing season is about as long as a sneeze. You can savor fresh flavors and heavenly scents year-round. Herbs aren't just for Fourth of July cookouts. Rosemary, bay, and bayberry are as closely associated with the Yuletide as mistletoe and balsam firs.

Indoor gardening isn't any more difficult than outdoor gardening, it's just different. In the case of herbs, you have to make sure that the timer has turned on your grow lights. You also have to be vigilant: Herbs that are almost never troubled by insects and diseases in the garden are easy targets when grown indoors.

The bare-bones essential for growing herbs indoors is artificial light. But even when you provide that, many plants balk at confinement, like kids in a classroom. Some herbs are too tall to grow under lights; some have deep tap roots; some require a period of chilling or complete dormancy during the winter months.

With other herbs, it's a matter of what we might call quality of life — for both of you. They'll survive, yes. You'll have enough parsley to garnish your lemon chicken but not enough to make tabbouleh. You'll have a sprig of basil to impart some personality to that grocery-store tomato, but pesto? Forget it.

Forget, too, any herbs that you're growing for flowers, fruits, or seeds, such as fennel or dill. Getting plants that far along indoors is impossible without a greenhouse . . . and darn hard even with one!

Gimme shelter

Many tender perennial herbs must come indoors during winter in the colder regions of North America. Leave aloe, bay, ginger, lemon verbena, rosemary, scented geraniums — and many more — outside in December and January, and all you'll have left in spring are a few dead stems and a pot of soil to dump on the compost pile.

Only a handful of herbs appear consistently on everyone's list of indoor favorites. Bay adapts fairly well to being indoors, yet for some it dies. However, if your bay (a symbol of honor) dies, evil may descend on your household — at least according to folklore.

Following are a few of the herbs that most gardeners must haul inside when the mercury dips:

✔ **Lemon verbena** can be a good indoor herb, but you should know that after you've wrestled it inside, your plant will ungraciously drop all its leaves. Don't panic, and don't fertilize. Because lemon verbena is deciduous, it's supposed to lose its leaves in autumn, so it's just going to sit there for a while and look ugly. Let it get a bit dry, and keep an eye open for spider mites and whiteflies. Resume fertilizing and watering in early spring.

✔ **Rosemary** is the summer vacation romance that palls when autumn comes around. Without gentle zephyrs and sunlight — and with too much fawning from a well-meaning owner — the death blow is usually root rot from too much water. Use a soil high in perlite, and keep it just *barely* damp. It also goes to meet its maker if it gets bone dry.

✔ **Scented geraniums** do well inside. They need plenty of light, good air circulation, daytime temperatures around 70 degrees Fahrenheit, and ideally, nighttime temperatures slightly cooler, around 60 degrees Fahrenheit.

Instant herbs

For (almost) instant gratification and no messy soil, try growing sprouts. Cress and mustard are two herbs you can harvest within a few days of sowing. Soak a couple tablespoons of seeds overnight, rinse well, and then put in a wide-mouthed quart jar with a cheesecloth-and-rubber-band "lid." Lay the jar on its side near an east or west window; rinse the seeds in water twice a day. When you see more leaves than seeds, dig in.

Many other herbs can survive indoors. Give them plenty of artificial light, and they'll struggle through winter. In their search for sunshine, many plants get leggy and impossibly tall and lean like Ichabod Crane, so prune stem tips frequently to keep them bushy. (Pinching off the ends tells the buds farther down on the branch to start growing.)

Gardeners have moderately good luck with growing these herbs indoors:

- Artemisia
- Basil
- Catnip
- Chives
- Costmary
- Curry plant
- Germander
- Ginger
- Lemon balm
- Marjoram (*Origanum majorana*)
- Mint
- Oregano
- Parsley
- Rue
- Santolina
- Winter savory

Caring for Herbs Indoors

So you've picked out a few herbs that you think deserve to share your humble home. Now think of your abode as a bed-and-breakfast and some-time-clinic for plants. Herbs reward you with their pleasant company, but you do need to cater to their appetites and whims.

Moving day

Psychologists say that for humans, moving to a new home is one of those events, like weddings and births, that's highly stressful, even when happy. The same is true for plants. Moving is a big change.

When you take plants from outdoors to indoors, they adapt by producing a different type of foliage: leaves that can make sugars and carbohydrates efficiently in lower light. An abrupt move makes their current "outdoor" leaves turn yellow and drop off or become brown around the edges.

You can ease your herbs' transition by moving them under a tree, an overhang, or a shelter of shade cloth (a mesh material available from garden shops or online) for a few days or a week. While the plants are in the transition area, check them carefully for any sign of insects. If you see any, try the pest-management treatments we talk about in the section "In sickness and in health," later in this chapter.

You also need to reduce both fertilizer and water. Less fertilizer slows high-energy top growth (but the roots will keep growing). Drier soil "hardens off" the foliage, preparing it to cope with your home's drier environment.

If you want to start new herb plants indoors — a quick crop of basil, for example — see Chapter 8, which tells you how to sow seeds indoors.

Bright lights, big payoff

In providing light for your indoor plants, the goal is to mimic the light spectrum of the sun as closely as possible. Several _indoor light gardens_ — special plant stands that have light fixtures suspended over each shelf — are on the market. Most gardeners use regular fluorescent bulbs, ideally a mix of "warm white" bulbs (to provide light from the red end of the sun's spectrum) and "cool white" bulbs (for the blue end). Alternatively, you can look for fixtures that use T-5 high-output fluorescent bulbs that provide full-spectrum light. Avoid incandescent bulbs; they give off too much heat.

You can make your own light garden by purchasing a standard "shop-light" fixture that holds two bulbs under a hood so the light is directed down at your plants instead of out into the room. The bulbs should be no farther than 6 inches apart.

Most of these fixtures hang from a chain or cable, which enables you to move them higher or lower. For seedlings and cuttings, the lights should be only a few inches away from the plants. Mature herbs should be about 10 to 12 inches away from the lights. Give your herbs 14 to 16 hours of light daily by plugging the light fixture into an inexpensive timer.

Air of superiority

Good air circulation is also essential to growing herbs indoors, where plants need air movement but not gale-force winds or even a cold draft. To encourage cross-ventilation, keep the door of the room where they're growing open. And don't crowd plants together — space them far enough from their neighbors so their leaves don't touch. If your house or apartment is well-sealed, use a small tabletop fan to get the air moving.

Because the air in most homes is very dry, especially in winter, set your containers in trays lined with pebbles and filled with an inch or so of water. The herbs should sit over the water, not in it.

Some may like it hot, but most herbs like it cool, around 68 degrees Fahrenheit during the day. Nighttime temperatures should be 5 to 10 degrees lower. Make sure that the leaves of plants sitting on a windowsill don't touch the glass — if the windowpane freezes, so will the leaves!

Eating and drinking

Just as outdoor containers tend to suffer from too little water, indoor plants often get too much. Plants that are growing rapidly use more water, but many perennial herbs go semi-dormant or completely dormant in winter. These plants need much less water than they did in summer.

Watering on a once-a-week schedule may help you remember, but like a good waiter or waitress, you should inquire first as to whether your service is needed. Water most herbs only when the soil surface is dry. Other watering tips:

- ✔ Water less often if your home is cool or if your herbs are growing in plastic pots rather than clay.
- ✔ Water less often if plants seem to be ailing (rapid growth adds to their stress).
- ✔ Don't let your plant sit in a saucer of water.
- ✔ Don't shock plants with cold tap water; water should be tepid — about room temperature.
- ✔ Let tap water sit overnight to dispel much of the chlorine.

Observation is key. Some plants are simply thirstier than others. For example, basil seems to need even more water when grown indoors than it does outdoors.

Currying flavor

For a handsome houseguest with a scent that will drive you wild with desire (for dinner), try cardamom. The ground seeds from this member of the ginger family are crucial to Indian cuisine. The white flowers, tinged with violet, are elusive indoors. But the perfume of the 2-foot leaves, which resemble thick lances, will have you pining for curry and kebabs.

Use less fertilizer — and use it less frequently — indoors than you would outdoors, because most plants are growing more slowly. If you're using fish or seaweed emulsion, which we recommend, this will be a relief, because they can smell of last week's halibut. Give the plants a monthly shot at one-fourth the recommended dose. (If the smell bothers you, put the plants on a tray and whisk them to a warm porch or garage at mealtime, or look for formulas described as odorless and hope for the best.)

In sickness and in health

Dry heat, overwatering, and especially the proximity of neighbors mean that when pests strike indoor plants, damage can spread like a plague. Vigilance is a must.

Although the list of indoor pests is shorter than the list of outdoor foes, some of these enemies are extremely difficult to control. Aphids, spider mites, and whiteflies are fond of herbs with succulent foliage and stems; bay and other woody plants are likely homes for scale. Mealybugs are equal-opportunity enemies. (For more information about the insects and diseases that attack herbs — and how to combat them — see Chapter 10.)

Integrated pest management, or IPM, is a practice in which you first do everything you can to prevent plant problems, and *then* take progressively more drastic steps to correct them.

Here's our IPM approach to gardening indoors:

1. **Keep it clean.**

   Remove dry leaves and other debris, use clean containers and potting mix, and clean the surfaces on which plants sit.

2. **Don't crowd plants.**

   Allow enough space between plants for good air circulation; this helps minimize disease problems and makes it more challenging for pests to jump from one plant to the next.

3. **Don't overfertilize plants.**

   Rapid growth makes plants weak and susceptible to disease and pests.

4. **Isolate anything you bring indoors — cut flowers or new plants — for at least two weeks.**

   Isolate any herbs that become infested while you're treating them, and don't put them near other plants until you're sure you have the pest under control.

5. **If plants become badly infested, consider getting rid of them.**

   Unless plants are particularly valuable (either moneywise or for sentimental reasons), sometimes it's best to start over with fresh, healthy plants.

6. **At the first sign of insect pests, begin spraying the plant frequently with water.**

   You can control some insect pests by simply knocking them off the plants with a stream of water. Wash small plants in the kitchen sink; bring larger ones into the shower for a good hosing down. Make sure to wash the undersides of the leaves, too. Let extra water drain from soil.

   To keep from drowning or dislodging the soil, cover it with aluminum foil.

7. **Dab infested areas with a cotton swab dipped in rubbing alcohol.**

   This is especially effective on mealybugs and scale insects.

8. **Try spraying with insecticidal soap.**

   Follow the directions on the label, and be sure to cover the entire plant, including the undersides of the leaves. Note whether it's safe for edibles.

9. **Sticky traps not only help control flying pests but also show you how heavy the infestation is.**

   These are colored pieces of plastic or cardboard coated with a sticky substance to catch pests. Different colors attract different pests.

10. **To smother insects, try summer-weight (light) horticultural oil.**

    This is especially effective for scale insects.

Part III
Getting Down to Earth

In this part . . .

In this part, we get down to the nitty-gritty of growing herbs, starting with the soil. We look below ground at the characteristics of soil and delve into how you can nurture the soil ecosystem so that it can in turn nurture your plants.

Then comes the fun part: planting. We consider the options of growing from seed or purchasing plants and then take you step-by-step through the planting process. We also talk about caring for your herb garden, including mulching, watering, fertilizing, weeding, and keeping pests at bay.

Chapter 7

There's No Place Like Loam: Preparing Your Soil for Planting

- -

- -

Some gardeners are downright contentious about the word *soil,* insisting that it's not the same thing as dirt. Soil, they insist, is the stuff in your garden; it's what you grow plants in. Dirt is what you wash off your hands or sweep under the rug.

Soil. Dirt. Even planting medium. It's the place roots call home. Call it what you want. The gardener's secret is never to treat soil like dirt.

Savvy gardeners continually improve their soil. It doesn't matter how long you've been growing herbs and other plants: Garden soil is always a work in progress. This chapter is all about soil and what it takes to get it ready for planting.

What Plants Need from Soil

Soil anchors plants to the earth and supplies the oxygen, water, and nutrients that they need to live. Good garden soil, according to the professionals, consists of about 25 percent air, 25 percent water, 45 percent mineral particles, and 5 percent organic matter.

That's right — although most people think of soil as a solid, about half the volume of a healthy soil is actually made up of air and water! Picture a glass filled with marbles; the spaces between the marbles are like the spaces between soil particles. Plant roots grow in these spaces — the same passageways through which air, water, dissolved nutrients, and soil organisms travel.

Soil provides plants with much of what they need to survive and grow, including air, water, and nutrients:

- **Air to breathe:** Plants need oxygen, and they absorb some of it through their roots. A few plant species thrive in ground so wet that it contains almost no air. That extra moisture may be okay for watercress, but not for most herbs (or for many of the beneficial macro- and microorganisms that live in your soil). If the roots of most herbs sit for too long in saturated soil — soil in which the spaces between the particles are filled with water — the roots will die, and when the roots die, the plant dies, too. So one of your goals in preparing the soil for an herb garden bed is to make sure that water drains well.

- **Water to drink:** Most plants are about 90 percent water (which is why plant leaves become limp during a drought). And most plants need a fairly constant supply of water, especially during hot, dry weather. So although you want water to drain from the soil after watering or a heavy rain, you don't want it to drain so quickly that plants are left thirsty. Another one of your goals, then, is to make sure the soil retains some water.

- **Nutrients for healthy growth:** As roots take in the water they need, they also take in the nutrients dissolved in that water — nutrients that the plants need for healthy growth. Some of these nutrients are leached into the water from minerals in the soil; some may be from fertilizer you've applied to the soil (more on fertilizing in Chapter 9). Water must be present for plants to take up nutrients.

Soils 101

Particles of rock make up most of the solid portion of garden soils. Soil scientists classify soil separates by their size (see Figure 7-1), beginning with boulders — any rock that measures about 10 inches across. That measurement may sound small to you if you thought a boulder was something big enough to sunbathe on. But those of us with lots of these boulders in our gardens refer to them as "those #%*!! rocks."

Progressively smaller in size, technically speaking, are stones, pebbles, and gravel, and we hope these items are scant in your garden. Smaller yet are sand, silt, and clay, and these particles constitute the mineral component of garden soil. Although most soils contain a combination of these particle sizes, often one size predominates. Here's a rundown of the characteristics of these soil particles:

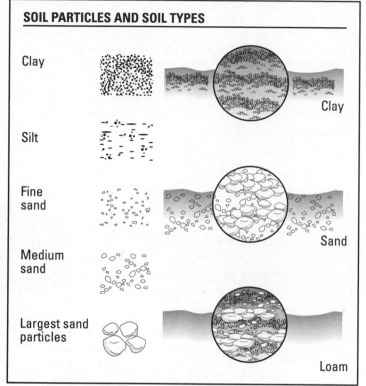

SOIL PARTICLES AND SOIL TYPES

Clay — Clay

Silt

Fine sand — Sand

Medium sand

Largest sand particles — Loam

Figure 7-1:
The size of the mineral particle determines the soil texture. Loam is the ideal soil for most plants.

✔ **Sand:** Sand particles, which can be fine or coarse, are the largest of the three, measuring from 0.5 to 2 millimeters across. You can see them clearly with the naked eye. Gardeners with sandy soil, which feels gritty, often call it light soil because it doesn't get saturated and soggy and is easy to cultivate whether wet or dry.

Because sand particles are relatively large and angular or round in shape, they don't cling together closely, leaving space for water and air to move between the individual particles. As a result, sandy soil drains quickly — too quickly for many plants.

✔ **Silt:** You need a microscope to see silt particles (0.002 to 0.5 millimeters), but you can recognize them by touch: When dry, silty soil feels smooth, like flour or talcum powder. Most silt particles have an irregular shape as sand particles do, but in soils, they're often thinly coated with clay.

Water tends to run off silty soil, but once it penetrates the surface, silt retains moisture better than sand does.

✔ **Clay:** Clay particles measure less than 0.002 millimeters across. Because of their size and flat shape, clay particles stick together — and feel sticky and slick when wet. (If you've ever made pottery, you know what clay soil feels like.) The particles in clay soil are tightly packed, and the spaces between them are small, so water drains poorly, leaving the soil saturated and depriving plants of the air they need.

Clay soil, which may be tinged red, black, gray, or blue, stays wet and cold in spring. Because clay is harder to dig when wet or dry, it's often referred to as heavy soil.

Your garden soil won't be all sand or all clay, however, but a mix. If that mix is 40 percent sand, 40 percent silt, and 20 percent clay, you have loam, the ideal soil for gardening.

A feel for texture

Most gardens don't come with loam. Luckily, loam isn't required for growing herbs. But it helps to know your soil's *texture* — that is, whether sand, silt, or clay predominates.

One way to get an idea of your soil's texture is to take a handful of damp soil from your garden plot. Take a pinch and rub it between your thumb and index finger. If it feels gritty, it's mostly sand. If it feels slick, it's mostly clay. Now grab a handful and roll it between your hands. If you can form a long cylinder, it's mostly clay (see Figure 7-2). If the cylinder starts to crumble as you roll, it's mostly silt. If you can't roll a cylinder at all, it's mostly sand.

Figure 7-2:
You can roll clay soil into a cylinder.

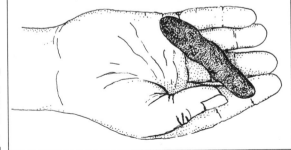

A sense of structure

When gardeners discuss soil *structure,* they're talking about how well or poorly the soil particles cling, or aggregate, together. The best garden soils have a loose, crumblike structure with spaces through which water, nutrients, and plant roots can readily pass. Healthy soil with good structure looks something like crumbled chocolate cake. It's moist and airy with clumps of various sizes. Compare this structure with a powdery cake mix, which represents soil with poor structure.

Although you can't change your soil's texture, you *can* improve its structure by providing an environment that supports the *soil ecosystem.* This amazingly complex array of organisms is responsible for recycling the nutrients in plant debris, in the process yielding *humus,* a sticky substance that helps bind soil particles into those crumblike aggregates.

It's a Jungle Down There: The Soil Ecosystem

If you think of garden soil as inert and lifeless, you couldn't be more wrong. There's an entire below-ground ecosystem filled with organisms that are busy tunneling and aerating the soil, as well as breaking down dead plant and animal matter.

You probably know about the merits of earthworms, but did you know that an uncountable number of other beneficial organisms (plant and animal) also dwell in your soil? We won't attempt to supply a directory of what's down there, except to say that there are billions and billions of residents, most of them too small to see. In the soil, good things come in small packages.

The macroorganisms (everything from voles, worms, and grubs to nematodes and plant roots) are world-class soil-openers, aerating it as they move. They do the initial breaking down of dead plant and animal matter. Then the microorganisms (bacteria, fungi, and more) go to work on the residue their larger neighbors leave behind. Most of these organisms live in the top 8 inches of soil, right where your herbs' roots are growing.

Your goal as a gardener is to keep the soil ecosystem healthy and functioning efficiently. And the best way to do that is to provide a constant supply of organic matter.

As the worm turns

Charles Darwin called earthworms the "intestines of the soil"; farmers call them "Mother Nature's plows." Earthworms feed on organic matter, depositing their castings, or excrement, as they burrow through the soil. Scientists estimate that a 1-acre garden with organically rich soil contains about 1 million worms; their castings are rich in nitrogen, phosphorus, and potassium, the three nutrients plants most need.

The equation is simple: Lots of worms equal good soil. In spring, dig a cubic foot of soil and count: Five worms is okay, but ten is excellent. And if, in the digging, you happen to cut a worm in half, don't worry. Earthworms grow new heads if no more than the first six or seven body rings are lost.

Do you have just a few worms in your soil? Add organic matter, and they will come.

Organic Matter: Rx for Soils

Although technically you can call all plant and animal matter, living and dead, *organic matter,* most gardeners use the term to describe materials they add to their garden, including leaves, kitchen scraps, grass clippings, animal manures, and compost. As soil organisms break down this organic matter, they release the nutrients it contains, converting it into a form plants can use. Everything you add to your soil helps, from carrot tops to cow dung.

The faster the material decomposes, the faster the nutrients it contains are recycled. Fresh matter decomposes more quickly than dry materials; chopped matter decomposes more quickly than materials that haven't been shredded. Organic matter that you dig into the soil breaks down more quickly than matter you spread on the soil's surface. Lastly, organic matter decomposes more quickly in warm soil than in cold.

Aim to add at least 1 inch of chopped or fine organic matter or 4 inches of bulky matter to your garden each year. In almost all cases, more is better. It's hard to imagine a garden with too much organic matter.

Organic matter improves different types of soil in different ways:

- ✔ **Sandy soils:** Sandy soil is the natural home of many herbs, but soil that's too sandy has few nutrients and drains too quickly for all but the most drought-tolerant species. The solution is easy: Add organic matter. Organic matter helps the soil retain moisture, provides a reservoir of nutrients, and nurtures soil life.

- ✔ **Clay soils:** To lighten clay soil or open up soil that has become compacted, dig in rough organic matter, such as half-decomposed compost, shredded bark, or roughly chopped leaves. Mixing in organic matter opens up pathways for air, water, and plant roots, and it helps wet soils drain better.

Make it manure

If you have access to manure — horse, cow, sheep, chicken, or rabbit — count yourself lucky. Animal manures are nitrogen gold mines that supply smaller amounts of phosphorus, potassium, calcium, sulfur, and other micronutrients. Manure also adds organic matter to the soil.

But fresh manures carry risks. Fresh manure can burn leaves and kill young plants. You're better off if you add fresh manure to the compost pile where it can age, or spread it on the garden in late autumn when the growing season is over. You can add well-rotted or composted manure anytime.

Avoid adding dog and cat manures to the garden because they may contain parasites and other unpleasant microbial surprises.

Don't cultivate clay soil when it's wet, or you'll end up with rock-hard clumps when it dries. And don't add sand: If you combine the right amount of clay and sand, you'll end up with something resembling concrete.

Whenever you have the chance, add organic matter. For example, you can mix in some leaf mold at planting time, spread a thin layer of grass clippings every few weeks, and apply organic mulch like shredded bark. Adding organic matter isn't a one-time proposition. Think of it as feeding the soil. You don't want your soil to go hungry, do you?

Compost Happens

The *crème de la crème* of organic matter is compost — a dark, crumbly mix that you can cook up yourself. You may have seen the bumper sticker that reads "Compost Happens." It really does! Making compost is like making a good stew. Add the right amounts of the right ingredients, let them simmer, and it just happens. In fact, millions of microorganisms actually do the work, but you can take the credit, if you want.

The easiest approach to composting is to throw all the organic matter you can get your hands on into a pile and wait. This *laissez-faire* method works — it's called *cold composting* — but it's darned slow. (On the other hand, ignore ads promising "Great Compost in Three Days.") You can speed up decomposition by providing the perfect working conditions for the herd of microorganisms living in your pile. When they're working flat-out, your pile's temperature will reach an ideal 160 degrees Fahrenheit.

Gathering the raw ingredients

Good ingredients for compost include animal manure, coffee grounds, conifer needles, eggshells, grass clippings, hair, hay, leaves, sawdust, seaweed, shredded newspaper (black and white only), soil, straw, vegetable and fruit scraps, and garden clippings — almost any plant matter. Compost made with a variety of materials contains the gamut of plant nutrients.

For fast decomposition, add a mixture of fresh and dry ingredients. Fresh materials, sometimes called *green matter,* are high in nitrogen and include fresh grass clippings, vegetable scraps, animal manures, and fresh plant debris. Dried materials, sometimes called *brown matter,* are high in carbon and include dried leaves, sawdust, straw, and dried plant debris. Aim for a ratio of 1:3, one part green matter to three parts brown matter. This ratio provides the best environment for decomposing organisms.

Not everything organic belongs in a compost pile:

- **Don't add bones, meat scraps, or kitchen debris with oil or sauce.** These items are likely to attract rodents and neighborhood dogs.

- **Avoid adding diseased plants.** The fungi or bacteria may not be killed during the composting process, and you'll just end up spreading the disease when you spread the compost.

- **Avoid pet feces.** It may contain parasites.

- **Don't add any vegetation that has been sprayed with a pesticide or herbicide.** The chemicals may survive the composting process.

- **Don't add weeds that are in flower or have gone to seed.** Most compost piles don't heat up enough to guarantee killing weed seeds.

Speeding up the process

If you're in a rush to have finished compost, try these techniques:

- Shred or chop materials before you add them to the pile.

- Keep the pile well aerated. This one usually means more work; you have to stir or turn the pile, so decide how much of a hurry you're in for finished compost.

- Alternate layers of green and brown ingredients.

- Add an occasional handful of soil, which is full of the same bacteria, fungi, and enzymes that commercial "compost starters" contain.

- Keep the pile small — the ideal size is 3 x 3 x 3 feet.

- Keep your pile damp, but not soggy; the usual description is "damp as a wrung-out sponge."

Time for tea

Watering with compost tea gives growing plants a nutritional boost. To brew, fill any large container half full of compost and half full of warm water (or fill a cloth bag with compost and immerse it in water), as shown in the figure. Let the mixture steep for several days and then strain it through a cloth or window-screen wire. If you use the bag method, straining is unnecessary. Dilute the liquid until it is the color of weak tea before using it to water plants.

The simplest compost pile is just that, a freestanding pile. Rake up leaves, shred them, and toss them on. Or you can use a bin. Our favorite is nothing more than three wood pallets, which you should be able to scrounge from local businesses (see Figure 7-3). Turn each on its end and wire (coat hangers work nicely) or nail them together to form a three-sided container. Leave the top, bottom, and front open. Or you can cover the front with a fourth pallet or wire mesh to keep the compost in and dogs out. To build double or triple side-by-side bins, add more pallets.

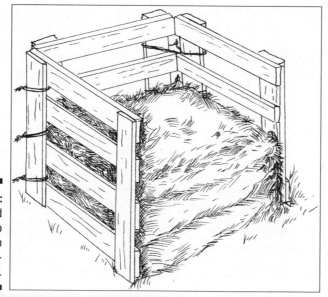

Figure 7-3:
Use wood pallets to make an easy compost bin.

An array of barrel and drum composters is available from garden centers and mail-order companies (see Figure 7-4). These composters are expensive, and their capacity is often small, but they produce compost quickly and are handy for gardeners in small quarters.

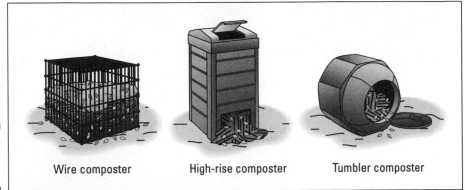

Figure 7-4: Commercial composters.

Wire composter High-rise composter Tumbler composter

P.S. . . . pH

Your soil's pH (potential hydrogen) is a measurement of acidity or alkalinity on a scale from 0 (extremely acidic) to 14 (extremely alkaline) with 7.0 as neutral. Technically speaking, pH is the actual measure of the number of hydrogen and hydroxyl ions, but all you need to know is that most herbs do fine in neutral or near-neutral soils, with a pH from 6.0 to 7.5.

The pH scale is *logarithmic,* meaning that each unit represents a power of 10. So a soil with a pH of 5 is ten times more acidic than a soil with a pH of 6.

If your soil is strongly acidic (below 5.0) or highly alkaline (above 9.0), your herbs will rebel or die on the spot. That's because soils at the extremes of the pH scale tie up mineral nutrients, making them unavailable to your plants (or the elements become too available, which can be toxic). Moreover, soil organisms also like neutral or near-neutral soil. There are no pH extremists among them, so keeping them alive and working requires your keeping the soil's pH in rein.

Testing your soil's pH

You can test the pH of anything organic. Once people got a pH meter and probe in their hands, there was no stopping them, so we now know that lime juice registers 1.8, near the bottom of the pH scale; ammonia is 11.5. (For the record, devil's food cake is 7.5.) Remember that gardening is always local:

Your soil's pH may be different from your region's pH or even your next-door neighbor's. It can even vary from place to place within a garden.

If you're adding herbs in an established garden where a variety of plants are doing fine, don't worry about testing for pH. But if yours is a new plot, checking out its pH level is a good idea. You can do this test yourself — simple to complex soil-testing kits are sold at garden centers and by mail-order suppliers. (Instructions will be included in the kit.)

We're dedicated do-it-yourselfers, but we recommend having an initial pH test done by the professionals, either through your local Cooperative Extension Office, local nursery or garden center, or a private laboratory. A professional test is more accurate than a do-it-yourself one; it can be expanded to test for nutrient deficiencies in your soil, with a written report that includes specific recommendations to remedy any soil problems or imbalances.

To find the Cooperative Extension Office nearest you, consult the U.S. Department of Agriculture's Cooperative State Research, Education, and Extension Service Web site at `www.csrees.usda.gov/Extension`.

Modifying pH

You can handle small pH problems — only slightly too acid or too alkaline — by regularly adding a generous amount of organic matter to your soil. Pine needles and composted sawdust lower the pH (make alkaline soil more acidic); wood ashes raise pH (make acid soils more alkaline).

If your soil needs a major-league pH adjustment, by a point or more on the pH scale, these are the general guidelines.

- ✔ **Soil that is too acidic:** Calcitic limestone, or calcium carbonate, is the standard material used to *sweeten* (lower the pH) garden soils. Pelletized lime is easier to apply than regular ground limestone. Fall is the best time to lime. The general rule is to add 6 pounds of lime per 100 square feet to raise the pH by one point. The amount of lime needed is affected by your soil's texture and by its initial pH number. Sandy soils need less lime, while heavy clay soils require more. Very acidic soils need more lime to raise the pH one point than moderately acidic soils do.

   In other words, one size doesn't fit all — another reason we suggest having a professional test yours.

- ✔ **Soil that is too alkaline:** Soils that are too alkaline are normally treated with elemental sulfur. Again, there is no hard-and-fast rule about amounts — both the soil texture and the degree of alkalinity affect how much sulfur you should add. One pound of sulfur per 100 square feet lowers the pH one point; but always read the application directions on the bag for specifics.

Few soils are wildly acid or alkaline, so if you're working without specific recommendations from soil experts, go slow and start small when adjusting pH. It's better to change pH gradually rather than making the entire correction with one application. Remember that soil is a work in progress.

Starting Your Garden from Scratch

If you're starting your herb garden in an area that has never been a garden — or if it hasn't been a garden in a long time — then before you can sow the first seed or set out the first plant, you'll need to clear the site.

Clearing the site means removing everything — plants, weeds, rocks, roots, and anything else in the way. Try to clear your garden site well ahead of planting time. Autumn is the best time to clear the site, but if you're someone who fills out income tax returns on April 14, don't close this book and decide to take up needlepoint. You can clear a garden site in spring, even on the same day you plant. Waiting until the last minute, however, means hand-digging and other hard labor instead of using some of the labor-saving methods we describe in this chapter.

Whether you're an early bird or a procrastinator, begin by marking your garden's boundaries. If the garden has straight sides, outline it with string stretched between small stakes and mark the boundaries with ground limestone, flour, or sand. For free-form designs, use rope or garden hose to lay out the boundaries and then mark them. Now remove all the large debris and woody plants (be sure to grub out the roots), mow the site, and remove the sod.

Sod, or turf, consists of all those ground-hugging plants, mostly matted grasses. You need to strip off the sod before you cultivate the soil. Getting rid of *every* plant and all its roots is essential. Leaving behind even a small piece of leaf, stem, or root tip — which is inevitable when you pull weeds by hand — usually means you've left enough to sprout the minute your back is turned.

Spade power: Clearing sod by hand

When you clear the sod, your goal is to remove *all* the vegetation but to take away as little soil as possible. Here's what you need to do:

1. **Before beginning, water the site thoroughly.**

   Start on one side of the plot.

2. Slice into the sod, about 1 or 2 inches deep and then lower the handle of the spade so that its blade is nearly parallel to the soil surface.

3. Now push forward until the spade face is completely buried and then lift the piece of sod, shake the soil back into the bed, and set the sod aside.

4. When you're done, add the sod (upside down) to your compost pile or use it to fill in low spots in your landscape.

If you want a giant-sized herb garden, check into renting a gasoline-powered sod stripper.

Shade power: Clearing sod with covers

Hands down, the easiest and most effective way to kill weeds is to turn off the sun. Plants (if you don't count mushrooms and a few other things that grow plump in the night) can't live without bright light. Flip off the solar switch by covering your site with black plastic or dark landscape fabric to stymie the sun; use bricks, boards, or U-shaped pins made from clothes hangers to secure the edges of the cover. (Rolls of black plastic are sold at garden centers and by mail-order firms.)

And don't dilly-dally: You need to cover the site for at least six months before planting time.

Herbicides — the last resort

If you face a plot of weeds, you may be tempted to reach for an herbicide, one of those skull-and-crossbones chemicals that kill vegetation as quickly as bad breath kills romance. Stop! All herbicides are toxic, and most are persistent, which means they stay around to do damage long after the weeds are history.

If you have a thick stand of poison ivy that isn't fazed by being cut back repeatedly, then an herbicide may be necessary. But in general herbicides should be a last resort. Handle them carefully and always read the directions: Not only are herbicides dangerous to you, they can be dangerous to adjacent plants (and wildlife). Choose a windless day and always spot-spray individual plants (even better, paint on the herbicide) rather than drench an entire site.

If you must use herbicides, consider these pointers:

- ✔ Look for organic herbicides derived from corn gluten, lemon juice, vinegar, or other natural substances. Most organic herbicides are slow acting and less effective than synthetic weed killers, but work moderately well on emerging annual weeds.

- ✔ Many gardeners consider Roundup, a glyphosate-based weed killer, to be the least harmful of the synthetic herbicides. Its persistence is brief, yet it's an effective assassin. However, Roundup is also nonselective, which means it will kill anything you spray. Aim carefully.

Preparing Beds

After you clear your site, it's time to ready the soil for planting. You'll be doing two things at once: loosening, or aerating, the soil and improving the soil by adding all that organic matter you've collected and composted. Fall is the best time to tackle this job — so you can let frost break up clumps and clods for you during the winter — but you can take it on any time that the soil's not frozen or soppy wet.

Begin by covering your garden with a generous layer — 3 inches or more — of organic material. Not only do you want to enrich your soil, you want to raise the soil level, because you lowered it an inch or two when you removed the sod.

Rototilling

If your garden is both new and large and your time is limited, consider renting a rototiller to turn the soil. Ask for a model with rear-mounted tines, which is much easier to manage than a front-tine tiller.

Rototillers, or just plain tillers, are real back- and time-savers, but they're too good at their job. Run one over a garden three or four times, and the soil looks terrific. Well, it looks terrific, but it isn't really terrific. Overtilling pulverizes soil, destroying the pore spaces that air, water, and nutrients use to travel to the roots of plants. The goal is soil with the consistency of bread stuffing, not flour. Don't overdo it.

Going overboard is all too tempting, so follow the rules of rational rototilling:

- ✔ **Don't till when the soil is wet.** Squeeze a handful of soil. If it doesn't crumble when you open your hand, it's too wet to be tilled.

Oh, my aching back

To avoid a date with a chiropractor, dig ergonomically, a fancy term that refers to a design or method to reduce "operator fatigue and discomfort." If you already have big-league back problems, consider buying ergonomic tools and follow this advice for all gardeners on the working end of a fork, shovel, or spade. Here's how to dig properly:

1. **Keep the handle of your tool straight up and down.**

2. **Put your foot on the tread, or footrest, and use your weight to drive the tines or blade into the soil.**

3. **Bend at the waist and knees to push the handle down and forward.**

4. **Straighten your waist and knees to lift and turn the dirt.**

✔ **Don't till when the soil is bone dry.** If you can't squeeze a handful of soil into a ball, it's too dry to be tilled. Water the plot thoroughly, wait a day, and then till.

✔ **Don't overtill the soil.** One or two passes is usually enough. If you do overtill, add organic matter to correct your mistake.

✔ **Don't use a rototiller for routine weeding or cultivation.**

Ideally, you'll need to rototill only once, the first time you prepare the bed; you don't need to do it every spring. Rototilling disturbs the soil ecosystem and brings buried weed seeds to the surface to germinate, so do it only when necessary to start or renew a garden.

Hand digging

Digging a small garden by hand is altogether manageable, even for rookies, the out-of-shape, and the over-50 crowd. The goal is to loosen the soil and mix in organic matter. A spading fork is the best tool for this work, but a spade is nearly as good. Unless your soil is extremely heavy (clay) or extremely light (sand), you need to loosen the soil to a depth of about a foot.

In loose soil, insert your fork and lift the soil to incorporate the organic matter; repeat over the entire bed. In heavier soils, you may need to lift out forkfuls of soil and break up the clods with the fork.

After the soil is loosened and the organic matter incorporated, put on the finishing touches. Use a garden rake to remove any debris and smooth the surface. The soil is ready to be planted. Now pat yourself on the back . . . and smile.

For peat's sake

Adding peat to garden soil at planting time is a recommendation you find and hear everywhere — in books, magazines, and newspaper columns, and even from garden-center employees. Peat is partially decayed organic matter; the peat you see in garden centers is harvested from peat bogs made up of sphagnum moss and other plants that have been decaying for millennia.

Yes, peat is a handy source of organic matter, but whether it's an environmentally friendly soil amendment depends on whom you ask. Some say it takes a peak bog just 25 years to regenerate after it's been harvested. Others say it takes a thousand years or more, and that harvesting process is more akin to mining. Either way, much of the peat we use is from northern Canada and travels hundreds, if not thousands, of miles to reach our gardens — a decidedly un-environmentally friendly, diesel-fuel-consuming trip. Consider looking for sources of organic matter closer to home (your compost pile, for example).

If you use peat, apply it sparingly as an additive to soil mixes or to amend planting holes when setting out individual herbs. Be aware that peat contains no nutrients and is devilishly difficult to rewet if it dries out. Spreading it on the soil surface is almost like laying down a layer of plastic; water runs off rather than sinks in.

Buying peat can be confusing; you can choose from several products for sale:

- **Black peat,** or peat humus (*terre noire* if it comes from Canada), looks like rich topsoil and is often sold in bulk. Sedge peat, like black peat, comes from sedge plants, but is less decomposed and reddish brown in color.

- **Sphagnum moss,** or floral moss, consists of moss plants harvested from the tops of peat bogs; it's sold in small, packaged quantities for lining hanging baskets and other decorative purposes.

- **Peat** — also known as sphagnum peat, brown peat, and peat moss — is the most common garden additive. Made of dried, partially decomposed sphagnum mosses, it is very acidic and can absorb 15 times its weight in water.

Raised beds

If all this talk about digging has you questioning your commitment to having an herb garden, consider growing in raised beds — slightly elevated garden plots. They ensure excellent drainage, warm more quickly in spring (a bonus for northern gardeners), and they're attractive and easy to maintain. Plus, you don't have to bend down as far — making cultivating and harvesting easier on your back.

Six inches is a good height for raised herb beds (an inch or two lower in hot, dry climates where the soil dries out quickly). Although they can be any shape, rectangular beds are the most practical. Make the beds no more than

4 feet wide so that you can reach the center of a bed from either side. After you've figured out the size of the bed, you need to decide if you want it to be freestanding or permanent. Freestanding, or mounded, beds are easy to build — use a rake or hoe to pull up soil from the surrounding area to create an elevated bed — and they're easy to modify, resize, or eliminate. On the down side, they also erode easily, which means you'll have to keep mounding up the sides to keep water and nutrients from running off the bed. A free-standing bed is a good first step if you're not sure raised beds are for you.

Permanent beds — wood- or stone-sided beds — take more time to build and are more expensive. Once built, they're more difficult to modify or remove. But they're largely erosion-proof and can add a decorative element to your landscape.

Lumber, timbers, flagstones, bricks, and concrete blocks are among the materials used to frame a raised bed. (Treat wood with a nontoxic preservative to resist decay or choose a naturally decay-resistant wood like cedar.) Dig the soil underneath the bed to a depth of at least 8 inches. Set up the bed, burying the frame about 3 inches in the soil to discourage weeds that spread underground and to provide extra support for the sides. Next, spread a thick layer of rough organic matter over the surface and then add soil that has been heavily amended with still more organic matter to within 2 inches of the top of the frame.

If you must purchase topsoil, be aware that it usually contains little organic matter and few nutrients, so be sure to mix it with compost or some other organic matter (50:50 ratio).

Chapter 8

It's Time to Plant

*E*verything's ready. You know what herbs you want to grow and where you want to grow them. You've prepared the soil in your beds, cleaned out the window boxes, and retrieved your terra-cotta pots from the garage and cleaned them. It's time to plant!

Whether you're ordering packets of seeds or purchasing plants, let us sow one idea now: Start small. Remember that the work doesn't stop after you plant your garden — you have to take care of these herbs! You probably don't need to start seeds for 100 cilantro plants or set out a dozen horseradish plants. Grow only what you'll enjoy and use, and only as much as you'll have time to care for. A weedy, out-of-control garden is more depressing than no garden at all. You can always expand your garden later.

Seeds or Plants?

We're fans of starting plants from seed, in part because growing from seed is one of the miracles of gardening. Every seed is a plant-in-waiting, a tiny package of roots, stems, leaves, flowers, and more seeds. Although they aren't foolproof, seeds want to sprout and grow: It's their destiny. As American writer Henry David Thoreau observed, you can have "great faith in a seed."

The seed-starting process is fun, interesting, and satisfying, and it's cheap — compare $1.50 for 100 basil seeds with $4 for six 3-inch plants. Moreover, you can get your hands on dozens and dozens of unusual herbs and herb cultivars only if you're willing to sow seeds. For example, Canadian seed company

Richters offers dozens of different kinds of mint. Trust us, you probably won't find grapefruit mint or variegated peppermint in pots at your local nursery. And you may not even find plants of common herbs like marjoram and fennel.

Starting from seed isn't required, however. Don't feel like a second-class gardener if you decide to begin with plants grown by someone else. Most garden centers offer the basic culinary herbs — basil, thyme, cilantro, chive, oregano, parsley, dill, mint, rosemary, and sage— and perhaps a modest selection of less popular plants. We can't debate the fact that buying plants is simpler, it saves you time, and the plants reach harvest stage sooner.

There is one plant you cannot grow from seed — tarragon. It rarely sets seed; all plants are propagated from stem cuttings or root divisions. *Caveat emptor* (buyer beware): French tarragon *(Artemisia dracunculus)* has the herbal flavor you want, while Russian tarragon *(A. dracunculus* var. *indora* —formerly *A. dracunculoides)* has more medicinal uses.

It's Seed Time

For us, each garden season includes the past and the future. We always purchase herbs we've grown before — herbs that we know we like and that will thrive in our gardens. Seed for 'Sweet Genovese' basil is an annual purchase, as is seed for broadleaf (Italian) parsley *(Petroselinum crispum* var. *latifolium)*. But we also try new things each year — a new cultivar or an herb we haven't grown before.

Planning your seed purchases

No one has time or room to grow everything, so ask yourself the following questions in order to rein in your purchases:

- **Will I use it?** You can grow herbs for their own sake — with no thought of using them — but if you're the practical sort, be realistic about what herbs you'll use.

- **Will it grow in my garden?** Every herb has peculiar needs. Basil will be a bust if your garden is a large pot on a cool, shady patio; angelica won't survive in southern Florida's heat. Be sure to check our plant encyclopedia in the appendix to see whether you have the conditions necessary for the herbs you'd like to grow.

- **Is it too much trouble?** The majority of herbs are like good friends: cooperative, undemanding, tolerant, even forgiving. But all herbs require some care. Marsh mallow requires lots of moisture — do you have time for watering? Do you have time to start chive seeds in January so that you'll have plants in June?

Seed catalog savvy

Mail-order and online seed catalogs are some of our favorite reading. They're also gold mines of gussied-up photographs and hyperbolic prose, designed to seduce even an experienced gardener. Every new cultivar is bigger or brighter or better, every seed guaranteed to grow faster and taller. For the record, every new cultivar *isn't* better, and every seed *won't* grow.

Having gotten that off our chests, we're still devoted mail-order and online shoppers for two reasons. First, you must start with seeds in order to grow more than the run-of-the-mill herbs. And second, to find more than the run-of-the-mill herbs, you often have to order them by mail or online. Seed racks at the supermar-

ket or garden center usually contain only a few common herbs.

With all their flowery prose, reading a seed catalog is not entirely easy. And invariably, there are too many herb choices. Don't be intimidated by all the possibilities, though. Think of seed catalogs as resources filled with information about herbs, as well as sources for buying seeds.

If you're like us, once you start turning the catalog pages, you'll want one of everything. We recommend that you pretend you're Santa Claus. After you've made your list, check it twice. Maybe three times.

✔ **How much should I grow?** Seed packets usually indicate how many seeds they contain — probably 50 times more than you need. Three basils are not enough if want to freeze batches of pesto to take you through the winter, but three sage plants are probably more than all but the most ambitious gourmet cook can use.

Be sure to start small. Beginning seeds indoors takes lots of room, especially as you start to move seedlings to larger pots. If you don't plant enough, there's always next year. (With some herbs, there's even time for a second crop this year.) Dyeing, drying, and craft projects require a hefty number of plants, but you can usually grow culinary herbs in smaller numbers unless you're planning to supply all your neighbors or to preserve your harvest.

Sowing seeds also requires a modest investment in equipment — flats, trays, and, for best results, supplemental lighting. Read through this entire seed-starting section to see what you already have and what you'll need to buy. Remember that you'll be able to reuse many of the items year after year.

Seedy business

"I've got to get some seeds, right away." That's what Willy Loman says in *Death of a Salesman,* and that's how we feel every winter. Yes, winter. Starting from seed also means starting early, as many as 12 weeks before the last spring frost for perennials, four to eight weeks for biennials and hardy annuals.

All-Americans

A few herbs have been awarded the designation of All-America Selection (AAS), which indicates that they have been grown in more than 60 trial gardens located throughout the country and judged superior to other cultivars. The AAS program, which identifies outstanding plants for home gardens, began in 1932. Past herb winners include anise hyssop 'Golden Jubilee', Thai basil 'Siam Queen', echinacea 'Powwow Wild Berry', basil 'Magical Michael', lavender 'Lady', cilantro 'Delfina', and dill 'Fernleaf'.

Winter also is when the seed catalogs arrive (once you're on mailing lists). If you're starting plants from seed, start with a seed catalog. Most seed companies send one without charge (or will deduct the dollar-or-so cost from any order you place); most companies now post their catalogs on their Web sites, too.

A seed company with a broad range of wares may be all you need for your first few orders. Before long, though, you may be looking for new forms of tri-colored sage or the 19th-century scented geranium you saw at Monticello. That's when specialist seed houses become indispensable.

Nonprofit organizations are another great source of herb seeds. If you belong to the Seed Savers Exchange, a laudable nonprofit group that works to preserve heirloom flowers, vegetables, and herbs, you'll also have access to hundreds of herb seeds, many available nowhere else. Some regional garden organizations and local garden clubs sponsor annual seed exchanges, as do plant societies.

Starting Seeds Indoors

All that most seeds need to germinate, or sprout, are oxygen, water, and heat. It sounds easy, and usually it is. Whether you sow seeds indoors or outdoors depends on what you're growing and where you live. Gardeners who live where the mercury falls well below freezing in winter — and especially those whose summers are short — start many herbs indoors. If your winters are mild and summer stretches on forever, you can *direct seed* many herbs — that is, sow them directly in the garden.

Starting your plants inside gives you a head start on the growing season: Instead of planting seeds on May 15 — or whenever your soil warms — you will be setting out the young plants you started indoors weeks or months earlier.

Sow most annual herbs from four to eight weeks before your frost-free date. Most perennial herbs grow more slowly than annuals, so you may need to sow them as many as 12 weeks before the last frost. (You can find planting recommendations on the back of seed packets.)

Containers, planting medium, and more

You don't need a greenhouse to begin your herb garden indoors, but you do need containers, planting medium, heat, and care.

You can sow seeds in almost any container if it has drainage holes in the bottom. Plastic cell packs are inexpensive and reusable (see Figure 8-1). If you're sowing lots of seeds, they're a good investment because they nestle neatly into their waterproof trays, maximizing the number of plants you can fit into a given area.

Want to use homegrown seed-sowing containers? Paper cups and yogurt and cottage cheese containers work fine. So do cardboard milk cartons and 1-gallon milk jugs (cut jugs off 3 inches from the bottom; staple the top of cartons and remove one side to form a rectangular container). With all of these containers, don't forget to make drainage holes.

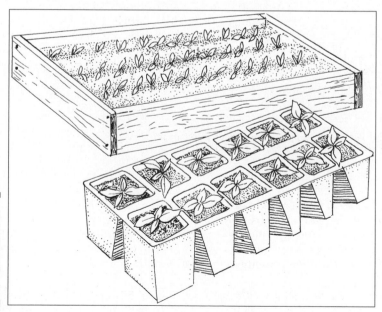

Figure 8-1:
Cell packs
and
matching
waterproof
tray.

A few seed-container don'ts:

- ✔ **Don't** pick huge, deep containers. Seeds germinate better in shallow quarters — no more than 3 inches deep.

- ✔ **Don't** be tempted to half-fill a deep container. Seedlings need fresh air, and they won't get it if the sides of a container surround them.

- ✔ **Don't** use a dirty container. Especially if you're reusing a container, wash it with soap and water, dip in a 10 percent bleach solution, and rinse in clear water.

- ✔ **Don't** sow different herbs in the same container. Each herb has its own needs and timetable.

Don't use soil from your garden — it contains weed seeds and diseases. Instead, use a soil-free commercial mix, usually called *seed-starting mix* or *germination mix,* that is made especially for starting seeds. Seeds don't need fertilizer to germinate, so commercial mixes usually are nutrient-free, sterile, and water-retentive, and provide the good drainage seedlings need.

Seeds need even warmth (most prefer 70 to 80 degrees Fahrenheit) to sprout quickly. Seeds can sprout at lower temperatures but do so more slowly. If your house isn't that warm both day and night, put your containers on top of a radiator or refrigerator or on an electric heating mat (a hot pad for sprouting seeds, available from garden supply companies) to speed germination.

Seeds sown indoors sprout more quickly than those sown outdoors, so don't start too early. Seedlings that have been grown too long indoors, especially without enough light, tend to be spindly and weak. Be patient. Clean the garage, sharpen your garden tools, varnish the canoe paddles. Do anything! Beginning the garden too soon is always a mistake.

A few herb seeds need special handling before they can germinate. Those of some species, such as sweet Cicely, must be *stratified,* or chilled for a period of time. The seed packet will provide instructions for any special requirements.

Sowing the seeds

Now you're ready to make the seeds meet the soil. Here's how:

1. **Wet the soil-less seed-starting mix in a bucket.**

   Use warm water and let the mix sit for a few minutes so that it can absorb the water. The mix should be completely moist but not soppy wet — aim for the moisture level of a wrung-out sponge. Moisten only as much as you can use at one time; in storage, damp mix attracts disease organisms.

Germination, not . . .

So you planted according to our directions, and nothing came up. If the seed you sowed was purchased recently, most likely poor germination isn't the seeds' fault. If, on the other hand, you planted year-old (or older) seeds or seeds that you collected yourself, you'll want to go back and test some of the leftover seeds to make sure that they're viable (capable of sprouting) before planting more.

To test the seeds, spread ten seeds on half of a damp paper towel, fold the towel over to cover the seeds, and place in a loosely tied plastic bag in a warm location (75 degrees Fahrenheit). Keep the towels moist (not soppy wet) and keep your eye out for signs of sprouting. If only a couple of seeds germinate, or none at all do, you'll know the seed isn't viable.

If you used viable seeds and nothing came up, the most likely explanation is that you've over-watered and the seeds have rotted or that you haven't given the seeds enough moisture to trigger germination. Other possibilities:

✔ Soil is too cold or too warm

✔ Seeds were set too deep or soil wasn't firmed around seeds

✔ Soil is contaminated

Whatever the reason, start afresh by using clean, sterile containers, sterile soil-less mix, and seeds you know are viable. Don't despair. As Big Bird from Sesame Street says, "Everyone makes mistakes." We know we have.

2. **Fill your cell-packs or containers to the top and then tap them on a solid surface or firm the soil mix gently to eliminate air pockets.**

   Don't compact the mix by pressing down hard. Leave about ½ inch of headroom in the pot.

3. **Sprinkle seeds on top of the mix.**

   Most herbs have a high germination rate (the percentage of seeds that sprout — the number usually appears on the seed packet), so sow sparingly. It doesn't take 50 seeds to get 15 plants. If you're using cell packs, three seeds per cell are plenty.

4. **Cover the seeds with seed-starting mix and firm gently.**

   The general rule is to cover seeds two or three times as deep as their diameter. Some herbs, including angelica, anise hyssop, chamomile, chervil, dill, echinacea, feverfew, lemon balm, savory, wormwood, and yarrow, prefer to have their seeds only partially covered. These seeds need some light to sprout: Lightly press them into the soil-less mix with your finger and mist them with water. The seed packet will provide this information.

5. **Label each container with the name of what you've sown and the date you sowed it.**

   You may think you'll remember what it is. You won't. For more advice on labeling, see the section "Remembering What's What," later in this chapter.

6. **Mist the container and then cover it with plastic wrap to retain moisture.**

   Remove the wrap for a few hours every day to ensure good air circulation and to avoid a seedling disease known as damping-off.

7. **Set your containers in a warm location out of direct sunlight.**

   Watch the containers carefully so that they don't become too damp (remove the cover if they do) or dry out. Water carefully so that you don't disturb the seeds. Pour off any water that accumulates beneath the containers.

Don't panic when all your seeds don't sprout in three days or at the same time. Germination for each herb is different: Lavender seeds can take a month, while German chamomile seeds sprout in less than one week. It's helpful to write the number of days to germination (listed on the seed packet) on the label so that you know when seeds should sprout and you don't mistakenly give up on slow germinators.

Once Seedlings Are Up

When green sprouts shove their way through the soil's surface, you must be ready to give them the new conditions they require.

If you can't provide seedlings with at least 14 hours of sun daily — or if you don't have artificial lights — you're better off buying plants at a local garden center or direct seeding.

The following sections show you what you need to set up an indoor nursery for your herb seedlings.

Good light

Young plants need light — bright light, and lots of it. Growing seedlings on a windowsill is possible, but windowsills usually get too hot during the day and too cold at night. Even a south-facing window rarely gets as much sun as your new plants need.

You'll be forever glad if you purchase two inexpensive items from the local hardware store: a fluorescent light fixture, one of the simple industrial types designed for illuminating a workbench (often called *shop lights*), and a timer. Pick a fixture that holds at least two bulbs (use both cool white and warm white bulbs) and is suspended on chains. (A 4-foot model with two bulbs will light a 12-x-40-inch area.) Set the lights between 2 and 4 inches above the seedlings — raise them as your seedlings grow — and keep the bulbs running 16 hours a day.

Beyond shop lights

If you're just starting out, a few sets of shop lights are a reasonable investment. But if you get bitten by the seed-starting bug, you may want to look into higher intensity grow-light options. High-output, full-spectrum fluorescent bulbs put out more light, use less energy, and last longer than regular fluorescent bulbs. And high-intensity discharge (HID) fixtures put out even more light, but are much more expensive, generate more heat, and use a lot more electricity.

Cool room temperature

Seedlings are young, tender, and vulnerable, but they don't need the heat that germination requires. Seedlings prefer cooler conditions — temperatures ranging between 65 and 75 degrees Fahrenheit and 5 degrees colder at night. Too much heat not only promotes spindly growth, it also encourages bugs and diseases.

Good air circulation

Stagnant air invites pest and disease problems. Set your seedlings where they can get plenty of fresh, circulating air, but keep them out of strong drafts. A small fan set on low aimed near, but not at, the plants can do the trick. Don't crowd seedlings. Give each plant enough room to grow without bumping into its neighbors to ensure good air circulation.

Water

Seedlings need water, but they're not fish. Check the soil daily. When the surface is dry to the touch, water gently, pouring off any water that accumulates in the drainage trays. Or water the plants from below by adding water to the drainage tray and letting the soil soak up the moisture; just remember to drain excess water. Use tepid water to avoid shocking the roots. Wilted leaves can signal too much moisture as well as too little, so always feel the soil before you water.

Fertilizer

If you've sown seeds in a sterile seed-starting mix, you must fertilize your seedlings shortly after their first true leaves appear. Feed them every week to 10 days with a diluted solution of equal parts of fish and seaweed emulsion (use 1 tablespoon of each per gallon of water); compost tea (see Chapter 7 for our recipe); or other liquid organic fertilizer.

Room for roots

Seedlings need room to grow below, as well as above, the soil surface. As soon as your plants start to develop their second set of true leaves — which look different from their original seed leaves, or *cotyledons* — they're ready to be on their own. If they're growing in cell packs, choose the biggest, healthiest seedling in each cell and remove the rest. This process is called *thinning*. You can thin by transplanting the extra seedlings to their own pots, but in most cases, it's better to simply snip off the extras with a pair of scissors.

If you're tempted to try to transplant the extra seedlings to new containers, consider two things:

- ✔ **Do you really need all those seedlings?** If you planted basil seeds in 2 cell packs, each with 6 cells, you probably intended to grow 12 basil plants (enough for all but the most ambitious pesto makers). If you sowed 3 seeds per cell and they all came up, you're looking at 36 basil plants. Unless you're planning to give some away or start selling pesto, that's too many for one garden.

- ✔ **Are you willing to sacrifice the best seedling?** Prying up and transplanting the extra seedlings invariably disturbs the roots of the remaining seedling, which can slow its growth or, even kill it. So, as painful as it is, in most cases, it's better to snip off the extra plants at the soil line and discard them.

Potting up

Depending on the type of plant and the size of the pot, you may need to transplant young seedlings from their cell packs into larger pots. Gardeners call this task *potting up,* or *potting on.*

When you pot up, use containers that are only a little larger than the ones your seedlings were growing in. Fill each with lightly moistened soil-less mix, and then use your finger or a pencil to make a planting hole.

Be gentle when removing the seedlings from their cell packs. Be sure to hold seedlings by the leaves, not the stems, and never pull them from the soil — seedling roots are small and easily damaged. Either prick seedlings out with the tip of a knife or turn the container upside down to dislodge the *root ball* (the roots and the soil that surrounds them). Inspect each seedling before you move it to larger quarters. If it's pale or sickly, toss it.

Set each seedling slightly deeper than it was growing before and gently firm the soil around the roots. Water, set the containers away from bright light for 24 hours to let the seedlings recover from being transplanted, and then move them back into bright light.

Buying Herb Plants

Purchasing young herb plants is a great idea if you don't have the space, energy, or patience to start from seed. You also may not have the time to take care of seedlings. Perennial herbs, such as bee balm and scented geranium, take a year or more before they're good-sized, so many gardeners purchase plants rather than grow them from seed.

You can find herb plants in a range of pot sizes, from cell packs (with four or six plants to a pack) to gallon pots. Usually, the smaller the plant, the less expensive it is, but that doesn't mean small plants are necessarily a better value than larger ones. Annual herbs usually grow quickly, so buying small plants makes sense, as long as the plants haven't outgrown their pots. Perennial herbs, on the other hand, tend to grow more slowly, so if you're in a hurry to start harvesting or to fill in a gap in the garden, larger plants may be a better bet, even if they're more expensive.

Just as important as size is the overall health of the plant. Small, healthy plants will often catch up to and surpass bigger, older plants that have received poor care at the nursery.

Here are some signs that plants haven't been properly tended:

✔ **Plants have yellowed or wilted leaves.** Both signal that bad things have happened to a good plant, probably over- or underwatering and/or lack of fertilizer.

✔ **Plants are tall and spindly.** You're not picking players for an NBA franchise. Tall and spindly means a plant has received too little light and/or has been growing too long in a too-small container.

✔ **Plants have lots of roots coming out the bottom of the container, or the root ball looks like a solid mass of roots with little or no soil.** This condition means the plant is *pot-bound* — it's been in cramped quarters longer than was good for it — and it's unlikely to flourish, even after you plant it in your garden.

✔ **Plants show signs of insects or diseases.** Look for bugs (especially on the undersides of leaves), leaves that are sticky or appear to have been munched on, or leaves with odd spots or blotches. All are warnings that you're not only buying an unhealthy plant, you're carrying problems back to your garden.

✔ **Plants that are already in flower.** Today, almost everything at the garden center is in flower, but if you have a choice, pick plants that haven't bloomed yet. These plants will adjust better to transplanting. If you can bear to do it, remove any blossoms before you set out your plants — removing flowers encourages root and leaf growth, giving you larger, more vigorous plants.

Moving Indoor Herbs Outdoors

Seedlings — whether you've grown them yourself or bought them — must be *hardened off,* or acclimated, before they go into your garden. Transplanting young plants too suddenly from their cozy indoor quarters to the harsher outdoor conditions can halt their growth for weeks.

Begin hardening off your plants a week or two prior to transplanting outdoors. To harden off, set the plants outdoors in a sheltered location, one where they're protected from direct sun and strong winds. A cold frame is ideal for hardening off plants. The *cold frame* is a bottomless box made of 2-inch pine lumber — typically about 4 feet wide and 8 feet long, 12 to 18 inches high in the back, 8 to 12 inches high in front — with a hinged glass or clear plastic lid.

You can build your own (cold frames are a classic way to recycle old windows) or purchase a high-tech model from a mail-order/online supplier, such as Gardener's Supply Company. If you use a cold frame, don't forget to raise the lid on sunny days to ensure that your herbs don't get cooked.

If you don't have a cold frame, harden off your plants by putting them in a protected outdoor location. Begin by leaving them out for only a few hours. (Be sure to bring them inside if temperatures drop suddenly.) Gradually move them into the sun, increasing their time outside to 24 hours daily.

When to move young plants outdoors depends on your climate — and the herb. Don't be in a rush with plants such as basil, which are frost-tender; hardy annuals and perennials, such as caraway and yarrow, can withstand colder temperatures and go out sooner. If you're unsure about frost-free dates in your area, ask other gardeners for advice or check with your local Cooperative Extension Service. And always be prepared to cover plants if a late cold snap threatens.

Transplanting is hard on young plants, even those you've hardened off. To make their change of address easier,

- **Soak your herbs' soil in a weak, balanced, organic fertilizer** a few hours before transplanting.

- **Transplant on a cool, overcast day;** if the sun always shines in your garden, transplant in late afternoon.

- **Gently remove the plant from its pot and untangle and spread out the roots** as best you can if your plant is *root-bound* (its roots have entirely filled its container). Otherwise, transplant the entire root ball, disturbing the roots as little as possible. If you're using a biodegradable pot — one made of peat, newspaper, or another material that decays in the soil — cut a few slits in the sides of the pot and be sure to bury the entire pot, including the rim. Otherwise, the exposed material acts as a wick and draws moisture away from the roots.

- **Make the planting hole only a bit wider than the container the plant was growing in** and set the plant at the same level as it was previously growing. Backfill around the root ball, firm the soil, and water gently.

- **Use compost, shredded bark, or other organic matter to mulch your transplants.** Mulch suppresses weeds, helps retain moisture in the soil, and keeps it cool. Keep the mulch an inch or two away from stems to help prevent stem rot.

- **Protect your transplants from sun and wind** during their first few days in the garden by covering them with floating row covers. Or use pieces of cardboard or wood shingles to shade them. Mist plants with cool water if they wilt.

- **Label the transplanted plants.** You'll want to be able to identify the variety of a plant you fall in love with.

Direct Seeding Herbs Outdoors

There are many good reasons to *direct seed* (sow seeds directly into your garden) outdoors. Seedlings with a *taproot* (a long single root with little side growth; think carrot), such as borage and fennel, resent transplanting. (You can start these herbs indoors, but grow them in individual containers so that you don't have to disturb their roots.)

Direct seeding (also called direct sowing) also makes sense if you want to grow a huge quantity of herbs — few of us have space indoors for 200 calendula seedlings. In fact, many herbs simply don't need a head start. Sow most hardy annuals outdoors in spring, and they'll mature in plenty of time to provide you with a bountiful harvest.

Direct sowing is also a lot less work if you heed two warnings:

- ✔ Don't sow seeds too early.
- ✔ Don't sow seeds too deeply.

Ignore our warnings, and you'll be replanting. Most seeds rot if buried in cold, wet soil. Be patient. Wait until the soil warms up (70 degrees Fahrenheit for most herbs); soil thermometers are available from garden-supply companies. Also, don't bury your seeds so deeply that the sprouts can't make their way to the soil surface. The general rule for planting depth is to cover seeds two or three times their diameter — a little deeper if your soil is sandy and dries out quickly. (Check the seed packet for specifics.)

You must clear the *seedbed,* the place where you're going to sow your seeds, of weeds and debris. (See Chapter 7 for details about preparing soil for planting.) After you rake the bed smooth, sow your seeds, either in rows (use stakes and string to keep the rows straight if that's important to you) or by *broadcasting* (spreading the seeds over the bed rather than in rows).

Weeding is easier if you sow seeds in rows, especially if you aren't sure of your ability to distinguish herb seedlings from weed seedlings.

Space seeds as evenly apart as you can, following the spacing recommendations on the seed packet. You'll need to sow more densely than you would if you were indoors planting in a container. (The percentage of seeds that sprout will be lower outdoors, where you can't always provide ideal conditions.) Use a hoe or rake to cover the seeds; *tamp,* or press down, the soil; and water gently. Label.

After seedlings are up, it's time to thin them. Thinning seems wasteful, but it isn't. Plants grown too close together rarely reach normal size, and crowding causes poor air circulation, which makes plants more susceptible to bugs and diseases. When they're growing too near their neighbors, more plants will give you less. The seed packet will tell you how to thin — for example, "thin to 6 inches apart."

Remembering What's What

Unless your memory is a lot better than ours — not filled with "senior moments" — you need plant labels to remind you what you've planted and where you planted it.

Dear Diary

In addition to knowing exactly what we're growing, we like to record when we planted it, how we grew it, and how successful we were — or weren't. A garden diary can hold all that information and more.

In addition to names and dates, you may want to note that catnip took 11 days to germinate or that the chervil growing in partial shade did a lot better than the plants you set in full sun. Or that using garlic chives to edge your perennial border was a mistake. Or that cilantro tastes like soap, and you never want to grow it again. Or that lemongrass did a lot better in a pot on the patio than it did in the garden. Or that monarda, appropriately named bee balm, attracts so many bees that you want to move it away from the picnic table.

Record anything that seems important — or strikes your fancy. Most gardeners like to include weather information, especially frost dates and rainfall amounts, and make notes on what's blooming in the wild. Jot down yields so that you'll know that six dill plants weren't enough and six rosemary plants were too many.

A garden diary can be a superb source of information for next year. It helps you repeat your successes and avoid repeating your failures. You don't have to write every day, but you'll be glad if you do.

Even if you plant only basil, knowing it's basil isn't enough. Not all basils are alike. You'll want to awe your friends with your herbal prowess and tell them your basil is 'Mrs. Burns' or 'Red Rubin' or 'Fino Verde'. More important, if you decide lemon basil isn't your cup of tea, you don't want to plant 'Mrs. Burns' again next year.

While you're at it, include the scientific name on each label. It will help you remember that lemon balm is *Melissa officinalis*. Knowing scientific names isn't required, but the more you know about plants, the more fun gardening becomes. Gardeners are a friendly bunch — even the rank beginner is welcome — but being able to spit out horticulture Latin will give you a certain cachet. It's like knowing the secret handshake or the *mot de passé*. (See Chapter 2 for an explanation of scientific names.)

Don't delay labeling and make sure that your labels are permanent enough to survive the garden season (use an indelible pen). Plastic isn't pretty, but plastic labels are inexpensive, and they last. A seed packet stuck on top of a stake is picturesque, but it doesn't last.

Chapter 9

Everyday Care and Feeding

. . . .

In This Chapter

▶ Gardening every day

▶ Nourishing your herbs

▶ Solving the weed problem

▶ Figuring out how to mulch

▶ Maintaining a tidy garden

. . . .

North Carolina garden writer Elizabeth Lawrence observed that a garden "demands as much of its maker as he has to give" — or she! Those words may sound ominous, creating a vision of hours on your knees grubbing out quack grass when you'd rather be reading the latest P. D. James mystery. But, Lawrence continued: "No other undertaking will give as great a return for the amount of effort put into it."

Occasionally, when the sun is directly overhead and it's hot enough to fry eggs on your patio, or when poison ivy is overtaking the chives, you may feel that you will never get an adequate return for your labor in the garden. But those moments are few, far outnumbered by the times you stand back and admire your work or by the times you race out 20 minutes before dinner to snip two cups of basil to make pesto.

New gardeners may be surprised to discover that they can derive great pleasure from garden work — from the processes of clearing, digging, planting, and caring for. Beautiful, healthy herbs are another reward. We're pretty sure that like us, you'll come to relish every moment you spend in your garden.

One of the great things about herbs is that most of them need only a few things from you as they grow to maturity. That doesn't mean herbs are no-care plants. But herbs (and herb gardens) are certainly low care, especially if you keep on top of the basic, routine jobs. That's what this chapter is all about.

Thyme Waits for No Gardener

You can't postpone gardening tasks, like you can hanging wallpaper in the guest bedroom or painting the fence. You can't walk away from gardening for six or eight weeks. A few thistles are easy to deal with — a five-minute job — but an herb bed overrun by thistles may be a lost cause. At the very least, it's many hours of work that can leave you prickly in more ways than one. Following are some thoughts on how to keep the time you spend in the garden under control to keep garden work fun rather than burdensome.

- ✔ **Check your plants every day or two.** Establish a routine, a regular garden tour. Getting to know what your plants look like when they're healthy will help you notice when something's awry. Watch for insect and disease damage, such as chewed or curled leaves. Poke your finger in the soil to see whether it's dry and needs watering.

- ✔ **Grow plants that do well in your region.** We don't mean that you must cultivate only native Southwest plants or indigenous New Englanders — after all, most herbs aren't North American natives. But if you're looking for an easy-care herb garden, choose plants that are adapted to your region — usually, they're species that originated in conditions similar to yours.

- ✔ **Don't wait until things get out of control.** Spend five minutes now hoeing a few small weeds. Cut back the mint before it overwhelms the sweet woodruff. Deadhead the garlic chives before their seeds mature and start sprouting throughout the garden. Hand-pick earwigs the first time you encounter them munching the angelica.

- ✔ **Don't create problems.** Wait until plant leaves are dry to work in the garden so that you don't spread diseases. Scrutinize new plants for bugs and disease before you add them to your plot. (You can find lots more on preventing pest problems in Chapter 10.) Don't overwater or overfertilize.

- ✔ **Use time- and energy-saving techniques.** We show you how in this chapter.

The H (How) of H2O

You can't make the sun shine, but you can make it rain. If your herbs sag during summer's dog days, they're telling you, "A little water, please." Plants, after all, are about 90 percent water, and even moderate wilting can damage them.

Wilting is an obvious red flag; curled or dull-colored leaves are two other signs that your herbs are thirsty. Because too much moisture also causes plants to wilt, check the soil before you water. If it's dry to a depth of 2 inches, you probably need to water. Keep an especially close eye on herbs growing in pots: You may need to water them every day — even more than once a day if they're in small pots.

How much water is enough?

Going out at noon to splash your herbs with a little cool water is a wonderfully mindless activity, one that refreshes the gardener but doesn't do diddly squat for plants. The water may wet the soil surface, but little or no moisture reaches the plants' roots. Indiscriminate watering just wastes water.

Many herbs need less water than garden flowers and vegetables require — ½ to 1 inch a week (provided by you or by Mother Nature) is usually enough. In fact, most culinary herbs have better flavor when they grow in moderately dry conditions. Annual herbs tend to need more water than perennial species, which have larger, deeper root systems.

Some herbs practically qualify as *xeriscape* plants (the word comes from the Greek word *xeros,* for dry), camel-like species that can survive in an arid landscape. Among the herbs that get by on very little water are catnip, chicory, hyssop, marjoram, oregano, safflower, santolina, southernwood, thyme, winter savory, and wormwood.

Just as you need to water more in hot climates and less in cool ones, you need to water differently depending on the texture of your soil. (See Chapter 7 for details on the different types of soil.) When you water, keep in mind that

- **Sandy soil** drains quickly, retaining water poorly. Plants growing in sandy soil usually require more water than those in clay soil and need to be watered more often.

- **Silty soil** retains water better than sand, but not as well as clay.

- **Clay soil,** which holds moisture well, also takes longer to move the water down to plant roots. Water slowly for long periods of time so that water soaks in rather than running off. Plants growing in clay soil need to be watered less often than those growing in sandy or silty soil.

Install a rain gauge and keep track of rainfall, but don't be a slave to numbers: If you had an inch of rain in the past week but your plants clearly show that they're thirsty, water them. If you've had no rain but your herbs look great and the soil is still moist, don't do a thing except feel grateful.

Water smart

If your herbs are begging for water, you need to respond quickly. When you do water, do it as efficiently and effectively — and be as environmentally smart — as you can.

Keep the following tips in mind:

- ✓ **Water the plants, not the plot.** Rather than spraying a large area with a hose or setting up an overhead sprinkler — both lose water to evaporation and often wet some areas, such as paths, that don't need moisture — make sure that the water goes where it's needed: the soil around your plants.

- ✓ **Use drip irrigation.** The most efficient way to water is to use a drip irrigation system, which is made up of flexible tubing with individual emitters for each plant and a computerized timer. A less expensive (but not quite as efficient) way to get water to your plants is to use a soaker hose (or drip hose), which has tiny holes from one end to the other. Lay it on the soil near plants; water oozes out, slowly and gently. In addition to conserving water — through reduced evaporation and runoff — drip irrigation and soaker hoses water without wetting foliage, reducing disease problems.

  You can make your own drip system to water a small area by punching a few small holes in the bottom of a 1-gallon milk jug and placing it next to the herbs that need water. And don't forget about hand watering. In this age of high-tech equipment, it's easy to overlook the watering can.

- ✓ **Water during the morning or early evening hours.** You'll lose less water to evaporation during these times. Morning is best so that the sun can dry foliage quickly.

- ✓ **Water deeply.** Plants take in water through their roots, so the soil needs to be wet to a depth of at least 6 inches. You may need to water young seedlings with shallow roots more frequently but less deeply.

- ✓ **Add organic matter.** Organically rich soil retains moisture well. It's never too late to add more organic matter to your garden; refer to Chapter 7 for details.

- ✓ **Keep weeding.** Weeds use water, too — keep them out of your garden so that they don't compete with your herbs for water and nutrients.

- ✓ **Don't overfertilize.** Plants that grow slowly use less water than those that grow rapidly.

- ✓ **Be aware of wind and sun patterns.** Wind and sun steal moisture from plants. Create a windbreak if your herbs are growing where hot summer breezes are constant. Locate herbs that don't want to be out in the midday sun, such as angelica or sweet woodruff, in a partially shaded spot.

- ✓ **Recycle water.** Capture runoff from your roof in a rain barrel and use it to water your garden. Some *gray water* (household wastewater from the laundry, kitchen sink, and bath) is safe to use in the ornamental garden, but is not recommended for culinary or medicinal herbs. Don't recycle water that contains borax or great amounts of chlorine bleach. Apply gray water to the soil; don't pour it directly on your herbs. Check your local natural resources department for regulations and guidelines before using gray water in your garden.

✔ **Mulch.** Mulch reduces the soil temperature and conserves moisture. You can find much more about this subject in the section "Mulch: The Great Cover-Up," later in this chapter.

Putting on the Feed Bag

Fertilizing plants is just a variation on the nursery rhyme about the house that Jack built: You add the organic matter that feeds the microorganisms that feed the soil that feeds the herbs that you plant. Regularly enrich your soil with compost and other organic matter, and your herb plants are unlikely to need any additional fertilizer. Healthy soil grows healthy plants. It's as simple as that. Check Chapter 7 for more information on building healthy soil. However, at times, you may need supplemental fertilizer, especially for herbs growing in containers.

Plants get some of the elements they need to live from air, sunlight, and water, but the crucial mineral elements must come from the soil. A soil test, in addition to giving pH readings, can tell you whether any of these nutrients are missing in your garden:

✔ **Macronutrients:** Nitrogen, phosphorus, and potassium. Herbs need a generous helping of the big three.

✔ **Secondary macronutrients:** Calcium, magnesium, and sulfur. Herbs need lesser amounts of these elements.

✔ **Micronutrients:** Boron, chloride, copper, iron, manganese, molybdenum, nickel, and zinc. Herbs need tiny amounts of these seven.

The big three

Nitrogen (N), phosphorus (P), and potassium (K) are the most important plant nutrients. The three numbers on the bags of commercial fertilizer refer to the percentage of each element that is immediately available to plants. A bag of 5-10-5, for example, contains 5 percent nitrogen, 10 percent phosphorus, and 5 percent potassium. The remaining 80 percent may contain some usable nutrients but consists mainly of *carrier* (scientific lingo for the inactive agents that the usable nutrients attach to).

Each macronutrient plays a vital role in plant growth:

✔ **Nitrogen:** Produces good growth and healthy green leaves.
✔ **Phosphorus:** Encourages plant growth, strong root development, and the production of flowers, fruits, and seeds.
✔ **Potassium:** Aids photosynthesis, encourages flowering, increases resistance to cold and diseases, and improves overall plant vigor.

Organic versus synthetic fertilizer

We believe that maintaining healthy soil is the key to healthy plant growth. But sometimes plants can use an extra boost — especially plants growing in containers whose root systems are confined. Although synthetic fertilizers line the shelves at most garden centers, we think it's worth the effort to find their organic counterparts — often less prominently displayed but still readily available — or to make your own in the form of compost tea. Here's why we think organic fertilizers (those derived from natural materials) are better than synthetic ones (those that are made by processing chemicals into concentrated nutrients).

Synthetic fertilizers

Your plants won't care off the bat if their meal came from a bag of synthetic fertilizer. To them, nitrogen is nitrogen. Synthetic fertilizers, however, are a second-best way to feed your herbs. These fertilizers work fast and give plants a nutritional lift, but this nutrient boost can lead to rapid, succulent growth that is very attractive to insect pests.

Synthetic fertilizers often contain only the big three: nitrogen, phosphorus, and potassium, and none of the secondary and micronutrients also vital for plant growth.

Finally, synthetics don't help the soil because they lack the organic matter that microorganisms eat. If you use only synthetics, then you inadvertently starve the billions of inhabitants that live and work in your soil. Having the microorganisms die off affects the fertility, structure, and pH of the soil. And because the soil is infertile you have to keep fertilizing. This cycle may be good for the fertilizer manufacturers, but it's not good for your soil.

Organic fertilizer

Most organic fertilizers, on the other hand, are derived from natural substances and contain a broad range of plant nutrients. You may not see the immediate growth spurt you'd see with synthetics, but that's actually a good thing because slow and steady growth is healthier for the plant and less attractive to pests. Plus, many organic fertilizers contain organic matter that feeds the soil ecosystem. The traditional saying is worth remembering: "Feed the soil, not the plant."

Our all-around favorite fertilizer is homemade compost tea, which gives your plants an immediate and complete nutritional boost. (The recipe is in Chapter 7.) You can either pour compost tea on the soil around the plant or spray it on the foliage — plants can take up some nutrients through their leaves. Compost tea is also showing promise in preventing diseases that affect plant foliage. Dilute the liquid until it is the color of weak tea before using on plant leaves.

No compost? Fish emulsion, which is sold in liquid and powered forms, is another good balanced fertilizer, as is *kelp,* or seaweed, emulsion. A meal of half fish emulsion and half kelp emulsion is the most complete and effective diet you can provide. You can mix your own spray or buy this dynamic duo already formulated to be used as a foliar spray, but check the package directions before you take aim. Even natural products can burn plants if they're too strong or applied when the temperature is above 80 degrees Fahrenheit.

Side-dressing, or *top-dressing,* which is spreading fertilizers on the soil surface around plants, also provides extra nourishment, but it doesn't provide immediate help. Compost is the best side dressing for herbs. Use a tined hoe or trowel to work it into the top 2 inches of soil.

At the risk of repeating ourselves, herbs growing in organically rich soil almost never need extra fertilizer. Too much is as bad as too little. Probably worse.

Keeping Weeds Under Control

Forget all those quotations about a weed just being a plant in the wrong place. In our gardens, weeds are a pain in the you-know-what, and we suspect you'll feel the same way when bindweed, a country cousin of the morning glory, uses your borage as a trellis.

You're more likely to win the lottery than to have a weed-free garden, though. We'll be forthright: Controlling weeds, like getting your kids to clean their rooms, is a never-ending battle.

So forget about eliminating weeds altogether. Instead, concentrate on keeping them in bounds so that they don't interfere with your growing herbs.

The basic approaches

Weeds can be annual, biennial, or perennial. Annual weeds live only a year; biennials live for two years. Each, in its allotted time on earth, produces enough seeds to cover your county.

To control annual and biennial weeds, stop them from producing seeds. Either pull them out of your garden or cut them off at the soil surface — an oscillating hoe is the ideal tool.

If you've caught them before they've started flowering, add them to your compost pile where they can do you some good. (If they've begun to flower, discard the weeds somewhere else. The flowers may have begun producing viable seed, and you don't want to add weed seeds to your compost, or you'll end up sowing them right back in the garden.)

Perennial weeds live forever, or seem to. Like annuals and biennials, they make seeds, but they also reproduce vegetatively with traveling roots and underground stems. With perennials, what you can't see will hurt you. It's usually fruitless to pull perennial weeds: Each bit of root left in the soil produces a new plant. So grab your hoe and slice them off at the soil surface. When they resprout, slice them off right away. And repeat. If you keep cutting them back before they have a chance to develop more than a leaf or two, you'll deplete their roots of stored energy.

Try these methods of weed control in an established garden:

- ✔ **Consider your design.** If you don't have time to spend with a hoe, grow herbs in containers or in raised beds rather than in a traditional vegetable garden or large ornamental border.

- ✔ **Don't help weeds.** Whole-garden watering and fertilizing makes your weed situation worse. Water and feed individual plants, not the entire garden.

- ✔ **Mulch.** Cutting off the light is a sure way to kill weeds. If you don't care about how your garden looks, black plastic, cardboard, and old carpet are first-rate sunblocks. If you do care, as we do, use an organic mulch. (Check out the section "Mulch: The Great Cover-Up," later in this chapter.)

- ✔ **Keep planting.** Bare ground is like a sign that says, "Weeds Welcome!" Keep the ground covered, either with plants or mulch.

- ✔ **Mow and hoe.** In the end, the best remedy is to keep cutting down weeds and going at them with a hoe. Eventually, they die.

Herbicides: The big guns

Unless poison ivy or another "untouchable" plant has invaded, you shouldn't need to resort to herbicides to control weeds in an established garden. There's no excuse to use a synthetic herbicide for ridding your garden of dandelions or even an unruly crop of pigweed — control these by hoeing, pulling, or mulching. Even if you're clearing out a new bed, herbicides should be a last resort. Refer to Chapter 7 for more on herbicides. If you do use herbicides, apply them selectively — spray individual weeds, not the whole garden.

Mulch: The Great Cover-Up

Mulching is the process of covering bare soil in your garden with either organic matter like compost or an inorganic material like marble chips. Mulching often makes a garden more attractive, and it does "mulch, mulch" more.

Let us list the ways:

- Moderates soil temperature, keeping it cooler in summer and warmer in winter
- In winter, reduces *heaving* (plants uprooting because of alternating freezing and thawing of the soil) by keeping the soil at a more constant temperature
- Conserves moisture in the soil
- Covers the soil and prevents mud from splashing up onto foliage when it rains or when you water; this not only makes plants look nicer and gives you a cleaner harvest, but also helps prevent soil-borne diseases from spreading
- Suppresses weeds
- Reduces soil erosion from wind and water
- Reduces soil compaction from pounding rains

And if your mulch is an organic one, such as compost, it also

- Adds nutrients to the soil
- Feeds soil organisms
- Improves soil structure

Mulch saves time and labor — *your* time and labor. As one busy Vermont friend always says when he shows off his lush gardens, "Brought to you by the miracle of mulch."

You get better results from mulching if you follow these steps:

1. **Remove all weeds — or as many as you can.**

2. **Loosen the top inch or two of soil with a hoe or rake.**

3. **Water thoroughly (until the top 3 inches of soil are moist).**

4. **Apply the mulch.**

The depth of your mulch depends on the time of year, your location, your soil, your herbs, and which mulch you're using. Usually, a layer of 3 to 4 inches is adequate to suppress weeds.

Mulch musings

Here are some tips and techniques we've gleaned from our many years of mulching:

- ✔ If you're growing annual herbs in a vegetable garden or separate bed, use an organic mulch, such as straw, in spring. Over the summer, the mulch will begin to decompose. Dig the mulch into the soil in autumn and then cover the bed with a winter mulch — more straw, or shredded leaves — to protect the soil.

- ✔ In perennial beds and borders, keep mulch an inch or two away from plant stems to discourage stem rot.

- ✔ In shady, moist spots apply organic mulches in a thin layer to prevent soil from staying too wet. Wet soil attracts slugs and snails.

- ✔ In spring, especially in cold regions, wait until the soil warms before you mulch; in hot, arid climates, mulch as soon as you plant. Don't mulch seedbeds until your herbs germinate, however, and be careful not to smother small plants.

Most mulches work well in any garden, so the materials you choose may depend most on what is available where you live, how you want your garden to look, and your pocketbook. For example, straw is valuable in a vegetable or cutting garden but may not give you the look you want in your ornamental border. There, shredded bark may be a better choice.

You can use a few layers of newsprint or cardboard underneath mulch to increase its effectiveness. This technique is best saved for paths and areas between rows, because the paper or cardboard can form an impenetrable layer that keeps water from reaching plant roots — or prevents soil moisture from evaporating, causing rot.

Any mulch is better than no mulch. To borrow a slogan from the athletic shoe company, "Just do it!"

Organic mulches

You have lots of choices when it comes to organic mulch: salt hay, oyster shells, rice hulls, ground corncobs, and peanut shells are five of the more unusual choices — but here are a few common organic mulches and some of their characteristics:

- ✔ **Bark:** Shredded bark, bark chips, and bark nuggets — all are widely available, easy to apply, and contain no weed seeds. They're slow to break down; the bigger the pieces, the longer it lasts. Large nuggets are lightweight; a heavy rain can wash them off slopes. Bark is attractive, and it's one of our favorite mulches.

- ✔ **Cocoa hulls:** Cocoa hulls are attractive and slow to decompose (and smell like chocolate when first applied). They have a tendency to mat if applied too heavily and blow away in windy locations. Spread them no more than 1½ inches deep. Cocoa hull mulch can pose a risk to pets if they ingest it; if you or your neighbors have a dog, cat, or other animal that may be tempted to nibble, play it safe and mulch with something else.

✔ **Compost:** A wonderful source of nutrients, compost can be expensive unless you make your own or buy it in bulk. Compost suppresses weeds well and is easily penetrated by water while conserving moisture in the soil. It breaks down quickly, and it may contain weed seeds. Apply up to 3 inches deep. (You've probably gathered by now that in our minds compost is the king of mulches.)

✔ **Grass clippings:** High in nitrogen, quick to decompose, and widely available for free, grass clippings may also contain weed seeds. Never use clippings that have been treated with herbicides. Use only a thin (1 inch or less) layer of fresh clippings; if spread too thickly, they tend to mat and then decay anaerobically (without oxygen), This process produces a smelly, slimy mess as well as chemicals that can harm your herbs. To avoid the problem, dry the clippings before using them as mulch or compost them first.

✔ **Hay and straw:** Hay is quick to decompose, inexpensive (ask for spoiled, or moldy, hay), easy to spread, and readily available everywhere. The bad news is that most hay contains thousands of weed seeds. A better choice is straw (the stalks of grain crops after seed heads have been removed). Straw is moderately slow to break down and widely available (although more expensive than hay). Light and easy to handle, both hay and straw can blow away in windy spots and both are flammable when dry. Spread 4 to 6 inches deep.

✔ **Leaves:** Leaves are a terrific soil additive, as well as an attractive mulch. To prevent matting, shred leaves before applying them. (You can use your lawnmower for this chore or fill a plastic trash container with leaves and use a string trimmer to chop them.) Apply shredded leaves up to 3 inches deep, less if leaves are whole. Even better than shredded leaves is *leaf mold,* leaves that are partially decayed.

✔ **Pine needles, also called pine straw:** Inexpensive (or free) and available almost everywhere, pine needles are easy to handle and add organic matter to the soil. They decompose slowly but lower soil pH in the process. (Sprinkle your soil with lime to offset their acidity.) In some regions, mulching with pine needles creates a fire hazard. Spread from 2 to 3 inches deep.

✔ **Regional mulches:** Depending on where you live, different mulches are available, including nut hulls — pecan, hickory, peanut — and ground corncobs.

✔ **Sawdust:** Slow to break down, sawdust is inexpensive and available from sawmills and lumber yards. Sawdust is a good source of carbon but lowers pH (add lime, to offset its acidity) and can rob the soil of nitrogen unless composted before it's used as a mulch. Fine sawdust can pack into an impenetrable layer; coarse shavings pose less of a problem. Spread fresh sawdust about an inch deep.

- **Seaweed.** Available for free in coastal areas, seaweed is slow to decompose; apply 2 to 3 inches deep. Seaweed, or *kelp,* is a good source of nitrogen, potassium, boron, and other trace elements, but it may contain more sodium than is good for your herbs, so rinse it first in fresh water.

- **Wood chips:** Wood chips, the roughly ground limbs of shrubs and trees, are another mulch possibility, particularly for perennial herbs. Water penetrates easily, and they're weed-seed free. Wood chips, however, can rob nitrogen from the soil as they decompose; bark chips are better in that respect because they decay more slowly. Apply up to 3 inches deep. You sometimes can get wood chips free from utility companies or public works departments.

Inorganic mulches

With the exception of stone mulches, inorganic mulches are mostly made of some kind of plastic or woven fabric. Inorganic mulches don't improve the soil as organic mulches do, but they're good for stopping weeds and retaining moisture.

- **Stone mulches:** Stone mulches, such as marble chips and pebbles, are uniform, attractive, and right at home with herbs. Not only do they look great together, many of the most popular culinary herbs, such as thyme and rosemary, crave the heat that stones absorb. Because stones don't absorb water, they reduce the risk of rot because they don't hold moisture against stems. Use stone mulches in permanent beds and borders, not in gardens that you plan to rototill each year.

- **Opaque plastic mulches:** Sold in different-sized rolls at garden centers, these mulches are ugly, but unsurpassed at killing weeds. Lay down the plastic right after you prepare your soil for planting. You can cut long slits to sow seeds or cut holes to set in seedlings. Make a few extra slits in the plastic so that rainwater can reach the soil. Plastic sheeting may hold in too much moisture for herbs that need excellent drainage, like lavender.

  Plastic sheeting is inexpensive but lasts only one season because sunlight degrades it; if you cover yours with an organic mulch, you may get another year's use. Pulling up the plastic can be a chore, and then there's the need to discard the bulky mess. For these reasons, some gardeners avoid it. Don't forget that dark plastic absorbs light, raising the soil's temperature. If you live in a hot climate, it may keep your soil too hot.

- **Fabric mulches:** Landscape fabrics are more expensive than plastic mulches, but they last longer (several years at least, longer if they're covered with another mulch). Also known as *geotextiles,* landscape fabrics suppress weeds while allowing water and air to reach roots. You can find them at your local garden center. They're normally laid around permanent plantings, such as shrubs and trees, and then hidden by a layer of wood chips, shredded bark, or stone. Be sure to bury the edges of the fabric, or you risk catching an edge in the lawn mower — and if you've ever had to extract a section of fabric that's wound around the blades of a mower, you know it's not an easy job.

Keeping Tidy

We don't want you to be compulsive about keeping your herb garden neat —
a couple of small weeds aren't going to ruin the lavender — but a little good
gardenkeeping goes a long way in producing healthy, vigorous herbs.

Thinning

Lush, spreading herb plants will crowd out most weeds, but you can have too
much of a good thing. Don't let your herbs shove up against their neighbors,
like passengers in a crowded elevator. If they grow too close to each other,
they fight for light, moisture, nutrients, and fresh air. Crowded plants are less
productive and more susceptible to insects and disease. Thin out crowded
plants throughout the season.

The first wave of thinning occurs when the plants are seedlings (see Chapter 8).
You may need to thin a second or third time when your herbs begin to reach
their full stature. It's hard to yank out good-sized plants. Go ahead. The remaining herbs will thank you. Transplant the extras elsewhere if you can or use
them in the kitchen or in making medicinal preparations. Pot up a few for
friends. At the least, compost them.

Pruning

Keeping plants in bounds usually makes them more productive and attractive.
Cut back some of the stem tips of most herbs, such as feverfew, to encourage
new growth and a bushy growth. (The exception is parsley or any other herb
that has a basal form, where all its leaves grow from the plant's base.) Don't
prune perennial herbs until they've lived in your garden for at least one season.

Woody plants, such as bay and rosemary, need less radical cutting back.
With these herbs, your aim is more to shape the plant than to encourage lots
of new growth. And if you're not after flowers, you may want to pinch off the
buds to keep plants producing new stems and leaves.

For plants that you allow to bloom, take time also to remove spent flowers —
gardeners call it *deadheading* — to keep plants growing and blooming as long as
possible. Like other living things, plants strive for immortality. If you allow them
to produce seeds after they flower, they sense their job is done and stop growing.

Don't be afraid to make the first cuts. Begin modestly — a few snips here and
there, always cutting just above a node, the spot where a leaf or stem grows.
As you get to know your herbs, you'll feel more comfortable pruning them. If
you can combine pruning and harvesting, all the better.

Cultivating

Roughing up the soil around plants dislodges young weed seedlings. If the soil around your herbs is well mulched, you can skip this item. But if any of the soil in your garden is bare, you need to keep it loose. Otherwise, a crust can form on the surface and water will run off rather than soak in.

Use a tined hoe if you have one or a common hoe. Cultivate shallowly, only an inch or two, so that you don't damage plant roots.

Cleaning up

Remove plant debris — all those dead leaves and flowers, plucked weeds, and over-the-hill plants — from the garden. As long as this refuse isn't infested with insects or disease, you can add it to the compost pile. Anything that looks suspect, such as leaves covered with a white, powdery substance, should go in the trash.

Going on pest patrol

Catching pest and disease problems early makes them a whole lot easier to control. Patrol your garden each day and be on the lookout for signs that your plants have become infested or infected.

Bugs especially like new growth and the undersides of leaves. Chewed foliage is a sign that someone besides you is harvesting your herbs. Other signs are stunted growth, yellowing leaves, and sticky residue or white markings on leaves.

Diseases are more difficult to identify — and usually more devastating. The most common early warning signs are yellowing foliage, white, yellow, or reddish-brown splotches on leaves, and wilting leaves and plants.

The ins and outs of keeping herbs free of insects and diseases are in Chapter 10.

Stretching the Season

We confess that we're ready to toss in the trowel by October or November. But if you want to extend your garden year, we have some ideas to help. Nothing can postpone winter forever, but you may get several more weeks' harvest from your herb garden.

Lengthen your growing season with these techniques:

- **Pruning and deadheading:** Harvesting is one way to keep plants healthy and vigorous. Pruning plants periodically and removing spent flowers are also methods for keeping plants growing actively, especially annuals.

- **Protective mulches:** Putting a little extra straw mulch around and over a plant can protect it from an early cold snap, extending your harvest. Uncover the plant in the morning when the air has warmed. (For more on mulching, see the section "Mulch: The Great Cover-Up," earlier in this chapter.)

- **Cloches:** You can find a truckload of *cloches,* or covers, available from garden-supply companies. The word *cloche* is French for "dish cover" and refers to the glass, bell-shaped jars that were used to protect plants in the Victorian era. Most modern cloches are made from polyethylene and range from individual water-filled teepees and square hot caps to both flexible and rigid polyethylene sheets that are used with metal frames or hoops to protect entire rows of plants.

  You have homemade versions of the cloche at your elbow: paper bags, clay and plastic pots, baskets, buckets, newspaper hats, gallon milk jugs (cut out the bottom), cardboard boxes, tomato cages wrapped with plastic or burlap, and more. Don't forget that you need to remove these covers after the sun comes up so that you don't fry your herbs.

- **Row covers:** Made from polyspun fabric and available in different lengths and widths, row covers give your herbs some frost protection — the usual number that manufacturers give is protection from 24 to 28 degrees Fahrenheit — while allowing sun and rain to reach the plants. Some are so light that you can lay them on top of your plants; these types are sometimes called *floating row covers.* Use hoops to support heavier fabrics, which are sometimes called *garden quilts.*

  Don't forget the homespun versions of floating row covers: old sheets and blankets. Remove them in the morning, when temperatures rise.

- **Cold frames:** We describe using a cold frame for hardening-off herbs in Chapter 8. You can also keep semi-hardy herbs going for an additional month or two by moving them into a cold frame. Cold frames can become hothouses when the sun comes out: Be sure to open the lid during sunny days.

- **Overwintering:** We're not enthusiastic about growing herbs indoors — our success rate is darn low — but you may be able to extend your garden season by bringing some of your garden indoors. To overwinter, dig entire plants (smaller is better) and pot them up well before the first frost.

Protecting plants with water

If you have an abundant supply of water, you can try a method that commercial growers use to protect plants from frost: Spray your plants with water as soon as the mercury falls below 33 degrees Fahrenheit. Keep the spray going — use an oscillating sprinkler — until the sun rises and the air warms to 33 degrees Fahrenheit. As water freezes it gives off a little bit of heat, which keeps the temperature of the water/ice mix at 32degrees Fahrenheit, even if air temperature is lower than that.

The idea is to provide a constant supply of water so that some freezing is always going on. This method can sometimes be enough to save plants, but it's tricky business. A row cover is more reliable.

Our focus here is on the end of the garden season, but you can use cold frames, plant covers, and other heat-enhancing equipment in spring as well as autumn. Encourage the ground to warm by covering it with clear plastic, which gives your plants some protection from the chilly air, and you can get outdoors as much as a month sooner than Mother Nature planned.

The first and last words on extending your garden season is *Four-Season Harvest: Organic Vegetables from Your Home Garden All Year Long* by Eliot Coleman, Barbara Damrosch, and Kathy Bray (Chelsea Green). Maine gardener Eliot Coleman focuses on vegetables, but the techniques are the same for herbs.

Bedtime for Borage

We wouldn't push this metaphor too far, but a garden is a lot like a sailboat: When the warm weather ends, you can't just walk away and leave it. Well, you can, but to keep it in good shape, you have to do some winterizing. Old timers call this process "putting the garden to bed." Before you winterize, gather what's left in your garden. Cut back annual herbs to the ground — the cold is going to kill them anyway — but don't harvest more than a few sprigs of perennials, such as rosemary, sage, and thyme. Heavy cutting triggers new growth, tender shoots that don't have time to harden off before the first frost.

It's not too late to dig and pot up tender herbs, such as rosemary, that have been growing in your garden. Growing herbs in your house is tricky at best, but bringing things indoors may give you another month of fresh herbs.

When the harvest season is over, turn your attention to your garden plot:

- ✔ **Clean up.** Remove all the dead plants and weeds — they can act as overwintering sites for diseases and pests — and add them to the compost pile. If plants look diseased or are loaded with insects, put them in the trash. Once their foliage has died and the soil has frozen, you can cut most perennial herbs back to a couple of inches above the soil surface to make things look tidy. If you can tolerate the unkempt look, leave the dead foliage to trap snow and blowing leaves to help insulate the plants against cold and wind.

- ✔ **Test your soil.** If your first herb garden has been more disaster than success, fall is a good time to discover whether the problem isn't in your stars or yourself, but in your soil. See Chapter 7 for details about testing your soil.

- ✔ **Adjust your soil's pH.** If you have reason to think — or a soil test to prove — that your soil is extremely acid or too alkaline, fall is the time to make corrections. Ground limestone, which raises pH, works slowly, so you should apply it in autumn. To lower pH, amend your soil with peat in the fall or use elemental sulfur, which leaches quickly, in spring. Flip to Chapter 7 for more on adjusting pH.

- ✔ **Improve your soil.** Consider planting a *cover crop* in empty beds. Also called green manures, cover crops are fast-growing plants that are sown with the intention of turning them into the soil. All cover crops aren't created equal — crimson clover and other legumes are especially good at improving soil fertility — but all help choke out weeds and protect, improve, and enrich the soil.

  Annual ryegrass is an especially good choice for northern gardens (Zones 3–6). You can sow it in late autumn, and it will make enough growth to curb weeds and create a dense cover. Gardeners in warmer regions have more choices for late summer or fall plantings, including barley, crimson clover, fava beans, field pea, hairy vetch, oats, winter rye, and winter wheat. Your local Cooperative Extension Service can help you choose the best cover crop.

- ✔ **Enlarge your garden.** One season of growing herbs is usually enough to make you want to grow even more herbs. Fall is the best time to dig a new bed or enlarge the one you have. Step-by-step instructions are in Chapter 7.

- ✔ **Mulch.** Don't leave bare ground to be invaded by weeds and eroded by winter winds and rains. Cover your plot with organic matter, such as chopped leaves or manure. If a bed contains perennial herbs, wait until the soil freezes before you mulch. (The mulch will keep the ground frozen, insulating your plants from freeze-thaw-freeze cycles that can heave them out of the ground.) Loosen the soil and then mulch around, not over, your plants; covering plant crowns with a heavy layer of mulch encourages crown rot and other problems. (You can cover marginally hardy plants with a layer of straw during the coldest part of winter to help insulate them from the cold.)

✓ **Plant.** Planting isn't exactly putting a garden to bed, but fall is a good time to sow some herbs, such as caraway, cilantro, fennel, and garlic. If you live in a very warm region, the list of fall-sown herbs is a hefty one.

Autumn is also the time to clean and sharpen hand tools — and don't forget to winterize your power equipment. Nothing is more frustrating in spring than a rototiller that doesn't start.

Chapter 10

Managing Pests in Your Herb Garden

Television ads for pest control products and services describe insects as evil threats to be annihilated at all costs. They use words like *war* and *enemy* and *battle,* but in reality, very few insects pose a problem. At least 95 percent of the insects you see in your landscape are either beneficial or harmless. And most of the time, the remaining 5 percent pose minor concerns that you can control without resorting to pesticides.

The American landscape is already up to its knees in toxins — chemicals blended to combat weeds, diseases, and pests large and small. Don't add to the problem by bombing bugs and drenching diseases with more poisons. Often, these "remedies" are more harmful than the pests and diseases you're trying to control. You may have to accept a few imperfections — an occasional hole in a leaf, a nibbled flower, even a dead plant or two — but the reward is a healthier harvest, and a healthier environment.

Fortunately, herbs are among the garden plants least bothered by diseases and pests. With help from you, they'll grow vigorously, untroubled by plagues or pestilence. This chapter takes you step by step through the process of managing pests in your herb garden.

Controlling Pests and Diseases Organically

The term *integrated pest management* (IPM) describes a commonsense approach to keeping gardens and landscapes healthy. While we're great fans of IPM, we're even keener about what we call OPM, *organic pest management.* We avoid using synthetic chemical products on our herbs. You, too, can take an organic approach to gardening by embracing the following techniques.

Start with prevention

Everything you do to make your plants strong and healthy increases their resistance to pests and diseases. Good gardening practices prevent most troubles.

Gardeners call these preventive practices *cultural controls,* and you should make all of the following part of your garden routine:

- **Choose resistant cultivars.** Some herbs are particularly susceptible to certain diseases or pests. For example, bee balm often gets powdery mildew, and in recent years, fusarium disease has become a problem on basil. When possible, choose disease-resistant cultivars, like 'Marshall's Delight' bee balm and 'Nufar' basil.

- **Keep your soil healthy.** We sing our anthem to the value of organically rich soil in Chapter 7.

- **Mulch plants.** Mulch protects plants from soil-borne diseases by keeping water from splashing from the ground onto stems and leaves. Mulch also suppresses weeds. (See Chapter 9 for more on mulch.)

- **Give plants what they want.** Planting sun-loving basil in shade is asking for sickly, diseased plants. Be sure you give each herb the conditions it needs to succeed — the right amounts of sun, space, food, and water. Refer to the appendix for information on individual herbs.

- **Rotate crops.** Rather than planting basil and other annual herbs in the same places year after year, move them around to different beds. This technique is called *crop rotation.* It confuses insects that have overwintered in the soil and are expecting a quick bite of their favorite herb when they emerge. Crop rotation also foils diseases whose spores are waiting for the right weather to infect your new crop.

- **Practice diversity.** Planting a large bed of nothing but lavender — or any one herb — makes it an easy target for marauding insects or incipient diseases. When possible, mix herbs with each other or with vegetables and flowers.

- **Practice restraint.** If a particular disease or pest is overwhelming your herbs, consider leaving the plants that attract it out of your garden for a year or two — at the least, move them to a new location.

- **Make friends with natural predators.** Insects, spiders, toads, and birds are among your allies in controlling pest problems. You can encourage beneficials to linger in your yard and garden by providing them food, water, and shelter and by refraining from using pesticides. You can find out more on this in the section titled "Attracting Beneficials" later in this chapter.

✔ **Keep foliage dry.** You can't stop the rain, but if you water plants, don't wet the leaves. (Many diseases are spread by water splashing from the soil to the leaves.) Instead, water herbs at their roots.

✔ **Take it easy!** Be careful. Bruised and torn leaves, snapped stems, damaged roots, or anything that stresses plants leaves them more open to diseases and pests.

✔ **Don't make things worse.** Be sure that you don't bring problems into the garden. Inspect new herbs and other plants for signs of disease and insects before you add them to your beds and borders.

✔ **Be a good housekeeper.** Diseases and pests lurk in weeds and plant refuse. Keep your garden weeded and cleaned up. Remove and destroy plants that are diseased or severely plagued with pests. Remove plant residue at the end of the garden season.

✔ **Clean your tools.** If you're cutting off diseased material from any plant, dip your pruners in rubbing alcohol or a 10 percent bleach solution between each cut.

Monitor the garden

Get to know what your herbs look like when they're healthy so that you'll notice when something changes. Visit the garden daily and occasionally give plants a close inspection. Focus on the new growth, the upper and lower surfaces of the leaves, where the leaves meet the stems, and the stems themselves. Look for discoloration, puckering, spots, fine webbing, holes, or anything else out of the ordinary that might indicate a pest problem. Look for insect activity, too, but keep in mind that by far most of the insects you see in your garden are either harmless or beneficial.

Don't jump to any conclusions just because you see an insect, especially if you don't see signs of a problem; just make a mental note of its presence.

Many insects are sluggish in the cool of the morning, making them easier to observe. And some critters, including snails, slugs, raccoons, and possums, are active at night, so grab your flashlight and head out after sunset if you want to see them in action.

Identify the problem

Catching a problem early can keep it manageable. If during your daily garden tour you see that something's amiss, determine what's causing the trouble.

Figuring out the issue can be challenging for new and experienced gardeners alike. Look for insect activity — and the insects themselves — and make detailed notes of the symptoms. In the "Identifying Common Pests and

Diseases" section, later in this chapter, you can find descriptions of some of the most common pests and the damage they cause, as well as suggestions for managing them.

Decide whether control is necessary

This step is one of the most important in any pest management strategy. Even if you identify a pest problem, control steps may not be warranted. Is the damage minor? Is it only cosmetic? Is the season almost over? You may decide that it's not worth the time, money, and effort (as well as the potential disruption to your garden's ecosystem) to use control measures. If, on the other hand, it's early in the season or you have a boatload of pests or you know that the pests will overwinter and come back in full force next spring, then you'll want to take steps to control them.

After you identify the culprit and determine that it warrants control, start with nontoxic, least invasive methods. Using *physical controls* like barriers, repellents, and traps can eliminate the need for spraying.

Let's Get Physical

Physical controls are the garden equivalents of a chain link fence to keep the neighbor's Jack Russell terrier from doing his business on your patio. Like chain link fences, physical controls are infinitely practical but not necessarily pretty.

A straightforward approach to solving garden problems is to remove the problem. It's not always 100 percent effective, but sometimes you can help your plants by simple subtraction. Here are some ways to make that happen:

- ✔ Remove any plant or plant part that looks diseased or infested.
- ✔ Dislodge pests with a strong blast of water from the hose.
- ✔ Remove any pests large enough to grab by hand. If you're squeamish, wear gloves and drop the pests in a jar of soapy water; if you're not, squish them with glee.

If this approach doesn't control the problem, the following sections describe a few other techniques to keep pests from reaching plants.

Beneficial barriers

Barriers stop diseases and pests from reaching plants. The trick is to erect them *before* you discover your lemongrass is under attack. There's no sense putting a paper collar around an herb after the cutworm has felled it.

Here are some simple ways to prevent pests from reaching your plants:

- **Floating row covers:** Floating row covers are one of the great garden inventions of the last quarter century. Initially, row covers were intended to protect plants from cold, but savvy gardeners discovered that while they were keeping the basil from freezing, they were also keeping the Japanese beetles and other flying pests at bay. Row covers are so lightweight, you can lay them directly over seedbeds, seedlings, and plants. Remove the covers, which are available in different lengths and widths, when the threat is gone.

- **Plant collars and shields:** Plant collars and shields are old-time, proven barriers. A *collar* goes around a plant stem — above and below ground — to protect against cutworms. A *shield* covers the ground around a plant to prevent root maggots and others from laying their eggs at the base of plants. Fashion collars from paper-towel and toilet-paper tubes or cardboard; the collar should be about 5 inches tall, with 2 inches buried in the soil. You can use a 6-inch square of heavy black plastic or landscape fabric to make a shield. Punch a hole in the center large enough for the stem and cut a slit to one edge to slide it around your plant.

    You also can cover small plants with plastic milk jugs (cut out the bottom and remove the cap) to protect them from pests. The jugs also serve as mini-greenhouses, giving tender young herbs protection against the cold. Don't forget that the jugs can heat up during the day and may need to be removed, or your herbs will be cooked.

Traps

Traps are an alternative to mashing bugs by hand or underfoot. Before you empty a trap, take a look at the contents to be sure that you're catching what you're after.

Don't measure success by the number of victims — instead, measure it by reduced damage to your herbs.

Among the arsenal of traps are

- **Pheromone traps:** *Pheromones* are chemicals secreted by females to attract males. Use these traps cautiously: Most research shows that unless all your neighbors also set out traps, you're likely to attract more pests than you capture. If you use them, locate them well away from the plants you want to protect.

- **Sticky traps:** The outdoor version of fly paper, you can buy sticky traps at garden centers and by mail, or you can make your own by painting a 1-foot-square piece of hard plastic or plywood yellow and then coating it with Tanglefoot or a similar sticky spray sold for this purpose. Nail the square to a stake and set it in your garden; clean and recoat as necessary.

- **Food and plant traps:** Some pests are attracted by specific foods (slugs and snails to beer, for example). You also can grow trap plants to lure pests away from your herbs (a hollyhock may divert Japanese beetles from your basil). After the trap plant is infested, either handpick the pests or remove and destroy the trap plant. (See our recommendations for trap plants in the upcoming section titled "Bad bugs" in this chapter.)

- **Shade traps:** Slugs and snails are shade lovers. To lure them, lay boards or shingles on the soil, checking under them each morning. Destroy your catch by dropping it into a can of soapy water.

Repellents

Repellents are physical controls, although most are less visible than collars or sticky traps. Garden suppliers sell organic products to ward off pests and diseases, or you can mix your own. You must reapply repellents after a rainfall.

Keep the following tips in mind:

- Many repellents use hot peppers to discourage pests. (The heat comes from flavorless chemical compounds in the peppers and is measured in Scoville Heat Units: zero for a sweet bell pepper and up to 200,000 for a mouth-scorching habañero.) Avoid sprinkling hot pepper powder or flakes from your spice rack on or around plants because animals, such as rabbits, squirrels, and even pets, can get the material in their eyes, causing excruciating pain. The Humane Society recommends using only wax-based hot pepper repellents because they stick to plant surfaces, discouraging feeding without harming animals.

   Wear gloves and keep your hands away from your face when you're working with any product containing hot peppers! And don't spray on any part of a plant you intend to harvest.

✔ Diatomaceous earth, a powdery substance that you sprinkle both around and on plants, is made from fossilized shells of diatoms. Its sharp particles abrade pests that come into contact with it, such as slugs, snails, and earwigs, but it is virtually nontoxic to mammals.

✔ Wood ashes discourage stem-attacking pests, such as root maggots. Spread them around but not on herb plants. Because wood ashes are alkaline and will raise your soil's pH, apply them sparingly. (See Chapter 7 for more information about pH.)

✔ To help repel fungal diseases, such as powdery mildew and blackspot, try a baking-soda repellent: 1 tablespoon baking soda, 1 tablespoon vegetable oil, 1 teaspoon liquid dish soap (such as Ivory liquid), and 1 gallon water. Mix and spray plants thoroughly. You can buy similar commercial formulations containing potassium bicarbonate.

✔ Evidence shows that commercial *antidesiccants,* or antitranspirants — products developed for helping plants retain moisture — also protect against a variety of plant diseases, including rust and powdery mildew. Follow label directions.

✔ Spraying herbs with compost tea (see Chapter 7 for brewing instructions) helps repel fungus diseases at the same time it provides nourishment.

✔ Slugs and snails avoid copper because they get an unpleasant sensation (akin to an electrical shock) upon contact. Use copper bands around individual plants or fasten a strip around the outside of a raised bed.

✔ Many plant extracts act as repellents, including citrus oils, garlic, tansy, marigolds, and mint. Use judiciously on herbs you plan to harvest.

Using Biological Controls

Biological controls use living organisms and are based on the theory that every pest has a mortal enemy. Biological controls are most often bacteria or fungi-control specific pests.

As synthetic pesticides come under more and more scrutiny (and more are restricted or banned outright), researchers are focusing their attention on biological controls. Expect to see new products in the coming years. Here are a few currently on the market:

✔ **Bacillus thuringiensis,** or *Bt,* is a bacterium that is safe for gardeners and other mammals but murder on larvae. *Bt* comes in more than one strain — each has a favorite target — so be sure you get the appropriate type. *Bt kurstaki,* for example, kills caterpillars; however, it doesn't distinguish between pest species and other butterfly and moth larvae, so use it judiciously. *Bt san diego* kills Colorado potato beetle larvae. *Bt israelensis* kills mosquito larvae.

- ✔ **Milky spore disease** *(Bacillus popilliae)* attacks Japanese beetle grubs. When the grubs ingest it, they become ill and stop feeding. When they die, the bacteria are released into the surrounding soil to infect other grubs. Milky spore is sold as a powder that you apply to your lawn. It can take several years for the bacteria to build up in the soil enough to achieve good control.

- ✔ **Beneficial nematodes** are microscopic, wormlike organisms that infect many soil-dwelling pests, including Japanese beetle grubs, cutworms, and sod webworms.

- ✔ **Spinosad** is a relatively new pest control product. It's derived from a naturally occurring soil-dwelling bacterium and is used to control caterpillars, beetles, leaf miners, thrips, and fire ants.

- ✔ **White muscadine fungus** is a promising new insecticide made from a type of soil-dwelling fungus. When spores of the fungus come into contact with an insect, the spores germinate and invade the insect's body, killing it.

- ✔ **Serenade, Sonata,** and **Mycostop** are three new fungicides derived from naturally occurring bacteria. **Serenade** and **Sonata** work by boosting plants' natural immune systems and by inhibiting fungal growth. **Mycostop** colonizes plant roots, helping prevent infection.

Attracting Beneficials

Good bugs, or beneficial insects (even though some aren't technically bugs or insects), greatly outnumber bad bugs. Beneficials not only pollinate flowers (remember the birds-and-the-bees talk with your mother?), they seek and destroy many plant pests. And they make the supreme sacrifice, giving themselves up as dinner for bats, toads, birds, and other FOTG (Friends of the Garden).

Bugs for sale

Believe it or not, you can buy beneficial insects for your garden Beneficial-insect companies won't ask you questions, but you should question them. Before you buy, be sure you know what it is you want to control and what the best bug is for controlling it. Know, too, when to release beneficials and what you need to do to keep them in your garden. One warning: Lady beetles, which are collected in the wild, are effective in greenhouses but rarely stay in the garden long enough to do much good.

Following is a short list, a beneficial top nine. These beneficials are flyers, creepers, and crawlers that you want to keep around. Most are native to the United States, so all you may have to do is make them feel welcome:

- ✔ **Aphid midges:** It's the midge larvae — tiny orange maggots — that commit "aphidcide."

- ✔ **Arachnids (spiders and mites):** Predatory mites prey on their less desirable relatives (spider mites and rust mites), thrips, and other pests; spiders lunch on anyone they can catch.

- ✔ **Beetles (lady beetles, rove beetles, ground beetles, and friends):** This army of pest-control beetles feeds on aphids, cutworms, mealybugs, root maggots, snail and slug eggs, spider mites, and more.

- ✔ **Dragonflies:** You need water to attract these flyers, one of the garden's most beautiful do-gooders.

- ✔ **Flies:** These flies are good flies, not the household type, whose larvae scavenge aphids, cutworms, caterpillars, and other pests.

- ✔ **Lacewings:** Lacewings give twice: They feed on aphids, mites, thrips, and other soft insects and insect eggs as larvae, and then they eat again, as adults. Like humans, they're much hungrier in their youth.

- ✔ **Parasitic wasps:** These tiny, nonstinging insects lay their eggs inside other bugs. Parasitic wasps control aphids, whiteflies, and some caterpillars.

- ✔ **True bugs:** Believe it or not, "true bugs" is the scientific name for a group of insects, which includes predatory members that attack aphids, beetle larvae, caterpillars, and thrips.

- ✔ **Yellow jackets:** If yellow jackets nest far enough away not to sting you, leave them alone to gather caterpillars, flies, and assorted larvae for their offspring.

Praying mantises are familiar and fascinating garden do-gooders, but it turns out they don't really do all that much good: Not only do they eat each other, they're as likely to eat beneficials as they are to eat pests.

In addition to these small pest-control champs, some larger animals are worth having on garden patrol. We don't suggest that you import these helpers — they may be inappropriate for your location or sensibilities — but don't discount the good they can do.

- ✔ **Bats:** Forget all the scare stories about rabies — scientists say the danger is remote — and remember that bats are champion insect-eaters. Maybe not the 500,000 bugs a night as some bat fans claim, but more bugs than we'd want to count.

How to keep 'em down on the farm

Increase your garden bounty by encouraging beneficials to stay around, be fruitful, and multiply. Here are our suggestions for turning your property into a five-star hotel:

✔ Use as few toxic controls as possible. Using none is best.

✔ Don't install an electric bug zapper — data now show they kill far more beneficials than mosquitoes.

✔ Keep your soil rich in organic matter.

✔ Provide beneficials with food, water, and shelter.

✔ Practice diversity by growing many different herbs and other plants in your garden, rather than just one or two species.

✔ Grow plants that attract and feed beneficials. Good host plants include angelica, anise, asters (*Aster* spp.) and other daisy-like flowers, baby blue-eyes (*Nemophila menziesii),* calendula, candytuft (*Iberis sempervirens),* coriander, dill, fennel, sunflower, and zinnia *(Zinnia elegans).*

✔ **Birds:** There are so many reasons to want birds in your yard that you'll forgive them a few transgressions, such as eating the cherries and blueberries. Keep in mind that the birds are also eating beetles, grubs, caterpillars, leafhoppers, and more. One estimate is that aphid eggs make up half a chickadee's winter diet. That's our little chickadee!

✔ **Snakes:** We're sympathetic if you draw the line at encouraging snakes to dwell in your herb garden. Just remember that some species keep rodent populations in check, and others eat slugs and insect pests. (If you live in a region with poisonous snakes, learn to distinguish them from their nonpoisonous relatives.)

✔ **Toads:** You didn't have to read *The Wind in the Willows* as a kid to love toads. They eat an almost exclusive diet of grubs, slugs, beetles, and other harmful insects, and no, they don't cause warts. To build your own Toad Hall, chip a doorway on the side of a terra-cotta pot and leave it, turned upside down, in a shady spot in your garden.

Turning to Organic Sprays and Dusts

We hope you won't have to use this section of the book — that all the precautions we recommend have meant that your herbs have been untroubled by pests or diseases. Using sprays and dusts in the garden, with a couple of exceptions, is never completely safe. Organic controls — the kind we're listing — kill beneficial as well as predatory insects. At the same time, they are safer than most synthetic products and break down quickly into harmless substances.

Beating bugs

This section shows you the safest, most common insect pest controls used by home gardeners. Many of these controls are contact poisons — they paralyze or kill pests when they encounter the substance; others are systemic poisons, which take effect when pests eat treated plants. All are widely available from garden centers or mail-order and online sources. Follow label directions exactly.

Try these organic controls for insect pests:

- **Horticultural oils** are used to kill immature insects and insect eggs. The two main types are *dormant oils,* which you spray on woody plants in winter to control eggs or overwintering pests, and *summer,* or *light, oils,* which you can use during the growing season to control aphids, mealybugs, scales, spider mites, whiteflies, and some caterpillars. Use a sprayer to cover the entire plant.

  Summer oils can damage fuzzy-leaved plants, such as betony, borage, and sunflower; use them only on herbs with shiny foliage and when the temperature is below 80 degrees Fahrenheit.

- **Insecticidal soaps** contain fatty acids that paralyze soft-bodied pests, such as aphids, mites, and whiteflies. You must spray insects directly for insecticidal soaps to work.

- **Neem oil,** a spray made from azadirachtin compounds extracted from neem trees, is both a contact and systemic poison. Neem oil controls a wide range of pests, including beetles, flies, and caterpillars, and it's most effective against immature insects. Neem oil may also act as a repellent. It appears not to be harmful to bees or most beneficials and breaks down quickly after it's applied.

Some formerly popular organic pesticides are now considered too toxic to be used safely. Avoid using rotenone, ryania, pyrethrin or pyrethrum, sabadilla, and nicotine sulfate.

Downing diseases

Curing plant diseases isn't easy for environmentally sensitive gardeners because only a few organic products control diseases. Many fungal diseases — powdery mildew is one — are more of a cosmetic concern than a life-or-death matter. Bacterial and viral diseases are more serious. Once plants are infected, you can do little except remove and destroy them.

Before you reach for disease-curing sprays and dusts, remember that the antibiotics produced in organically rich soil help your herbs ward off disease organisms; compost tea also appears to have some disease-fighting properties.

The most common organic controls for plant disease that appear in the following list are in the order from least to most potent. Again, organic doesn't mean nontoxic. We hope you never use any of them.

- **Sulfur-based fungicides:** These are the safest of the fungal controls, but they're still toxic to many beneficial organisms. Don't use sulfur in temperatures over 80 degrees Fahrenheit, or you'll burn the leaves of your herbs.

- **Copper mixtures:** Copper-based fungicides are effective but nonspecific — they kill the good with the bad. Used repeatedly, copper fungicides will stunt plants. They could stunt yours, too, if not used cautiously.

A mixture of copper sulfate and hydrated lime, *Bordeaux mixture* has been used by gardeners since the 1870s. (Its fungicidal powers were serendipitously discovered by French viticulturists who reputedly sprayed their vines to keep people from stealing their grapes.) Timing is important to keep from damaging your plants, so read instructions carefully. Use at half the recommended rate on culinary herbs.

Playing it safe

You won't find any pesticide that is completely safe, even if it's organic. If you purchase or make any products to kill diseases, pests, or weeds, follow these guidelines:

- Keep pesticides away from children.

- Read the label and follow its instructions exactly.

- Never mix different pesticides together.

- Use pesticides in the early evening, when beneficials are less active.

- Wear protective clothing and equipment to keep pesticides from reaching skin, eyes, nose, and mouth.

- Wash hands and face after handling pesticides.

- Don't use pesticides near water or in windy conditions.

- Always treat specific plants, not the entire garden.

- Store pesticides in their original container in a cool, dry place and dispose of them according to label recommendations and local ordinances.

Identifying Common Pests and Diseases

See some holes in the marsh mallow's leaves? Did your cilantro seedlings keel over just five days after they sprouted? Before you can remedy the problem, you need to know what's causing it.

You may be facing a slew of possible causes. Take a look at our short list of bugs and plant illnesses. These adversaries are the ones you're most likely to find in the herb garden.

If none of these pests and diseases fit the symptoms, consult reference books, Web sites, a gardening neighbor, and/or the experts at your local Cooperative Extension Service or Master Gardener program.

Bad bugs

You can find these herb pests indoors and out. Some, such as spider mites, mealybugs, scale, and whiteflies, are most troublesome inside. Borers, beetles, caterpillars, leaf miners, slugs, and snails are pretty much outdoor problems, while aphids and nematodes visit both house and garden.

Figure 10-1 shows many of the bad bugs mentioned in the following sections.

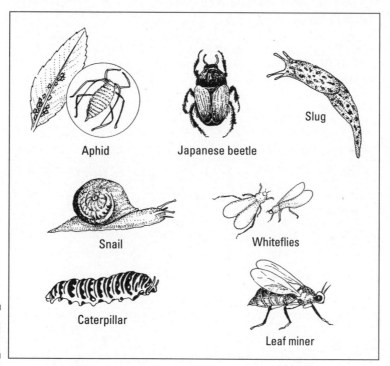

Aphid   Japanese beetle   Slug

Snail   Whiteflies

Figure 10-1:
Bad bugs!

Caterpillar   Leaf miner

✔ **Aphids:** Tiny black, green, or pink insects the size of a pinhead, aphids cluster on the undersides of leaves, especially angelica, basil, caraway, chervil, chive, lovage, nasturtium, oregano, scented geranium, and southernwood. In addition to damaging leaves, they carry diseases that distort and yellow foliage.

Prevention and control: Cover herbs in spring with floating row covers; encourage or release lacewings, ladybugs, or aphid midges. Plant nasturtiums as a trap. To control, spray plants with a strong stream of water. Spray with an insecticidal soap every two days until aphids are under control.

✔ **Beetles:** All sorts of beetles (insects with wings and wing covers that meet in the middle of their back) may feed on herbs. Most range between ¼ and ½ inch long. Metallic-green Japanese beetles are especially fond of basil, echinacea, elecampane, roses, and sorrel. Look for foliage that have holes or have been skeletonized. Mint flea beetles (very small dark beetles that leap when disturbed) feed on mints. Flea beetles attack horseradish.

Prevention and control: Cover herbs in spring with floating row covers. Weed and cultivate regularly. Plant traps include borage, grapes, hollyhocks, and white zinnias for Japanese beetles; flea beetles flock to Chinese cabbage and radish. To control, handpick. Apply milky spore to control beetle grubs. For crop-threatening infestations, apply neem or spinosad.

✔ **Caterpillars and borers:** The color and size of these critters vary, but you'll recognize a caterpillar. Parsleyworms (a 2-inch-long green character) and hornworms prefer chomping on parsley, dill, and all members of the carrot family; cabbage loopers are also fond of parsley. Cutworms are gray caterpillars that live in the soil, emerging in spring to feed on tender shoots of emerging plants.

Prevention and control: Surround new plants with collars to discourage cutworms. Carrot and Queen Anne's lace are good food plants for attracting caterpillars. To control most caterpillars, handpick.

Every caterpillar is a butterfly-in-waiting. Parsleyworms become swallowtail butterflies, so you should move rather than destroy them.

✔ **Leaf miners:** Leaf miners are tiny black flies that lay their eggs on plant leaves. The maggots burrow into the foliage, leaving irregular white markings on leaf surfaces, especially on angelica, lovage, madder, oregano, and sorrel.

Prevention and control: Cover herbs in spring with floating row covers. Keep the garden weed free. Attract parasitic wasps and other beneficials. Grow radish or beet as a trap plant. Spray with spinosad or neem in spring, before adult flies lay their eggs. To control, remove and destroy infected leaves.

✔ **Mealybugs:** Mealybugs are tiny, sucking insects that band together to form colonies that look like bits of cotton, usually on leaf undersides. Indoors, almost any plant is a target, but mealybugs are especially partial to rosemary.

Prevention and control: Apply horticultural oils. To control, spray plants with a strong stream of water. Dab the insect clusters with rubbing alcohol; treat with insecticidal soap or neem.

✔ **Mites:** You need a 10-power hand lens to see spider mites, microscopic web-spinning arachnids that show up as red dots. They suck on plant leaves, especially those of angelica, germander, lavender, lemon verbena, mint, oregano, rosemary, sage, savory, and thyme. Watch for their telltale webs.

Prevention and control: Spray plants frequently with cool water. Encourage lacewings, ladybugs, and predatory mites. To control, apply an insecticidal soap or a horticultural oil.

✔ **Nematodes:** Also known as eelworms, nematodes are soil-dwelling, microscopic worms that feed on plant tissue. (Not to be confused with the beneficial nematodes described in the "Using Biological Controls" section, earlier in this chapter.) The root-knot nematode occasionally troubles lavender, parsley, and rosemary. Look for stunted growth or yellow or wilted foliage.

Prevention and control: Practice crop rotation and amend soil with organic matter. Plant castor bean as a trap plant. To control, solarize soil by covering it with clear plastic secured at the edges for an entire summer. The sun will heat up the soil, killing nematodes. (Solarization works best in regions with long, hot, sunny summers.)

✔ **Scale:** Sucking insects fond of bay and rosemary leaves and stems, scale appear as brown oval bumps and are horribly difficult to get rid of. Sticky sap residue is another sign your herbs are infected with scale.

Prevention and control: Spray plants with a horticultural oil in spring and summer. Wash leaves and stems with insecticidal soap. To control, dab with rubbing alcohol. Remove and destroy infected leaves.

✔ **Slugs and snails:** You'll recognize a snail; a slug is a snail without its shell, a 1- or 2-inch slimy gray-brown mollusk. Both creatures are nocturnal, so you must stay up late to handpick. Slugs and snails munch on basil, calendula, sorrel, and violets.

Prevention and control: Encourage predatory beetles and invite toads to take up residence. Keep your garden free of plant debris; reduce mulching. Apply diatomaceous earth around herb plants. Grow hosta as a trap plant. To control, handpick. Leave out shallow trap containers of beer or lay boards in the garden.

✔ **Whiteflies:** Primarily an indoor problem, especially in greenhouses, whiteflies cluster on leaf undersides, where they also lay their yellow eggs. They're hard to miss — bump a leaf and the tiny, moth-like insects fly off en masse. Their feeding weakens plants, and they can also transmit harmful viruses. Favorite leaves are those of lemon verbena, mint, rosemary, and sage.

Prevention and control: Use yellow sticky traps. Encourage lacewings and ladybugs. Grow flowering tobacco (*Nicotiana* spp.) as a trap plant. To control, spray herbs with insecticidal soaps or horticultural oils.

Disturbing diseases

Plant diseases are sometimes tough to identify — a 10-power hand lens is indispensable for seeing signs of diseases, as well as the small pests that can spread them — and the list of possible herb ailments is substantial. Most can be avoided by following the prevention strategies at the start of this chapter.

Don't let this litany of common diseases put you off — with any luck, plenty of sunshine, and organically rich soil, your herbs won't even develop the sniffles. If necessary, spray with one of the organic fungicides listed in the section "Downing diseases," earlier in this chapter.)

Here's a rundown of some of the plant diseases you might encounter in your herb garden:

✔ **Bacterial wilt:** Bacterial wilts cause leaves, then entire plants, to droop and die, especially coriander, nasturtium, sage, and scented geranium.

  Prevention and control: Practice crop rotation to control cucumber beetles, which spread the disease. Cover plants with floating row covers in spring. There is no safe control. Remove and destroy infected herbs.

✔ **Crown rot:** A fungus that attacks the base of plants, crown rot turns plants yellow, followed by wilting. Angelica, parsley, and violet are likely victims.

  Prevention and control: Practice crop rotation. There is no safe control. Dig and destroy infected herbs.

✔ **Damping-off:** Diagnosing this fungal disease is easy. Healthy seedlings — practically all herbs are susceptible, especially those sown indoors — suddenly fall over and die.

  Prevention and control: Use sterile seed-starting mix and containers. Don't overwater. Give seedlings bright light. Dust the soil surface with milled sphagnum moss. Spray emerging seedlings with chamomile tea. (Steep 1 cup dried chamomile flowers in 1 quart water.) There is no control. Discard the soil, sterilize the containers, and start over.

✔ **Downy mildew:** Most common when conditions are cool and humid, downy mildew is a particular foe of calendula, coriander, germander, tarragon, and violet. The fungi leave yellow spots on leaf tops, gray mold on their undersides.

  Prevention and control: Space plants far enough apart to have good air circulation. Don't work among plants when foliage is wet. Practice crop rotation. Remove and destroy infected plants.

✔ **Powdery mildew:** Another fungal disease, powdery mildew prefers warm, humid weather and is partial to agrimony, calendula, coriander, germander, lemon balm, monarda, sunflower, tarragon, and yarrow. You'll know it by the white, powdery splotches it leaves on plant foliage.

Prevention and control: Give plants plenty of elbow room. Clean up plant debris when the garden season is over. To control, remove and destroy infected leaves and plants.

✔ **Root rot:** Root rot occurs underground, but yellowing foliage and slow growth are symptoms that your herb is infected with this fungal disease. Clary sage, fenugreek, lavender, mullein, myrtle, oregano, rosemary, sage, tarragon, thyme, and winter savory are most likely to be struck down.

Prevention and control: Aerate your soil by adding organic material, such as compost. Wait until the soil has warmed before planting in spring. Practice crop rotation. Clean up plant refuse when the garden season has ended. There is no safe control. Remove and destroy infected plants.

✔ **Rusts:** Rust diseases come in many forms, all spread by wind-borne fungi that leave reddish brown marks on leaves. Affected plants, such as germander, mint, bee balm, sunflower, and yarrow, often drop their leaves.

Prevention and control: Space herbs so that they have good air circulation. Remove plant residue at the end of the garden season. To control, dust herbs with sulfur. Remove and destroy infected plants.

✔ **Verticillium wilt:** A fungal disease common throughout North America, verticillium wilt causes foliage to yellow and die. Eventually, it kills the plant. Coriander, mint, nasturtium, and sage are common victims.

Prevention and control: To prevent, enrich soil with organic matter. Don't use high-nitrogen fertilizers. Practice crop rotation. Clean up plant refuse. There is no safe control. Remove and destroy diseased plants.

Outwitting Wildlife

What to do about Bambi, Thumper, and their friends? As usual with garden pests, there are no easy solutions for keeping them out of the garden. Stores are well stocked with repellents against deer and other wildlife. We've tried them all, as well as sacks of human hair, bars of soap, homemade hot pepper and garlic sprays, dried blood, castor oil, even urine (thanks to family members who prefer to remain anonymous). Nothing seems to work longer than a day or two, if that.

If wildlife damage is a sometimes thing in your garden, grin and bear it. Or frown and bear it. But if marauding animals trample or munch your entire basil crop three years in a row, here are some suggestions. Good luck!

✔ **Scare tactics:** Birds and some other animals are frightened by unexpected sights and sounds. Scarecrows are worth trying (even if they don't work, they are ornamental and a good way to recycle your spouse's wardrobe), as are Mylar scare tapes, inflatable scare-owls, mirrors, whirligigs, aluminum pie tins hanging from strings, and a radio tuned to a heavy metal station. Animals habituate, or become accustomed, quickly, so move these items every few days. Or use a motion-activated sprinkler or radio to startle them.

✔ **Fences:** Gardeners who have big-league problems with deer or other four-legged wildlife usually conclude that a fence is the only effective and permanent deterrent. A 2-foot fence will deter rabbits, but deer can easily scale any fence less than 8 feet tall. A fence plus electricity is even better. There are now "low impedance" controllers that make electric fences safer.

✔ **Traps:** Trapping wildlife — and we're talking about live trapping — is a mixed blessing for you and the trapee. The fact is that many animals are unable to adapt when dropped off in a new environment, so live trapping may not save a life. Still, trapping seems more humane than guns and poisons, and much safer. Frankly, it's the only break a hungry woodchuck deserves.

Call your Department of Natural Resources for rules and regulations about trapping and releasing wildlife. Be careful when using live traps: Wear heavy gloves, don't handle the animal, and choose a release site that is both appropriate and legal. Mammals and rodents are good travelers. Relocate rabbits, woodchucks, and other small animals at least 3 miles away, skunks and squirrels 5 miles, and raccoons at least 10 miles.

Part IV

Cut and Dried: Handling the Herbal Bounty

The 5th Wave   By Rich Tennant

©RICHTENNANT

"That part of the garden is called 'Area 51' because we don't know what's going on over there."

In this part . . .

In addition to enjoying their beauty in the garden, most herb gardeners end up using herbs in some way. In this part, we cover the basics of harvesting and preserving herbs for different uses. We also delve into specifics on using herbs in the kitchen, as well as harnessing their powers to heal. We consider ways to use herbs in beauty products and around the home, too.

All photos by Cathy Wilkinson Barash

This colorful herb and flower garden includes English daisy, pansy, and chamomile.

Gently rub the leaves of scented geraniums to release their fragrance.

Oregano is associated with the cuisines of many hot, sunny countries, including Mexico, Italy, Greece, and Spain.

Pretty bottles filled with homemade herbal vinegars make welcome gifts.

Herbs like this anise hyssop are right at home in a perennial garden.

This fragrant garden includes lemon balm, thyme, and lavender.

This decorative window box includes pansies, rosemary, and an ivy topiary.

These herbs look right at home in their kitchen-themed containers.

Parsley is packed with vitamins and minerals.

Basil comes in more than 30 varieties.

Rosemary's robust flavor complements hearty foods like stews and roasts.

Tuck herbs into the empty spaces in your vegetable garden.

Lavender and fennel spread freely in this informal garden.

Confine mint to a container to keep it from taking over your entire garden.

A close relative of oregano, marjoram has a milder flavor.

Chamomile flowers are used to make a relaxing tea.

Echinacea is right at home in perennial gardens and wildflower meadows.

Thyme makes a beautiful edging plant.

Look for tri-color, variegated, and purple sage, in addition to the common green-leafed variety.

Yarrow flowers are popular in dried arrangements.

Purple-leaved basil, dill, and marigold are a striking combination.

Chapter 11

Harvesting and Preserving

. . . .

. . . .

*W*hen you buy your first tiny herb seedlings or see them sprout from seed, it may seem inconceivable that you will ever have enough chamomile flowers for a single cup of tea or enough cilantro for a south-of-the-border fiesta. But if the fates are kind (and you faithfully follow all of our helpful tips), before you know it, your beds will runneth over.

Overwhelmed by the bountiful harvest? As they say in Australia, "No worries." In this chapter, we describe what, how, and when to harvest, as well as many methods for preserving your bounty. We show you how to add herbs to other foodstuffs to spice up your cooking and impress your friends. And we also suggest ways to mix and match your herbs to keep things lively.

Note: Always use untreated (chemical- and pesticide-free) blossoms and herbs for anything that is meant to be eaten.

Bringing in the Sheaves

Just as different herbs are ready to be harvested at different times, different parts of your herbs — leaves, stems, flowers, fruits, seeds, and roots — need to be collected at different times. The timing of your harvest also depends on how you expect to use the herb — to make tea, for example, or to make a wreath or a nosegay.

Fortunately, the rules for harvesting are pretty simple and straightforward. Here are some basics. (You can find more information under the individual listings in the appendix.)

Gathering leaves and stems

Don't be afraid to snap a few stems or pick a bouquet any time you want — your herbs are there for you to enjoy. Most herbs thrive with frequent, light harvesting because it keeps plants bushy and promotes tender, young growth.

If you want herb leaves to use as salad greens, harvest as soon as the leaves are large enough to be used but still tender and succulent. You know first-hand what we mean if you've ever eaten leaf lettuce that was picked past its prime — it's tough and bitter.

Mid-morning is by far the best time to harvest herbs, after the dew dissipates but before the day starts to heat up. That's because the oils that make herbs taste and smell wonderful and work medicinally are at their most power-ful then. Moreover, wet leaves take far longer to dry, if drying is your aim. Morning is a pleasant time to visit your garden, anyway, and to inspect plants for problems.

Keep a wicker basket handy when you visit the garden. (We suggest having a cup of coffee — or herbal tea — in your other hand.) Invariably, you'll see or smell something you'll want to snip for the kitchen or a vase. Your fingers will be adequate to pinch off soft stems, but keep florist's shears or pruners in your basket for woody herbs.

When you harvest, don't just strip off leaves so that you leave a bare stem waving around. Think pruning. Instead of pinching off leaves or stems willy-nilly, make all your cuts above the *node* — the point where they attach to the stem or branch — and you'll also stimulate new growth. And of course you want to harvest only healthy green foliage, not leaves that look diseased or discolored (though you may want to remove that foliage and discard it).

If you need large amounts of material for a family feast or a major craft proj-ect, a general rule is that you can harvest up to one-third of the tops of most annual and biennial herbs, and they'll continue to grow. Harvest more than that amount, and they may not recover from the shock. Of course, if an immi-nent frost is going to kill the plants, harvest all you can.

After perennials are established — at least a year old — you can take a third of their top growth in late spring and another third in mid-summer. Six weeks before your expected first frost, resist the urge to pinch more than a leaf or two. Perennials are a bit like bears and need time to collect extra "fat" in their roots to survive winter hibernation.

If you're like us, you discover something new almost every time you harvest your plants — a shortcut, perhaps, or something not to do again. Here are some tips we've picked up in our gardens and from gardener friends:

- ✔ Don't get carried away on harvest day and pile your basket high, because tightly packed, newly cut herbs generate heat. The effect is similar to what happens in a compost pile when you add a big load of fresh grass clippings. Harvest only what you can reasonably deal with right away, whether it's bagging up to refrigerate or hanging up to dry.

- ✔ If you harvest more than one herb at a time, use labeled paper bags instead of a basket. Herbs can look alike once they start to dry. (Avoid plastic bags; they hold in too much moisture, which leads to rot.)

- ✔ Many herbs bruise easily, so don't handle your harvest any more than you must.

- ✔ Don't rinse your herbs. Dampness can invite mold. Dust off dirt and dust specks with a soft brush; if plant leaves are muddy, rinse them off with a garden hose the day before you collect them. Mulching under plants helps prevent rain-splashed mud, too.

- ✔ If you're going to dry your herbs, keep the leaves on their stems. For details on drying herbs, flip to the "Cut and Dried: Proper Drying and Storage" section later in the chapter.

Salvaging other parts

Although foliage is the big draw for growing most herbs, sometimes the seeds, flowers, or roots are more tasty or potent, or have value for dried arrangements and other uses. Just as with foliage, the rules about when and how to collect them are pretty much the same, no matter the plant.

Seeds

Seeds are the real reason to grow some herbs, such as anise and caraway. With others, such as cilantro/coriander and dill, both the leaves and the seeds are often harvested. Seeds begin forming after the flower is pollinated and the petals fall off. The seeds are ripe and ready for collecting when they turn from green to brown or black. Watch, too, for seedpods to swell or change color. Shake the ripened flowerhead into a paper bag, and the seeds will fall into the bag. Be sure to label the bag with the name of the plant and the date you gathered the seed.

Some seeds are in a hurry to go forth and multiply and will shoot off the plant without notice. Others are hard to see within the drying flower head.

A common trick is to tie a small paper bag around the flower head before the seeds drop. (Use a twist tie or rubber band to secure the bag.)

In the case of herbs with only a few large seed heads, such as fennel, you can do this bagging while the plant is still in the garden. In other cases, you need to bag the head after you've cut and hung it upside down. The seeds of a few herbs — anise is one example — ripen over a period of time. Cut the entire head, shake the ripe seeds off, and let the rest ripen in a warm, dry, dark place.

If you've dried an entire seed head, you may find you have nearly as many pieces of pod and other plant bits, called *chaff,* in your paper bag as you have seeds. In her infinite wisdom, Mother Nature made seeds heavier than chaff. To separate the two, pour the mixture in a shallow dish and use a hairdryer, small fan, or plain old pucker power to blow away the chaff.

Flowers

For most uses — such as eating fresh in salads and making medicinals, cosmetics, and potpourris — harvest herb flowers just as they start to open. Essential oils that provide flavor, fragrance, and healing qualities are all at their peak as the bud is swelling. Cut the flower off with a bit of stem (which helps keep flowers from falling apart) above the top set of leaves.

For dry arrangements, wreaths, or crafts in which you use entire flowers, you can achieve a more natural-looking result if you pick flowers at different stages — unopened, partially opened, completely opened. Harvest them with at least 6 inches of stem. Potpourri, too, has a more interesting texture if you include a few tight buds along with petals. (For more on making potpourri, see Chapter 15.)

If you're going to press flowers, let them open a bit more before you cut them — enough that you don't have to wrestle them to lay flat. After they've fully opened, don't leave them in the garden or anywhere their color will fade or that insects can damage them.

Roots

The ideal time to harvest roots (and rhizomes, which are horizontal stems that travel on or just below ground) is in fall, after the foliage has died back. That's when roots are at their most potent. (If you forget, you can harvest the next spring before growth starts, but you may have a harder time finding the plant. In addition, the roots may be more full of moisture and take longer to dry.)

Herbs harvested for their roots include angelica, burdock *(Arctium lappa),* chicory, comfrey, dandelion, elecampane, ginger, horseradish, madder *(Rubia cordifolia),* marsh mallow, orrisroot, soapwort, sweet Cicely *(Osmorhiza longistylis),* and valerian. These roots have a variety of uses. Horseradish, one of the herbs most commonly grown for its roots, was an often-prescribed medicine in the 17th century to "wonderfully help" sciatica, gout, arthritis, and liver ailments. It also wonderfully helps hot dogs.

Here are a few rules for underground harvesting:

✔ Be patient with roots. Don't harvest perennials before the autumn of their second year. (A couple of exceptions are chicory, which you can harvest the first year before it goes to seed, and marsh mallow, which is better when harvested in the fall of its third year.) Biennials, such as angelica, begin wearing out and become woody in their second year, so harvest them in their first fall or second spring.

✔ Your job will be easier if you dig roots when the earth is damp but not sopping wet. Use a spading fork (which will be less likely to damage the roots) and delve deep. Cut off the plant tops; if you can't use them, then add them to the compost pile. Roots, unlike herb leaves, need washing after harvesting; if necessary, scrub them with a brush to remove dirt.

✔ In most cases, gardeners dig the entire plant when they harvest roots. But if you want that perennial in the same spot next year, remember to slice off a hefty section of root containing an eye, or bud, and replant it.

Cut and Dried: Proper Drying and Storage

For short-term storage of harvested leaves (a week or less), place the stems in a glass of water as you would a flower bouquet; cover with a plastic bag and refrigerate. (Basil is an exception; leave the glass out on the counter because basil leaves turn black if they get too chilled.)

If you aren't sure how you'd like to use your herbs — as seasonings, as medicines, or to keep ants out of the cupboard and fleas off Rover's belly — drying them allows you to decide at a later date. If you love to cook, you'll probably want to try more than one approach to drying to find one that best suits your taste buds. Just make sure to store the herbs properly and label them.

Most dried herbs (with the exception of a few oddballs like bay leaves) lack the flavor of fresh ones. But if you dry them carefully, they far surpass the bottled ones you buy at a grocery store. And you can feel comfortable about their quality because you know they weren't irradiated or doused with chemicals to get rid of hitch-hiking pests.

The rest of this section offers guidelines for drying herbs using various different methods.

Just hanging around

You've seen country shops or photographs in which bundles of herbs hang from the ceiling on tidy twists of twine. They always look quaint and homey. Hanging is actually a good and relatively easy way to dry herbs — as long as you remember a few basics. The goal is to dry your herbs quickly in order to retain as much of their fresh flavor as possible. Fast drying keeps medicinal properties intact, as well.

A warm, dry place

The key to drying herbs this way is location. The perfect place to hang your herbs must be

- ✔ **Dark:** The sun bleaches and discolors herbs, stealing their precious oils and making them ugly, to boot. This effect pretty much rules out outdoor locations, except perhaps a roofed porch on the north side of your house. Even indoors, you may need to block sun coming in windows.

- ✔ **Dry:** It seems silly to say that a place for drying herbs should be dry, but some gardeners think a kitchen is a logical place to dry culinary herbs, forgetting how humid that room is. Ditto the bathroom. Humidity is another reason most outdoor sites don't work, except perhaps in the southwestern United States. Even overnight dew can retard the process. Attics are often good, but if you live in a humid climate, you need to hook up a dehumidifier there as well.

- ✔ **Warm:** Herbs dry best where the temperature stays between 80 and 85 degrees Fahrenheit. Near the end of the process, which averages about 2 weeks, 90 degrees Fahrenheit is okay. This high heat is another reason why many people choose attics to dry their herbs. Just keep an eye on the temperature to make sure that it doesn't get much hotter than 90 degrees Fahrenheit, or the quality of the dried herbs will decline.

- ✔ **Clean:** Steer clear of sheds or rooms where you fill your lawnmower or use other chemicals, or any areas where mice may play periodically. And that attic that was looking so good — how often do you vacuum or dust it? To keep culinary herbs sanitary, many herb gardeners envelop them loosely in cheesecloth or in paper bags punched full of holes.

- ✔ **Well ventilated:** Moisture is the biggest enemy of herbs that are doing their darnedest to dry. Cross-ventilation from open doors and windows is the most natural solution. If all else fails, a fan set on low helps to stir the air.

Some elbow room

Don't hang bunches of herbs against a wall or too close to each other — 6 inches apart is a minimum distance. You can bunch together as many as ten stems of a single herb if it has small leaves, as thyme does, but if you're drying succulent herbs, such as basil, borage, or comfrey, keep the bundle to six stems or fewer.

Hang down your head . . .

The best herbs for hanging in bundles are those that have long stems, such as lavender and yarrow. Other good candidates to suspend, batlike, in a cool, dark, dry location are anise, artemisia, borage, caraway, chamomile, cost-mary, feverfew, hyssop, and lady's bedstraw *(Galium verum)*. You can also hang marjoram, mint, oregano, parsley, rosemary, rue, sage, santolina, savory, sweet Cicely, sweet wood-ruff, tansy, tarragon, and thyme.

For the record, many flowers also air-dry well. Flowers for hanging in bundles include alliums (garlic, onion, chive), artemisias, calendula, clary sage, goldenrod, hop, lavender, sage, tansy, and yarrow.

Although hemp twine looks charming, rubber bands are a more practical way to tie herb stems together. Unlike twine, rubber bands contract as the stems dry and shrink, so stems are less likely to fall out.

You can hang the bundles from individual hooks in the ceiling, but it's more efficient to set two hooks several feet or yards apart, string a clothesline between them, and suspend the bundles of herbs from the line. To expand that space even more, use clothes hangers and clip three or four bundles of herbs to the hanger with clothespins. You can also clothespin bundles of herbs to a portable drying rack.

Now wait and watch. Check your harvest often, because herbs can take any-where from a couple of days to several weeks to dry — it all depends on the plant and the weather. Leaves are dry when they feel stiff and crumbly, like a cornflake.

Plant leaves are quick to reabsorb moisture from the air, so the minute they're completely dry, put the herbs into airtight containers and store in a cool, dark place. (Most experts agree that flavors last longer if you keep the leaves whole rather than crushing them.) Opaque glass containers are best, but clear glass is fine as long as your storage cabinet is a certified black hole. Light and moisture erode herbs' freshness. As a last safeguard against any undetected moisture, wrap a tablespoon of dried milk in an unscented facial tissue to act as a desiccant and place it in the container.

Even when stored properly, herbs lose much of their oomph after six months. But by then, of course, you'll be started on next year's seedlings!

Rack 'em up

For some herbs, hanging isn't good enough. Their stems are too short, too soft, too skinny, or wiry to make bunching them an easy process. For these guys — as well as for individual leaves, flowers, seeds, and roots — you need a drying rack.

You can buy a rack, but they're easy to make, as shown in Figure 11-1. Just staple some window screening or cheesecloth to a wooden frame made by screwing together the corners of four pieces of 1-x-2 lumber. Be sure to set the frame on bricks so air circulates beneath it. (For a bountiful harvest, make several racks the same size and then stack them by setting wooden blocks on each corner.) You can also repurpose an old window screen. Or, if you have only a few leaves or petals to dry, spread them in the bottom of a basket or on a paper towel laid on a cake rack or wooden dish rack.

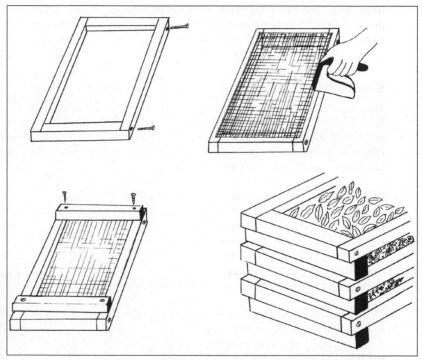

Figure 11-1:
Making
racks for
your herbs.

Spread out your herbs in a single layer on the drying surface. Stir or turn them every day or two to avoid excessive curling and to discourage mold from developing. How long does drying this way take? As always, it depends on what you're drying and where you live, but plan on five days to two weeks. Most flowers take longer to dry — a week or more depending on the size and type.

Because roots are thick and must be washed after they're harvested, they can take weeks to dry. To speed drying, slice them into 2-inch lengths or peel long taproots and cut them lengthwise. You know roots are ready for storing when you bend them and they snap the way a crisp stalk of celery does.

To dry seeds, lay cheesecloth over a drying rack (in a dry, well-ventilated location) and cover it with a single layer of seeds or ripe seedpods. After your seeds are dry and you've blown off any chaff, store them in airtight containers in a cool, dark place.

Modern methods

All right, they're not faster than a speeding bullet, but some devices do help speed herb drying. Some serious herbalists create drying cabinets by grouping racks around an electric heater. Others purchase commercial food dryers. You can speed the process of drying herbs by using equipment that you probably already own.

Conventional ovens

Some experts are adamantly opposed to using a conventional oven to dry herb foliage and flowers because getting an oven to stay at the ideal 80 to 90 degrees Fahrenheit temperature is so difficult. Gardeners with gas stoves say the pilot light emits just enough heat. An oven thermometer can tell you if your oven can heat in the right range.

To dry in the oven, spread leaves and flowers in a single layer on a baking sheet and place them in an oven set as low as possible. Leave the oven door partway open to let moisture and excess heat escape. Keep a close eye on the temperature, opening the door more or turning off the oven as necessary to keep the temperature between 80 and 90 degrees Fahrenheit. Drying can take from 10 minutes to several hours. Check the herbs often, especially if they have delicate leaves, and turn them periodically.

Most people agree that ovens are a good option for roots, which can take several weeks to air-dry. Many gardeners like to start drying roots in the oven — a single layer spread on a baking sheet at 90 degrees Fahrenheit — and then transfer them to a drying rack so the oven's free for Sunday's pot roast.

Be sure to allow herbs to cool before you bottle them; store them as you would herbs that have been air-dried.

Microwave ovens

Most culinary herbs dry in a microwave in a minute or less. The downside to this convenience is you have to watch like a hawk to make sure that your herbs don't become too hot, which gives them a burned flavor.

Begin by spreading a single layer of herbs on a paper towel and then cover them with a second towel. Set the temperature to high and microwave the herbs for 45 seconds. If the herbs haven't dried completely, give them another microblast of 10 or 20 seconds. Continue blasting away until all moisture is gone. Allow the herbs to cool and then store them as you would if they had been air-dried, in airtight containers set in a cool, dark place.

Refrigerators

This "cool" approach to preservation is becoming increasingly popular because drying herbs this way retains both their flavor and color. Spread a single layer of leaves or flower petals on a baking sheet covered with paper towels and place it in the main section of the refrigerator (not the crisper). Drying usually takes two to four days, depending on the herb and the refrigerator. This technique works especially well for herbs that can be challenging to dry in other ways — parsley, dill, and chives, for example.

Dehydrators

These gizmos are sold primarily for drying fruit and making beef jerky. They're also good for drying herbs; they operate like low-level toaster ovens that rotate their contents on racks. In terms of drying speed, dehydrators fall between the microwave and air drying. Herb foliage dries in three to ten hours, but roots can take several days. Most machines come with specific instructions for drying a variety of herbs.

The Big Chill: Freezing Herbs

Freezing is an option for preserving delicate culinary and medicinal herbs that tend to go all to pieces when they're dried. Some herbs seem to retain their fresh flavor better with this method, but your experience may differ. Depending on who's talking, freezing may be as good as or better than drying for basil, chervil, chives, cilantro, dill weed, fennel, garlic greens, lovage, marjoram, mint, oregano, parsley, sage, sorrel, sweet Cicely, tarragon, and thyme.

Just as people disagree about the wisdom of freezing herbs at all, people also disagree about whether to blanch herbs before freezing them. *Blanching* means to plunge the herb into boiling water for no more than a second or two. (Gardeners who freeze vegetables usually blanch them to keep them firm, colorful, and fresh tasting.) Gwen Barclay, coauthor of *Southern Herb Growing,* observes, "Any instructions you have that say to blanch herbs are heresy. You might as well throw the herbs away and keep the blanching water." (Anti-blanchers often make an exception for basil, which blackens if frozen unblanched.)

A large blob of herbs stuffed into a bag can freeze unevenly, retaining moisture that changes the flavor and makes pieces stick together. To freeze quantities, spread herbs in a single layer on a baking sheet. Place the baking sheet in the freezer for a couple of hours, or until the herbs are frozen, then transfer the herbs to freezer bags, pressing out as much air as possible, and return them to the freezer.

Salting herbs

In the days when folks' home freezers were smaller than their radios, Grandma would salt down her tender herbs. If you have some space in your own pantry or root cellar, you may want to experiment with this method, which leaves herbs tasting surprisingly fresh.

Cover the bottom of a glass or ceramic container (which has an airtight lid) with a layer of uniodized or kosher salt and then add a single layer of herbs. Barely cover the herbs with salt and add another layer of herbs. Continue alternate layering, ending with a salt layer. You can leave dill or flat-leaf parsley on its stems, but strip the leaves of other herbs to make sure that they lie flat. Seal and store in a cool, dark place. Rinse the salt off the herbs as you use them.

Frozen herbs should keep for six to eight months. Don't refreeze them. When you use frozen herbs in recipes, measure as though they were fresh.

If you use herbs to flavor soups and stews, try freezing them in ice cube trays, as shown in Figure 11-2. Pack chopped fresh herbs in the tray divisions and top with boiling water. (Remember to use slightly less liquid in your recipes.) For sauces, puree the herb in a blender or food processor with enough oil or water to make a paste and fill your ice cube tray with the mixture. If you often use a certain herb combination, such as basil and oregano, freeze the premeasured herbs together in cubes or freezer bags.

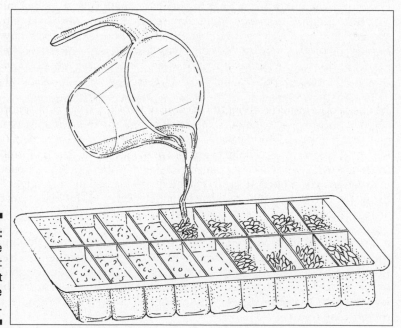

Figure 11-2:
Ice cube trays: They're not just for ice anymore.

Getting Crafty with Decorative Herb Parts

If you want to use herb leaves, flowers, and fruits for crafts, you have even more preservation options. You can air-dry herbs for potpourris, which don't require perfect flowers or leaves in the same manner that you dry culinary herbs. You can leave a few varieties of flowers outdoors on their stalks until they dry — tansy and yarrow are two examples — but you must pick and dry most flowers.

To keep herbs shapely or to keep stems, flowers, and foliage all in one piece — which is important in making dried wreaths and arrangements — you need to use special techniques. To air dry flowers, for example, use a mesh wire rack and slide the stems down through the holes so that the flowers dry upright. Following are several additional solutions for preserving herbs for bouquets, baskets, and more.

Desiccants for decorations

Desiccants are moisture-absorbing substances, such as borax, kitty litter, and cornmeal, that are used to dry plants, especially delicate flowers that don't air-dry well. Silica gel is far superior to other desiccant substances because it's lightweight, won't crush delicate plant parts, and works quickly. Available at craft and florist shops, silica gel is fairly expensive but reusable. The powder turns blue when it's full of moisture; dry it by putting it in a covered pan in a 200 degrees Fahrenheit oven for about 20 minutes. Store in an airtight container.

Until you discover how long it takes a desiccant to dry different species, work with flowers and foliage of the same kind and size so that they dry at the same rate. If you're using silica gel, drying should take only a few days; other desiccants may take a month or more. Whichever desiccant you use, the technique is similar. Use flowers that are not completely open. (If a wire stem is necessary, attach it before you dry the blossom.) Then follow these steps:

1. **Sprinkle about an inch of desiccant in the bottom of a glass or plastic container.**

2. **Arrange your blooms on top so that they don't touch.**

   Make sure that the flowers are relatively flat. You may want to push some extra crystals between the petals of double blossoms, such as calendula or roses.

3. **Top the blooms with enough desiccant to cover the flowers or leaves completely.**

If you're using silica gel, seal the container; otherwise, leave it open. Be careful not to breathe the silica gel fumes, which can irritate mucus membranes. Never eat herbs or flowers that have been dried using silica gel.

4. **Place the container in a warm, dry place, checking it frequently so that blossoms don't overdry.**

Leaves and flowers dried in most desiccants have a tendency to reabsorb moisture over time. A spot over the living room fireplace is a better home than a humid kitchen for that dried wreath you spent hours making.

Microwave blossoms

You can use a microwave oven to preserve foliage and flowers for crafts. (See the guidelines for microwave drying that appear in the "Microwave ovens" section, earlier in this chapter.) Better still, especially for preserving flowers or any plant parts that you don't ingest, you can use the microwave oven and silica gel. Be sure to dry similar flowers together so that everything is done at the same time.

Fill a microwaveable container with 1 inch of silica gel. Spread the flowers or leaves in a single layer and cover them with more gel. Microwave the open container for 1 minute on high. If drying isn't complete, continue microwaving in 15-second intervals until all moisture is gone. Let the flowers or leaves sit in the oven to cool for about 10 minutes and then carefully empty the container onto paper towels.

Remember, you can't consume anything that has been dried with silica gel.

Pressing business

You can use pressed flowers, foliage, and seed heads to make wall hangings and greeting cards. Commercially made presses are inexpensive and easy to use. Simply arrange the material in a single layer in the press between two sheets of blotting paper and turn the thumb screws. You can also press flowers in a city phone book or between the pages of newspapers, weighted with a couple of dictionaries or a copy of *War and Peace*.

Good candidates for pressing include single-flowered roses and the flowers of calendula, chives, lavender, bee balm, pansies, and nasturtium. Incorporate the foliage of chervil, chamomile, dill, feverfew, sweet Annie, rue, and violets, or the seed heads of dill, parsley, or rue. Most flowers dry in a week or two, but if it's warm and humid, drying can take more than a month.

Chapter 12

Culinary Concoctions

In This Chapter

▶ Making your own herb combinations

▶ Crafting herbal vinegars and oils

▶ Preparing herb butters and spreads

*I*t's a fair guess that most gardeners delve into the world of herb growing so that they can harvest a fresh sprig or two for their favorite dishes. In some recipes, you can make do with dried herbs, but in others, there's no substitute for fresh herbs — pesto just isn't pesto without handfuls of fresh-picked basil leaves. Fresh herbs are ridiculously expensive in supermarkets (and the word "fresh" is relative — they may have been harvested days or weeks ago). Plus, who knows what they've been sprayed with? It just makes good sense to grow your own herbs, especially the one's you'll be eating.

Some of the recipes in this chapter use fresh herbs; others make use of the herbs you've dried or otherwise preserved (see details in Chapter 11). The recipes in this chapter are just the tip of the herbal iceberg — once you start experimenting with food/herb combinations, you'll be on your own culinary adventure.

Note: Unless otherwise noted (as dried), fresh herbs are called for in all the recipes.

Mixing It Up

Combining herbs with foods and each other is obviously a matter of personal taste, as are the proportions to use. Just like some people, some herbs, such as basil and parsley, get along famously in almost any situation. And some foods, such as beef and potatoes, are amiable companions for most herbs. Other herbs like cilantro or sage can be a bit more persnickety about their partnering. Here are some of our favorite herb-food pairings:

- **Asparagus:** Chervil, chives, lemon balm, savory, tarragon
- **Beans (dried):** Basil, bay, cilantro, fennel, garlic, marjoram, oregano, rosemary, sage
- **Beans (fresh green):** Chives, garlic, rosemary, thyme
- **Beef:** Bay, cayenne, cumin, fennel, garlic, horseradish, marjoram, oregano, rosemary, thyme
- **Cabbage:** Caraway, dill, fennel, oregano, savory
- **Carrots:** Caraway, chervil, coriander, poppy seed, savory
- **Cauliflower:** Coriander, cumin, rosemary, mustard
- **Chicken:** Allspice, cardamom, chervil, lemony herbs, marjoram, nutmeg, oregano, tarragon, thyme
- **Eggplant:** Chili peppers, garlic, marjoram, oregano, sage
- **Eggs:** Basil, chervil, chives, French tarragon, mustard, nasturtium
- **Fish:** Chervil, chives, dill, lemon herbs, lovage, parsley, rose, savory, tarragon
- **Lamb:** Coriander, cumin, garlic, mint, rosemary
- **Pork:** Basil, caraway, chervil, coriander, cumin, fennel
- **Potatoes:** Caraway, chervil, dill, lavender, marjoram, nasturtium, oregano, rosemary, savory
- **Rice:** Dill, fennel, marjoram, mint, parsley, rosemary, saffron, sage
- **Turkey:** Marjoram, pepper, tarragon, thyme, sage

Creating Classic Combos

Just as certain foods go with certain herbs, some herbs mingle well. Choosing which ones to combine, to use immediately or later, is "quite a matter of fancy," to borrow from Carol Campbell, an Ohio herbalist.

If you're unsure about where to start when mixing and matching herbs, we suggest that you begin with some of these traditional herb combinations:

- ***Bouquet garni:*** A bunch of fresh herbs tied together with string in a cheesecloth bag is a *bouquet garni.* It's also a French culinary classic, used to flavor broths, soups, and stews. It usually includes bay leaf, parsley, and thyme and is removed from the dish before it's served.

✔ *Fines herbes:* This famous French combination of chopped fresh herbs calls for equal amounts of chervil, chives, parsley, and tarragon. Some cooks include marjoram or savory. It's especially good with eggs, fish, and poultry. You should add it near the end of cooking so that the herbs retain their color as well as flavor.

✔ *Herbes de Provence:* This mix of dried herbs works for almost every-thing, from pot roasts to potatoes, from beans to cheese spreads. Dozens of recipes don this name, but even the most egocentric chefs pretty much agree that *herbes de Provence* should contain equal parts of basil, fennel seed, lavender, marjoram, rosemary, sage, summer savory, and thyme.

Crafting Herbal Vinegars and Oils

When it comes to homemade gifts, a fancy bottle of homemade tarragon vinegar or citrus-basil oil is always a hit. Even better, the recipient likely has no idea how easy they are to make. Herb vinegars and oils are a way to capture and preserve the flavor of fresh herbs, and the flavor combinations are endless.

Of the two, vinegars are the safer choice, especially for gift-giving. Because vinegar is acid, it keeps bacteria in check; oil is not acidic, and illnesses have been traced back to flavored oils. Take the precautions set out in the following sections.

Making flavored vinegar

You can use herbal vinegars in salad dressings, marinades, and a hundred other items that call for regular vinegar. You can combine any vinegar with pretty much any culinary herb or herb combination. Rice and white wine vinegars are the usual choices for more reticent herbs, such as tarragon, while bold herbs, like rosemary and sage, can stand up to cider or red wine vinegar.

To make an herbal vinegar, start with a squeaky-clean glass container (wide-mouthed jars are the easiest to fill) that has a nonmetal cover. Now cram it full of fresh, clean herbs. Don't be stingy — really pack them in there. Next, fill the jar with vinegar, making sure to cover the herbs. (Our first choice is rice vinegar because it's milder and lets the herb flavors shine through more than stronger-tasting vinegars.) There's no need to heat the vinegar — room temperature is fine. Use about 1 cup of fresh herbs (or ½ cup dried herbs) for each 2 cups of vinegar.

Allow the vinegar to steep: Seal the filled container and set it in a cool, dark place for two to three weeks. Then strain the vinegar into a clean storage bottle and discard the herbs. (You can add a few fresh herb leaves and edible flowers for decoration.) We love to store vinegar in those imported beer bottles with lids held on by wires, but you can use any bottle for which you can find a tight-fitting top or cork. Although the acidic vinegar acts as a preservative, to be on the safe side, store herbal vinegars in the refrigerator and use within one year.

Tarragon and Garlic Vinegar

Use this vinegar in salad dressings, marinades for chicken, and sauces for mild fish and chicken dishes.

enough tarragon to loosely fill the jar — 4 to 6 stems

1 clove garlic

2 cups white wine vinegar

Place the tarragon and garlic clove in the jar and cover with the vinegar. Allow to steep, as described above, and strain into storage containers.

Citrusy Basil Vinegar

Use this vinegar in dressings for fruit and vegetable salads and in sauces for salmon and trout.

2 cups white wine vinegar

zest from one lemon and 1 orange (use a zester to remove in thin strips)

1 cup basil leaves, packed

Combine ingredients in a glass jar and allow to steep for a week or two. Strain into storage bottles. Add a strip of citrus peel for decoration, if desired.

Some other favorite herbs for vinegars include basil, bay, cilantro, fennel, garlic, lavender, and thyme. Chives and pinks flowers as well as purple basil produce a pink tint; while bright nasturtium blooms give a red to orange hue.

(Put these in clear bottles to show the colors.) Spices, such as chilies, cloves, and peppercorns, add zip to meat dishes. A few more tasty combinations are

- Bay, garlic, rosemary, and thyme — for marinating beef
- Cilantro, garlic, and hot peppers — for marinating Tex-Mex meats
- Lemon-flavored herbs, mint, and rose geranium petals — for dressing spring greens
- Basil, cilantro, ginger, and lemongrass — for Thai stir-fries
- Chives, fennel, and marjoram — for dressing cooked vegetables

Making flavored oils

Now that so many people are trying to cut back on animal fats, spout-topped bottles of herbal oils are replacing "the other spread" on restaurant tables. In addition to being drizzled on breads, these oils are great for sautéing meats and vegetables or mixing salad dressings. Any high quality oil makes a good base. Olive oil is the usual choice, but some herbs and oils, such as lemon herbs and walnut oil, make particularly harmonious marriages.

Many people have had a change of heart about herb oils since several botulism deaths were traced to garlic stored in oil. And garlic is not the only suspect. All herb oils are easily contaminated and must be prepared, handled, and stored carefully. Blanching herbs before adding them to the oil is not an adequate protection against toxic bacteria forming.

Cooperative Extension Services suggest following these guidelines when making herbal oils:

- *Always* add acid, either vinegar or lemon juice.
- *Always* keep herbal oils refrigerated.
- *Always* use the oil within one week.
- *Always* play it safe; many toxins can't be detected by sight, so if the oil clouds or just looks funny, heed the adage — when in doubt, toss it out.

If our warning hasn't scared you off, fill a sterile, wide-mouthed jar loosely with fresh herbs that have been thoroughly washed. Aim for a 1:2 herb-to-oil proportion (1:4 for dried herbs).

Add the oil and 1 tablespoon of vinegar or lemon juice for each cup of oil. Seal the bottle, give it a shake, and refrigerate. After one week, remove the bottle from the refrigerator (if necessary, let it sit briefly at room temperature for the oil to reliquify), and strain the oil through a coffee filter or cheesecloth. Return it to a sterile container, seal, label and date it, and refrigerate. Use the oil within one week.

Mint-Infused Olive Oil

Use this flavored oil on lightly steamed vegetables (especially fresh green peas) and in Middle Eastern–inspired recipes, such as tabbouleh, couscous, and lamb dishes.

1 cup mint leaves

2 tablespoons lemon juice

a few strips of lemon zest

2 cups extra-virgin olive oil

Pack the mint, lemon juice, and zest into a jar and cover with oil, making sure all the leaves are covered. Follow the directions for steeping, straining, and storing.

Living It Up with Herbed Butters and Spreads

Now that we've mentioned butter being unhealthy, we'll 'fess up — we love the stuff. Not slathered willy-nilly on instant mashed potatoes, but saved for fresh-baked muffins at Sunday brunch or garlic bread with Friday night's spaghetti. Ahhh!

If plain butter is good, herbed butter is better. Good herb choices include basil, chives, marjoram, rose, rosemary, thyme, and sage. For each quarter pound of unsalted butter (one stick, at room temperature), mix in 2 or 3 teaspoons of minced fresh herbs. Let the butter sit at room temperature for an hour and then cover and refrigerate overnight to let the flavors meld.

Don't even think about substituting margarine or another butter alternative; the flavor won't be up to par. Besides, a little bit of herb butter goes a long way.

You can give soft cheeses a similar treatment. Cream cheese with chives is the classic combination, but try your bagels with dill, oregano, or even minced horseradish in your spread. For a lighter touch, use whipped cream cheese.

Store herb butters in the refrigerator and use within three days. Herb butters freeze wonderfully — use your hands to form the softened butter into a log and wrap tightly with freezer paper or plastic wrap. Once the butter is frozen, slice it off as needed; use within three months.

Soft cheeses don't freeze well; store them in the refrigerator and use them within three days, tops. (Unlike commercial products, yours don't contain preservatives.)

Savory Herb Butter

Fresh herbs are best; choose the youngest, most tender leaves. You can also substitute the fresh herbs with half the quantity of dried herbs, crushing the herbs into small pieces before mixing. Use on chicken, fish, hot biscuits, hot vegetables, and in scrambled eggs.

½ teaspoon sage leaves (or sage flowers)

½ teaspoon tarragon leaves

½ teaspoon rosemary leaves (or rosemary flowers)

½ teaspoon minced chives or onion (or the same amount of onion powder)

1 stick butter, at room temperature

Finely mince the herbs and then mix all ingredients together, mashing the herbs into the butter.

Herbed Horseradish Spread

Serve over hot foods like roast beef, grilled meats, and steamed vegetables or use cold as a sandwich spread and in potato salad and cole slaw. If you're not used to eating spicy horseradish, start with the smaller amount, then add more to taste. You can also use prepared horseradish; omit the vinegar and sugar.

½ cup cream cheese, softened

½ cup mayonnaise or sour cream

2 to 4 teaspoons horseradish

2 teaspoons cider vinegar

1 teaspoon sugar

1 teaspoon Italian (flat leaf) parsley, or ½ teaspoon dried

1 teaspoon thyme (or ½ teaspoon dried)

1 teaspoon prepared mustard

Combine everything together and let sit overnight so flavors can blend.

Boursin Dip

Boursin is a brand name but has come to describe any mild, soft, herbed cheese. Serve this dip on freshly baked bread or toasted baguette slices or use as a dip for raw vegetables.

1 teaspoon dill

1 teaspoon Italian parsley

1 teaspoon marjoram

¼ teaspoon black pepper

3 tablespoons plain yogurt

8 ounces soft goat cheese

Finely mince the herbs and mix with yogurt and cheese.

Blending Herbal Salad Dressings

Herbs add zing to any salad — even something as simple as a wedge of iceberg lettuce. If you have more flavorful mixed greens, such as a mesclun mix or a variety of vegetables mixed with lettuce, the right herb dressing will enhance the overall blend. You can simply mix a single herb like tarragon, chives, garlic, or mustard into oil and vinegar or get creative with dressings. The following recipes are a few of our favorites.

Harvest Dressing (with Fresh Herbs)

Fresh salad greens deserve the freshest, most flavorful dressings, and this one is bursting with herb flavor.

2 cups mayonnaise

1 scallion, chopped

2 teaspoons chopped Italian parsley

1 teaspoon chopped basil

1 teaspoon chopped tarragon

1 tablespoon white wine vinegar

1 teaspoon honey

Combine all the ingredients in a blender for one minute. Chill for a few hours so flavors can blend.

Italian Dressing Blend

Use this classic dressing over greens and on vegetables as part of an antipasto plate.

1 cup extra-virgin olive oil

½ cup balsamic vinegar

1 tablespoon white sugar

1 teaspoon minced oregano

½ teaspoon minced thyme

½ teaspoon minced Italian parsley

¼ teaspoon celery salt

salt and pepper to taste

Combine all the ingredients in a tightly sealed jar and shake. Let it sit for an hour so flavors can blend. Shake again before dressing the salad.

Lowfat Green Goddess Dressing

This creamy dressing has the green tint of its full-fat relative, but far fewer calories.

½ cup packed baby spinach

1 tablespoon chopped Italian flat leaf parsley

1 tablespoon basil, chopped

⅔ cup nonfat plain yogurt

⅔ cup buttermilk

1 tablespoon fresh lemon juice

1 teaspoon sugar

2 tablespoons extra-virgin olive oil

salt and pepper to taste

Purée all ingredients in a blender or food processor for your own "green goddess" dressing.

Marinating in Style

We marinate food to impart extra flavor, and herbs shine in this regard. Most marinades contain an acid, such as vinegar or lemon juice, which helps tenderize meats in addition to adding flavor.

In general, the longer you marinate (within reason) the more flavor is imparted. Overnight is best for most red meat, a few hours will do for chicken. Seafood is the exception: Marinate for no more than 30 minutes or the acid in the marinade will start to change the texture of the fish.

Sweet-and-Sour Herb Marinade

Use to marinate meats and vegetables before grilling.

½ cup cider vinegar

½ cup olive oil

⅛ cup light brown sugar

⅛ cup ketchup

1 teaspoon prepared mustard

¼ cup chopped fresh herbs (any combination, such as thyme and rosemary)

2 cloves garlic

Mix everything together.

Lemony Herb Marinade

Use to marinate chicken or fish.

⅓ cup olive oil

⅛ cup lemon juice

⅛ cup cider vinegar

1 tablespoon chopped basil

1 tablespoon chopped lemon verbena

2 teaspoons chopped thyme

¼ teaspoon salt

¼ teaspoon pepper

Mix everything together.

Savory Herbal Rub

Rub on meat before cooking.

4 tablespoons sweet paprika

2 tablespoons brown sugar

1 tablespoon dried oregano

1 teaspoon dried sage

1 teaspoon dried rosemary

1 teaspoon salt

½ teaspoon pepper

Mix all ingredients.

Preparing Dried Herb Mixes

Dried herb mixes are handy — you reach for one herb container instead of all the individual jars in the mix. They're also fun to package up and give as gifts. The classic dried herb blend is *herbes de Provence,* described in the section "Creating Classic Combos," earlier in the chapter. Here are a few other blends to try.

Poultry Seasoning

Use as a dry rub to season chicken and turkey before grilling or baking, and as a seasoning in stuffing and any dish containing poultry.

1 tablespoon dried parsley

1 teaspoon dried thyme

1 teaspoon dried sage

1 teaspoon dried rosemary

½ teaspoon sweet paprika

1 teaspoon onion powder

1 teaspoon garlic powder

½ teaspoon celery seed

½ teaspoon salt

½ teaspoon pepper

Mix everything together, crumbling dried herbs into small pieces.

Tex-Mex Mix

Use to flavor any Mexican-inspired dishes.

2 tablespoons paprika

2 tablespoons ground mild chilies or chili powder

2 tablespoons dried oregano

2 tablespoons dried cumin

1 teaspoon dried thyme

1 teaspoon garlic powder

dash (or more) of cayenne and/or hot red pepper flakes

Mix all ingredients.

Dill-Citrus Blend

Use on fish — especially salmon — or mix with sour cream for a delicious dip.

2 teaspoons dried dill weed

2 teaspoons dried parsley

1 teaspoon onion powder

1 teaspoon finely ground dried lemon peel (preferably Meyer lemon)

½ teaspoon finely ground dried orange peel

½ teaspoon salt

½ teaspoon pepper

Mix everything together, crumbling herbs into small pieces.

Herb Salt

Although herbs are often used instead of salt, we like to keep herb salt on the table.

1 cup non-iodized salt

2 tablespoons of mixed dried herbs (perhaps marjoram, oregano, sage, and thyme)

Combine salt with dried herbs. Grind the salt and herbs together in a blender or food processor and place in a shaker. Or, use coarse or kosher salt and pour the salt/herb mixture into a salt grinder so that you can grind the mix onto any dish that needs a dash of flavor.

Making an Herbal Cuppa Tea

Herbs are sometimes combined for teas based on medicinal effects, such as chamomile and mint for indigestion. More likely, or perhaps simultaneously, you'll want to mix your herbs based on flavor.

If your tea is exclusively herbal (you also can add herbs to packaged black, white, or green teas, such as English Breakfast), the usual formula is 2 tablespoons chopped fresh herbs or 1 tablespoon dry herbs for each cup of water. Of course you know how to make tea, but just in case:

1. **Warm your teapot with hot water and then pour the water out.**

2. **Add the herbs to the empty pot.**

3. **Pour boiling water over the herbs and cover the pot.**

4. **Let the tea steep for 5 to 10 minutes, depending on desired strength.**

5. **Strain the tea, pour a cuppa, stick up your pinkie, and sip.**

In addition to the following recipes, here are some other herbal tea blends we like: borage flowers and lemon balm; rose-scented geranium and lemongrass; fennel and savory; dill, cardamom, and mint; sage and rose hips.

Soothing Chamomile Tea

Chamomile makes a soothing tea perfect for sipping before bedtime. Avoid chamomile tea if you're allergic to ragweed.

1 tablespoon dried chamomile flowers   *1 tablespoon fresh lemon balm*

Brew the tea according to the instructions in the "Making an Herbal Cuppa Tea" section. Makes 1 cup.

Invigorating Iced Hibiscus Tea

Flowers of *Hibiscus sabdariffa* (also called roselle) make a tart brew with a beautiful red hue. Harvest the calyces (the fleshy red portion just behind the petals) while they're still tender and juicy, about 10 days after the flowers appear. You can also buy dried hibiscus flowers in Mexican markets, where they're known as jamaica (pronounced ha-my-kah).

2 dried hibiscus flowers   *½ cinnamon stick*

½ teaspoon fresh ginger root   *sugar*

Place the first three ingredients in a small teapot and add 8 oz. boiling water. Let the tea steep, then strain and add sugar to taste. Enjoy it hot or allow it to cool, pour over ice, and you have a refreshing iced tea. Makes 1 cup.

Mint Tea for Indigestion

One of the most common herbal teas, mint tea has a refreshing flavor; it also aids digestion and helps settle an upset stomach.

¼ cup mint leaves honey

1 green tea bag

Pour 8 ounces boiling water over the green tea and mint leaves and allow to steep. Strain and add honey to taste. Serve hot or cold. Makes 1 cup.

How Sweet It Is

Most people associate herbs with *savory* (in the sense of piquant, or non-sweet) food. But herbs also offer something for those with an insatiable sweet tooth. The possibilities include sugars, honeys, syrups, cordials, jellies, jams, cakes, tarts, ice cream, and sorbets, for starters.

Combining herbs with sugar and honey is really just another way to preserve the herbs (the sweetener acts as a preservative), but if you're the kind who finishes all the Valentine candy before Presidents' Day, you may find yourself consuming more herbal confections.

Jolly jellies

Herbs lack the pectin that is found naturally in many fruits and which causes them to gel after a period of heating. Therefore, most herbal jelly recipes call for adding pectin, although some cooks substitute fresh apples or apple juice. Pectin won't work unless it is combined with the right amount of sugar and acid (usually provided by vinegar, but lemon juice also does the trick). Most jellies begin with a strong infusion of fresh or dried herbs. (An infusion is really just a tea; we talk about it more in Chapter 13.)

Mint is probably the most popular herb for jelly, but you can also use basil, lemon verbena, rose hips, rosemary, sage, tarragon, thyme, violet flowers, or even garlic.

Herb Jelly

This master recipe uses pectin and is a good place to begin if you haven't made jelly before. Vary the amount of fresh herbs according to the strength of the herb and your taste.

1 cup chopped fresh herbs

1 cup cider vinegar

3 cups sugar

3 ounces (1 packet) pectin

1 Make an infusion by pouring 1 cup boiling water over herbs. Steep for 15 minutes. Strain, reserving the liquid.

2 Pour the infused liquid into a non-aluminum pan and add vinegar and sugar. Bring to a full boil, stirring constantly. Stir in the pectin all at once and continue cooking for another minute.

3 Remove the mixture from heat, skim off any foam, and pour the liquid into clean canning jars. Wipe the jar rims clean with paper towels and seal. Let the jelly stand at room temperature until cool, and then store it in the refrigerator.

Warning: *Because this recipe does not require processing in a water bath or pressure cooker, the jelly must be stored in the refrigerator. Once opened, any leftover refrigerated jelly should be discarded after two months.*

Heavenly honey

Making herbal honey is so simple a child could do it. It's marvelous spread (thickly) on hot breads, biscuits, muffins, and bagels — anything that stands still, according to a couple of our children. Lemon- and mint-flavored herbs (including hyssop and bee balm), lavender flowers, marjoram, rose geranium, rosemary, sage, rose petals, and violet blossoms complement honey wonderfully. Use these and other herbs, singly or in combination.

Herb Honey

Store this honey in the refrigerator and use it within one month.

1 tablespoon washed, chopped herbs (1 tea-spoon dry herbs), tied in a cheesecloth bag   *2 cups honey*

1 Place the herb bag into a heavy pan and pour the honey over it. Heat until just warm and then pour the mixture into a sterilized glass jar and seal. Store it in a dark location at room temperature for one week.

2 Pour the herb-honey mixture into a pan and rewarm it over low heat. Remove the herb bag and pour the flavored honey into sterilized jars. Wipe the jar rims with paper towels and seal them tightly.

Crystallized confections

You can candy edible herb flowers — especially those with flat petals, like borage, pansy, and violets —to decorate pastries, drop in drinks, or liven up fruit trays. For a complete plant package, treat the leaves of mint or lemon-flavored herbs this same way.

Crystallized herbs are traditionally made with uncooked egg white, which is no longer considered safe. An easy and safe substitute is pasteurized egg whites, which are available in both liquid and dehydrated form. Just Whites is one brand name; directions and equivalents are included in the package.

Edible Herb Flowers

Begin with flowers that have just opened, and be sure to leave enough stem so that you have something to hold on to. The results are certain to bring oohhhhs and ahhhhs.

1 egg white

½ teaspoon vodka (optional)

assorted herb flowers, such as borage, pansies, and violets

superfine granulated sugar

1 In a small bowl, gently beat the pasteurized equivalent of 1 egg white with the vodka until it's foamy. (The vodka isn't essential but it aids in drying.) Using a soft artist's brush (the kind that comes in a child's watercolor set), paint the petals, flowers, or leaves with egg white — tops and bottoms. Sprinkle superfine granulated sugar on the herb until it's evenly covered.

2 Lay the coated flowers or leaves on waxed paper and allow to air dry. Or place them in an ovenproof dish and set the dish in an oven (on its absolute lowest setting) for 10 to 15 minutes, turning the herbs a few times. Don't let the coating turn brown. Cool.

Note: You can store candied herb flowers and foliage between layers of waxed paper in sealed, airtight containers for up to one month.

Chapter 13

Herbs for Healing and Soothing

*I*f you tried just a few of our ideas from Chapter 12, you know that herbs can make a world of difference in cooking. But even if you followed all our gardening tips, you probably still have bushels of herbs left over. That's why in this chapter, we explore ways to use those herbs to improve your health and your environment.

It's true that if you've got your health, you've got everything, but sometimes everything can be even nicer when you spruce up your surroundings. Your quality of life goes way up when the house is clean and filled with beautiful things you've made yourself and when you take time to pamper yourself with long, luxurious baths and little catnaps, surrounded by fresh natural smells.

In this chapter, we show you how to make infusions, poultices and salves. We also share ideas for using herbs to beautify yourself and your home. (You can find more details about specific herbs in the Herb Encyclopedia in the appendix.)

We're just touching on the basics in this chapter. If you want to find out more about using herbs as remedies for various ailments, seek out an experienced herbalist in your community — your local college may even offer classes. Remember that some herbs are potent and, like pharmaceuticals, can have negative effects if used improperly. But they can have almost miraculous powers, too.

Proper Use of the Herbal Pharmacy

Today you can buy capsules of the most popular herbs from the local supermarket and various forms of even the weirdest ones from health-food stores and organic grocers. But you get a special kind of satisfaction when you whip up your own herbal infusions and salves; the process alone can make you feel better.

Making herbal remedies isn't an exact science, and even experts disagree over precise measurements. But everyone agrees that your equipment should be clean (sterilize glass storage containers and their lids) and that you should label any remedy, noting the ingredients and the date it was prepared.

Following a few simple rules

Before you're tempted to do all your own doctoring — which we don't recommend — we offer a few general cautions:

- ✔ *Never* ingest large doses of any herbal preparation.
- ✔ Stop taking any preparation if you experience side effects, such as dizziness or nausea.
- ✔ Seek a physician's advice before you combine herbal remedies and medical prescriptions, if you're experiencing more than minor pain, or if your problem is chronic.

A word for moms (and moms-to-be)

The list of medicinal herbs to avoid when you are pregnant or nursing is so long that we suggest avoiding all herbs at that time unless you discuss them with a doctor who is herb savvy. Even herbs as common as basil contain some substances that can cause uterine contractions and miscarriage.

A couple of exceptions may be raspberry leaf tea — said to be the pregnancy herb for both morning sickness and preventing miscarriage — and ginger, which allays motion sickness and may help morning sickness.

Also, do not give any herbs to children younger than 3 years old. Even chamomile, which is extremely mild, can cause an allergic reaction in someone disposed to hay fever.

Dazed and Infused: Herbal Remedies to Drink

Infusions, decoctions, tisanes — you would think there was some kind of conspiracy to make herbal remedies mysterious and baffling. Psssst, c'mere: They all mean "tea," and they're all made with hot water.

You make an *infusion* by steeping the soft parts of the plant — leaves and flowers. You make a *decoction* by boiling the hard parts — seeds and roots. That's it. What's a *tisane?* It's a synonym for infusion, but mainly, it's pretentious.

A *tincture* is also tealike, but it's made with alcohol instead of water. A *syrup,* often given to children, combines sugar or honey with herbs to disguise their flavor.

In Table 13-1, we list many medicinal herbs and indicate which ailments they relieve.

Table 13-1	Common Medicinal Herbs Taken Internally	
Herb	*Parts Used*	*Ailment*
Angelica	All parts	Indigestion
Anise	Seeds	Bad breath, respiratory ailments
Catnip	Aerial parts	Insomnia, indigestion
Chamomile	Flowers	Insomnia, indigestion
Dandelion	Roots	Healthy liver, diuretic
Fennel	Seeds	Heartburn, indigestion, flatulence
Feverfew	Leaves	Migraine
Garlic	Bulb	Healthy heart, allergies, respiratory ailments
Ginger	Roots	Motion sickness
Lemon balm	Leaves	Insomnia, headache
Marsh mallow	Roots	Sore throat, cough, indigestion
Mint	Aerial parts	Heartburn, indigestion
Mullein	All parts	Respiratory ailments
Parsley	Leaves, seeds	Bad breath, diuretic
Valerian	Roots	Insomnia, headache

Infusions

Okay, if you want to get picky, an infusion taken as medicine is measured a bit more precisely than a tea to sip with scones — but not much more. Most herbs taken for common woes like indigestion and insomnia are so mild and safe that your main worry is not getting enough of them.

The usual proportions are 2 to 6 teaspoons of fresh herbs (1 to 3 teaspoons of dried herbs) per cup of water. Boil the water, remove it from the heat, and pour it over the herbs in a warm teapot or a non-aluminum container. (Some evidence exists that aluminum releases toxins that herbs and other foods can absorb.) Cover, let steep 10 to 20 minutes, and strain.

If you make more than one dose (normally you drink a cup or less at a time), put the rest in the refrigerator in a sealed glass container, where it will keep for up to two days. You can take up to about three cups a day of most herbal infusions.

Decoctions

For a decoction — the liquid made with the tough parts of herbs, such as roots, seeds, and bark — the usual proportions are 1 tablespoon of dried plant material per cup of water. In a non-aluminum pan, combine the herbs and water and bring to a boil. Cover, reduce heat, and simmer for 20 to 30 minutes. (If you're making a small amount, check the pan frequently to make sure that all the liquid hasn't evaporated.) Remove from heat and strain into a cup to drink immediately or strain into a sterilized glass container, which you can seal and store in the refrigerator for up to two days.

Tinctures

A tincture is an herbal medicine made with alcohol and taken by the teaspoon rather than by the cupful. A tincture is more convenient to take than a tealike remedy (on trips, for example), and it stays potent for up to two years. You can make a tincture with vodka or, if you find certain herbs unpalatable, use brandy or rum to cover the taste. The usual proportion is 1 ounce of dried herbs to 5 ounces of alcohol.

To make a tincture, combine herbs and alcohol in a large glass jar. Seal the jar and set it in a cool, dark place for two to six weeks. (Shake the jar occasionally.) Strain the liquid into a dark glass container and seal. The usual dose is ½ to 1 teaspoon of tincture up to three times a day.

Syrups

You won't want to give alcohol-based tinctures to children, so make a syrup instead by combining one part herbal infusion or decoction with an equal measure of honey or sugar.

Simmer over low heat, stirring gently, until the sugar or honey dissolves and the mixture has a syrupy consistency. Cool. Pour into dark glass bottles sealed with cork stoppers (syrups occasionally ferment — using a cork prevents the container from exploding) and store in the refrigerator for up to three months.

The standard dose is 1 to 2 teaspoons up to three times per day.

Salved by the Bell: External Herbal Medicines

Many herbs in your garden, such as rosemary and thyme, have antiseptic properties, meaning they help to prevent infection of cuts and scrapes. Other herbs with at least some antiseptic properties are angelica, calendula, chamomile, and garlic. Some, like calendula, comfrey, ginger, bee balm, and yarrow, are anti-inflammatory — they reduce redness and swelling. Aloe, basil, chamomile, fennel, oregano, tarragon, thyme, and yarrow contain natural antihistamines, which work against the allergic reaction that makes insect bites itch.

Some herbs contain tannins and other substances that have an *astringent* effect (tightening and contracting the skin). Witch hazel is the best known; aloe is another. Other herbs, such as marsh mallow and mullein, are *emollient.* They contain mucilage that expands like a sponge when it gets wet, soothing conditions as varied as chapped skin and hemorrhoids.

Hot peppers, or chilies, may be the most surprising plants in our gardens. Herbalists usually refer to them as cayenne, although the term in cooking and horticulture indicates one particular type of hot pepper or the powder that is made from that pepper.

As much as they burn your mouth (or your eyes, if you're not careful), hot peppers also work against pain in several ways. Hot peppers contain salicylates; these chemicals, which the plant produces as a defense against pests, are similar to the pain-relieving chemical in aspirin. The capsaicin that makes the peppers hot stimulates the body's own pain-quelling endorphins. And finally, hot peppers are one of the herbs known as *rubefacients,* which speed healing by drawing blood to the skin where they're applied.

In Table 13-2, we list these and many other healing substances that you can use externally. You can put any of these substances to work by applying them in one of the ways described in Table 13-2.

Table 13-2	Common Medicinal Herbs Used Externally	
Herb	*Parts Used*	*Ailment*
Calendula	Flowers	Skin problems
Cayenne	Fruits	Pain
Chamomile	Flowers	Wounds
Garlic	Bulb	Insect bites
Lavender	Flowers, leaves	Insomnia, burns, pain
Lemon grass	Leaves	Preventing insect bites, treating fungal infections
Marsh mallow	Roots	Wounds
Mustard	Seeds	Pain
Pennyroyal	All parts	Preventing insect bites
Sage	Flowers, leaves	Body odor
Yarrow	Flowers, leaves	Wounds

Poultices

The easiest way to use herbs externally to treat bruises, sprains, cuts, and scrapes — especially in an emergency — is as a *poultice*. To make a poultice, just crush the herb (diehard herbalists would tell you to macerate it), moisten it, and apply it to the skin. If your situation is not an emergency, whirl the herb in a blender with a little water or chop it. Simmer it over low heat — with just enough water to cover — for about five minutes and apply. And if you want to go about your business with the poultice in place, cover and tie it with a strip of gauze or other cloth.

Compresses

To make a *compress,* start with an infusion or decoction. Dip a strip of absorbent cloth in the liquid and apply it to the affected area. For aches and pains, a hot compress feels good. Keep it cold for swelling or a headache. Compresses also feel wonderful on poison ivy and tired eyes.

Aloe out there

If aloe could be interviewed, it might say it wants to be a doctor and heal the world. Indeed, aloe could enter the medicinal talent competition in several categories. You've seen aloe in all kinds of skin-care products, and this herb is no mere marketing gimmick. Aloe contains an enzyme that reduces swelling and an antihistamine that relieves itching. As an antiseptic, it seems to work against both bacteria and fungi. And it also contains an immune-stimulating substance powerful enough to be studied for use against the HIV virus.

Although aloe is best known for healing burns (including radiation burns from cancer treatment, as well as sunburn and frostbite), scientists aren't sure how it works in this regard. One theory is that aloe speeds oxygen to the injured area, helping to heal connective tissue.

The greatest thing about aloe is that it's a ready-made poultice: Just pull off a leaf, strip the outer covering, and apply the moist inner gel to your boo-boo.

One word of caution: You may see aloe products sold as laxatives, but don't take them internally. Even the commercial preparations can cause painful cramps.

Oils

Steeping or simmering herbs in oil lets you use them to massage sore muscles or arthritic joints. (We're not talking about essential oils here; essential oils are highly concentrated oils distilled or expressed from herbs and often used in aromatherapy. See the "Essential oils" sidebar for more information.) Because the quantities of herbs used are much larger than with infusions or decoctions, recipes are usually given in terms of weight instead of measuring spoons or cups, so it's handy to have a kitchen scale. The standard proportion is 4 to 6 ounces of chopped fresh herbs (2 to 3 ounces of dried herbs) for each cup of a pure vegetable oil, such as olive, safflower, almond, and jojoba.

To create a soothing oil, use one of the following methods:

- **Slow 'n' easy method:** This approach is best if you're using flowers or delicate-leaved plants. Put the herbs and oil in a covered glass container and leave them where they receive as much sun as possible. Give them a good shake or vigorous stir at least once a day. At the end of two weeks, strain, reserving the oil; store in a sealed glass jar in the refrigerator for up to six months.

- **Quick ('n' also easy) method:** Combine the oil and herbs in the top of a double boiler and simmer on very low heat for two to three hours. Even easier, simmer them in a crock pot — use a candy thermometer to make sure that it's about 100 degrees Fahrenheit — for 12 hours. Cool; strain into a glass jar and store in the refrigerator for up to six months.

Essential oils

If you read other books on herbal crafts, cosmetics, and medicines — particularly aromatherapy — you know that many recipes call for essential oils. These oils are made in a laboratory through distilling or expressing various parts of the herb plant.

Scented oils vary in quality, and some are made synthetically. If you see a display of different scented oils and all are the same price, it's a clue that they are synthetic. (Some essential oils are much more difficult to make and, therefore, more expensive.) Synthetic oils are called fragrance oils.

Warning: Never use any essential oil internally. A few are extremely toxic, and all of them are highly concentrated and can burn skin. Keep them away from your eyes, nose, mouth, and genitals. Always dilute them before using.

Salves

Making herbal salves is more fuss than making oils, but you may like them better because they're easier to apply. Most recipes call for beeswax, which you can buy in 1-ounce cubes at health-food stores. Some recipes also suggest adding a few drops of oil of benzoin as a preservative; you can find oil of benzoin at craft supply stores, herb shops, and some health-food stores, along with handy items like small tins for salves and tubes for lip balm. Begin with 1 cup of infusion or decoction, made double strength, and 1 cup of cooking oil. Combine them in a saucepan over low heat and simmer, stirring constantly, until the water evaporates. You should have about 1 cup of liquid. Melt 1 ounce of beeswax in a double boiler, pour it into the herbal oil, and stir thoroughly. Add a drop or two of essential oil for fragrance (see the "Essential oils" sidebar). Store in a glass container in the refrigerator for up to six months.

Who Ya Gonna Call? Stress Busters

When Kathy was a cub reporter about a million years ago, she got one of those stock assignments to interview a man on his 100th birthday. She asked the usual question: To what did he owe his longevity? It wasn't his diet, he said, and he had smoked since he was 12. "I don't let anything worry me for long," he said. "Worry'll kill ya, girl."

Today, we all know the toll that stress takes on our health, yet modern life makes it inescapable. So use some of those wonderful herbs you've grown to help alleviate stress. Apply them during the moments of relaxation you owe yourself: during a long bath or while you sleep. Or just breathe in their fragrances when you need a pick-me-up after a long, hectic day.

Stop and smell the roses

Teas made from chamomile, hops, lemon balm, passionflower, and valerian are well known as herbal tranquilizers. But a whole school of thought
exists that says herbs can affect our moods just by our smelling them — an
approach called *aromatherapy*. (For in-depth information on how aromas
affect our bodies as well as our spirits, check out *Aromatherapy For Dummies*
[Wiley], by Kathi Keville.)

Advocates of aromatherapy explain the phenomenon by observing that odors
stimulate olfactory nerves (pathways for our sense of smell), which in turn
trigger the release of different chemicals in our brains. We also have what are
called *learned odor responses,* which cause us to have emotional reactions to
the aroma of lilacs or cinnamon buns. Whatever the explanation, most people
would agree that the scent of certain herbs is relaxing (lavender) or exhilarat-
ing (rosemary).

Essential oils (see the sidebar "Essential oils" earlier in this chapter), which
you can't make at home with your garden-grown herbs, have the most concentrated fragrances. But you can still get a therapeutic kick from the fragrance of fresh and dried herbs and from your own herbal preparations.

Aromatherapists put most herbs into broad categories of being either calming (for when you're jittery or worried), uplifting (for when you're blue), or
stimulating (for when you're tired or facing a challenge). Some practitioners
go so far as to make much more specific recommendations, such as sniffing
rose oil when you're in a funk over lost love. If the nose truly knows, here are
some of its secrets:

- Basil clears the mind and lessens mental weariness.
- Chamomile calms anxiety.
- Clary sage induces euphoria.
- Bee balm and lemon balm lift depression.
- Peppermint stimulates.
- Rose calms nervous tension and may stimulate sexual appetites.

Perchance to dream

Most sleep pillows are based on aromatherapy: You stuff a pillow with a mix
of herbs with scents believed to induce sleep (for example, chamomile and
violet) or fragrances, such as honeysuckle, jasmine, lavender, lemon balm,
and rose, that are reputed to calm frazzled nerves.

Getting steamed

Steam is a great way to put herbs to work for respiratory or skin problems. Fill a large bowl with boiling water — or fill your bathroom sink with the hottest water possible. If you use a bowl, crush a handful of fresh or dried herbs right into the water; if you use the bathroom sink, cleanup is easier if you add a strong infusion of the herb. Lower your face over the steam, and make a tent around your head with a bath towel. To clear sinuses, use eucalyptus or peppermint. For cleansing skin — the steam opens pores for follow-up treatment with astringents or emollients — use chamomile or mint.

Hops is another traditional ingredient in sleep pillows. Some scientific evidence exists for the soporific effect of the female flowers from this vine that is usually connected with making beer. When hops are stored, they oxidize and produce a volatile substance that depresses our central nervous systems when we inhale it. Skeptics say even the biggest pillow can't hold enough hops to deliver more than a couple of effective doses, but you might want to make hops a major ingredient in your herbal pillow mix. (Moisten the hops with some glycerin so they don't crackle and keep you awake.)

A pillow of dried herbs can't compare to goose down for comfort. We recommend making a small herbal pillow to tuck inside a bigger, softer one, or a long bolster to lie alongside.

Chapter 14

Herbs for Beauty

*I*f you read the label on commercial shampoos, conditioners, and liquid soaps, you'll find a long list of ingredients, many of them with unpronounceable names. Some are derived from natural ingredients, but some are chemicals synthesized from petroleum. Especially common are synthetic fragrances, made from a blend of "aroma chemicals." As a result, a product with a lavender fragrance may or may not contain any lavender at all. Fortunately, you don't have to be a chemist to make chemical-free products that keep you looking and feeling your best.

This section describes a variety of body care products you can make from the herbs you grow. Generally speaking, it's best to make them in small batches, keep refrigerated, and use within a week or so.

Having a Herbal Hair Day

You can use herbs to give your hair more shine and color, correct oily or dry hair, and even combat dandruff.

✔ **To make an herbal shampoo:** The easiest approach to using herbs in shampoos is to add them to a commercial product, preferably a mild, all-natural baby shampoo. Fill a glass jar with the herbs of your choice and cover with the shampoo. Infuse for a week and strain before using. (Refer to Chapter 13 for instructions for infusing herbs.)

✔ **To make an herbal rinse:** Begin with apple cider vinegar, which is a folk treatment for dandruff. (Vinegar also works wonders with oily hair and helps remove soap.) Steep the herbs in vinegar, just as you would for culinary use (see Chapter 12), and then strain the vinegar into a bottle.

✔ **To make an herbal conditioner.** The Chinese believe that safflower and sesame dilate vessels in the scalp and help prevent hair loss. You can use either of these cooking oils as the base for an herbal conditioner. Prepare it as you would a culinary oil (see Chapter 12) and then strain the mixture, discarding the herbs. You can massage it into the scalp, which also stimulates blood circulation, or treat dryness and split ends by combing it through your hair and wrapping your head with hot towels for about 15 minutes — a great excuse to put your feet up and relax.

Here are some common herbs to help problem hair. Use them in the preceding recipes by making infusions for shampoos or by steeping them in vinegar or oil for rinses and conditioners.

✔ **Oily hair:** Use yarrow.

✔ **Dry hair:** Use marsh mallow.

✔ **Dull or limp hair:** Use rosemary.

✔ **Dandruff:** Use burdock or comfrey.

You can mix and match these with herbs that help you color your hair: To darken graying locks, add sage. For better color highlights, blondes should add chamomile; brunettes can try rosemary; redheads should opt for calendula. Is your hair blonde and dry? Use both chamomile and marsh mallow in the recipes.

Creating Skin Cleansers and Soothers

Herbs not only add fragrance, but they also provide other benefits in soaps, lotions, and other skin-care products as well.

If you have sensitive skin, start with simple recipes with just a few ingredients. Evaluate their effectiveness (and note any unwanted side effects). Add new ingredients to your recipes one at a time so that you can monitor how your skin reacts to each one.

Bewitching hazel

Witch hazel is a wonderful native American shrub, worth including in your ornamental garden for its yellow flowers, which appear in fall and look like Lilliputian streamers. (You also can buy other species of witch hazel

[Chinese, *Hamamelis mollis;* Japanese, *H. japonica;* Ozark, *H. vernalis;* and hybrids, *H.* x *intermedia*] that bloom in winter in other shades of yellow, red, or orange.)

The tree's bark and twigs are the source of the pleasant-smelling astringent witch hazel lotion. Today, however, witch hazel lotion is made by distilling the wood with steam, which removes the tannins that give it a powerfully cooling kick.

If you're lucky enough to have a large witch hazel, try making your own old-fashioned tincture. Never remove bark all the way around a tree because that will kill it; instead, remove small pieces from the tree's north side, where its bark tends to be most dense. Use mostly twigs and add some leaves if you still don't have enough material.

To make your own tincture, use 8 tablespoons ground fresh witch hazel bark, twigs, and leaves (4 dried tablespoons) for each cup of vodka. Combine in a glass jar and set in a cool dark place for one month, shaking the mixture frequently. Strain, discarding the herb material; store as you would any tincture, in a sealed, dark glass container, for up to two years.

Apply the tincture full strength to cuts, scrapes, and bites. To use it cosmetically as a lotion, add a drop or two to ¼ cup water. Witch hazel lotion is especially soothing applied to tired eyelids with cotton pads (you can add some infusion of borage, calendula, or chamomile) or wiped over hot, tired feet.

Comin' up roses

Rose water is another brew for which you can find numerous uses. You can use rose water to sweeten herbal vinegars or splash it on your face and neck as a cleanser and coolant. (You can also use it in the kitchen with fruit salads or baklava.)

To make "real" rose water, you must first make an *attar,* a fragrant oil, of roses. (Rose essential oil is one of the most expensive essential oils on the market because it takes several thousand damask roses to produce 1 ounce of oil.)

Here's an old-fashioned recipe for a similar product that serves as a basis for rose water. You need a glass or ceramic container that you can cover, 2 to 3 cups of fragrant rose petals (preferably damask rose petals), and some rock or kosher salt. Start with a layer of petals and alternate thin layers of salt and petals. Cover the container and set it in a cool, dark place for about a month until you see liquid — this is the attar — in the bottom of the container. Strain the liquid through cheesecloth and compost the petals. To make rose water, add a few drops of the rose essence to 1 cup distilled water.

Scented soaps

An easy way to add the fragrance of herbs from your garden to bath and hand soap is to melt chunks of glycerin soap in a double boiler over low heat. Remove the double boiler from the heat and add ⅓ cup of an herbal infusion for each 3 ounces of soap.

A waxed 1-quart paper milk carton makes a great mold because you can slice it up for several "bars."

Down the primrose bath

Gardeners know that nothing beats a long, hot soak in the tub after a day of pushing around cartloads of mulch, digging planting holes, or weeding among bugs and briars. You can compound the pleasure by adding the fragrance of herbs. Just put fresh or dried herbs in a muslin bag or a double wrap of cheesecloth and tie it to the bath faucet, letting the hot water flow over it as the tub fills.

Good herbs to try (alone or in combination) include comfrey, lavender, lemon verbena, lemongrass, orange mint, rose, rosemary, scented geranium, and sage (which has the double benefit of reducing body odor). Marsh mallow acts as a moisturizer.

Here are a few ideas for other preparations:

- ✔ **Bath water:** Make an infusion of fragrant herbs as you would for herbal tea (see Chapter 12). You can make the infusion as strong as you like because you won't be drinking it, but allow at least ¼ cup of herbs for each pint of water. Then add the infusion to your bath water.

- ✔ **Herbal vinegar:** No, it won't pickle you. Vinegar offsets alkaline water and soaps, helps remove flaky skin, and balances both oily and dry skin. It helps heal acne and is even reputed to lighten freckles.

  Make a vinegar infusion as you would culinary vinegar, using about 1 cup of fresh herbs (½ cup dried herbs) for each 2 cups of vinegar. Start with 2 cups of vinegar infusion in the tub, adding more if you want. (Refer to Chapter 12 for details on making culinary vinegar.)

- ✔ **Bath oil:** Oil is a soothing addition to your bath, especially if you suffer from dry skin. Choose a light, sweet-scented oil, such as almond, jojoba, or vitamin E oil, and infuse it with herbs just as you would for culinary use. (Instructions for making culinary oils are in Chapter 12.) Use a couple of tablespoons per bath.

Kiss a Little Longer

Fresh breath and smooth lips add up to a kissable mouth. Instead of sugary breath mints and sticky-sweet lip balms, try these homemade herbal versions.

- **Breath fresheners:** A number of herbs are known for their prowess in sweetening breath and improving oral hygiene. Among those you can grow in your home garden are coriander, dill, and parsley, which sweeten breath because they're rich in chlorophyll — that stuff that makes them green. You can just chew on a leaf or two if you like. You can also make an herbal mouthwash by steeping 1 tablespoon each of dried peppermint and sage and 1 teaspoon cardamom seeds per 1 cup of vodka. Dilute the vodka with water before you gargle.

- **Herbal lip balm:** Keep lips soft and kissable with this soothing balm, which is similar to the salves described in Chapter 13 but dries a little harder due to relatively more beeswax. Melt 1 ounce of beeswax in a double boiler and then add ¾ cup herb-infused sweet almond oil. (Peppermint and calendula are two good herb choices.) You can replace some of the oil with shea butter or cocoa butter. Pour it into small tins or special lip balm tubes, both of which are available at herbal supply stores.

Herbal Fragrances

An aroma can stop you in your tracks and bring to mind long-forgotten memories. Maybe lavender conjures up images of Grandma, or lemon verbena inspires you to call home to Mom. Capture the sweet fragrances of your garden in these scented delights:

- **Solid perfume:** Use the recipe and technique for lip balm (see the section "Kiss a Little Longer," earlier in this chapter), using sweet almond oil infused with the herb you desire. You can add a few drops of essential oil to enhance the scent — choose the same herb or a complementary one. Don't overdo the amount of essential oil, however; it can irritate skin. Pour the warm mixture into small tins and rub a small amount in the usual perfume spots (behind the ears, on the inside of the wrists).

- **Lavender powder:** Start with a base powder — cornstarch is a good choice, on its own or combined with white rice flower or arrowroot powder. Mix with ground herbs. It's that easy!

Chapter 15

Herbs for Hearth and Home

*Y*ou can put the power of herbs to work around the house. Not only do they smell better than last night's fish and whatever the cat dragged in, but they smell better than most of the air fresheners on the market.

The *strewing* herbs that medieval housekeepers spread on their floors served to repel bugs and vermin as well as mask odors. Insects (unlike humans) find many of them absolutely repugnant. If all that weren't enough, antiseptic herbs, such as rosemary, thyme, and sage, help sanitize whatever you spread them on.

Keeping Your House Clean

Instead of buying a heavily scented, "new and improved" (synonyms for expensive) cleaning product, why not use the scent and germ-clobbering capabilities of herbs around your house? We encourage you to experiment. Here are a few ideas to get you started:

✔ **Glass and other surfaces:** Vinegar is wonderful for cleaning glass. Infuse vinegar with one of the antiseptic herbs or mix 1 to 3 teaspoons of Murphy's Oil Soap in about four cups of a strong herb infusion. You can use both mixtures on painted wood, ceramic and vinyl tile, and plastic. (Flip to Chapter 13 for details on making herb infusions.)

✔ **Rugs and carpets:** Sprinkle crushed dried herbs under the rug, where they also deter fleas. Or dump a handful of dried herbs on the rug and sweep them into your vacuum bag, where they'll whoosh out a pleasant fragrance as you clean. (Do it again whenever you change the bag.)

> ## Getting in a lather
>
> Plants in the carnation family contain a substance called *saponin* that lathers when wet, notably the appropriately named soapwort. Sometimes called bouncing bet, soapwort is a native of Europe but has made herself at home in the East and Midwest.
>
> Two feet tall with pink, red, or white fragrant flowers with five notched petals, soapwort is ornamental, too. With a little pinching, you can keep it blooming from summer through fall. Soapwort grows in USDA Zones 3 to 9; don't give it rich soil or it flops over. Nurseries usually sell the double-flowered form, 'Rosa Plena'.
>
> If you've inherited or planted a patch of soapwort, try whipping up some suds with some crushed root or chopped stems. (If the stems are dry, soak them overnight first.) Use about ½ cup of fresh herb for each 3 cups of water. Add the stems to boiling water. Reduce heat and simmer, covered, for about 20 minutes.
>
> The gentle cleanser that results is recommended for upholstery, carpets, clothing, and tapestries. (Test it first in an inconspicuous place.) Apply with a sponge or soft brush, and then rinse with cool water.

> If your carpet already smells a bit, uh, funky, mix a box of baking soda with a cup of lavender and a tablespoon of crushed coriander seeds. Spread the mixture over your carpet, leave overnight, and vacuum it up in the morning.
>
> ✔ **Laundry:** Make an infusion of your favorite herb and add it to the last cycle of your wash. The floral scents of rose or lavender are especially nice.

Getting the Bugs Out

You can also use herbs outdoors to keep chiggers and fleas from chomping on you and your pets, and indoors to keep critters out of your pantry.

Pennyroyal is the crown prince of insect-repelling herbs, but it's also one of the most toxic herbs, especially its essential oil. Just a few drops can be lethal if you should accidentally take it internally. Although pennyroyal is a component of some insect repellents, you should also avoid using it in any form, even externally, if you are pregnant.

Other good (and safer) anti-insect herbs are the artemisias, mints, and tansy.

As a moth repellant in the sweater drawer, lavender is the classic, in no small part because of its clean fragrance. You can also try costmary, rosemary, and santolina. Wormwood is said to be an especially good addition for repelling silverfish.

Here are a few sample formulas:

TIP

✔ **Moths:** In the section called "Herbs to Dry For" later in this chapter, we talk about potpourris and sachets intended only for fragrance. You can make a sachet with any combination of the herbs just mentioned for protection from moths in a closet (or silverfish in the study). Put the herbs in small muslin bags, which you can buy for making tea, or tie them in a man's plain white handkerchief.

✔ **Ants:** Crush or grind dried tansy or wormwood, mix it with a little cream of tartar, and sprinkle it under your sink or wherever you find ants. Or make a spray with 2 tablespoons of dried, crushed red pepper in 6 drops of dishwashing liquid added to a gallon of water. Spritz it around drainpipes and other potential entry points.

✔ **Fleas:** The artemisias, eucalyptus, and lemon verbena may help deter fleas. To keep fleas out of your pet's bed, stuff it with a mix of cedar chips and dried, crushed eucalyptus.

✔ **Biting bugs:** In a pinch, you can get some protection from mosquitoes and other stinging insects by snatching up a handful of fresh basil and rubbing it on your skin. Or try the same with lemongrass, which is related to the plant from which we get citronella essential oil, the fragrance used in commercial bug candles and other bug-defense products.

Even better than rubbing fresh herbs on your arms and legs is adding an infusion of the herbs to sweet almond oil or witch hazel. You can rub on the oil or use a recycled pump spray bottle and spray the mix on your skin and clothes.

Herbs to Dry For

Now that you're in peak health, you're looking great, and your house is so clean you can eat off the floor, how about some projects purely for sensual pleasure? We're talking about potpourris and sachets for your nose and dried arrangements and wreaths to please the eye.

Potpourris and sachets

The great thing about potpourri is that it's quick and easy to make, and you don't have to follow many rules. We aren't going to tell you what herbs are good for potpourri, because almost all of them are. Your nose knows. Mix together small portions of herbs until you get a combination you like.

In addition to herbs, here are a few other things you probably want to include in a potpourri:

- **Fixative:** A *fixative* is a substance that helps pull all the separate aromas together and keep the less robust ones from fading out.

   The most commonly used fixative is orris root. You can find it in craft stores, but you can also grow it in your garden: It's the rhizome of the Florentine iris (*I. germanica* var. *florentina*). The flowers are white with touches of purple or blue. As with most roots, you harvest them in the fall of their second year.

   Chop the roots immediately because they quickly turn into botanical rocks. In craft stores, you find orris in powdered form, but you can grind your harvest in a coffee grinder if you don't let it harden completely. Standard recipes call for using anywhere between a tablespoon per cup to a tablespoon per quart of dried herbs and spices. Some folks may be allergic to orris root and should not handle it.

- **Un-garden ingredients:** In addition to herbs, you can find countless potential potpourri participants by raiding your spice rack, the nearest woods, or a craft store.

   For example, try combining one or more of the following with the herbs: citrus peels, cinnamon sticks, cloves, cedar chips, sandalwood chips, pinecones, and vanilla beans.

   For texture and color, consider everlasting flowers, such as gomphrena or statice, dried lichens or moss, and berries like those of juniper (blue), bittersweet and pyracantha (orange), and holly and nandina (red).

- **Essential oils:** These oils strengthen and complement the ingredients in your potpourri without overwhelming them. As little as one drop per cup of dried materials is enough. Once you have a theme — floral, citrus, woodsy — you can find an oil to match.

Choosing pleasing combinations

Anything goes when making a potpourri. Still, most experienced potpourri producers choose herbs that have similar fragrances — for example, sweet or citruslike. Here are a few combinations to get you started, but don't stop with these suggestions:

- **For a bedroom:** Sweet flowers, such as carnations, catmint, lavender, and rose. The rose is reputed to be an aphrodisiac. (In fact, early Christians kept it out of churches because of its ribald reputation.) You might throw in a teaspoon of another aphrodisiac — cardamom — for good measure.

- **For a bathroom:** Mix lemon herbs — lemon verbena, lemon geranium, lemon balm, and lemon grass — with orange peel, mint, and cinnamon.

- ✔ **For a kitchen:** Culinary herbs, such as bay, rosemary, sage, and thyme, plus a pinch of crushed cloves.

- ✔ **For a study:** Woodland scents, such as pine, juniper, and bayberry. Add basil, mint, or rosemary — all believed to sharpen mental acuity.

Shakin' it up

You can make potpourri two ways: the old-fashioned wet method and the slightly lazier dry method. We offer a quick run-through on the wet method, which supposedly yields a stew of dried herbs that remain fragrant for half a century. However, the extra work may not be worth it — in our experience, even potpourris made with the dry method can remain fragrant for years if kept in sealed containers.

- ✔ **The wet way:** You need non-iodized (kosher or sea) salt; a fixative, such as orris root; essential oils; and either brandy or an alcohol-based perfume. Don't let your herbs dry out completely; they should be slightly limp, not crisp.

  Mix ½ cup salt with ½ cup of fragrant spices (cinnamon, bay, cloves, cardamom). In a separate bowl, mix 3 cups fragrant herbs with one tablespoon orris root. In a large crock, make a layer of herbs and top with a layer of the spiced salt. Continue layering, ending with a salt layer. Pour the brandy or perfume over the layers and weigh down with a plate. You should stir daily for a month, and then transfer to permanent containers.

- ✔ **The dry way:** You need 2 quarts of dry, fragrant herbs; 6 to 8 tablespoons of spices (such as crushed cinnamon sticks, cardamom seeds, allspice, or whole cloves); 2 to 4 tablespoons of orris root; and 20 drops of one or several essential oils. In a ceramic container, combine the herbs and orris root. Add the spices and toss gently, then add the essential oils. Cover tightly, give the container a shake every few days for four to six weeks, and then transfer to a permanent container.

Most people keep potpourri in a container with a lid, opening it when they need an olfactory lift, when the dog has an accident, or when company comes. If you have an endless supply of herbs, you can leave potpourri in an open container and then pitch it onto the compost pile when it loses fragrance.

Making sassy sachets

A *sachet* is simply potpourri in a fabric bag. (Some people grind or crush the ingredients to make the sachet lay flat.) In addition to making a sachet to repel insects, you also can make a sachet just for its pleasant aroma, although lavender — Grandma's favorite — repels moths while it perfumes the surroundings.

Your sachet can be as pretty as you please, with appliqués and lace. Sachets are a great way to use antique handkerchiefs, as long as the fabric is heavy enough for the coarser herbs. Just tie the top with a ribbon. Make a loop with the ribbon and hang it in a closet or garment bag, or tuck it in a drawer.

Decorating with dried herbs

If you're like us, you like gazing at your herbs even when you can't scratch and sniff them. You can add them to fresh arrangements throughout the growing season, of course, and you can also dry them to enjoy almost indefinitely in a vase, a basket, or a wreath for the wall, door, or tabletop.

You need only a container to hold herbs, fresh or dried, but making arrangements is a whole lot easier if you have some of the following items, all of which are widely available from florists' shops:

- **Foam blocks:** You can put blocks of white Styrofoam or a finer textured green foam called oasis in the bottom of a vase to help hold stems upright for arrangements. You can also buy circles of foam to serve as the base of a wreath.

- **Floral picks:** These are little wooden stakes attached to a length of wire. You wrap the wire around weak plant stems — or several very fine stems — and stick the sharp bottom end of the pick in your foam block.

- **Floral wire:** You can buy different thicknesses (gauges) of wire in various lengths or on a spool. Use it to strengthen stems, wire stems together, or shape wreaths.

- **Floral tape:** This tape comes in browns and greens and lets you wrap stems together or fasten stems to wires.

- **Floral pins:** These pins look like old-fashioned hairpins and help you fasten dry material to a wreath base.

A nice arrangement

We're not about to dictate which herbs to use in arrangements. Beauty is in the eye of the beholder. Still, we can't resist offering a few tips.

- **Keep stems long.** When picking flowers, seed heads, or foliage, keep stems as long as possible. You can always shorten them, but you need the extra length for a tall vase. You can also make informal wreaths for tabletops simply by braiding stems together.

- **Use wire and tape.** Spiral florist wire around weak stems to make them stand upright, or around short stems to lengthen them. You can stick wire directly into the base of dense flowers, such as calendulas and roses, and dispense with their stems. If necessary, use tape to hide the wire.

✔ **Hide the foam.** If you use a clear or shallow container for your arrangement — or no container at all — you can conceal the floral block or oasis with sphagnum moss.

✔ **Preserve your work.** Keep dried arrangements out of direct sunlight so colors don't fade. Hair spray makes the dried materials tougher.

Wreaths

You can buy wreath frames (made either of foam or wire) at craft and florist shops — they're easy to use and inexpensive — but if you want to make your own, try these ideas:

✔ **Chicken wire:** Make a roll of chicken wire — the same stuff you use to fence in your herb or vegetable garden. Then bend it into a circle and use the wire ends to secure the shape. Fill the wire frame with sphagnum moss, which gives you additional material in which to secure the stems of your herbs.

✔ **Straw:** What about a frame made of fresh straw? This isn't the straw that comes in bales, but long stalks. Gather together enough to make the wreath the thickness you want and then form it into a circle, securing it every few inches with floral wire.

To attach herbs to the wreath, first create small bunches of herbs (securing them with floral wire). Starting with the inner part of the wreath, attach the herbs with floral pins, being careful not to cover the center hole. Once you've made your way around the inner part of the wreath, attach a circle of herbs around the outside. Finally, fill in between the two rows.

Cut and dried

In Chapter 11, we offer you tips for harvesting and drying herbs, including some special instructions for drying herbs to be used in decorations. Table 15-1 shows a few of our favorite candidates for dried arrangements.

Table 15-1	Good Candidates for Dried Arrangements	
Flowering Plants	*Foliage Plants*	*Seed Heads*
Artemisia	Artemisia	Dill
Basil	Bay	Epazote
Borage	Dill	Fennel
Calendula	Fennel	Rose hips

(continued)

Table 15-1 *(continued)*

Flowering Plants	Foliage Plants	Seed Heads
Catnip	Geranium	
Chive	Germander	
Horehound	Rosemary	
Mullein	Santolina	
Oregano	Wormwood	
Tansy		
Yarrow		

Herbs to Dye For

Until about 150 years ago, we all would have been the man (or woman) in the gray flannel suit if it hadn't been for plants. That's when synthetic dyes were developed. Still, there's a certain appeal to dyeing with plant extracts.

Keep in mind that the colors may run and fade on fabrics colored with natural dyes, and that the colors are usually more subtle and earthy. If you're hoping for Day-Glo orange, stick with synthetic dyes.

Dyeing with plant extracts requires the use of a *mordant* — a substance that helps bind the dye to the fabric. Historically, mordants sometimes included poisonous metals, such as chrome. Today, the most commonly used — and far safer — mordant is alum. Dyeing with plant extracts is an art and a science; it's best to study up on the subject before embarking on your first dye project. You can find lots of books and Web sites on the subject.

Table 15-2 presents a short list of dye plants and the colors they render when using alum as a mordant.

Table 15-2	Plants to Dye With	
Plant	**Parts Used**	**Color Rendered (Using Alum)**
Bayberry	Leaves	Yellow
Betony	All parts	Chartreuse
Catnip	Fall leaves	Yellow

Plant	Parts Used	Color Rendered (Using Alum)
Chamomile	Flowers	Yellow
Dandelion	Flowers	Yellow
Dandelion	Roots	Orange-brown
Goldenrod	Flowers	Yellow
Lady's bedstraw	Roots	Dull red
Lady's bedstraw	Flowering tops	Yellow
Madder	Roots	Red
Marjoram	Tops	Green
Mullein	Leaves and stalks	Yellow
Parsley	All parts	Yellow-green
Rosemary	Leaves	Yellow-green
Safflower	Flowers	Yellow
Sage	Leaves and stems	Lemon yellow
Sorrel	All parts	Yellow
Tansy	Young leaves	Yellow-green
Tansy	Flowers	Yellow
Thyme	Fall leaves	Gray-gold
Yarrow	Flowers	Yellow

Part V
The Part of Tens

The 5th Wave   By Rich Tennant

"I used an all natural method of pest control, but we're still getting an occasional vacuum cleaner salesman in the garden."

In this part . . .

We scattered projects and lists throughout this book, but in this part, we offer still more helpful and inspiring information. You find ways to use the herbs you grow to make gifts and suggestions of herbs for different gardening situations and intended uses.

Chapter 16

Ten Gifts to Make from Herbs You Grow

A great side benefit of growing herbs is that they offer abundant opportunities for gift-giving. Here are ten ideas, but don't limit yourself — the possibilities are endless! A few require sewing, some use materials available at craft shops or natural food stores, and some can be made simply with items you're likely to have around your home.

TIP

Keep track of the herbs you use for each project so that you can let the recipient know the ingredients, in case of allergies.

Herb Wreaths

Start with a premade grapevine wreath, available at craft stores. Choose a variety of attractive dried herbs and flowers — good choices include artemisia, calendula, catnip, oregano, santolina, and yarrow. Gather the herbs into small bunches, and tie or wire the stems together. Then tuck the stems into the wreath in the spaces between the vines. You can decorate the whole wreath or just use a few bunches of herbs — the grapevine is pretty all by itself, so you don't have to hide it like you would other wreath forms. Use a hot glue gun, if necessary, to secure the herbs. Add a few dried everlasting flowers and attach a pretty ribbon bow as the final touch.

Dried Culinary Herb Blends

Anyone who likes to cook will be happy to receive a gift of dried, garden-grown herbs. By all means, use your own special blends if you have favorites. Or, go with these reliable, traditional combinations:

- **Bouquet garni:** Gather a few stems of each of the following dried herbs, and tie them together with cotton string or place them in a cheesecloth bag. Tradition calls for bay leaf, parsley, and thyme, but you can also add chervil, rosemary, and/or tarragon. Place the bundles in plastic bags to preserve their flavor and aroma. Include a note stating that the recipients can use the herb bouquets in soups and stews. You might even include a favorite recipe.

- **Fines herbes:** Combine equal amounts of dried chervil, chives, parsley, and tarragon, and pour into attractive glass jars. (Some cooks include marjoram or savory.) Let recipients know that this mixture is especially good with eggs, fish, and poultry.

- **Herbes de Provence:** Mix together equal parts of dried basil, fennel seed, lavender, marjoram, rosemary, sage, summer savory, and thyme, and package in glass jars. This is an all-purpose mix that works for a variety of dishes, including meats, potatoes, and beans.

Scented Herb Soaps

Making soap from scratch is a messy and exacting process and requires you to wear gear to protect yourself from caustic lye, one of the main ingredients. The good news is that you can buy premade soap base (sometimes called "melt-and-pour" soap) at craft stores, and add your own dried herbs and other ingredients. You'll find plain clear and white soap bases (usually sold in blocks), as well as soaps with goat's milk, aloe, and olive oil. While you're at the craft shop, pick up some soap molds in pretty shapes. (You can use ice cube trays or muffin tins in a pinch.)

You'll be using dried herbs; good choices include calendula, chamomile, lavender, mint, and rosemary. Grind the herbs using a mortal and pestle or blender until they're a coarse powder. You'll want ½ to 1 tablespoon of herbs per 4-ounce bar of soap. You can also add a tablespoon of finely ground oatmeal to each bar. A drop or two of essential oil adds a stronger fragrance.

Cut the soap base into chunks, put it in a microwave-safe bowl, cover it, and melt it in a microwave for about a minute. Stir, and if there are any chunks left, repeat in 15-second bursts until the soap is just melted. You can also melt it in a double boiler. Keep a close eye on the soap as it melts so that it doesn't get too hot or boil over. After it has melted, stir in the ground-up herbs, oatmeal, and essential oil. Pour the soap into soap molds (if the molds are intricate shapes rather than plain bars, give them a light coating of vegetable oil before pouring soap to make removal easier).

After pouring, let the soaps cool for an hour or two before popping them out of the molds. Let them cool completely, then wipe them down and wrap them in plastic. Make nice labels, listing all ingredients. Wash the equipment you used by hand, so any soap remaining in the pans and molds doesn't overwhelm your dishwasher with suds.

Drawer and Closet Sachets

Tucked into dresser drawers and closets, sachets infuse stored clothing and linens with a delicate scent and, depending upon the herbs inside, they may also deter moths. You can often find small muslin bags at natural food stores and herb shops, but for gifts it's nice to make something a little more decorative. If you can't (or don't want to) sew, start with a piece of pretty, tightly woven fabric (so herbs don't leak out) and wash it to be sure it's colorfast (so color doesn't bleed onto stored fabrics). Cut the fabric into 9-inch squares. Place ¼ cup of dried herbs in the center (see suggested combinations later in this section). Gather the edges up over the herbs and tie with a ribbon, leaving a long loop so the sachet is easy to hang in a closet.

If you can find them, you can use antique handkerchiefs. Those adorned with embroidery are especially pretty.

To sew fabric into sachets, cut the fabric into 5-x-9-inch rectangles, and, if you're feeling creative, decorate the sachets by sewing pretty ribbons or appliqués on the right side of the fabric (the side that will show in the finished sachet). Take one piece of fabric and fold it in half crosswise, with the wrong side on the outside. Sew two of the edges and then turn the sachet inside-out so that the right side of the fabric is on the outside and the seams are on the inside. Add ¼ cup dried herbs, and then sew the bag closed. Tie three sachets together with a pretty ribbon for a nice gift.

Dried lavender flowers and rose petals are classic fillers for sachets. If you include some dried artemisia, eucalyptus, lemon verbena, mint, rosemary, tansy, or thyme leaves, the sachets will also help repel moths.

Herb Bath Salts

Bath salts help soothe aching muscles, relieve joint stiffness, stimulate circulation, and transform a regular bath into a spa treatment. Most bath salts start with mineral-rich sea salt and Epsom salt, and may include baking soda, aromatic oils, dried herbs, and essential oils. Look for coarse-grained salts, which look especially sparkly and pretty.

The use of bath salts is not recommended for pregnant women, people with diabetes, or people with high blood pressure.

Herb Bath Salts

Chamomile, lavender, lemon verbena, mint, and/or rosemary are all good choices for bath salt mixtures. You can also add a few drops of different essential oils.

1 cup coarse sea salt

1 cup Epsom salts

½ cup baking soda

½ cup dried herbs, ground fine in a coffee grinder or blender

Place all the ingredients in a bowl and then stir until thoroughly combined. Place the salt mixture in decorative jars — cork-topped glass apothecary jars are especially nice. Include a small stainless steel scoop if you like, and add a label with the ingredients and instructions to use about ¼ cup per bath.

Bath Sachets

Another type of herbal bath gift is the bath sachet. Like a tea bag for your bath, these sachets hold dried herbs and other soothing ingredients.

Bath Sachet

Use any of the following herbs, either singly or in combination: chamomile, lavender, lemon balm, lemon verbena, mint, rose, and/or rosemary.

1 cup dried herb

1 cup rolled oats

½ cup powdered milk

1 Combine all ingredients. Place a few tablespoons of the mixture in small muslin bags, usually available at natural food stores and herb shops. Or, cut 9-inch squares of cotton fabric, place the mixture in the center, gather the fabric around it and tie tightly with ribbon.

2 Add a long loop of ribbon to the bath sachet so that the recipient can hang it from the faucet underneath the running water and let it steep in the bathwater.

Dream Pillows

If you can sew a simple seam, you can make a sweet dream pillow filled with dried herbs. The idea is to place the dream pillow inside the pillowcase of a regular bed pillow; during the night, the herbs release their soothing aroma and inspire sweet dreams.

Start with a piece of cotton fabric. If you're making multiple pillows, look for the square pieces of fabric sold for quilting. Sometimes called "fat quarters," they usually measure 18 x 22 inches and are sold in bundles of complementary colors and patterns. Cut them in half crosswise to get two 18-x-11-inch pieces; each piece will yield a pillow that's about 8 x 10 inches. You'll also need some fiberfill stuffing.

Fold the piece of fabric in half with the wrong side facing out. Sew two of the edges, and then turn the resulting pouch inside-out (so the right side of the fabric is on the outside and the seams are on the inside).

Next, blend a mixture of dried herbs together. Most herb pillows include lavender flowers to promote relaxation, but they can also include a variety of herbs reputed to induce pleasant dreams, including chamomile, hops, jasmine, and rose flowers, as well as mint, mugwort, and verbena leaves. Place about ½ cup of dried herbs into the pouch, and then fill it loosely with fiberfill stuffing so it's ½ to 1 inch thick. You want the pillow to be quite flat. Now sew the pillow closed. Add a tag explaining how to use the pillow: Slip it inside your pillowcase, and as you move during the night, the herbs will release their dream-inducing scents.

Eye Pillows

Filled with flaxseed or buckwheat and dried herbs, you can chill these little pillows in the freezer to make a cooling compress or use them at room temperature. The weight of the filling creates a gentle, therapeutic pressure. Both flaxseed and buckwheat are available at natural food stores.

Begin by sewing a 4-x-10-inch bag from smooth cotton fabric or cotton flannel, leaving one end open (see directions for sewing in the "Dream Pillows" section). Fill the bag with a combination of flaxseed and/or buckwheat filler and dried herbs, in a ratio of about 4 to 1. (You don't want the scent to be overpowering.) Don't overfill the bag; it should lay flat. Chamomile, eucalyptus, lemon balm, lavender, mint, and rose petals are good herb choices. Store the pillows in a sealed plastic bag when not in use to prolong the life of the herbs.

Herb-Infused Honey

One of the easiest herbal gifts you can make is herb-flavored honey. You can spread it on muffins and biscuits, drizzle it over ice cream or breakfast cereal, or use a spoonful to jazz up your tea.

Herb-Infused Honey

Any of the following herbs are good choices: bee balm, hyssop, lavender, marjoram, rose geranium, rose petals, rosemary, sage, and violet blossoms.

1 tablespoon of chopped fresh herbs, or 1 teaspoon dried   *2 cups honey*

1 Place the herbs in a cheesecloth bag and tie it tightly. Put it in a saucepan and pour the honey over it, then heat until the honey is warm (not hot).

2 Pour the mixture (including the herbs) into a sterilized jar, and let it steep at room temperature for a week.

3 Warm up the honey again, remove the herb bag, and pour the honey into sterilized jelly jars. Seal them tightly. Store in the refrigerator and use within a month.

Pressed-Herb Notecards

With most of our correspondence coming through our computers and cellphones, handwritten notes are especially welcome. You can use your harvest of herbs to make stationery for your own use and to give as gifts.

Start by selecting the herbs and flowers you want to press. Leaves are easy because they're flat; flowers are more challenging. Choose flowers that are relatively easy to flatten, like pansies, yarrow, and lavender, rather than voluptuous rosebuds.

Place the leaves and flowers on a sheet of white paper, arranging the petals and stems carefully. Then cover with another sheet of white paper and cover with something heavy and flat — a big book weighed down by a few other big books, for example. In a few days, remove the weights. The flowers and leaves have to be flat, but they don't have to be completely dry. Here's why:

You'll be making photocopies of the arrangement and attaching them to plain notecards (available at craft and art stores).

Take a fresh sheet of paper, and trace around one of the cards in the package. Arrange the flowers and leaves in a pleasing shape within those lines. Sometimes, the simplest arrangement is the most pleasing — a sprig of sage with a few carefully spaced leaves, for example. Use a clear glue stick to tack the plant material to the paper. Now photocopy the page, trim it to size, and use double-sided tape to attach it to the front of the notecard.

Chapter 17

Ten Lists of Herbs for Different Uses and Garden Situations

In This Chapter

▶ Collecting culinary must-haves

▶ Matching herbs to specific garden situations

▶ Finding the easiest herbs to start from seed

*O*verwhelmed by the sheer number of herbs to consider for your garden? Narrow down your choices with these lists. They give you a feel for what works best depending on your gardening conditions and how you intend to use the herbs you grow.

Classic Kitchen Herbs

These herbs have a place in every kitchen — and every herb garden:

- ✔ Basil
- ✔ Chervil
- ✔ Dill
- ✔ Fennel
- ✔ Marjoram
- ✔ Parsley
- ✔ Rosemary
- ✔ Sage
- ✔ Savory
- ✔ Tarragon
- ✔ Thyme

Herbs for Sweets

If you have a sweet tooth, be sure to grow these herbs. You can use these herbs to flavor desserts. Stevia adds a strong dose of sweetness without adding calories. Drop a few leaves in hot or iced tea or any other drink you'd like sweetened.

- Anise
- Lavender
- Mint
- Stevia

You can candy and use borage, rose, and violet flowers to decorate cakes; refer to Chapter 12 for instructions.

Herbs for Containers

These herbs adapt especially well to growing in containers:

- Basil
- Lavender
- Mint
- Nasturtium
- Oregano
- Parsley
- Rosemary
- Sage
- Tarragon
- Thyme

Herbs that Attract Butterflies

Include a few of these herbs in your vegetable garden to attract pollinating insects — cucumbers and squash are two vegetables that require insect pollination.

- Anise hyssop
- Basil
- Bee balm
- Catnip
- Dill
- Fennel
- Feverfew
- Lavender
- Nasturtiums
- Sage
- Thyme
- Yarrow

Herbs for Sunny, Dry Gardens

These plants are relatively drought-tolerant and need little irrigation once established. Group them in low-maintenance gardens.

- Anise hyssop
- Catnip
- Lavender
- Oregano
- Rosemary
- Sage
- Thyme
- Yarrow

Pretty Herbs for Ornamental Gardens

We think all herbs are pretty, but these top our list:

- Basil
- Bay

- Bee balm
- Calendula
- Catnip
- Chamomile
- Chives
- Lavender
- Nasturtium
- Parsley
- Pinks
- Rosemary
- Sage
- Thyme
- Yarrow

Herbs with Edible Flowers

Add a few petals or blossoms from these herbs to salads for a colorful kick:

- Anise hyssop
- Basil
- Bee balm
- Borage
- Calendula
- Chamomile
- Chicory
- Chives
- Cilantro/coriander
- Dill
- Fennel
- Hibiscus (roselle)
- Lavender
- Lemon verbena
- Mint

- Mustard
- Nasturtium
- Pinks
- Rose
- Rosemary
- Sage
- Savory
- Scented geraniums
- Thyme
- Violet

Herbs for Tea

These herbs make a tasty addition to black or green tea, or you can use them on their own to make a caffeine-free cup. Use them individually or in various combinations.

- Anise hyssop
- Bee balm
- Borage
- Chamomile
- Fennel
- Lemon balm
- Lemongrass
- Mint
- Rose hips
- Scented geranium

Easiest Herbs to Grow from Seed

If you're new to starting seeds, try these. They germinate reliably and grow quickly.

- Basil
- Calendula

- ✔ Cilantro
- ✔ Dill
- ✔ Fennel

Herbs That Should Not Be Ingested

Avoid ingesting these herbs, and don't grow them if you have pets or children who might be tempted to nibble on them.

- ✔ Aconite
- ✔ American false hellebore
- ✔ Angelica
- ✔ Black cohosh
- ✔ Black hellebore
- ✔ Carolina jasmine
- ✔ Castor bean
- ✔ Comfrey
- ✔ Foxglove
- ✔ Ipecac
- ✔ Madder
- ✔ Pennyroyal
- ✔ Pokeweed
- ✔ Rue
- ✔ Water hemlock
- ✔ Wormwood

An Encyclopedia of Herbs

*This part of the book is the herbs' coming-out party, except that there are more than 65 of them and only one guest — you (and you can dress any way you please). We take you around to each herb and introduce you one by one. We also clue you in to some family history (including look-alike plants that you may want to grow or avoid) and some juicy (albeit often ancient) gossip — full of witches and curses and advice to the lovelorn.

We also suggest more modern uses for the herbs, but we don't go into great detail. Getting more information on using specific culinary herbs is easy; recipes using fresh herbs abound. Using herbs medicinally requires more exacting knowledge than we can supply here; consult with an experienced herbalist if you plan to make any but the most basic remedies, especially those taken internally.

After you've sized up each character, you can decide whether the herb is worthy of adorning your garden. To that end, we include what you can do to keep the herbs healthy and happy, and pass along any quirks the herbs may have regarding soil, sun, and starting seeds.

Agrimony (Agrimonia eupatoria)

The leaves may be prettier than the flowers on agrimony, a 3- to 5-foot-tall perennial. Heavily toothed with prominent veins, similar to a raspberry leaf, the leaves are deep green and a bit hairy. Each leaf is divided into six or eight pairs of leaflets and a terminal leaf, with tinier leaves in between. The effect is eye-pleasingly complex. In fact, the plant's genus name comes from a Greek word, *argemone,* meaning "healing for the eyes." The Greeks meant this medicinally, but we think it works aesthetically, as well.

Beginning about midsummer and continuing for a couple months, agrimony produces spikes of ⅜-inch, five-petaled, apricot-scented, yellow flowers. The blossoms face out and up as though glued around the spike. When the flowers drop off, they leave a three-part calyx that develops into that friendly little bur.

Despite the nice foliage — which is slightly fragrant — you may want to put this herb in an out-of-the-way place where pets and people won't brush against it.

*Agrimonia
eupatoria.*

How to grow

Hardy in USDA Zones 3 to 6, agrimony is happy in ordinary, well-drained soil, is unparticular about pH, and is among the few herbs that prefer a bit of shade. Its seeds can be hard to germinate, even though the plant readily seeds itself where you may not want it. Sow seeds outside in early spring and thin to 8 inches, or start with a division.

Cultivars and related plants

In some herb books you may come across the plant hemp agrimony *(Eupatorium cannabinum)*. Five-feet tall with fuzzy pink flowers, it's not related to *Agrimonia eupatoria,* but to the Joe-Pye weed that's popular as a butterfly-garden plant. Hemp agrimony is toxic to the liver (so just let the swallowtails sip from its blossoms).

Lore and usage

Agrimony, a member of the rose family and native to the British Isles, sometimes fails to show up in herbal hit parades. But who can resist a plant that smells like apricots and wants to follow you everywhere you go? Philanthropos, an ancient name for this herb, is thought to refer to its seeds' inclination to cling passionately to the pants or fur of every passerby. Other common names include church steeples — for its spires of little yellow flowers — and also cockeburr, cocklebur, cockburr, and, for a little variety, sticklewort.

Another explanation for the "philanthropic" nickname was that agrimony received credit for a boatload of spiritual and health benefits. The Anglo-Saxons plucked the herb for snakebites and warts. In the Middle Ages you might have put it under your pillow for a sound night's snooze. The Chinese have used it for a millennium to control bleeding and as a tonic for the digestive system and liver.

Agrimony does contain tannins, which are good for diarrhea, and mucilage that can take the scratch out of a sore throat in a gargle and soften skin in the bath. Or you can just enjoy the fruity-scented leaves in a tea or as a garnish for fruit dishes.

Angelica (Angelica archangelica)

Even if you don't harvest angelica, you might want to cultivate the herb for its statuesque form. The plant grows up to 6 feet tall — 4 feet across — and has shiny, 2- to 3-foot leaves. Each toothed leaf is divided into thirds, which are again divided into thirds, and the leafstalk has a puffy base that looks like a starched collar. The thick, ribbed stems are usually tinged purple.

Softball-sized, off-white, starburst flowers open early to mid-summer, usually in the plant's second year. The seed heads that follow are even more dramatic — clusters within clusters — and the ribbed seeds are ¼-inch long with papery wings. All parts of angelica are musky smelling.

Angelica contains furocoumarins, which can make people highly sensitive to sunlight, and there's some evidence that it contains carcinogens, so limit your consumption. An occasional bite of candied angelica should be fine, but other than that, avoid ingesting it. Fresh roots are poisonous.

How to grow

Angelica is one of the few herbs that can thrive in the dank and dark — and the cold (it's hardy from Zone 3 to 6). This plant likes its soil deeply dug, loamy, acidic, and very moist (but still aerated). It likes sun or shade but not heat.

Angelica self-seeds freely, but seeds need light to sprout and can take up to a month to germinate. Just tamp the seeds into the soil; once your plants emerge, thin the seedlings to 2 feet in all directions.

Angelica is a biennial-like plant that dies after it goes to seed in its second or third season. Harvest leaves from the stem the first fall, and roots the next spring or second fall. Roots rot quickly once seeds have ripened.

Cultivars and related plants

The Chinese use the roots of Chinese angelica, *A. polymorpha* var. *sinensis,* which they call *dong quai,* to cure all types of "women's problems." Ornamental gardeners put another Asian angelica also known as purple or Korean angelica, *A. gigas,* at the back of their perennial border to enjoy its 3-to-4-inch, reddish-purple flowers and their purple stems; you'll find it abuzz with bees and beneficial wasps. This species does best where humidity is low and nights are cool. American angelica, *A. atropurpurea,* is a native of the central United States and has dark purple stems and white flowers.

Don't try to collect angelica in the wild. It looks all too much like the lethal water hemlock, *Cicuta maculata,* which also grows in wet places.

Lore and usage

The botanical name of this giant member of the parsley family (sometimes called wild parsnip) practically conjures up choirs of cherubim and seraphim.

In fact, angelica was once deemed so holy it was thought to be the only herb that witches never used. If Inquisitors came knocking, you could prove your innocence merely by showing them that angelica grew in your garden.

Legend has it that during the days of bubonic plague, an angel came to a monk in a dream and suggested this herb as a cure. The results aren't known, but the celestial name stuck. Angelica does have some antibacterial properties. Native Americans used a Plains species for both internal and external ills.

To remember its most common culinary use, think of "angel" as a term of endearment. Cooks candy angelica and use it to decorate cakes and other desserts. The herb is also used commercially to flavor alcoholic beverages, including gin, vermouth, Benedictine, and Chartreuse.

To crystallize, or candy, angelica, make a simple syrup by simmering equal parts water and sugar (1 cup each) until the sugar disappears. Use tender angelica stems cut in the plant's second spring. Blanch the stems in boiling water for two minutes, peel, and slice into 2-inch pieces. Simmer the pieces in the syrup for 20 minutes, cool, and store stems and syrup in a covered container in the refrigerator for three or four days. Reheat syrup and stems; remove stems from any remaining syrup and cool them on a rack.

Anise (Pimpinella anisum)

A lank and floppy 2-foot annual, anise begins life with round, toothed leaves; but on a mature plant, the leaves are feathery and ferny. The midsummer flowers are airy, flat, yellowish-white clusters about 2 inches across, followed by tiny gray-brown ribbed fruits shaped like commas.

Pimpinella anisum.

How to grow

Anise can be a bit touchy in the garden. It won't set seed in climates with fewer than 120 frost-free days. Anise needs full sun but also rebels against heat and humidity. For the best results, the soil should be light and fast-draining, of average fertility. Give your plants shelter from wind and don't make anise compete with weeds or other plants.

A long taproot makes anise hard to transplant, so start it outdoors once the soil and air have warmed. Sow seeds ¼- to ½-inch deep, and thin seedlings to 8 inches apart. (Close spacing enables plants to support each other.) If you live in a cold climate, try starting seeds in peat pots. In the Deep South, sow anise seeds in the fall.

Cultivars and related plants

Although common anise is a star in Southeast Asian cuisine, the Chinese may use one of their native evergreen trees, star anise *(Illicium verum)* to get an anise flavor. An ingredient in five-spice powder, this magnolia relative bears star-shaped brown fruits. In addition to treating indigestion, the Chinese use star anise to treat hernias, rheumatism, and back pain.

Lore and usage

Anise is native to the Mediterranean and Egypt, where it was first used some 1,500 years ago. To quell indigestion, the Romans baked it in after-dinner cakes called *mustaceum.* In Biblical times, citizens used this herb — along with mint and cumin — to pay taxes, and in the 14th century, King Edward I levied a tax on anise to help pay for the London Bridge.

A member of the parsley family, anise tastes like licorice. In fact, licorice candy is likely to be flavored with anise, which is easier to grow and safer to consume than true licorice. Several cultures use anise in liqueurs — the Greeks in their famous *ouzo* and the French in the strong aperitif called *pastis.* Anisette is flavored with fennel, coriander, and anise.

Dogs love its scent, and anise has been used to mark trails for foxhounds and to scent hares for greyhounds. Mice like it, too. If you're out of cheese, try smearing your traps with anise oil.

Use fresh anise leaves in salads, soups, and stocks, or as a garnish. Bake the tasty seeds in breads, cookies, or cakes; stew them with apples and pears; or steam them with cabbages, onions, carrots, or turnips. Anise is a good breath freshener, used commercially in toothpaste and mouthwash.

Anise hyssop (Agastache foeniculum)

Anise hyssop is from a clan of aromatic perennials native to arid parts of the United States, Mexico, and Asia. All produce spikes covered with whorls of tubular, two-lipped flowers, similar to other members of the mint family. But unlike other mints, *Agastache* species are happy in a drought.

Anise hyssop has relatively tiny pale lavender flowers. But the flowers are so tightly packed on the spike that the overall effect is fuzzy, like a mauve bottle brush. When several 2- to 2½- foot, multistemmed plants are blooming in mid- to late summer, it's a refreshing sight, especially because they're usually swaying to the ministrations of butterflies and bees. The toothed leaves look similar to those of lemon balm and some other mints, but smell like anise when crushed.

*Agastache
foeniculum.*

How to grow

Anise hyssop, which is hardy in Zones 5 to 9, is happy in dry, relatively poor, slightly alkaline soil and full sun (shade makes them floppy). Plants are easy to start from seed and will bloom in their first year. You may or may not be pleased by their tendency to reseed.

Cultivars and related plants

Almost any *Agastache* is worth having in your herb garden, butterfly garden, or perennial bed — especially if yours is a dry climate. Most cultivars have purplish flowers, although some bloom in white, blue, or orange; our favorite is Tutti-Frutti, which is the color of raspberry sherbet. All anise hyssops have aromatic leaves, and those with bigger flowers are hummingbird magnets.

Anise hyssop is easily confused with hyssop (described later in this chapter), which also has tubular flowers but is semi-evergreen, more compact, and camphor-scented.

Lore and usage

There isn't a wealth of ancient lore or alleged medical wonders surrounding this herb. It just does its modest bit to bring long-lasting texture and color to the garden, whereas its flowers and leaves lend a minty-anise flavor to foods or honey. The flower spikes dry well for arrangements and wreaths, and the scent is worthy of your potpourri.

Basil (Ocimum basilicum)

We're going to stick our necks out and say that if you already grow or use one fresh herb, it's likely to be basil. The most commonly grown type, sweet basil, grows 1 to 2 feet tall, 1 foot wide, and has bright green, oval, somewhat puckery leaves. The flowers are spikes of small, white tubular flowers, sometimes tinged with pink or purple, especially in the purple-leafed cultivars.

Ocimum basilicum.

How to grow

Give basil plenty of sun and moderately rich, well-aerated soil that also retains moisture. Plants wilt easily in drought, so mulch your basil and water it when rain is scant. You can sow seeds in your garden — it germinates easily — but we always start ours indoors 4 to 6 weeks before the last frost date.

Space plants about 1 foot apart. Basil is pretty enough to plant among your flowers, which will help protect the herb from wind. Just as on the table, basil is a fine companion for tomatoes in the vegetable patch because it's reputed to repel tomato hornworms.

As soon as plants are 6 inches tall, begin pinching off stem tips and tops that are threatening to bloom; the pinching encourages more branching and leaf growth.

Cultivars and related plants

Basil comes in well over 30 varieties. For quantities of the sweet-tasting type, you can choose big-leafed selections such as 'Mammoth', 'Lettuce-Leaved', 'Large Leaf', or 'Genovese'. 'Green Ruffles' has deeply cut, ornamental foliage. To bring burgundy foliage to the garden, try 'Dark Opal', 'Osmin', 'Red Rubin', or 'Purple Ruffles'. The small spheres of 'Spicy Globe', 'Green Globe', or 'Piccolo Verde Fino' basil can make an interesting edge for the herb bed or echo topiary in a formal garden. For the kitchen, experiment with subtle variations in flavor, such as lemon, lime, and cinnamon basils. 'Siam Queen', which won an All-America Selection (AAS) award, and other Thai basils complement Thai and Vietnamese cuisine. Relatively new to cooks and gardeners are two tender perennial basils. 'Aussie Sweetie' (also known as 'Greek Columnar' or 'Lesbos') grows to 3 feet tall with a distinct upright habit and soft green leaves. 'Pesto Perpetuo' has a similar growth habit in addition to its striking green-and-white variegated foliage.

Lore and usage

Basil is such a nice, friendly plant — sort of peppery and sort of sweet. Who would connect it with scorpions, madness, and evil? Yet more than one tale of scorpions has been found in the brains of people too fond of smelling basil (according to one account from a physician aptly named Hilarius). Basil was said to breed "venomous beasts" if tossed on a pile of horse manure. One reputed source of its name was "basilisk," a creature whose look would literally kill. The Greeks and Romans thought it symbolized insanity and anger, and passed down to the French a belief in cursing while sowing its seeds. *Semer le basilic,* the French idiom for ranting, translates literally as "sowing the basil."

On the flip side, Italian women put a pot of basil outside to give the thumbs-up to a suitor; Indians consider it sacred to Hindu gods; and Haitian shopkeepers sprinkle it about to ensure a good cash flow.

In today's kitchens, basil goes far beyond pesto. It's great in almost any pasta topping. Snip leaves into soups, stir-fries, marinades, or over meat on the grill. Add the flowers to salads. The purple-leafed cultivars lend color (as well as flavor, of course) to vinegars.

Bay (Laurus nobilis)

Bay is technically a tree, and in its native Mediterranean home it can grow 40-feet tall. In the United States, even where it can stay outdoors all year, it's rarely half that size; with the indoor-outdoor treatment many of us have to give it, bay stays at around 5 feet or less.

Bay's narrow oval leaves are leathery, glossy, pungent, and pointed at the tips. Mature plants may produce little pale yellow flowers in early summer, followed by dark purple berries.

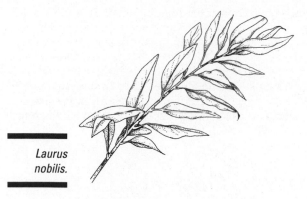

Laurus nobilis.

How to grow

Bay requires good drainage, but doesn't mind fairly poor soil. Give your plant protection from wind and full sun, which can scorch the leaves, and don't let it go thirsty in a drought. Bay is an ideal container plant, which makes it easy to bring inside in Zones 3 to 7, where it can't survive winter. Gardeners in Zones 9 to 11 can leave it outdoors year round, while those in borderline Zone 8 should sink its pot in the ground and mound soil and mulch around it to keep the roots from freezing.

Bay seeds are notorious for turning moldy. Most gardeners opt for starting with a small, purchased plant. Indoors, bay can tolerate temperatures from 45 to 80 degrees Fahrenheit, but it needs a sunny window. Keep the soil just barely moist, and don't feed it in winter.

Cultivars and related plants

Few plants offer a better illustration of the need for botanical names than bay, which is also widely known as laurel and sweet bay. Among trees and shrubs with similar names are the mountain laurel, cherry laurel, laurel oak, laurel poplar, laurel willow, laurelwood, bat willow, bar star, and bayberry — and each of these plants is known by still other common names.

Lore and usage

Even the gods suffered the agonies of unrequited love. Take the case of Apollo, god of medicine, and Daphne, foxy nymph: Boy meets girl. Girl loathes boy. To hide her from this stalker, Daphne's father, Peneus, turns her into a laurel (bay) tree. Apollo vows to worship the evergreen evermore, and uses wreaths of its leaves to crown champions in all pursuits, from triumphant generals to spelling-bee champions.

In addition to being the official herbal headgear of champs, bay has been credited with protective powers — against lightning and thunder, and general evil and mayhem. If nothing else, if you crumble it on pantry shelves it may protect them from evil insect pests, thanks to a substance called cineole.

Bay is a must for Creole and Spanish cuisine and mixed spices for steaming shellfish. It's a good addition to stews, soups, or bean dishes. Because bay leaves are tough and sharp, they're usually used whole and removed before a dish is served. Use bay in moderation — too much makes food bitter.

Bee balm (Monarda didyma)

Like other mints, bee balm has tubular, two-lipped blooms. Those of the species are usually scarlet with red-tinged bracts. Whorled atop the stem, the flowers have a raggedly charm, like a red daisy trimmed with pinking shears. You can find natural white forms, and cultivars and hybrids extend bloom colors into pink, lavender, and shades in between. Bee balm grows 2 to 4 feet tall, and the pointed oval leaves have fairly pronounced veins.

Monarda didyma.

How to grow

Bee balm grows naturally along moist stream banks, usually in dappled shade, so not surprisingly, it demands rich, moisture-retentive soil. It does best in Zones 4 through 9. In humid areas, or when drought-stressed elsewhere, it often becomes disfigured by powdery mildew — not a pleasant prospect when you want a few leaves for tea. Watering only at the roots and spacing plants generously will help prevent mildew, but your best protection is to buy mildew-resistant cultivars.

Flowering starts in midsummer and continues for two months if you remove spent blooms. A valuable addition to a butterfly/bee/bird garden, bee balm also is a natural for pondside plantings and other damp spots.

Bee balm may self-seed and it spreads by underground stems, although at a more leisurely pace than other mints. Clumps die out in the center, so you need to divide it every couple of years. You can start it from seed, but division in spring is easier.

Cultivars and related plants

You can find more than 30 bee balm cultivars and hybrids available, and if your climate isn't conducive to powdery mildew, you can pick whichever shade suits your fancy.

'Croftway Pink' and 'Cambridge Scarlet' are two old forms still widely available. For disease resistance, look for 'Marshall's Delight', a deep pink, or 'Gardenview Scarlet'. 'Adam' (white) and 'Blue Stocking' (violet) do better in heat and drought than most cultivars.

For your lemony herb garden, look for *M. citriodora,* lemon bergamot. Other *Monarda* species contain more medicinal compounds. *M. punctata* (spotted bee balm, or horse balm) is high in antiseptic compounds. It has whorls of cream-colored flowers spotted with purple. *M. fistulosa* (wild bergamot) is high in geraniol, which helps prevent tooth decay.

Lore and usage

Members of this mint-family genus — all native to North America — go by a slew of common names. "Oswego tea" honors its discovery by early American botanist John Bartram near Oswego, New York, and "liberty tea" recognizes its use by revolutionaries in the wake of the Boston tea party.

You're also likely to see the name bergamot; the scent of monarda leaves is evocative of the bergamot orange, the peel of which is used in Earl Grey tea. And the name bee balm is for the siren song it sings to those fuzzy little pollinators. Hummingbirds love it, too.

Many people just call the plant monarda. It has been a popular garden plant in England since it was carried there from Virginia in 1637 — "far too decorative to banish to the kitchen garden or even the herb garden," one British writer observed.

In addition to its charm in the garden, bee balm makes a tangy tea, more citrusy than minty. In cooking, use it with anything that benefits from a touch of citrus — fruit salads, fish, pork, duck, cucumbers. The red-flowered varieties have tasty blooms — spicy and sweet. They deliver color and flavor to sweet and savory dishes, from sorbet to pound cake and from potato salad to curries.

Betony (Stachys officinalis)

If you're already an enthusiastic gardener, you probably know or grow lamb's ear, *Stachys byzantina,* beloved for its soft fuzzy foliage. Betony, or bishop's wort, is its cousin, and comes with more flamboyant flowers and a history as a cure-all. Betony is a 2-foot-tall European perennial that is, like bee balm, a member of the mint family. In late spring or early summer it erupts into spikes of small, neon violet, tubular blossoms that continue opening until early fall.

The leaves are worthy of attention, too, textured as they are with veins, wrinkles, and oil glands, scalloped and hairy along the edges. The lower leaves are roughly heart-shaped, whereas those near the top are narrow ovals without any stalks.

Stachys officinalis.

How to grow

Hardy in Zones 5 to 8, betony likes its soil deep, rich, and moist but well draining. If its feet get wet in winter, it will turn up its toes and die. Happy plants spread to form handsome mats that should be divided every two or three years to keep them from *flagging* (diminishing). Betony prefers full sun but can take some shade, especially in the South.

You can start the species from seed or by division. Plant them at least a foot apart.

Cultivars and related plants

In addition to the popular lamb's ear, you can grow big betony *(S. macrantha/ S. grandiflora)*, which is almost identical, but as a native of the Caucasus is hardy farther north, in Zones 4 to 7. It flowers in several colors: white ('Alba'), pink ('Rosea'), purple-pink ('Superba'), and violet ('Violacea').

Lore and usage

Ancient Egyptians believed betony had magical powers, and the Romans listed some four dozen ills it would allay. It would shield you against both evil spirits and bad dreams, at least if you harvested it without using iron and dried it in the shade with the root still attached. It was said that snakes would fight to the death if surrounded by it, and other beasts would search it out when injured.

Betony tea is bland, but the tannins in it are good for diarrhea. You won't waste your time gargling a betony infusion for a sore throat. The jury is still out on its reputed power against what herbalist Mrs. Grieve calls "languid nervous headaches," but it contains some chemicals that might do the job.

Borage (Borago officinalis)

Borage is an annual that can reach 2 to 4 feet high, but it tends to sprawl in a laid-back mound. Tiny white hairs on the leaves and on the hollow, succulent stems create something of an aura around it, totally in keeping with the star-shaped, heavenly blue, edible flowers that open in humbly drooping clusters. Five long stamens with black anthers heighten the drama.

Borago officinalis.

How to grow

Borage is tough, but it is happier when you add well-rotted manure to your soil. This herb also needs good drainage and doesn't like competing with weeds; mulching helps retain essential moisture.

Add full sun, and your plants will repay you by reseeding in perpetuity. Plant your first seeds where you want the borage to grow, because it has a long taproot and can be hard to transplant. Given borage's floppy nature, you should space plants at least 18 inches apart, mingled with plants of a similar devil-may-care habit, in a wildflower garden, vegetable patch, or among casually arranged herbs.

Cultivars and related plants

Borage blooms ought to be blue, but if you need a white flower in your garden, look for *Borago officinalis* Alba; *B. officinalis* Variegata has green leaves marked with white. If you live in Zone 5 or warmer, you can try another species, *B. pygmaea,* creeping borage, a short-lived perennial that has pale blue flowers.

If you love blue-flowered plants as much as we do — here's where all that scientific botany stuff gets to be fun — get to know borage's extended family, a Who's Who of the cerulean class: forget-me-not *(Myosotis sylvatica),* lung-wort *(Pulmonaria officinalis),* Virginia bluebells *(Mertensia viginica),* alkanet *(Anchusa azurea),* and Siberian bugloss (also known as perennial forget-me-not *Brunnera macrophylla).*

Lore and usage

If even a fraction of the reputation that borage has for "making men and women glad and merry" were true, college fraternities would have borage blasts and radio psychotherapists would have to seek new careers. Borage sprigs, a late 17th-century herbalist wrote, "are of known virtue to revive the hypochondriac and cheer the hard student."

Borage has been a welcome garden plant in Britain since the 1400s, perhaps because English gardeners knew the popular Latin saying, "I, Borage, bring always courage." That quality was one reason why impatient maidens of yore added borage to the drinks of slow-to-propose suitors.

Or perhaps the popularity of borage is due to the sky-blue color of its blooms and the cool-as-a-cucumber flavor of its leaves, stems, and flowers. According to ancient sources, it's a good addition to "drinkes that are cordiall." Appropriately, one of its common names is cool-tankard.

Freeze the flowers in ice cubes for your own cool tankard, candy them, or toss them in a salad. If the fuzz doesn't bother you, you can eat the leaves, too, steamed or raw (just be sure to peel the stems). Borage is difficult to dry and impossible to freeze. Use it fresh, or preserve it in vinegar. Despite fears that borage may be toxic to the liver, trusted experts assure us it is safe to drink and eat as long as you avoid "chronic consumption." Women who are pregnant or on the pill should avoid borage because it can stimulate lactation (its traditional medicinal use).

Burdock (Arctium lappa)

This biennial, a member of the daisy family, is an attention-getter at 5 feet tall. Burdock is made even more commanding by magenta, thistle-type flower heads and wavy, spade-shaped lower leaves (gray with down on the under-side) that can be a foot long. Upper leaves are smaller and more oval. The flowers give way to round fruits bristling with hooks. The taproot, the part most often used, grows as long as 3 feet.

How to grow

Some gardeners may bristle at the thought of deliberately planting a prickly thistle on their home ground, but burdock won't look out of place in a wildflower area, and will peer protectively over shorter plants from the back of a border.

Most people grow burdock as an annual. You can start it indoors from seed, but the huge taproot doesn't allow it to be confined for long. Give it rich, moisture-retentive, and — most important — deeply dug, loose soil. Some gardeners create a mound for it so it will be easier to harvest. You can dig the root at the end of the growing season, or wait until the following spring, when you won't have the prickles to contend with.

Cultivars and related plants

Chalk up another one for using botanical names, because there are a lot of plants with "bur" or "dock" in their common names. Common burdock or lesser burdock *(Arctium minus)* often grows just as big as its "great" cousin but has shorter flower stalks and hollow leaf stalks.

Lore and usage

You just know that a plant with nicknames as diverse as cockle buttons, beggar's buttons, hareburr, and love leaves (not to mention pig's rhubarb) has to have a mixed reputation. Burdock, a native of Europe and Asia Minor, is a prickly pest in fields and along roadsides. Even Shakespeare, who knew his flora, called upon its image several times to represent woe or annoyance.

Burdock once was considered a first-rate blood purifier and cure for skin diseases. The 17th-century English physician Nicholas Culpeper, often given to unbridled inclusiveness, credited it with power over everything from "shrinking in the sinews" to rabies. Five hundred years ago, burdock was mashed into wine to treat leprosy. From the Middle Ages to modern-day Asia, it has been used to treat cancer, and it does contain some anti-tumor substances.

The fresh root contains some antibiotics, which may explain burdock's reputation for skin disorders, including dandruff and acne. You can dry the root to make a tea, which, as a diuretic, may lessen PMS symptoms. The herb also has a long-standing reputation as a liver tonic, which is one reason the Japanese (who call the root *gobo*) cook it in soups and stews.

Every part of burdock but the flowers and — of course, the bur — can be eaten fresh or cooked. The root tastes a bit like celery and a bit like potato, faintly sweet, and should be scrubbed or peeled like a potato and used in much the same way. If you're going to eat the stem (which also should be peeled) or leaves, pick them while they're young and fresh.

Calendula (Calendula officinalis)

A member of the daisy family, calendula grows about 18 inches tall with numerous branches and sports cheerful yellow-orange flowers. The leaves are aromatic when crushed, and tiny hairs cover the plant all over.

How to grow

Start calendula from fresh seeds in early spring; it germinates better in slightly cool conditions. In the Deep South and Southwest, it can sometimes be sown in fall. Transplant seedlings into full sun or part shade in moderately fertile soil. Space plants at least 10 inches apart so they have room to branch and good air circulation — they're prone to powdery mildew.

Calendula usually starts blooming about six weeks after germination, but it may peter out during the hottest part of the summer. Keep pinching off the flowers for their many uses, and they'll oblige you by making more.

By all means, include calendula in the ornamental garden with other hot colors or, for a vivid contrast, with blues or purples.

Cultivars and related plants

If your favorite use of calendula is looking at it — whether to lighten your heart or to see fairies — you may want to collect some of its many cultivars, which look great planted together. Most of them are double-flowered. New ones become available almost every year, some with a second color on the petal tips or edges, and many with a contrasting center. A few, like the dahlia-look-alike 'Radio', border on gaudy. Many seeds come in mixes, such as 'Art Shades Mixed' (apricot, orange, and cream) or 'Kablouna Mixed' (tall crested flowers that include gold, orange, and lemon, all with dark centers).

Lore and usage

Often called pot marigold, calendula was loved by gardeners (and Romantic poets) long before the marigolds that are now planted at every hamburger franchise ever came on the scene. Calendula was both a clock and a calendar. Linnaeus, the guy who came up with botanical names, wrote that the pot marigold flower was open from 9 a.m. to 3 p.m. (making it appropriate land-scaping for modern banks). Its name came from the observation that it was open the first day of each calendar month.

Calendula's traditional uses were as much magical as medicinal. One herbal declared that if the planets were properly aligned, and if the gatherer was sin-less and said Our Fathers and Hail Marys (three each), wearing a calendula blossom would give him a vision of anyone who robbed him. It might also grant visions of fairies and a faithful husband-to-be. Culpeper recommended a plaster of calendula flowers, hog's grease, and turpentine for strengthening the heart.

Calendula flower tea was prescribed for treating measles (12 flower heads steeped in 1 pint boiling water) as late as 1900 in some parts of England, where it was known as measle-flower.

Today, you can put calendula's antiviral and antifungal properties to work in oils and creams for treating wounds, skin problems, and bug bites. In the kitchen, it's known as the poor person's saffron. Use its petals in paella, polenta, and other dishes that call for that costly spice — which is kept in the safe at our grocer — and you'll get a similar color, if not taste. Calendula petals are not water-soluble; chop calendula petals and sauté in oil to allow them to release their color and flavor. Boil potatoes in water with oil and calendula petals for golden potatoes. Or just toss flowers in a salad to make it sizzle with summer color. You can dry and crush the petals for off-season use.

Caraway (Carum carvi)

Like its relatives, fennel and dill, caraway has delicate, fernlike leaves, which have the same anise scent as the seeds do. Once a plant reaches 18 to 24 inches tall, it produces an *umbel* (umbrella) of tiny, white flowers — usually in the summer of its second year but occasionally at the end of the first. Then come the famous seeds with five ribs and pointed ends. The long taproot is like parsnip, both in appearance and taste.

How to grow

Sow seeds ½ inch deep in spring (if you live in the South or Southwest, you can sow in the fall as well) in loose, fertile soil that retains moisture well. Thin seedlings to 8 inches apart. Caraway prefers full sun, although a bit of shade is your only hope in hot, rainless, humid summers. If you've given it the right spot and don't collect all its seeds, it may surprise you with a return visit.

You'll have to plant many rows to stock the cabinet for a season of caraway cookery, so if space is limited, make your meager harvest a festive occasion.

Lore and usage

Grow caraway if you're into billing and cooing. Cultivated for five millennia, this biennial in the carrot family has been deemed capable of keeping both pigeons and lovers from straying. Shakespeare's contemporaries dipped roasted apples in the seeds. Then the Scots, who called caraway salt-water jelly, dipped buttered bread in the seeds. English herbalist John Parkinson wrote that such uses would dispel colds or "wind in the body." The Germans still use it to make *kummel,* a liqueur.

Caraway and cabbage aren't just alliterative. Caraway is great in slaw and a must for sauerkraut and the pork that often accompanies it. Caraway and apples are as popular today as they were with the Elizabethans. Try caraway in applesauce, apple pie, or Waldorf salad.

Parkinson wasn't full of hot air, either: You can make a caraway tea to combat flatulence, bloating, and other digestive miseries.

Catnip (Nepeta cataria)

Okay, it's our age. We always associate catnip with cartoon cats like Tom, the archenemy of Jerry, or Sylvester, the bane of Tweety Bird, because mouse and bird, respectively, so often used the herb to make their escapes. In about two-thirds of domestic cats — and also the big, fierce ones like lions — the volatile oils contained in catnip leaves induce utter ecstasy.

Catnip is a 2- to 3-foot erect, branching perennial with downy gray-green toothed leaves shaped like stretched-out hearts, 1 to 3 inches long. Like other mints, it has square stems and spikes of tiny two-lipped, purple-spotted white flowers from mid- to late summer. Native to Europe and Asia, catnip has naturalized in parts of the United States, especially the mid-Atlantic.

How to grow

Unlike many mints, catnip likes fairly dry, even sandy soil — good drainage is a must. It will develop its pungent scent best in full sun, although some southern growers urge a little shade. There's a saying that if you plant catnip from seed, the cats won't know it's there. That's because handling the plant is what sends out the "come and get it" signals. Propagation from cuttings or root division is much easier than starting from seed, however. Plants tend to die out after about three years, so if you and your cat are addicted, take some insurance cuttings.

A word to the wise: Keep catnip well away from other valuable plants because they're likely to get flattened in any feline free-for-all.

Cultivars and related plants

All members of the *Nepeta* genus are called catmints, and we like having them in the ornamental garden for their blue flowers and gray foliage. The most commonly planted cousins are an 18-inch-high hybrid, *N.* x *faassenii* (often called *N. mussinii*), and a cultivar, 'Blue Hills Giant', which gets twice as big. Catmints tend to flop over, so they perform prettily at the edge of a raised bed, in a large container, and in rock gardens.

Lore and usage

Herbalists of old claimed that the root had a more unpleasant effect on humans than on felines, making "the most gentle person fierce and quarrelsome." Folklore also has it that hangmen chewed the root to work up enthusiasm for their job. Fortunately, catnip tea is made from the leaves, not the root, and has yet another result: It makes most people tranquil or sleepy. It may also aid digestion as do many other mints.

In addition to using dried catnip leaves in little stuffed toys for Fluffy or Snowball, you can toss some in your potpourri if the smell appeals to you. Just don't open the lid while Mittens is on the prowl. And if you like the taste of the fresh leaves, include them in salads, or candy them.

Chamomile (Matricaria recutita, Chamaemelum nobile)

The story of chamomile is complicated by the fact that there are two plants that go by that name. The Germans think that a 2-to-3-foot-tall annual from Europe and western Asia (*Matricaria recutita*, or German chamomile) is the only true chamomile, and that the other is a weed; the English think that a 9-inch creeping perennial from western Europe and Ireland (*Chamaemelum nobile,* or Roman or garden chamomile) is the only true chamomile, and that the other is a pest. Fortunately, this issue hasn't sparked a major war; the plants not only look and smell a great deal alike, but are also used the same way — to make a relaxing tea.

Both chamomiles have delicate, threadlike leaves and daisylike flowers with white rays and an endearing, cone-shaped button center. Besides being taller, German chamomile is more upright and produces more flowers per plant. The leaves of Roman chamomile are thicker and flatter, but the acid test is to tear open the receptacle — the swelling behind the flower head — and see whether it's hollow (German) or solid (Roman). Roman chamomile is hardy in Zones 4 to 9.

Chamaemelum nobile.

How to grow

You can grow both chamomiles from seed, but the annual German chamomile is easier to find on seed racks and easier to germinate. It prefers light, moisture-retentive soil but is forgiving, and tolerates drought and alkaline soil. Heat launches the flowering season, and you should be able to get about three good harvests every two weeks.

When conditions are right, German chamomile reseeds into every nook and cranny. Because you won't get more than two or three cups of chamomile tea from a single plant, you'll want to cheer on all the volunteers. And fortunately, having chamomile as a companion is said to make every plant healthier. Set it wherever you can use its cheery face and ferny foliage, but be ready for offspring.

Roman chamomile also grows almost anywhere. It doesn't like hot, dry weather, though, which is why American gardeners can rarely pull off the English tradition of a chamomile lawn. (Queen Elizabeth has one at Buckingham Palace.) In very hot regions, give plants some afternoon shade; elsewhere, plant it in full sun. Start Roman chamomile from seed, cuttings, or division, and space plants about 1 foot apart.

Cultivars and related plants

If your garden conditions are right for Roman chamomile (impossibly mild like the Pacific Northwest), you can grow a variety developed for lawns, 'Treneague', which never flowers. (We love the idea of a flowering lawn, but bees are a disadvantage if you like to go shoeless.) Want more flower rather than less? A double form, 'Flora Plena', was bred for twice the tea.

Breeders tinkering with the German form have put their money on chamomile as medicine; several newer cultivars, such as 'Bodegold', are said to contain more essential oil.

Lore and usage

Most people compare the scent of the chamomile flowers and foliage with apples. The Greeks must have thought so, because they gave the plant that evolved into chamomile a name meaning "earth-apple." The Spanish call it "little apple" — *manzanilla* — and use it to flavor a sherry of the same name.

As everyone from the herbalist Dioscorides to Peter Rabbit's mother knew well, chamomile makes a soothing tea. The plant does contain some sedative chemicals, and many herbalists are convinced it's also good for heartburn. Antiseptic and anti-inflammatory compounds make a chamomile compress or ointment worth trying for rashes and other skin problems. Try an infusion in your bath if you have poison ivy.

If you drink chamomile tea daily as a calmative, it can suddenly have a strong stimulant effect.

Chervil (Anthriscus cerefolium)

Chervil may be the Rodney Dangerfield of herbs. Even though it's a key ingredient in the famous French herb mixture *fines herbes,* some otherwise sterling cookbooks and gardening books swear it's the same thing as sweet Cicely — which it's not. It gets no respect, or, at least, not nearly enough.

Chervil does have a good deal in common with sweet Cicely. Both are members of the carrot family and have white umbrella flowers and somewhat ferny leaves, similar seeds, and an aniselike flavor. But while sweet Cicely is a perennial, chervil is an annual. Growing 1 to 2 feet tall, with thin, branched stems, it has divided leaves that are easily mistaken for parsley's. And like parsley, it comes in both flat-leaf and curly varieties.

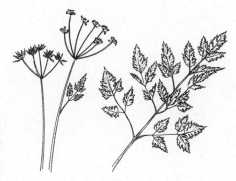

Anthriscus cerefolium.

How to grow

In hot sun, chervil either goes to seed early or shrivels faster than the Wicked Witch of the West when Dorothy doused her with that bucket of water. Plant it where it will get some summer shade, near a deciduous tree or shrub, or among taller herbs, vegetables, or ornamentals. You can begin harvesting this herb about eight weeks after germination, and you can harvest it continually if you sow seeds every couple of weeks in spring and again in late summer. Harvest leaves just before the flower clusters open. (Better still, remove flower stems to encourage new foliage.)

Chervil seeds need light to germinate, so just press them into the soil with your hand and keep the soil moist. Once the seeds sprout, thin plants to 10 inches. (Chervil seeds don't age well, so don't keep them over winter.)

Note chervil's delicate nature if you dry it: Expose leaves to high heat and they will be as tasty as yesterday's newspaper.

Cultivars and related plants

Breeders haven't tinkered much with chervil, but you might look for the curly leafed form, 'Crispum'. Avoid cow parsley *(A. sylvestris),* which is a noxious weed, outlawed in many states. You can try the lacy form 'Ravenswing' with purple-brown foliage. Use it to give airy grace to a border, but when it reseeds, you'll have to cull the green-foliaged interlopers.

Lore and usage

People have been growing chervil almost forever. By one account, a basket of its seeds was found in King Tut's tomb. The Romans took it with them as they expanded their empire. Both they and the Greeks cooked it, including the root (which was candied to treat stomachaches), but the Saxons used it raw in soups and salads. Once prescribed to prevent plague and to cure hiccups, chervil's reputation as a blood purifier has made it a traditional spring tonic in central Europe.

Follow the tonic tradition and use chervil with spring vegetables for a subtle anise note. Later in summer, chervil is good with cold soups and salads. Preserve it in spreads such as cream cheese, butter, or sour cream. Eggs are another popular destination for chervil, which is high in protein and contains calcium and magnesium. Herbalists say it may reduce high blood pressure.

Chicory (Cichorium intybus)

Chicory, the bonnie-blue roadside denizen and sunflower cousin, can grow to 3 feet or more from a clump of leaves that look like a dandelion's. As it grows upward, it branches with sparse, smaller leaves, leaving its stem nearly naked. Then, from midsummer to early fall, it glows with 1½-inch-wide, true blue flowers. The ray petals have squarish, ragged tips. Many blue flowers glow at dusk, but Linnaeus, the Swedish botanist, included chicory in his flower clock because it closes midday.

Cichorium intybus.

How to grow

Succory, an old common name for chicory, stems from Latin for "run under." That's because chicory's taproot can grow 2 feet down and 2 inches across. If you're growing it for its roots, loosen soil to a depth of at least 18" and mix in lots of compost. Plant this perennial at the edge of your vegetable or herb plot where it won't be disturbed, perhaps near a trellis that will shade it from summer heat. While it's hardy in Zones 2 to 9, southern gardeners may struggle to grow it well.

Sow seeds ¼-inch deep in early spring, and thin the plants to about a foot apart. Plants usually flower in their second year. Some growers blanch the leaves — covering them with a newspaper or cloth — to reduce their bitterness.

Cultivars and related plants

If you don't want to dig a roadside plant, try 'Biondissima Trieste' or 'Spadona', traditional Italian cutting chicories ready to harvest in 50 days.

Once upon a time, radicchio was what you got if you cut back chicory and let it regrow in cooler weather. Today, you can buy radicchio cultivars, such as 'Red Verona' and 'Early Treviso' that blush prettily from the get-go. Northern gardeners plant them in the spring, while southerners start seeds in summer and harvest them in fall or winter.

Witloof chicory is a relative that produces a tight cone of pale leaves and usually goes by the name of Belgian endive. It's an outdoor-indoor crop (the hybrid 'Witloof Zoom' is a good cultivar). Sow seed in spring, then lop off the aboveground plant parts after the first frost and dig the roots. Store the roots in damp sand in a cold place for at least one month, then reset upright in moist, organically rich soil. Similar to mushrooms, endive needs to grow in the dark (with temperatures in the 50s and high humidity). If you don't have a dungeon, cover the roots with flowerpots in your basement.

Lore and usage

Chicory has endured an up-and-down reputation. Relished by the Romans and commended by such notable writers and poets as Virgil, Ovid, and Pliny (who mixed it with vinegar and rose oil for headaches), it has long been popular as a coffee substitute or additive. You find chicory coffee mostly in New Orleans and in upscale restaurants, where it's right at home with its trendy salad greens cousins, radicchio and endive. Chicory fans believe that adding the toasted, ground root to regular coffee creates a smoother taste. There's some scientific evidence that chicory is a mild sedative, so chicory-laced coffee also smoothes out the coffee drinker.

The azure flowers once hinted at chicory's value as an eyewash, at least in regions where most everyone had blue eyes. Early colonists carried its seeds from their homelands to North America, where it won praise primarily as livestock fodder. In a letter to George Washington, Thomas Jefferson wrote that it was "one of the greatest acquisitions a farmer can have." Today, state road crews sipping real coffee mow it down with nary a thought.

Chicory leaves not only look like a dandelion's (they're in the same family), but have a similar taste and health benefits. (Modern herbalists believe that the herb benefits the liver and may have heart benefits.) But while dandelion leaves are gathered in spring, you should collect chicory's in fall. Most people enjoy the bitter edge of fresh chicory greens, but if it isn't your cup of tea, cook them in several changes of water. They're too ethereal to freeze or dry. The flower petals are also edible, with a slightly bitter taste. Combined with whole cherry tomatoes and cubes of fresh mozzarella, they make a patriotic red-white-and-blue salad. And of course, don't pick the chicory growing by the roadside; who knows what pollutants it has inhaled.

Chives (Allium schoenoprasum)

Those who crave chives on their baked potatoes and bagels lop the flowers off as mercilessly as the Red Queen in Wonderland. But those round, fuzzy, purple-pink heads are one of our favorites for the spring garden. Plant lots and lots of chives because you'll want plenty of leaves and blossoms.

Chives are hardy perennials, closely related to onions and garlic. They grow from bulbs in clumps of grasslike, onion-scented hollow leaves, pointed at the tip and usually about a foot tall. In mid-spring, on stems roughly the same height, the plants produce pretty balls of tightly packed lavender blossoms, rather like clover flowers.

Allium schoenoprasum.

How to grow

If ever there were a beginner's herb, chives is it. (Or rather, *are* it. You'll note that it's always plural, like scissors and pants.) Chives are hardy in Zones 3 to 10, can take sun or partial shade, and grow in almost any soil that's not off the chart in pH. As with most plants, organically rich soil and good drainage suits them best.

Chives seeds need temperatures of 75 degrees Fahrenheit or less to sprout, and they take two to three weeks. Like most perennials, they're pretty sleepy the first season — dare only to take a snip or two. A better approach is to buy young plants or bulbs, or find a friend who will dig you a clump or two. Should you get more than one clump (6 to 10 bulbs each), set them 8 inches apart. And don't let grasslike weeds get near them, or you may not be able to separate the good guys from the bad guys.

Chives are similar to other grassy plants: Grazing makes them grow. You may hear that you shouldn't harvest all the leaves from a clump at once, but commercial harvesters do — just leave about 3 inches. Clumps need dividing every three or four years, so you'll have plenty to share with friends — or spread them around your own spread.

To bring chives indoors for a short-lived winter crop, dig a small clump (or divide a large one) three or four weeks before your first expected frost. Pot it up but leave it outdoors for a couple of months in a protected location to go dormant (the tops should die back). When you bring it in, the bulbs will think it's spring and send up shoots.

Cultivars and related plants

Although chives seem pretty perfect just the way they are, breeders have given us 'Forescate', which has more intensely rosy flowers, and 'Sterile' (trademarked as Profusion Chives), which has more flowers and is seedless. (As a rule, cultivars easily cross-pollinate, so you can't plant them close together if you want to collect seed and grow the same plant next year.)

Garlic, or Chinese, chives, *Allium tuberosum,* have solid, flatter leaves and star-shaped, sweet-scented white flowers that bloom in late summer or fall; taller than common chives, they can reach 2 feet. Garlic chives can be invasive — every seed the flowers produce seems to sprout. They're good with the same foods as regular chives, but use them with a lighter hand the first time around because they have a zingier, hotter flavor.

Lore and usage

Nicholas Culpeper believed that only a professional "alchymist" could prepare chives safely. Raw leaves, he wrote, emit "vapours to the brain, causing troublesome sleep and spoiling the eyesight." On a more positive note, chives are a folk remedy for whooping cough (taken in a bread-and-butter sandwich). Today, some herbalists feel that chives can help lower blood pressure and even help prevent cancer. If nothing else, they're full of vitamins A and C. And they taste great. Even the flowers are edible. Always break up the chive blossom into individual florets; the flower head can pack the same wallop as an entire bulb of raw garlic.

Use chives fresh. The freezer will turn them to mush, and they don't dry well either. (Commercial chives are freeze-dried.) Culinary possibilities include omelets and other egg dishes, cooked vegetables of all kinds, butter, and soft cheeses. Make them a last-minute addition to sauces and soups.

Cilantro or coriander (Coriandrum sativum)

Cilantro/coriander leads a double life, technically speaking, as both an herb and a spice. Cilantro leaves taste musky, whereas coriander seeds taste lemony. The leaves have a starring role in Asian and Latin American cookery, whereas the seeds are key ingredients in Middle Eastern staples, such as curry.

Cilantro is an annual herb with divided leaves that look very much like flat-leafed parsley (appropriately, Chinese parsley is one of its other monikers). Its bottom leaves are rounded, whereas those near the top are smaller and ferny. Plants grow to about 20 inches tall — 8 inches wide — and bear flat clusters of small white or pale purple flowers followed by round, beige fruits.

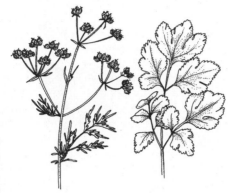

Coriandrum sativum.

How to grow

Cilantro wants only what you give all your favorite plants: full sun (or light shade in very hot regions) and soil full of organic amendments that drains readily. After spring's last frost date, sow seeds directly in the garden. After they sprout in about two weeks, thin seedlings to 10 inches apart. If you have the space (and the need), sow successive crops every three weeks into summer. Because cilantro bolts in heat, Southerners usually plant seeds in fall and give their plants afternoon shade. Cilantro is day-length sensitive, so plants started in spring will go to flower and seed quickly, whereas those planted after the middle of July will remain in leaf much longer.

Cilantro won't ruin the looks of your ornamental bed, but it's no raving beauty. Most people relegate it to the herb or vegetable patch where they can plant as many as they want to consume. Harvest plants for leaves when they're about 6 inches tall.

Cultivars and related plants

If you're growing this herb for foliage, look for strains called long-standing or Chinese, and cultivars such as 'Leisure', 'Santo', or 'Slo-Bolt'.

Vietnamese coriander *(Polygonum odoratum)* is an unrelated perennial with the same taste as coriander, but to keep it going for next season you need to overwinter it indoors. Southern and southwestern gardeners may succeed with another unrelated plant, Mexican or Cuban coriander *(Eryngium foetidum)*. From Central America, it's related to the spiky ornamentals called sea hollies, and one of its common names is thorny coriander.

Lore and usage

Cilantro comes from the Mediterranean. Its seed, known as coriander, has been toted around the world for some 5,000 years. It has appeared in Egyptian tombs, in the Old Testament, and in *The Thousand and One Nights,* where it played the role of an aphrodisiac. Pliny described its medical use for such appalling conditions as spreading sores, diseased testes, carbuncles, and "fluxes of the eyes, too, if women's milk be added."

The green herb seems "new" to many Americans who are just discovering ethnic cuisine. Today you can find it next to its kin, parsley, in many groceries, although the flavor still isn't universally adored. The ancient Greeks were among its detractors, comparing its aroma to that of a bed bug. Coriander's name stems from *koris,* the Greek word for bug.

A must in dishes such as guacamole, salsa, and gazpacho, cilantro also enhances sauces for fish, chicken, and lamb, and is good tossed into a green salad. (It adds needed zip if you're trying to cut down on dressing.) Growing your own cilantro also lets you use the root, which offers a crunchy variation on the flavor of the foliage. The flowers can be used in the same way as the leaves; try stuffing a chicken with a handful of flowers and cook in a covered clay baking dish — a great fall meal.

Although curry is the destination of much coriander seed, the sweet citrusy tang adds a lively note to otherwise rather tame vegetables, such as cauliflower, potatoes, parsnips, and other root vegetables. Try it in rice and pasta dishes, baked in fruits, or in soups and stews.

Clary sage *(Salvia sclarea)*

Clary sage (also know as clary) is a biennial and resembles common sage and other members of the mint family with its square stems and spikes of two-lipped flowers, which are either pale lavender-blue or white. Even while still in bud in early summer, the flowers are made showy by surrounding bracts of white, lavender, or pink. Growing 2 to 3 feet tall, clary sage bears leaves shaped like elongated hearts, fuzzy, wrinkled, and up to 9 inches long. The aroma is variously described as musky, balsam, fruity, and disgusting.

Salvia sclarea.

How to grow

The last thing you want to do for clary sage is fuss over it. Give it average soil with very good drainage and full sun. It tolerates both drought and a wide pH range.

Clary sage is easy to start from seed, indoors or out. Space seedlings 10 inches apart in the garden. After the first killing frost, cut back the plant tops. Northern gardeners should mulch plants to prevent frost heaving. (It is hardy in Zones 5 to 9.) Plants may self-sow after they bloom in their second year, but collect a few seeds, just in case.

Many people think clary is far prettier than common sage. Set it in the middle of an ornamental bed and its big, textured leaves will turn heads at the same time that its long-lasting flower spikes draw legions of butterflies and bees.

Cultivars and related plants

Turkestan clary *(Salvia sclarea* var. *turkestanica)* is sometimes described as a naturally occurring variety, but it's also sold as a cultivar of clary sage and labeled *S. sclarea* 'Turkestanica'. Its stems are taller and pinker than the species, and its flowers are white specked with pink. You can also choose a white cultivar, 'Alba'.

Another aromatic salvia sometimes used the same ways as clary sage is meadow clary, *S. pratensis.* It typically has violet flowers, although they can be white or pink. Cultivars bloom in rosy-red, deep blue, and dark purple.

Lore and usage

Before the advent of the Breathalyzer, inebriation was measured more subjectively. Clary sage used to be a substitute for hops in beer, but also served to make intoxicating drinks more bitter and potent, "fit to please drunkards, who thereby, according to their several dispositions, become either dead drunke, or foolish drunke, or madde drunke." Another writer described the effect as "insane exhilaration." The herb was added to Rhine wine along with elder flowers, which changed the flavor to that of muscatel without benefit of Muscat grapes.

Clary sage's common name derives from "clear eye." Its seeds, when wet, ooze a mucilage, and a seed put in the eye was said to extract any foreign matter — at a cost, we would think, of even greater discomfort. Today, clary sage has fallen by the way as a mainstream herbal medicine, but perfume-makers continue to use it as a fixative to keep other odors on track, and aromatherapists claim that its scent alone can induce euphoria — that old insane exhilaration.

Some herbalists still use clary to treat for gas and indigestion, but it is not recommended as a culinary herb.

Comfrey (Symphytum officinale)

Opinions are mixed on the eye-appeal of this herb, a kin of borage. Erect and brawny, it rises to at least 4 feet tall and is equally wide, is floppy in wind and rain, and bears 10-inch lower leaves covered in itch-producing hairs. The stems have pronounced "wings." Even those left cold by comfrey's charms thaw a bit when it blooms — from late spring to early summer, occasionally much longer. Its forked tassels of bell-shaped flowers in blue-violet, pink, or pale yellow are hard to resist.

How to grow

Consider long where you put comfrey, because it's not only large but made quite permanent by a taproot that can burrow as deep as 6 feet. Comfrey doesn't produce many seeds, so most gardeners start it from divisions or root cuttings. With that long root, it needs soil that's loose, deep, and rich with organic matter. Hardy in Zones 4 to 9, comfrey can grow in partial shade, but full sun makes the stem stronger and less apt to fall over on blustery days.

Cultivars and related plants

Common comfrey has a red-flowered form, 'Rubrum'. There are 34 other species in this genus, all smaller than common comfrey, and most are hardy through Zone 4. One is Caucasian comfrey *(S. caucasicum)*, which has bright blue flowers. Foot-high 'Goldsmith' has leaves edged in gold. Russian comfrey *(S. x uplandicum)* grows 3 to 4 feet tall and has a cultivar with lavender flowers and white-edged leaves, 'Variegatum'.

Lore and usage

You may know of the 1957 case of Sam Sheppard, the Cleveland physician found guilty of murdering his wife and the inspiration for the film, *The Fugitive*. He steadfastly maintained his innocence, and his claim is, well, a lot like that of comfrey.

For more than 2,000 years, comfrey, or knitbone, had a reputation as a healer of wounds and broken bones (because its parts were so mucilaginous and sticky). The 17th-century herbalist Nicholas Culpeper claimed that it was so powerful a knitter of broken bones that "if they be boiled with dissevered pieces of flesh in a pot, it will join them together again." It was used internally as well, for a host of ailments.

More recently, we've learned that comfrey contains allantoin, a substance that causes cells to multiply — which should be good in healing wounds and knitting bones. But it also contains pyrrolizidine alkaloids, or PAs, and beginning in the late 1970s, researchers began to connect PA with a disease that causes major blood vessels from the liver to clot.

Ever since, most herbalists advise never to use comfrey internally. Anyone with liver problems and pregnant and nursing women shouldn't use it externally, either. Others can use it as a compress or poultice for about any insult to the body's outer covering, from bruises to cuts and scrapes. Many herbalists recommend a comfrey infusion to soothe hemorrhoids.

Costmary (Tanacetum [Chrysanthemum] balsamita)

A perennial native to Europe and central Asia, costmary grows 3 feet tall, is woody at its base, and forms mats with its rhizomes. Silvery hairs cover the serrated leaves. The leaves at the bottom of the plant are up to a foot long, those toward the top rarely half that. The negligible yellow ray flowers bloom in late summer or early fall, and not at all in partial shade. The species name advertises costmary's redolent scent; appropriately, balsam herb was another of its common names.

Tanacetum balsamita.

How to grow

Costmary is hardy from Zone 5 to Zone 11. Buy small plants or start from divisions, setting them out in spring in the North, early fall in the South. Give costmary plenty of space — 18 inches is a bare minimum. Plants need only average soil as long as it drains well; grow in partial shade or sun. Locate costmary where it can show off its handsome foliage, perhaps among long-blooming annuals.

Cultivars and related plants

Two other herbs, feverfew and tansy, were shuffled into the *Tanacetum* genus along with costmary. You find out more about them elsewhere in this section. All these plants have daisylike flowers and scented foliage. The best known is probably the painted daisy *(T. coccineum).* Also called pyrethrum (it's the basis of the well-known organic insecticide), it has both single and double forms in red, pink, and white.

Lore and usage

Over time, costmary has been used for a plethora of quaint problems, including "quotidien ague, catarrhs, and rheumes," as well as consumption and vermin. One recipe for a skin ointment called for boiling costmary with a snake's tongue in olive oil, then mixing it with wax, resin, and turpentine.

Poor costmary has lost much of its élan since colonial times, and like many of the chrysanthemum clan, it has had to endure a change of name to *Tanacetum* by picky botanists. A native of Asia, its common name comes from the word *costus,* a term meaning "from the orient." Some English gardeners have called it mace, but it's not related to the spice you buy under that name, which comes from the red covering of nutmeg seeds.

Other common names are more telling: Alecost, because it was used to flavor ale, and Bible leaf, because American colonists used it as a place marker in the Good Book. The "mary" in its name linked it to the Virgin Mary, but its use went beyond symbolism. Churchgoers sniffed or nibbled it to revive themselves during long, dull services.

Some people compare the smell and taste of costmary to wintergreen — minty, cool, and powerful. Use its leaves in cooking as you would other mints, but with a lighter hand. Its camphor scent makes it a pleasant addition to a bath or facial steam.

Dill (Anethum graveolens)

Dill is an annual from the Black Sea and Mediterranean regions. It looks a lot like its cousin fennel, except that it gets only 2 to 3 feet tall. Plants have a single, hollow stalk, and the feathery leaves divide into hair-thin, blue-green leaflets. The tiny yellow flowers appear in 6-inch compound clusters that look like exploding fireworks. That's appropriate, because the pods, filled with ribbed, aromatic seeds, explode readily when ripe.

How to grow

Like the rest of the carrot clan, dill doesn't like to be transplanted. Direct-sow its seeds, just barely covered, as soon as you can work the ground in spring, preferably in full sun and light, in sandy soil of average fertility. When seedlings are about 2 inches tall, thin them to 8 to 10 inches apart. Sow more seed every three or four weeks to keep the dillweed coming.

Protect dill from winds, or stake plants to keep them from snapping. You can cut about one-fifth of a plant's foliage as soon as the leaves are big enough to use. The foliage will brown soon after the plant flowers (in hot weather, dill bolts quickly). Collect seeds as soon as they darken.

Dill is a graceful foil for plants with dense foliage, and it's a friendly companion for cabbage. It's a favorite food for the larvae of the swallowtail butterfly. Plant enough dill so you and butterflies-in-waiting can both have your share.

Cultivars and related plants

For more thrills from dill, pick cultivars bred for special uses. 'Bouquet', a standard cultivar, produces large seeds early in the season. 'Dukat' is slow to bolt so it offers more dill foliage, especially where summers are hot. 'Fernleaf', winner of the All-America Selections award, is also slow to bolt. Bushy and only 18 inches tall, it's perfect for a flower bed or container.

Lore and usage

Dill — its common name comes from a Norse word meaning "to lull to sleep" — is a friend to the digestive system from stem (bad breath) to stern (gas). Across time and cultures, from the Egyptians some 3,000 years ago, to the Chinese 1,000 years ago, and into modern times, dill has come to the rescue as "a gallant expeller of wind" in the words of Nicholas Culpeper.

Another traditional use of dill was in "gripe water," a drink cherished by new fathers whose turn it was to tend the crying baby. (One suspects that the gin added to gripe water was more efficacious than the dill.) Today, of course, most of us know dill for flavoring the pickles that buddy up with burgers and decorate deli platters.

Dill, which is packed with vitamin C, calcium, magnesium, iron, and potassium, is especially good on salmon and is a regular addition to sour cream. Toss it into your food at the last minute because heat, like drying, steals its zip. The opposite is true of the tangy seeds; simmer them in soups, stews, and sauces to your heart's content. The flowers are great tossed in salads, salad dressings, or sauces.

Elecampane (Inula helenium)

Elecampane is an imposing perennial when it reaches its full height of 6 feet. Its bright yellow, 3- to 4-inch daisylike flowers have narrow petals, and while few at a time, they keep coming from late spring until frost. The leaves are rough on top with soft fuzz on the underside.

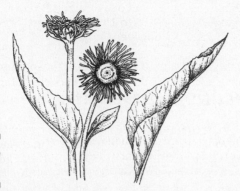

Inula helenium.

How to grow

Native to Europe and western Asia, elecampane is at home in damp, partly shady places and is hardy in Zones 3 to 9. It is most easily propagated from 2-inch pieces of root harvested in the fall of the plant's second year. Each piece of root should have a bud, or eye. Plant the pieces in containers of damp sand and overwinter them in a cool room, about 50 degrees Fahrenheit; set the sprouted roots out in spring (once the danger of frost has passed) in soil that is rich in organic matter, moist, and well-draining.

Space plants at least 2 feet apart. After that, you need do little more than make sure the soil doesn't dry out. Enjoy it in your garden much as you would sunflowers, at the back of an informal border, among wildflowers, or to protect vegetables from sun and wind.

Cultivars and related plants

Showy elecampane *(Inula magnifica)* can get even taller than elecampane, and most gardeners find it more attractive. The 6-inch flowers have an orange tinge to their central disks and bloom in clusters. Growing to 2 feet or less are swordleaf inula *(I. ensifolia)*, Himalayan elecampane *(I. royaleana)*, with spidery orange-yellow flowers, and Caucasian elecampane *(I. orientalis)*, which has fuzzy buds and wavy outer petals.

Lore and usage

Both the genus and species names of elecampane come from the same root word, which legend links to Helen of Troy. She was supposedly clutching fistfuls of elecampane — rather than a make-up bag for her ship-launching face — when Paris whisked her away from Sparta.

We don't know which of elecampane's reputed virtues inspired Helen's behavior. Common names such as horseheal attest to its use by veterinarians. But elecampane was most revered for curing respiratory system ailments. "It amendeth the cough . . . ceaseth the hard fetching of breath," gardener Thomas Hill wrote in 1577. The herb was also popular in candy, consumed not so much as a treat, but sucked for asthma symptoms and "when travelling by a river . . . against poisonous exhalations and bad air." Modern research supports some of elecampane's longtime uses for respiratory distress — for asthma, laryngitis, and as an expectorant.

Fennel (Foeniculum vulgare)

A non-gardening friend visiting coauthor Kathy's weekend escape in Virginia was so enchanted by this tropical-looking giant, waving in the wind in an old farm field, that he dug some up to grace his patio. Thread-thin, blue-green foliage on a 6- to 8-foot plant does make an arresting site, although in Virginia, California, and other warm areas, fennel self-seeds and is a pestiferous weed. Like closely related dill, it has tiny yellow flowers in a flat umbrella, followed by the famous ribbed seeds.

How to grow

Fennel is hardy in Zones 6 to 9; northern gardeners grow it as an annual. Other than sun and humus-rich soil with good drainage, it needs little attention. Start it from seed where you want it to grow, ideally when the soil is around 60 degrees Fahrenheit, and thin seedlings to at least a foot apart. Like other carrot relatives, fennel may attract swallowtail butterfly larvae, but on a plant this big, there's plenty for everyone.

Cultivars and related plants

Foeniculum vulgare is usually divided into two varieties, var. *dulce* and var. *azoricum,* and the horticultural community is hotly divided about which scientific name to attach to which plant. This may be a rare case where you're better off going with a common name. Grow common or sweet fennel if you want primarily foliage and seeds. If you want to eat fennel bulbs as a vegetable, you want finocchio, or Florence fennel, which is an annual or biennial. The "bulb" is actually the swollen base of the stem. Its leaves can be used in the same way as those of common fennel. The same goes for bronze fennel, *F. vulgare* 'Purpureum', a cultivar of sweet fennel often grown as an ornamental for its bronzy-red foliage.

Lore and usage

Coauthor Karan, who is much less tolerant of snakes than Kathy, has considered banishing fennel from her garden. It may ward off evil spirits, but according to the ancients, snakes rub against it to sharpen their eyesight — the better to spot gardeners bearing hoes. On the other hand, it was also reputed to heal snakebites.

This sweet-tangy perennial also was recommended "to helpeth digest the crude qualitie of fish and other viscous meats," and was used in drinks "for those that are grown fat, to abate their unwieldiness and cause them to grow more gaunt and lank."

You can take your pick of explanations for why the Puritans called fennel fruits "meeting seeds" and chewed them at church: A) to keep them awake, B) to dull their appetites, or C) to cover the scent of whiskey. (***Note:*** Recent research shows that fennel may actually stimulate the appetite.)

If anise speaks too loudly of licorice for you, try fennel, which is sweeter and lighter. The stalks hold up better than leaves in cooked dishes. The seeds are popular in cabbage, sauerkraut, and potatoes, and the flowers are delightful in salads or sorbets. Fennel is still recommended for "crude" or oily fish. Cosmetically, fennel helps soften skin and appears frequently in recipes for skin creams and lotions.

Fenugreek (Trigonella foenum-graecum)

Fenugreek is a member of the bean family, but with its three-part leaves, it more closely resembles clover. It grows up to 2 feet tall. In midsummer, this annual plant begins producing fragrant, off-white flowers that can keep reappearing for several months. The seedpods look a lot like those of green beans, but they point up instead of drooping down.

How to grow

A Mediterranean native, fenugreek asks only for a sunny spot and well-drained, organically rich soil. Sow seeds in spring after the soil has warmed (in cold, wet soil, seedlings are likely to rot). Thin seedlings to 4 inches apart. Seeds ripen about four months after germination.

Lore and usage

You have to sink pretty low to adulterate hay, but this is fenugreek's claim to fame. Its species name comes from a term meaning "Greek hay," because its maple flavor and scent were used to disguise mold. Earlier, the Egyptians used fenugreek in the mummification process, and other cultures burned it in religious rites. In the Middle Ages it was used to treat liver and kidney diseases, and in the 19th century, it was a common ingredient in patent medicines. Today, it pops up as an ingredient in artificial maple flavoring, and it may play a valuable role in treating diabetes.

Fenugreek is popular in African, Middle Eastern, and East Indian dishes. Yet cooking with this herb can be a challenge. It walks a fine line between a bitter, celery-like flavor and the sweetness of maple. Experiment, a bit at a time, with using the ground seeds to season meats and poultry, and try it in chutneys, curries, and other stews. You can also sprout the seeds for salads.

Feverfew (Tanacetum parthenium)

Feverfew, a perennial native to southeast Europe and the Caucasus, looks a bit like chamomile. Both have divided leaves and daisylike flowers, but the leaves of chamomile are extremely narrow and fine, while the individual leaflets of feverfew are rounded, with feathery edges. The central cone of the feverfew flower is flat, while that of chamomile is a raised cone.

Woody at the base, feverfew at first forms a tidy mound, then sprawls when flowers begin blooming. It usually grows to about 2 feet tall and tends to be somewhat short-lived.

How to grow

Feverfew's original habitat is scrubby and rocky, and today it has made itself at home in English hedgerows and along U.S. roadsides and forest margins. In other words, you won't have to baby it in your garden. Give it full sun or partial shade and ordinary soil that drains readily, and it will be happy. It's hardy in Zones 5 to 9.

In mild areas, you can sow feverfew seeds directly in the garden. In the North, start them indoors in March for planting out after the last-frost date. Once you grow feverfew, it's likely to self-seed. If not, you can propagate new plants by division or taking cuttings. Space plants about a foot apart.

Bees dislike feverfew, so don't plant it among vegetables or other plants that need pollinating. The plant is handsome near the front of an ornamental border if you keep it deadheaded.

Cultivars and related plants

Scientists have made great sport of the chrysanthemums, renaming them in spite of public outcry. Those that have been shuffled into *Tanacetum* with feverfew include costmary, tansy, and the painted daisy.

You can buy feverfew cultivars with more golden foliage ('Aureum'), many with double flowers ('Snowball', 'White Pompon', 'White Stars'), and dwarf types suitable for rock gardens or smaller containers ('Golden Moss', 'Santana', and 'Silver Ball').

Lore and usage

This daisy-flowered perennial is a good example of the cyclical whims of fashion. Feverfew once was used to reduce fevers, as its common name suggests; to treat toothaches, vertigo, kidney stones, and opium overdoses; and to act as a remedy for those "such as be melancholike, sad, pensive and without speech." The species name *parthenium* stems from the account by the Greek historian Plutarch that the herb had saved the life of a worker who fell from a great height while working on the Parthenon. Over time, however, feverfew's popularity waned until it was used only for problems relating to menstruation and pregnancy, if it was used at all.

A few herbalists, such as England's John Parkinson, continued to recommend it for headaches — Nicholas Culpeper espoused a rather unorthodox approach of bruising the leaves and applying them to the crown of the head. Then in the late 1970s, its folk use for migraines was brought to the attention of English researchers, and a series of ever-more-detailed clinical trials substantiated its effectiveness.

The camphorlike taste of feverfew, while pleasant, is not a flavor you necessarily want in your salad dressing. If you want to try feverfew to prevent migraines, chew three or four of the leaflets daily.

Keep in mind that there are no good studies on the effects of long-term use. Feverfew leaves cause mouth sores in a few people, and you shouldn't experiment with them if you're pregnant.

The leaves lose their medicinal punch when dried; freeze them instead.

Flax (Linum usitatissimum)

Flax is a wispy annual, 18 inches tall with an erect stem bearing narrow 1-inch leaves. The stem branches near the top, holding a five-petal, blue flower at the end of each branch. The flowers are only ½ inch across but numerous enough to create a star-spangled effect above these graceful plants. Flax begins blooming in midsummer, and keeps it up for more than two months. Seeds develop in round, brown capsules.

How to grow

Flax can be fussy about soil. It can't be too sandy, too heavy, too rich, or too lean, and of course, it must drain well. Adding plenty of organic matter to whatever nature gave you should give it what it needs (except sun).

You can start flax from seed in either spring or fall in warm-weather regions. Weed the bed well, because flax's shallow roots make cultivation difficult. Thin seedlings to 4 inches apart.

Cultivars and related plants

Linum usitatissimum 'Regina' was bred especially for weavers. 'Omega' is a cultivar grown for its seeds, which contain higher amounts of omega-3 oil, a compound that helps prevent cardiovascular disease. *L. perenne* is a perennial look-alike with uses similar to common flax's. Other flax for the ornamental garden include the perennials *L. flavum,* with yellow flowers, and *L. narbonense,* with blue flowers; and an annual, *L. grandiflorum,* which has rosy pink flowers.

Lore and usage

Throughout much of history, flax, or linseed, has been something of a one-man band.

The Egyptians wrapped their mummies in cloth woven of its fibers. Fishnets, bowstrings, sheets, purses, and bandages were just a few of its destinations. "[I]n what production of the Earth are there greater marvels to us than this?" the Roman scholar Pliny asked. It was popular for ship rigging, until the Tudors concluded that *Cannabis sativum* yielded stronger rope. There's no report on whether it got both sails and sailors higher.

A constituent of linoleum, linseed oil is a drying agent in oil paints, varnishes, and inks. The seeds can be used whole or ground into a flour and used in place of eggs as a thickener. Like other mucilaginous herbs, they can soothe the digestive tract and normalize either constipation or diarrhea.

If, like us, you just like its sky-blue flowers, they have lore of their own, offering protection from sorcery. The Bohemians believed that 7-year-olds who danced in a field of flax would become beautiful people. (Perhaps you know a second-grade teacher who could use a flax bouquet.)

Be sure that flax seeds are brown before you use them, because unripe seeds are toxic. Try sprouting the seeds for salads, or sprinkle them on cereal to add a nutty flavor. Crushed seeds are good in bread and are used in tea to treat constipation, as are other fiber laxatives; follow your cup of linseed tea with a big glass of water.

Garlic (Allium sativum)

Some lilies may be too regal to admit it, but garlic is family, along with chives, leeks, onions, and shallots. Garlic is unexciting in the garden, but valuable when harvested. The useful part — the compound bulb that is divided into cloves — is hidden underground. The gray-green, bladelike leaves are solid and grow 1 to 2 feet tall; the tiny white or pinkish flowers, which pop out of a pointed, papery pouch in rounded clusters, are ho-hum even by allium standards, but tasty. Many garlics developed for eating don't bloom at all.

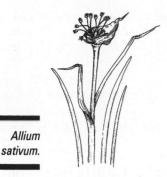

Allium sativum.

How to grow

This underground power pack needs a deeply worked bed of fluffy, generously amended soil that both retains moisture and drains well. Slightly acidic soil is best, as is full sun. Get rid of the weeds before you plant bulbs, because you'll have a hard time separating grass blades from garlic blades.

Don't be tempted to plant supermarket garlic. Buy cloves intended for planting from a garden center, online, or from a mail-order supplier. Plant them in fall, unpeeled, pointed end up, 2 inches deep and 5 inches apart. Side-dress the rows with compost and mulch to keep weeds at bay; mulch again once the ground is frozen. When growth begins in spring, pull the mulch back. Clip off any flower stalks that appear so that the plant's energy goes to the bulb.

Dig garlic when the plants' leaves begin to turn brown — and don't forget to save the biggest, outer cloves for replanting.

Cultivars and related plants

As with any popular plant, there are a lot of options with garlic (and mail-order and online companies that sell nothing else). Broadly, they're divided into softnecks and hardnecks. The easiest to grow are the softneck type known as artichoke garlics (try 'California Early', 'California Late', 'Inchelium Red', or 'Mudci').

Many cooks prefer a hardneck type called rocambole, but it doesn't store as well as the softnecks do. Good cultivars are 'Purple Rocambole', 'Spanish Roja', 'German Red', and 'Killarney Red'. Elephant garlic is a different species, *A. ampeloprasum,* and is more closely related to the leek. It has larger bulbs and milder flavor than that of garlic but doesn't overwinter in the North.

Lore and usage

Whether you love to cook French, Mexican, Asian, or Italian dishes; can't resist a good yarn about gods or monsters; or want to prevent aging or heart disease; you need more garlic in your life.

Many of the stories surrounding garlic associate it with evil, or at least an evil odor. According to an Islamic legend, garlic sprung up where Satan's left foot trod as he left the desecrated Garden of Eden. Wearing it in foot and horse races was said to keep competitors behind you. Garlic breath has been a mark of lower classes. But, hey, it saved Ulysses from being turned into a pig, and we all know we should string some around our necks when vampires are in the neighborhood.

In the past, garlic was used to treat such dread ailments as leprosy, smallpox, and anthrax in cattle. But unlike many herbs, its medicinal reputation may have increased in the scientific age. Among many potential health applications of garlic — one recent book suggests using it to treat 33 conditions, from allergies to yeast infections — the best-documented use is prevention and treatment of cardiovascular disorders, such as high blood pressure, hardening of the arteries, and stroke. It appears to work by preventing blood coagulation.

Ginger (Zingiber officinale)

Accept no substitutes! When a recipe calls for fresh ginger root, you won't find the same mingling of sweet, spicy, and hot in a bottle. You might guess ginger's tropical origins from its narrow, lance-shaped leaves, up to a foot long in a grass-like clump. Compared to other members of the genus, the blooms are rather unexciting green cones with tiny, dark red flowers. The leaves and flowers both have a ginger scent, however. You're probably familiar with the knobby mature root, which has a tan skin covering a cream-colored and crunchy interior.

Zingiber officinale.

How to grow

You can buy a plant or the root from a nursery, or buy a root (called a hand because of the way it branches) from the grocery store. Make sure it's plump and smooth, not dry and wrinkled, and that it has several eyes like those you see on potatoes. You may have better luck with one of the green roots sold in Asian markets.

Whether in the ground or in a container, ginger needs loose, organically rich soil, warmth, and humidity. Set the hand 2 inches deep (about 1 foot apart, outdoors), keep the soil moist, and feed your plant monthly with compost tea. In eight to ten months, you can harvest the root. Save a plump piece to start your next crop.

Cultivars and related plants

The foliage and flower of ginger are both lightly fragrant, but if it's strong aroma you want, try white butterfly ginger *(Hedychium coronarium),* the plant used in Hawaii for leis.

Lore and usage

A native of tropical Asia, this herb appeared in Chinese herbals as long as 5,000 years ago. Chinese sailors discovered its most popular medicinal use, preventing seasickness. Cooks of that country sometimes use it with a heavy hand in seafood dishes in the belief that it prevents shellfish poisoning.

The Greeks ate it tucked in bread to help them digest heavy meals, thus paving the way for gingerbread. In the Middle Ages, fair maidens gave the spicy breads to knights preparing for tournaments.

Today ginger is grown commercially in Jamaica, as well as in India, Africa, and China. Fresh ginger is a must for stir-fries and marinades (especially for salmon and swordfish), and is good in dressings for cold, cooked vegetables. Try it grated on steamed carrots or summer squash. If you need to keep it longer than three weeks, peel and slice it into a bit of sherry, and store in the refrigerator. The sherry will add its own sweet tang to sauces and soups.

Ginger works so well against motion sickness that some cruise ships now make it available for passengers. It also seems to ease symptoms of morning sickness, and most herbalists consider it safe to use in pregnancy if you don't have a history of miscarriage.

Horehound (Ballota [Marrubium] vulgare)

The British once spelled the common name hoarhound, referring to the herb's woolly looking stems and leaves. Its musky fragrance, which disappears with drying, may remind you of an artemisia.

In other respects, this perennial bears many mint family hallmarks, such as square stems and two-lipped flowers. The white blooms, which appear in whorls along the stem in mid- to late summer, are followed by capsules containing four barbed seeds. Bushy and up to 2 feet tall, horehound is hardy in Zones 4 to 9.

How to grow

If you see a plant described as tolerating a wide range of conditions, look out, because it can take over like neighbors who've heard about your new swimming pool. That's horehound. It grows in poor soil without much extra water, and in sun or partial shade. Plant the seeds with a light covering of soil in spring or fall; thin seedlings to 12 or 18 inches apart. Don't expect your plants to flower until their second year. You can also start new plants from division, but more likely, you'll need to weed out volunteers.

Cultivars and related plants

No cultivars of this aggressive plant exist, but it does have an even more aggressive distant cousin: black horehound, *Ballota nigra.* You're unlikely to find it for sale or even in gardens due to its "very unpleasant smell." Also called black stinking horehound, even cattle refuse to eat it.

Lore and usage

This herb's common name comes from the ancient Greeks, who called it "the seed of Horus" (the Egyptian god of light) and espoused its use for fending off rabies from a dog bite. Also used (no doubt disastrously) as a poison antidote, horehound was also recommended for intestinal worms and was soaked in fresh milk to repel flies. Otherwise, horehound has been used with amazing consistency for coughs and colds, having been recognized as an effective expectorant for more than 2,000 years.

Then in 1989 the U.S. Food and Drug Administration caused a huge flap among herbalists — even the most conservative — by decreeing that while horehound is safe, it doesn't work very well as a cough medicine. Buy or make some horehound candy the next time you're wheezing and hacking, make a tea with its leaves and flowers, and put it to the test.

Most people disguise the bitter flavor with sugar or honey, and possibly some lemon. Don't consume too much, because this herb is also a laxative.

Horseradish (Armoracia rusticana)

The lower leaves of horseradish, a perennial hardy in Zones 3 to 9, are more than a foot long with wavy edges. As the plant reaches its mature height of 3 feet or more, the leaves become smaller and more lance-shaped. Each tiny white flower, borne in clusters, has four petals. The roots can extend 2 feet into the soil.

Armoracia rusticana.

How to grow

If you want good-sized roots, make sure your soil is rich with organic matter, deeply dug, and well-draining so that the fleshy taproot can grow without rotting. The root has brittle side-shoots, and any pieces left in the ground are likely to sprout. For that reason, you may want to consider planting it in a container sunk into the ground.

Start horseradish from roots in spring or fall, spaced at least a foot apart in full sun. If your growing season is shorter than 150 days, plant in fall or wait until the second year to harvest the root. Take cuttings from your harvested root and replant them for a new crop.

Cultivars and related plants

There are two cultivars: 'Big Top', a large-leafed variety, and 'Variegata', with variegated leaves. If you like Japanese food, you may have noticed the green paste that comes with paper-thin ginger when you order sushi. This is wasabi *(Wasabia japonica),* an even hotter relative of horseradish. You can buy wasabi ready-made, as a powder to be mixed with water, or fresh in Asian groceries.

Lore and usage

Beginning in the Middle Ages, this eastern European member of the mustard family was used widely to cure worms in children and applied as a plaster for "sciatica, gout, joint-ache or hard swellings of the spleen and liver. It doth wonderfully help them all," Nicholas Culpeper gushed.

But as a condiment, horseradish was popular only in northern Europe, not the British Isles. As late as the mid-17th century, English herbalist John Parkinson dismissed the herb as too coarse for refined tastes and delicate constitutions. In fact, the "horse" in its name meant "coarse."

The English and French came around, of course. In today's kitchens, horseradish's use is generally limited to slapping on roast beef sandwiches and hot dogs, although spring leaves can be eaten like spinach. Modern herbalists recommend it for blowing open clogged sinuses.

Store harvested roots in a perforated bag in the refrigerator. We like to add a dab in mayonnaise-based salads, such as potato salad, and chicken, tuna, and ham salad for sandwiches. Try a pinch in a cream-based soup, sauce for vegetables, or spreads for bread. By tradition, horseradish is the "bitter herb" at the Passover Seder (also delicious with matzo and gefilte fish).

Hyssop (Hyssopus officinalis)

A native of Europe and Asia, hyssop grows up to 2 feet tall and 3 feet wide and bears 6-inch spikes of intense blue-violet flowers from midsummer to early fall. The flowers are not only brighter but also larger than those of anise hyssop, up to ½ inch across with two upper lips and three lower lips. The leaves differ from the typical mint in being smooth and lance-shaped.

Hyssopus officinalis.

How to grow

Hyssop needs plenty of sun to keep it from becoming leggy. Otherwise, it needs only light, well-drained soil, and a bit of deadheading and pruning now and then to stimulate growth and keep it tidy. You can start it from seed, planted a week or two before the first frost date, or from cuttings or root divisions. Attractive to butterflies and hummingbirds as well as bees, it's hardy in Zones 5 to 9.

Cultivars and related plants

Need a break from blue? Look for *Hyssopus officinalis* var. *alba* for white flowers, var. *roseus* for pink. There are also strains selected for being more compact in size. A perennial called hedge hyssop *(Gratiola officinalis)* is planted for historical interest, but it should never be used as a home remedy.

Lore and usage

Confusing hyssop with anise hyssop is easy. Both have spikes of purplish flowers, are members of the mint family, and are irresistible to bees. But there are more differences than similarities. (Hey, we warned you about common names.)

Hyssop is a shrubby evergreen that, instead of smelling like tasty anise, smells like something you might use to clean the bathroom floor. The fragrance is pleasant enough but clearly medicinal, although the plant once was used as a potherb. Hyssop was once used to clean holy places; the word hyssop stems from the Greek *azob,* meaning "holy herb."

In spite of its medicinal scent and taste, many cooks use hyssop in tomato sauces. It marries especially well with cranberries, other fruits, and stuffing. The flowers are less pungent, tasting more like quinine. When you have a cold, try inhaling hyssop in steam, or prepare it as tea or a gargle. For cleaning, add a strong hyssop infusion into a solution for scrubbing down the kitchen or bathroom floor.

Lady's bedstraw (Galium verum)

This delicate perennial lends an airy note to the garden, with thin leaves that climb the stem in whorls, and clusters of tiny yellow flowers from spring to late summer. It averages about 2½ feet tall, although it tends to sprawl instead of growing upright, especially in a partly shady location.

Galium verum.

How to grow

Start lady's bedstraw in spring, either from seed or by dividing an established clump. Space plants about 18 inches apart. Not particular about soil, the plants do well in sun or partial shade. The plants are hardy in Zones 4 to 8. Keep an eye open for slightly invasive behavior.

Cultivars and related plants

You might want to look to the entry for another member of the *Galium* genus, sweet woodruff. A third *Galium*, cleavers *(G. aparine)*, is an annual that also answers to the name goosegrass. It has bristly leaves and a long-standing reputation among herbalists for curing skin problems.

Lore and usage

Once used by both rich and poor for stuffing mattresses, *Galium verum* is sometimes called Our Lady's bedstraw, an allusion to the legend that the Virgin Mary used it to line the manger in Bethlehem. Another name, maid's hair, came from the little yellow flowers that reminded some people of peroxided tresses. The genus name has its root in *gala,* the Greek word for milk, because the herb once was used to curdle milk and give the resulting cheese a yellow tint.

Medicinally, lady's bedstraw is linked to urinary problems, such as kidney stones and bladder infections, although not favored by most modern herbalists. No question about its efficacy as a dye, though: the leaves for yellow and the roots for red.

Lavender (Lavandula spp.)

Is any herb better known for its scent than lavender? From lingerie drawer sachets and expensive soaps to lavender wands and just short of a million aromatherapy products, lavender is a scent most people find clean and refreshing.

There are at least 25 species of lavenders, not to mention many, many cultivars. As a rule, the plants are small (less than 3 feet), many-branched, woody shrubs with gray-green or silvery 2-inch leaves, narrow and lance-shaped. In late spring to midsummer, lavenders produce lovely 6- to 8-inch spikes of tiny, two-lipped purple flowers.

How to grow

Lavenders require full sun and soil that has a neutral or slightly sweet pH, is rich with organic matter, and that drains in minutes. (Some growers believe that sandy, less fertile soil produces plants with more fragrance.) Buy plants rather than seeds, because you can't count on species coming true, and seeds usually take forever to germinate. Other options are to start from cuttings or by layering.

Space plants 2 to 4 feet apart, depending on the species and how much pruning you want to do. Provide some shelter from wind to protect the flower stalks. Unfortunately, very few lavenders can survive a winter colder than Zone 6.

Lavenders also play myriad roles in an ornamental garden — edging walkways or borders, scattered among other perennials for contrast of form and foliage, or as residents in rock gardens. They're classic companions to roses, helping to hide thorny or bare stems, and send bees into a frenzy.

Cultivars and related plants

English lavender *(Lavandula angustifolia),* the most commonly grown species, is hardy in Zones 6 to 9 and offers numerous cultivars, including 'Hidcote', 'Munstead', and 'Twickel Purple', all with purple flowers and growing 18 to 24 inches tall. For pink, choose 'Hidcote Pink' or 'Miss Katherine'; for white, select 'Nana Alba', a fine dwarf cultivar, only 10 inches tall. 'Lady' blooms in the first year when grown from seed.

Spike lavender *(L. latifolia)* is a more upright species that is hardy in Zones 7 to 9. *L. dentata,* or fringed lavender, has gray-green foliage and dark purple flowers; it's hardy only in Zones 8 to 10.

Worth looking for and trying to grow indoors or outdoors in Zones 7 to 9 is French lavender *(L. stoechas),* which has extremely narrow leaves. The flowers are not only a vibrant rosy purple, but appear in tight little cylinders topped by a flag of pink petals. A variety, *L. stoechas* var. *pedunculata,* has even more dramatic, elongated blooms.

Lore and usage

A famous story about lavender involves Rene-Maurice Gattefosse, a French perfume chemist who discovered its healing properties in the 1920s when he burned his hand and plunged it into a vat of lavender oil. This successful move is credited with launching aromatherapy.

The Romans thought that the asp — that little Egyptian snake that snuggled up with Cleopatra — lived among lavender plants. But that didn't keep people out of the lavender patch. After all, it was also believed to be an aphrodisiac, good for "the panting and passion of the heart."

We think lavender tastes like perfume and has enough to do without masquerading as food. You can use lavender in virtually any cosmetic or cleaning agent that you want to scent, and of course, in potpourris, sachets, and sleep pillows. Toss a few petals or leaves in the rinse water of your lingerie or sheets.

Lavender cotton (Santolina chamaecyparissus)

A small, evergreen shrub from the Mediterranean, the species name means "dwarf cypress," and the arrangement of its thick, slender leaves might very well remind you of the neighbor's Leyland cypress hedge. Equally descriptive is the common name, the first part capturing its aroma (more medicinal than most lavenders, however) and the second, its soft, silvery white leaves. Hardy in Zones 6 to 9, these plants can grow up to 2 feet tall and up to twice as wide. Lavender cotton is crowned with little yellow button flowers from early to mid-summer, although many gardeners whack them off. Lavender cotton is also called santolina.

How to grow

Lavender cotton germinates somewhat unevenly, so sow more seeds than you think you'll need when the temperature warms to about 40 degrees Fahrenheit, and give them up to a month to sprout. Starting with plants is easier, especially for a knot garden, because they spread slowly.

This herb prefers slightly alkaline soil but drainage is the crucial factor, because lavender cotton abhors dampness in the soil or the air. Prune in early spring and again after flowering so that the plants maintain their shape and don't become too woody.

Even if you don't have a knot garden, you'll find lavender cotton the perfect edging plant, ideal for creating a low hedge or defining a path. The delicate gray leaves contrast becomingly with almost anything else you might grow.

Cultivars and related plants

'Lemon Queen' is a dwarf cultivar with lemon-colored flowers, whereas 'Pretty Carol', another dwarf, has silver foliage and bright yellow blooms. *Santolina chamaecyparissus* var. *nana* is extremely small — only 6 inches tall.

Rosemary santolina *(S. rosmarinifolia),* looks a lot like rosemary and smells a little like lavender cotton. The cultivar 'Primrose Gem' has pale yellow flowers, and is hardy in Zones 7 to 10.

Lore and usage

Lavender cotton, or santolina, has such a knockout camphor aroma that you wouldn't be tempted to eat it, but would guess it had medicinal uses. Yet the ancient herbals are strangely silent about this herb, except to note its brief fling with treating bites, dispelling worms, treating skin problems, or discouraging moths. (Try a sprig of lavender cotton or a bag of clippings in your drawers and closets.)

Blame the Elizabethans for dandifying lavender cotton. Noting the pleasing shape of its foliage and its amenity to pruning — "for it will abide to be cut in what forme you think best" — they used it by the cartload to tie up their knot gardens.

Lemon balm (Melissa officinalis)

This scraggly perennial grows up to 18 inches tall. Its leaves are somewhat heart-shaped with toothed edges, and make it look like a diminutive nettle. Sporadically through summer it produces the small clusters of yellow or white flowers that bees love so much. Let your fingers check for the signature scent of lemon and mint.

How to grow

It's hard to go wrong with lemon balm. It's happy in any ordinary soil, although your plants will have bigger, plumper leaves if you add generous amounts of organic matter and water during a drought. Hardy in Zones 4 to 9, this herb needs midday shade in the South. If it gets beat up in hot weather, shear it back to the ground; it will regrow. Lemon balm doesn't spread rampantly like other mints but does self-sow. Remove the spent flowers if you don't want more lemon balm — or more bees.

You can start lemon balm from seed, but it's easier to take stem cuttings or divide an established plant (its shallow roots are thick and matted). Space plants about 18 inches apart.

Cultivars and related plants

If you want a lemon balm you can show off to friends, look for one of the variegated cultivars, such as 'Aurea', or the appropriately named 'All Gold'. (These cultivars need protection from hot sun even more than the species.)

The balm of Gilead, *Cedronella canariensis,* has a balsam rather than a lemon scent. It's appropriate for potpourri but not for the teacup. Vietnamese balm *(Elsholtzia ciliata)* combines lemon and floral flavors — it's not our cup of tea, but you might feel differently. Beware, it's quite invasive.

Lore and usage

So you've spilled hot coffee on your computer's hard drive, discovered that you threw away those records the IRS wants, and received an irate phone call from your teenage son's girlfriend's father (all before noon). Sounds like you could use a cup of the beverage "esteemed of great use in all complaints supposed to proceed from a disordered state of the nervous system." You need some lemon balm.

Three centuries ago, people believed that a morning glass of wine flavored with lemon balm would "renew youth, strengthen the brain, relieve languishing nature and prevent baldness." The Roman scholar Pliny went so far as to suggest that a warrior could stanch a wound merely by tying lemon balm to his sword. Sixteenth-century writer John Gerard reported that beekeepers rubbed it onto their hives to keep the swarm together. (The genus name *Melissa* is Greek for "bee.")

Science has borne out lemon balm's antibacterial and tranquilizing effects, although these are less pronounced that those of other herbs. Today we know the herb, sometimes called just balm, as a soothing tea, a too-eager colonizer in the garden. Another common name is sweet Melissa, which the Allman Brothers borrowed for their 1972 hit song, "Melissa."

Use this delicately flavored herb fresh in salads — vegetable, fruit, or meat — or add it at the last minute to foods that benefit from a hint of mint, such as seafood, broccoli, asparagus, rice, or couscous. Lemon balm's combination of relaxing and healing qualities make it a fine addition to bath water and facial washes.

Lemongrass (Cymbopogon citratus)

This perennial from India and Sri Lanka forms a clump similar to many of the ornamental grasses popular in today's gardens. Its narrow, blue-green leaves shoot up to 3 feet from the plant's onionlike base and are tough-textured with razor-sharp edges. The late-season flower panicles can add another 2 feet, but only gardeners with subtropical conditions are likely to ever see them. Worry not: It's the hollow stems that are most often used in cooking.

Cymbopogon citrates.

How to grow

Give lemongrass full sun and organically rich, moisture-retentive soil. To get started, beg or buy a division; plant it at the same depth it was growing. (If you're using a container, choose one that is at least 12 inches across.)

Hardy only in Zones 9 to 11, well-watered lemongrass growing in the garden forms a clump 3 feet wide. Yours is unlikely to be that large, but you can still divide clumps to obtain more plants. Divide during the growing season (cut the leaves of the new division down to 3 or 4 inches to reduce stress) or well before the first fall frost to overwinter indoors in pots. Or just grow it as a potted plant to begin with. Harvest young lemongrass stalks while they're still tender.

Use lemongrass to give height to large containers, or as a support for delicate annual vines such as nasturtium.

Cultivars and related plants

Another *Cymbopogon,* citronella grass *(C. nardus)* is more famous for its mosquito-repelling properties than lemongrass is. You'll find its essential oil in those familiar yellow patio candles. Oils from members of this genus also are used in perfumery, especially for a synthetic violet scent. The best source of these oils is said to be palmarosa (*C. martinii,* sometimes called geranium grass or rosha). The scent, comparable to that of a rose geranium, is worth trying to capture in potpourri or homemade cosmetics.

Lore and usage

If you buy an herb book more than 15 years old, it probably won't list lemongrass. That's because a decade ago, you couldn't find a good Thai or Vietnamese restaurant anywhere in North America outside large coastal cities. Lemongrass is a key ingredient in those cuisines, which have the twin virtues of being low fat and exquisitely spiced. You can chop the stems into soups, sauces, seafood, and poultry, for a lemon taste without the tang of citrus.

Lemongrass has medicinal properties as well. Traditional uses are for inducing sleep (Brazil), for controlling fever (in the Caribbean, where it is called fever grass), and for treating ringworm (India). It does contain a mild sedative and shows power against fungal infections, such as athlete's foot and ringworm, when taken either in tea or applied as a compress. Lemongrass also has insect-repelling properties, so is worth including in homemade bugbanes.

Lemon verbena (Aloysia triphylla [Lippia citriodora])

Why do we struggle to grow this tropical shrub? The nose knows. In the garden it only takes a gentle touch to trigger the release of its lemon-lime scent. In a potpourri, the aroma lasts for months.

Lemon verbena is a deciduous shrub that grows to a dozen feet or more on the Isle of Wight or in Florida but stays under 5 feet in most gardens. Its narrow, lance-shaped leaves appear in whorls along the stem and are a bit hairy.

Aloysia triphylla.

How to grow

Lemon verbena prefers organically rich, well-draining soil that keeps its roots moist but never soggy. Plants rarely produce seed, so start with a purchased plant or stem cutting. Most gardeners grow this herb, hardy only in Zones 8 to 11, in a container, moving it outdoors in summer and back inside for winter. Feed plants with diluted fish emulsion while they're actively growing, and be firm about keeping small weak branches pruned off.

In winter, remember the word deciduous: Plants drop all their leaves and go dormant, which means no fertilizer and just a dribble of water now and then.

Cultivars and related plants

All the members of the verbena family have traditional medical uses, including the *Lippia* species from tropical America and Africa (used by native peoples for stomach upset and cramps, gas and bloating). You can use Mexican oregano *(L. graveolens)* like other oreganos in cooking. It's big enough to be used as a hedge in Zones 9 to 11. Other verbena family members are in a genus of the same name and include vervain *(Verbena officinalis),* once used by the Druids in religious ceremonies, and recommended by today's herbalists for anxiety and stress.

Lore and usage

Brought from South America to England in 1784, lemon verbena was once all the rage as a tea in France and Spain, and as a cure for indigestion, flatulence, lethargy, and depression. In Colonial and Civil War America, it was popular in perfumes and the little nosegays called tussie-mussies.

You can use lemon verbena — leaves and flowers — as you would any of the other lemon herbs. The flavor won't fade in cooking and makes a pleasant tea, or add it to marinades and dressings. An infusion of lemon verbena lends a squeaky-clean scent to cosmetics or cleaning agents.

Lovage (Levisticum officinale)

Lovage is celery to the max — both in stature and in flavor. In fact, people who've never tasted unblanched celery and think of that vegetable as all crunch and no flavor are in for a surprise when they try this big, brawny cousin.

To envision this carrot-family perennial, multiply celery by a factor of two or three. Lovage has the same ribbed, U-shaped stems and the same compound, toothed leaves, dark green and shiny, but it grows up to 5 feet tall and 3 feet wide. The root, as might be expected, is stout — up to 6 inches long. The minuscule edible flowers are in umbels, about 3 inches across; the small seeds are grooved. Plants are hardy in Zones 4 to 9.

Levisticum officinale.

How to grow

Celery has a reputation for being difficult to grow. Not so with lovage. Start it from seed, indoors or out. One plant will be more than enough for the average family. Remember that big root and give it deeply worked soil, preferably with lots of organic matter and a bit acidic. Site it in full sun (a bit of shade is fine in the South) where it can spread out, and top dress it with compost each fall. A floating row cover protects it from aphids and swallowtail caterpillars.

Should you need more lovage, divide the clump in spring. Lovage seeds don't remain viable for long; if you collect your own, sow them in autumn, or store them in the refrigerator until spring. To produce large roots for medicine, hold back on manure (which promotes leaf growth) and keep flowers pinched off.

Cultivars and related plants

Carrot-family plants in the sound-alike genus *Ligusticum* are sometimes called lovage. Scots lovage *(L. scoticum)* has been used like celery and lovage in that country. Osha *(L. porteri),* which sounds more like a workplace watch-dog federal agency than an herbal medicine, is a Rocky Mountain denizen that Native Americans used to boost the immune system. (***Note:*** Even nurseries that sell the seeds say this plant is a challenge to grow.)

Lore and usage

And you have to like a plant with a common name — it was once called love parsley — derived from being used as an aphrodisiac. It could also be considered something of a deodorant. Travelers used to put it in their shoes to keep their sweaty feet from stinking. Others chewed the seeds to dispel flatulence. Modern herbalists recommend a decoction of the dried root as a cure for bloating.

As a medicinal herb it was never such a giant, although 17th-century physician Nicholas Culpeper liked it for agues, quinsy, and pleurisy, and advised, "The leaves bruised and fried with a little hog's lard and laid hot to any blotch or boil will quickly break it." The "old writers," according to British herbalist Maude Grieve, used it for kidney stones and urinary problems; modern studies show that it is an effective diuretic.

In the kitchen, use lovage stems, leaves, and seeds like celery: Chop the raw stems and leaves for salads, steam or lightly sauté the stems for stuffings or stir-fries. But not so much! This herb easily overwhelms other ingredients. Lovage makes an especially happy marriage with tomato. Snip it into spaghetti sauces, or use the hollow stem to sip tomato juice — or a Bloody Mary.

Marjoram, sweet (Origanum majorana)

Oh, what a tangled web! Someone should have held an Herbal Peace Conference, agreeing to call all of the *Origanum* genus either marjoram or oregano. But no such luck. A mishmash of common names prevails. Some species are called marjoram, some oregano, and a few flop back and forth. The best we can do here is to focus on the plant that is always called marjoram, or sweet marjoram. The word "sweet" distinguishes its sweeter, more delicate flavor from the robust, pizza-esque tang of other culinary oreganos.

In its native Mediterranean, sweet marjoram is a shrubby, evergreen perennial, growing up to 2½ feet tall. But because it is hardy only in Zones 9 to 11, in most of the United States it is treated as an annual. A member of the mint family, sweet marjoram has many branching square stems; its oval leaves are gray-green and fuzzy. Marjoram's most distinguishing characteristic is the knotlike look of its buds before they open — it's also called knotted marjoram. The tiny white, lavender, or pink flowers have round, oily bracts and (if you look very closely) a one-lipped calyx with a slit down one side. Plants bloom from early to late summer.

Origanum majorana.

How to grow

You can try starting marjoram from seed, indoors four to six weeks before your last frost date, or sow directly in the ground when that date is past. Many gardeners buy plants, though, because of the name confusion, because cultivars or hybrids won't come true from seed, and because wet conditions make seedlings susceptible to damping-off. Set plants in full sun, about 6 inches apart, in good garden soil amended with plenty of organic matter.

When established, sweet marjoram grows quickly, although plants may sulk in the humidity and clay soil found in the far South. Begin harvesting in mid-summer to supply your kitchen and to keep your plants shapely and productive. To overwinter marjoram indoors, pot up a division (cut the top back to 2 inches) in the fall, well before the first frost.

Cultivars and related plants

Closest in flavor to sweet marjoram is its hybrid cousin Italian oregano, or hardy sweet marjoram, *Origanum* x *majoricum*. This evergreen perennial, winter-hardy in Zones 5 to 9, grows to about 15 inches. The edible flowers are like those of common oregano; the leaves are similar to, but less fuzzy than, marjoram.

Pot marjoram, or Cretan oregano *(O. onites),* is another little evergreen shrub, hardy in Zones 8 to 11. Its taste lies somewhere between marjoram and oregano but with a biting edge. Use it with restraint.

Lore and usage

In the Middle Ages marjoram was used in perfumes and cosmetics. The Greeks lay it on graves to assure sweet dreams for the dead; and because the herb was associated with Aphrodite, the goddess of love, they also used to wreathe the heads of newlyweds.

Marjoram is a staple of Greek and Italian cuisines. German cooks grind the herb into sausage and add it to potato soup. Sweet marjoram is also great with squash, mushrooms, eggplant, and most root vegetables. Its clean, fresh scent makes it worth adding to homemade cleaning agents.

Marsh mallow (Althaea officinalis)

No, you won't find any part of this plant in those white bits of fluff that are burnt to a crisp by kids at summer camp. But marsh mallow was a sweet treat (made by boiling the peeled root many times and adding sugar) your great-great grandparents would have recognized.

Brought from Europe by early American colonists, marsh mallow is a hardy perennial, often growing more than 5 feet tall and covered from stem to stern with tiny hairs. Its velvety leaves are spade-shaped with teeth and several lobes. The flowers are typical of the mallow family (which include rose-of-Sharon, hollyhock, and hibiscus); up to 2 inches across with five notched petals, they are lilac-pink with brighter reddish-purple anthers.

How to grow

With the common names marsh mallow and water mallow, you can guess that this herb grows in boggy and wet places in the wild. But you get more mucilage from roots if they are growing in soil that drains well but is watered frequently. If you start from seed, plan on not harvesting roots until the third year; if you plant divisions in spring, you can collect some roots in the second fall. Save root pieces with buds (eyes) to replant. Set them 18 inches apart in a sunny location. Marsh mallow is hardy in Zones 3 to 9.

Cultivars and related plants

Marsh mallow has escaped to swampy places in the United States, especially salt marshes in the mid-Atlantic and lower New England. However, if you see a mallowlike plant growing in shallow water with white flowers, it's probably common swamp mallow *(Hibiscus moscheutos)*. Up to 8 feet tall, swamp mallow may have red or pink flowers, and there are many showy cultivars. Roselle or jamaica (pronounced ha-my-ka, *Hibiscus sabdariffa)* has showy red flowers. The dried calyces are used to make a beverage common in the Caribbean and Africa; they give Red Zinger tea its color and citrus/cranberry flavor. Less ornamental but used medicinally in the same way as marsh mallow is common mallow *(Malva sylvestris)*. It is a native of Europe and Asia and has five-lobed scalloped leaves and 2-inch magenta flowers. Naturalized in the United States, common mallow self-sows readily in the garden.

Lore and usage

Consumed at least since the days of the Egyptians, marsh mallow was considered a delicacy by the Romans; in other cultures, it was a food for the poor, who boiled the herb and then fried it with onions and butter.

This desultory history as food is at odds with the marsh mallow's sterling reputation as a medicine (the genus name stems from *altheo,* meaning "to cure"). It is champ when it comes to mucilage — the stuff that swells up when wet — and its ability to soothe the body inside and out has been touted for centuries. The Roman Pliny enthused that whoever consumed a spoonful "shall that day be free from all diseases."

Make a decoction from dried, powdered marsh mallow root to drink for a sore throat, or make a thick gel to treat wounds, burns, or sunburns. For a face and body lotion, combine marsh mallow with rose water and lavender.

Milk thistle (Silybum marianum)

A thistle — particularly one whose botanical name looks like "silly bum" — would seem to be the last thing you'd want in your garden, kitchen, or medicine cabinet. All the same, a host of well-respected gardeners adore this annual. Every part of it is edible: young leaves in salads; mature leaves boiled like spinach; shoots peeled and steamed like asparagus ("Surpasses the finest cabbage," one early writer enthused); the root prepared like a parsnip. Even the unopened flower heads were once eaten.

An annual or biennial native of the Mediterranean and southwest Europe, milk thistle shoots up from a basal rosette to 5, even 7, feet, stout and branching to 2 or 3 feet across. The smooth, shiny leaves clasping the stem are scalloped and dramatically veined and marbled with white. (Common names such as Mary's thistle refer to a legend that the white color comes from the milk of the Virgin Mary.) The thistlelike flowers, 2 inches across, are flaming magenta.

How to grow

Milk thistle is one of those plants that grow too easily. It is a noxious weed in warm climates such as in California, and has naturalized in old fields and along roads in the eastern United States. This plant is happy in poor, dry soil (as long as drainage is good) and germinates from seed in one or two weeks.

The late Fred McGourty, noted Connecticut garden author, grew milk thistle in his famous perennial borders, calling it "pure elegance when planted among the summer phloxes of similar tint." The leaves alone can add some excitement to your herb garden. But he said that his passion for it has put something of a strain on his marriage, ever since his wife made the mistake of tossing its spent stalks in the compost — 2,000 seedlings germinated there and 2,000 more where the compost was spread. In a wildflower meadow you worry less about stray seedlings — and possibly not at all, because the seeds are a favorite treat for goldfinches.

Cultivars and related plants

Also known as Our Lady's thistle (and as blessed thistle or holy thistle) is *Cnicus benedictus.* In the Middle Ages this herb was deemed excellent for "old rotten and festering sores." It does have antiseptic properties, and as a bitter herb is sometimes used to stimulate the appetite. (A bitter herb on the tongue gets your gastric juices flowing.)

Two more cousins are yellow-spine thistle, *Cirsium ochrocentrum,* which some Native American Indians used as a cure for syphilis, and pasture thistle, *C. pumilum,* a favorite plant of Henry David Thoreau, who was astonished by the number of bees it attracted.

Lore and usage

Known as a liver protector since the first century A.D., the active ingredient in milk thistle seeds is silymarin. Modern laboratory and clinical studies have shown silymarin to protect the liver and help it recover from hepatitis, cirrhosis, and even the highly poisonous death's cap mushroom.

If you want to help ensure a healthy liver, buy the readily available capsules. You can certainly try eating parts of the plant, as gourmands of old did. But keep those prickly edges in mind. Wear gloves when stripping the edges off mature foliage before you steam the leaves.

Mints (Mentha spp.)

We're fairly sure you won't want to grow all the mints. About 20 species exist, but between bees and breeders, you can avail yourself of more than 1,000 hybrids. For beginning herb gardeners, the choice usually comes down to spearmint *(Mentha spicata)* and/or peppermint *(M.* x *piperita).*

Spearmint and peppermint are easier to tell apart by taste than by appearance. Peppermint is stronger and has a "bite" to it — hence the "pepper" in its name. Both are perennials, growing between 2 and 3 feet tall. Peppermint leaves tend to be more lance-shaped and less wrinkled; its stem is reddish, and it spreads along the top of the ground. Spearmint is a subway herb, traveling underground. Spearmint may bloom a little earlier in summer than peppermint, with white flowers rather than the pink or lilac of peppermint blooms. The flowers of both are tiny, bell-shaped, and held in whorls.

Mentha.

How to grow

Some mints don't produce viable seeds, and many of the plants you may want are hybrids — which don't come true from seed. Buy plants or beg some divisions in spring or fall. You can let them run amok as a groundcover — an olfactory rush to walk on — but be aware that mints will overtake anything in their path. It's better to restrain them in aboveground containers or tiles sunk into a garden bed. Divide mints about every three years because, like some middle-aged men, they get bald in the middle.

Set mints just below the soil surface. The best soil is moist, relatively rich, and slightly acid. Keep them from drying out and prune or harvest them regularly for bushier plants and plumper leaves. Hardiness varies: peppermint from Zones 3 to 8, spearmint from Zones 4 to 11.

Cultivars and related plants

Many mints are said to mingle with another flavor — lemon, lime, grapefruit, chocolate, ginger, even banana. They may not always perform as advertised — just another fluke of mints' highly varied nature.

Mentha x piperita 'Citrata' (which has orange, lemon, and lime strains) is sometimes called the eau-de-cologne mint because it's an ingredient in perfume. Hardy in Zones 3 to 7, it's off-putting in foods but superb in potpourri.

If you have a pond (or just a soggy spot), you might grow water mint *(M. aquatica)*. Hardy in Zones 6 to 11, it can grow submerged up to 6 inches. Water mint is rich in menthol, giving it extra punch in medicines and cleaning solutions. Like other mints, it can be invasive.

Looking for variegated leaves? Try pineapple mint. A cultivar of apple mint *(M. suaveolens),* you'll find it listed as *M. suaveolens* 'Variegata'. It's highly ornamental and has a wonderful fruity scent, but is hardy only in Zones 6 to 9.

For culinary uses, try curly spearmint, *M. spicata* 'Crispa'; it has round, crinkled leaves, a mild taste, and is hardy in Zones 6 to 9. Corsican mint *(M. requienii)* is more strongly flavored. This groundcover has tiny round leaves, needs protection from hot sun, and is hardy in Zones 6 to 9.

Lore and usage

Until 300 years ago everyone thought all mints were alike. The Pharisees demanded mint (along with anise and cumin) as a tax. In the first century A.D., mint was thought to "stir up the minde and the taste to a greedy desire of meate" and to incite lust. The Greeks rubbed it on their bodies after a night at the baths. Centuries later, European herbalists recommended mint for everything from the "bitings of mad dogs" and "all manner of breakings out on the head" to upset stomachs, tearing eyes, and "nervous crudities."

By that measure, modern medicinal uses of mints are limited. Mints are good for aiding digestion, so don't hesitate to reach for the after-dinner mints. The Roman scholar Pliny suggested hanging mint in sickrooms to "reanimate the spirit." Use mint anywhere you want yourself and others to feel clean and refreshed: in a steam tent when you have a cold, or in facial lotions when you're itchy or tired.

Mint is a must for Middle Eastern dishes, such as tabbouleh and cucumber riata, and is especially good with carrots. Or try it with fish, beans, and creamed soups. Try adding an infusion of mint instead of water — or add a handful of flowers — to a brownie or chocolate cake mix. And of course, add it to ice tea on a hot afternoon or to a mint julep as the sun goes down.

Mustard, black (Brassica nigra)

Mustards — there are dozens — are leafy annuals, ranging up to 6 feet tall in the case of black mustard (the spiciest and most often grown for its seeds). Most have stout stalks and broad, usually dark green leaves that are frequently puckered or wrinkled and lower leaves that have lobes or teeth. Each of the bright yellow flowers, which appear on tall spikes, has four petals arranged in a cross shape.

Brassica nigra.

How to grow

Mustard greens get hotter or more bitter when the plants are hot and dry. That means they may need some midsummer shade from taller plants or a vine-covered trellis. Otherwise, give them full sun and soil that is moisture-retentive, well-draining, and slightly acid. Start with seeds outdoors a couple of weeks before the frost-free date, then thin the plants to 18 inches apart (for black mustard), less for other types. Top-dress with manure or compost because mustard plants gobble up nitrogen in their brief but enthusiastic growing season.

Because mustards bolt (quickly go to seed) in hot weather, southern gardeners often plant them as a winter crop. Plants mature in about 50 days, so depending on your climate, you can try planting in both spring and summer (for a fall crop). Of course if you're growing mustard for seed, bolting is the goal, rather than a problem.

In either case, don't let the seeds fall on the ground unless you plan to start making mustard for the neighborhood. This is one prolific plant.

Cultivars and related plants

You can find a world of mustards. Asians cook with wrapped mustards, which curl inward to form heads, and mizuna, a mild *Brassica juncea* variety. There are curled mustards with frilly leaves, and green-in-the-snow types that are small, quick maturing, and hardy. You can buy big-leaf mustards with purple veins or foliage, and the foot-tall, quick-maturing common leaf mustards. If you want a mustard for seeds, look for 'Burgonde', 'French Brown', and 'Tilney'. The last is the source of most commercial yellow mustards.

Many *Brassica* species aren't mustard at all, but cabbages, kales, or broccoli.

Lore and usage

Mustard was born to snuggle with hot dogs. Of course it's not likely that the Romans, the first to pound mustard seeds and soak them in wine, enjoyed red hots at the Coliseum. But the basic mustard sauce recipe — calling for vinegar, honey, and a pinch of spice — has remained pretty much the same through the centuries. Lively Dijon types are made with black mustard seeds, milder American yellow mustards with yellow or white mustard *(B. hirta),* or a middle-of-the-road brown mustard *(B. juncea).*

In the sickroom, a mustard plaster was a time-honored poultice for respiratory ailments. Externally, mustard preparations were used for neuralgia, rheumatism, headaches, aching feet, and even epilepsy. (Because mustard paste alone can feel too hot too quickly, it is traditionally applied on top of paper.) Nicholas Culpeper said mustard seeds would cure laryngitis, mushroom poisoning, bruises, toothache, "the falling of the hair . . . also the crick in the neck."

Sautéed mustard seeds added to rice, potatoes, or other vegetables provide a Middle Eastern punch. Use them crushed or powdered in salad dressings, in rarebits, and in other white sauces. The traditional Southern recipe for greens is to steam or cook them with bacon or salt pork and onions, accompanied with cornbread. White mustard greens are good in salads and sandwiches.

Nasturtium (Tropaeolum majus)

Slip a few peppery nasturtium leaves in your dinner salad, and guests will be wide awake for the main course, even it it's meatloaf. You can use the flowers as well, but their emergency-beacon colors will give away the surprise.

The nasturtium, an annual vine growing to 10 feet, is charming even before it blooms. The leaves look like a tiny water lily pad with wavy edges, each attached to its stem in the middle, like an umbrella. Then, from summer to fall, the show begins with 2-inch spurred flowers, most often in hot orange, yellow, and red. (You can rebel and buy more pastel shades, such as 'Primrose Jewel'.) The species is a climber, but most of the cultivars form bushy mounds, perfect for containers or trailing over a ledge.

Tropaeolum majus.

How to grow

Sow seeds (which germinate quickly and easily) outdoors in early spring, or in the South in fall. In the far South and Southwest nasturtiums grow through winter and then peter out when heat arrives.

Nasturtiums like full sun and poor to average soil that drains quickly. Don't overdo the fertilizer or you'll have more leaf than flower. Water plants well, and don't hold back when pinching off leaves to munch, which will make plants bushier. Plant vining types about 1 foot apart, mounding types 6 inches apart.

The climbers are lightweight enough to hang on thin wires, strings, netting, or heavier vines, or to weave through shrubs. The mounders are ready-made for containers; give the trailers a hanging basket or window box, wind them between other plants, or plant them around steppingstones as a groundcover.

Cultivars and related plants

This genus includes several semihardy or tender vines. Flame flower *(Tropaeolum speciosum),* which likes cool, moist growing conditions, has notched vermilion petals that are arranged like the blades of a ceiling fan, followed by bright blue fruits. Anu or perennial nasturtium *(T. tuberosum)* has edible red and orange flowers, whereas those of Bolivian nasturtium, also known as three-colored Indian cress *(T. tricolorum)* are tubelike, red with a maroon edge and yellow petals. These are all hardy in Zones 8 to 10. Canary creeper *(T. peregrinum)* gets its name from its sulfur yellow color and fringed petals that look like a cockatoo's topknot. It's hardy only in Zones 9 to 11. All of these species have lobed leaves.

Confusingly, the plant with the botanical name *Nasturtium* is watercress, which you find out about in this chapter.

Lore and usage

The nasturtium is a native of Peru; native Andean tribes used the plant to heal wounds and relieve chest congestion. All parts of the plant are antibiotic. But ever since the Spaniards introduced nasturtiums to Europe in the 1500s, their primary use has been to add zip to salads and sandwiches. You can feel virtuous about using nasturtiums as salad greens because they're packed with vitamin C. Try the flowers and leaves to flavor and decorate vinegar. Unopened flower buds pickled in wine are a substitute for capers.

Oregano (Origanum vulgare)

Greek oregano is a perennial, 2 feet high with round leaves less than an inch long and unexciting whorls of tiny white flowers. Botanists say it can be distinguished from the wild oregano by the tiny oil glands or hairs on the leaves, calyxes, and stems. The flowers of wild oregano are usually pink. But out of flower, the most telling characteristic of Greek oregano is the aroma, which herb expert Art Tucker unfortunately compares with creosote. Yum!

How to grow

Always obtain oregano as a plant so you can determine for yourself if it has a pungent odor. Then, just give the plants full sun in average, well-drained soil, spacing them about a foot apart, preferably among other perennial herbs. If volunteer seedlings pop up, pitch them on the compost unless you decide they're as flavorful as the parent. Division is the best way to get new plants, which are hardy in Zones 5 to 9.

Origanum vulgare.

Cultivars and related plants

Some oreganos (including wild oregano) are worth growing primarily as ornamentals. The purple-pink flowers of showy oregano *(Origanum laevigatum),* which is not quite as hardy as Greek oregano, attract butterflies and are pretty in arrangements, fresh and dried. Its cultivar, 'Herrenhausen', has reddish purple leaves that become even more colorful in fall.

O. vulgare has several mild-flavored variegated cultivars, such as 'Aureum Crispum' and 'Polyphant', which droop handsomely from a hanging basket or window box. *O. vulgare* 'Compactum' is a dwarf, ideal for containers or the rock garden. It has dark green leaves and pink-violet flowers. All of these are hardy in Zones 7 to 9.

Dittany of Crete *(O. dictamnus)* is sometimes called hop marjoram because the dangling flowers — soft, green, and liberally painted with pink — look like hop strobiles. You may find the leaves too strong-flavored for foods, but try the flowers in tea. It's hardy only in Zones 8 to 11.

Cuban oregano *(Plectranthus amboinicus)* has rotund, scalloped, fuzzy leaves. 'Well-Sweep Wedgewood' has white-edged foliage. Neither plant tolerates freezing, but each makes an eye-catching houseplant, and you can batter and fry the leaves. See the entry on lemon verbena in this chapter to read about Mexican oregano, a tender plant with an oregano flavor.

Lore and usage

Given the interchangeable use of the names marjoram and oregano (see the entry for marjoram earlier in this chapter), there's reason to question which one is being referred to in various "duste olde" herbals. Most experts say the "true" Greek oregano that can make your kitchen smell like a trattoria is *O. vulgare* ssp. *hirtum* 'Greek'.

What grows wild in the eastern United States is *O. vulgare* ssp. *vulgare.* The name may sound doubly vulgar, but the plant doesn't smell or taste like much of anything. It doesn't even live up to its name: *Origanum* comes from the Greek word for "bitter herb." But you'll be bitterly disappointed if you plant the wrong oregano.

Oregano, which contains vitamin A and niacin, is associated with the cuisines of many hot, sunny countries — Mexico and those of Central America, Italy, Greece, and Spain. Most famous in tomato sauces, it's often a star at breakfast in egg dishes and in homemade bread; and it marries splendidly with beans, zucchini, and potatoes.

Like other mints, oregano is reputed to help settle "wambling of the stomacke," as Nicholas Culpeper put it in 1653. Medicinal plant expert Jim Duke includes it among herbs that may stop bacteria that cause body odor, although you may want to use a commercial product before your big job interview.

Parsley (Petroselinum crispum)

Parsley is a biennial usually grown as an annual, about a foot tall and wide, with deep green, divided leaves. The names of the two most common types speak for themselves. The leaves of the more flavorful flat, or Italian, parsley (*Petroselinum crispum* var. *neopolitanum*) look like they could have just come off the ironing board; those of curly parsley (*P. crispum* var. *crispum*) form crinkled little bunches. If you leave the plant in your garden for a second season, it will put up umbrellas of tiny yellow-green flowers.

How to grow

If you have a slightly shady garden, parsley is one of the herbs that will thrive. It likes cool weather, and in the South needs a sunscreen; in the North, it prefers full sun. Parsley seeds are so slow to germinate, legend says they go to the devil and back seven times before sprouting. To speed germination, soak the seeds overnight before sowing. You can start seeds indoors in individual peat pots (so you don't disturb the root when you transplant), but most people find it easier to plant seeds directly in the garden in early spring (or in autumn, in mild climates).

Space parsley plants about 8 inches apart in organically rich, slightly acid soil. Parsley is a favorite of swallowtail caterpillars; remove the caterpillars to a faraway plant if you can't bear to sacrifice a few sprigs of this herb. You can start harvesting leaves when the plant is about 8 inches tall. Cut off the outside leaves to stimulate new growth.

Parsley leaves left over-wintered can be bitter, but if you live in Zones 6 to 10, your plants will survive and provide a second-season crop.

Cultivars and related plants

You can buy cultivars of either form of parsley. In flat-leaf parsley, some have been bred for bigger leaves ('Giant Italian' which grows to 18 inches tall), sweeter flavor ('Titan'), stronger flavor ('Italian Dark Green'), or heat resistance ('Sherwood'). Curly parsley 'Forest Green' has stiff stems, whereas 'Favorit' has very curly, dark green leaves. Hamburg parsley *(P. crispum* var. *tuberosum)* is grown for its roots, which have a nutty, carrotlike flavor when cooked.

Lore and usage

Believe it or not, this healthful little herb was once associated with death. The Greeks dedicated it to Persephone, goddess of the underworld, and wove it into funeral wreaths. Morbid superstitions clung to it well into the Middle Ages, when Europeans were careful to plant it only on Good Friday.

On the other hand, John Gerard said that parsley seeds or roots, boiled in ale, would "cast foorth strong venome or poyson." Early in this century, it was a popular means of inducing abortion. Its most well-documented, medicinal use has been as a diuretic, and as a remedy for urinary problems.

The Romans munched this member of the carrot family after a feast to sweeten their breath — or perhaps mask exhalations of wine. Remember that the next time you eye the parsley sprig that decorates your dinner entrée.

Parsley — packed with vitamins A and C, plus calcium, iron, and magnesium — deserves better treatment than a neglected garnish. It's one of the key ingredients in Middle Eastern tabbouleh and makes an incredible pesto mixed with lemon and walnuts. And, of course, parsley is one of the triumvirate (along with thyme and bay leaf) in a bouquet garni. As a diuretic, it might help with menstrual or post-dinner bloating. But pregnant women should avoid more than a nibble now and then because it can stimulate uterine contractions.

Pennyroyal (Mentha pulegium, Hedeoma pulegioides)

"It creepeth much upon the ground," with stems up to 2 feet long, and in midsummer produces tiny lavender flowers in small whorls, 6 inches or more above the leaves. European pennyroyal is a perennial with half-inch leaves, whereas the American species is an annual, less sprawling with leaves up to twice as big.

Mentha pulegium.

How to grow

Pennyroyal needs rich, moisture-retentive, well-worked soil in either sun or shade. Start the European perennial from cuttings or divisions. Although it is hardy in Zones 5 to 10, it needs winter mulch in Zones 5 and 6. Plants spread by underground runners. Because it is no beauty (old nicknames include lurk-in-the-ditch), confine it where it can hang over the edge of a raised bed or container, or tuck it between rocks.

Launch the American species from seed; germination is iffy everywhere, so sow generously and then thin plants to 6 inches apart.

Cultivars and related plants

Australian, or Brisbane, pennyroyal *(Mentha satureioides)* is a Down Under relation, a perennial species that has a pungent aroma and is used to improve digestion. Like other pennyroyals, pregnant women should not use it.

Lore and usage

Since at least the first century A.D., European pennyroyal *(Mentha pulegium)* has had two claims to fame: repelling insects and inducing abortions. The Roman scholar Pliny thought it was a good flea repellent (for dogs and for homes, as a strewing herb), and in honor of this reputation, it earned its species name from *pulex,* the Latin word for flea. One ancient text, however, claims that drowning insects could be revived in ashes of pennyroyal. (Perhaps useful if you had a flea circus.)

And as early as the fourth century B.C., the playwright Aristophanes was making puns in his works that alluded to the plant's birth-control/abortive abilities. Sadly, more than a few desperate women have died ingesting powerful pennyroyal essential oil.

Native Americans used the American species of pennyroyal *(Hedeoma pulegioides)* to cure headaches, chills, and upset stomachs. After the Civil War, it was used to induce sweats in fever victims and to promote menstruation.

Pennyroyal is used in some commercial product insect repellants. Try braiding some around your pet's neck or hanging a bag from his collar. Stuff some in Snowball's and Rover's beds — if nothing else, the beds will smell great. You can make an insect repellent for yourself by spritzing on an infusion, or make a lotion. If you have trouble with ants in your garden, try growing a plant near their hill.

The herb and homemade pennyroyal products are safe for most people in small amounts, but err on the safe side and avoid ingesting the herb. And most definitely, you should not ingest pennyroyal or use any product containing it if you're pregnant. Although no essential oil should ever be taken internally, ingesting even tiny amounts of pennyroyal oil can cause convulsions, coma, or death.

Rose (Rosa spp.)

Seeds from the dog rose *(Rosa canina)* were found inside a 2,000-year-old skeleton in England. That suggests that he/she knew what we know: That the hips (or fruits) of this many rose species are especially high in vitamin C. During World War II, Englishmen (and women) used rose hips to help prevent scurvy when the Germans cut off their citrus supply. If you want roses for hips or fragrant petals, look to old species roses and their cultivars. Herbalists are most likely to grow the following:

- **The apothecary's rose** *(R. gallica* var. *officinalis)*. Grown in gardens for at least 400 years, this rose once was a popular tonic and purgative. This shrub rose grows 3 to 5 feet tall and wide, with rough, deep green leaves and dark pink, semi-double flowers in late spring or early summer. It has a nice, rounded shape but may sucker to form a thicket. Hardy in Zones 4 to 9.

- **The dog rose.** Native to Europe and cultivated from the early 1700s, this plant grows 8 to 12 feet tall and is smothered in late spring by single pale pink or white flowers, followed by shiny, dark orange hips — the ones you're likely to find in a health food store. Hardy in Zones 3 to 8.

- **The eglantine or sweet briar rose** *(R. eglanteria [R. rubrignosa])*. This relative of the dog rose was cultivated about 200 years longer, and is notable not so much for the single, bright pink spring flowers, but for the foliage, which releases a fruity aroma with every rain. Growing at least 6 feet tall and wide, it has curved prickles that make pruning an uninviting prospect. Hardy in Zones 4 to 8.

- **Rugosa roses** *(R. rugosa)*. Rugosas rebloom throughout the growing season, with a scent redolent of cloves. Each flush gives you more of the dark orange-red hips that earned the species the nickname "tomato rose." The hips are higher in Vitamin C than oranges. The leaves are wrinkled (rugose) and disease-resistant. The rugosas are famous as seaside plants because they tolerate wind and salt. The thorns are small but numerous. Another common name is "beach rose." There are scores of named rugosas, some hardy from Zone 2 to Zone 8.

Rosa.

How to grow

Although you can root roses from cuttings in roughly two months in spring or fall, or in about four months from layering during the growing season, most gardeners begin by buying a potted or bare-root plant.

Roses are greedy feeders that need excellent drainage, so don't skimp on the soil amendments. In spite of roses' reputation as sun lovers, all of these roses — and especially the dog and eglantine roses — tolerate some shade, particularly during hot afternoons in warm regions. Give them a monthly top-dressing with compost, regular mulching to keep the roots cool, and generous watering during droughts.

Black spot is the most common disease of roses, especially in humid areas. Alliums of all types — garlic, onions, chives, as well as the purely ornamental species — are a traditional companion plant, apparently because they ooze sulfur into the soil. A spray of compost tea is another good preventive.

For more information on growing roses, take a look at *Roses For Dummies,* by Lance Walheim and the Editors of the National Gardening Association (Wiley). Southern gardeners should see *The Organic Rose Garden* by Liz Druitt. Cold-weather gardeners can learn a lot from Robert Osborne's *Hardy Roses.* A good general reference on roses is *Easy Roses for North American Gardens* by Tom Christopher.

Cultivars and related plants

For fragrant petals, try one of the roses long cultivated commercially for perfume: the damask rose *(R. damascena),* which grows to 6 feet tall with semi-double, pale pink to white flowers in summer (Zones 5 to 8), or the cabbage rose *(R. x centifolia),* which grows to 5 feet tall with fully double, rose-red flowers in summer (Zones 4 to 9). For recurrent blooms to produce hips, consider 'Dortmund', a graceful shrub usually trained as a climber, with single, frilly, bright red blossoms (Zones 5 to 9), or 'Old Blush', which grows to 5 feet with semi-double, baby pink flowers (Zones 6 to 9).

Lore and usage

Hippocrates recommended rose petal oil for problems with the uterus. India's Ayurvedic physicians took advantage of the rose's astringent properties to soothe wounds and inflammations. In the Middle Ages and during the Renaissance, attar of roses was a cure for depression; today that expensive essential oil is one of aromatherapy's favorite mood lifters. Use rose water in the bathtub, splash it on your face, or mix it with any other cosmetics. Like witch hazel, rose water can be soothing to irritated eyes.

You can eat rose hips fresh, but Texas rose expert Liz Druitt warns that some people are allergic to the achenes (the hairy seeds inside the hips). Too many achenes can also cause diarrhea. It's better to use the cleaned hips to make tea, syrup, or topping for fruits and yogurt (Druitt suggests flavoring the sauce with orange liqueur, or spices such as ginger and cinnamon). You can make rose hip jelly or use the petals in salads and vinegars. Rose water is traditionally used in baklava and other Middle Eastern dishes. Candy the petals or use in desserts and beverages.

Rosemary (Rosmarinus officinalis)

Rosemary is a tender evergreen shrub from the western Mediterranean, known for its signature aroma (and flavor) that combines pine, mint, and ginger. The needlelike leaves are a shiny bluish-green on top and downy white or gray underneath. In summer to fall, it compounds its charms by producing little two-lipped flowers, usually ranging from soft lilac to bright blue. A typical plant holds its branches upright and can grow up to 6 feet in warm climates, less than half that where it lives indoors all or part of the year.

How to grow

Rosemary is slow and difficult to start from seed, so buy a plant. (For a named cultivar, you must begin with a plant, or at least a sprig of a plant.) More challenges await you. Rosemary's name means "dew of the sea." Native to scrubby hills near the Mediterranean, this herb needs warmth, good drainage, and humidity, a combination rarely found in gardens.

In Zones 7 to 11, where you can grow rosemary in the ground, give your plant near-neutral soil, only slightly enriched but with excellent drainage. Wet feet mean sure death, but never let plants dry out completely. Rich soil makes its branches flabby and prey to insects and disease. Site it in full sun, or allow it a bit of afternoon shade if your region is extremely hot.

Rosemary has a long root. It doesn't like to be moved and needs a deep container — established plants need a pot at least a foot deep and wide. Use light potting soil that drains well, and feed your plant monthly (spring through midsummer) with compost tea.

Indoors, rosemary will feel abused in dry, overheated air. Give it a sunny window where the air is cool and circulation is good. Keep the soil damp enough that the foliage doesn't wilt, and mist the plant once or twice a week with room-temperature water. Prune off any limp new growth. In spring, harden it off again, just like a seedling, before it goes outdoors.

If you've made it this far, congratulate yourself. Make more rosemary by taking cuttings when new growth has firmed up, or by layering.

Cultivars and related plants

You can choose rosemary cultivars with golden foliage ('Golden Rain', aka 'Joyce DeBaggio'), variegated foliage ('Aureus'), a stronger pine scent ('Pine'), trailing forms suited to hanging baskets ('Lockwood de Forest', 'Irene', 'Prostratus'), and knockout pink flowers ('Majorca Pink', 'Roseus', and 'Pinkie'). 'Arp' has grayish foliage and ice-blue to white flowers but is a hit because of its hardiness — Zone 6 with protection; 'Hill Hardy' is equally hardy and has pale blue flowers. 'Tuscan Blue' is upright with bright violet-blue flowers; 'Foto Blue' is semiprostrate with dark blue blooms; and 'Primley Blue' and 'Sudbury Blue' are upright cultivars with clear blue flowers.

Lore and usage

Even if you know nothing else about the "language of flowers," you've probably heard that "rosemary is for remembrance." This adage includes all types of remembrance, from being faithful in love, loyal in friendship, and honoring the dearly departed, to helping meats and wine "remember" their flavor and encouraging our stomachs to remember their appetites and our brains to remember what day it is. Rosemary contains antioxidants that appear to put the brakes on free-radical molecules, which may cause Alzheimer's disease and wreak other havoc on aging bodies.

Whether inspired by rosemary's evergreen nature or its long-lasting smell, the herb's link with memory began with Greek students who wore garlands of it in hopes of acing their finals. The herb has been woven into bridal wreaths, burned as incense (both in religious ceremonies and with juniper, to purify the air of sickrooms), and considered "very medicinable for the head" and for "weyknesse of ye brayne." The herb's ashes were used as a toothpowder.

About the only people who haven't loved rosemary were men of the 16th century, who thought (where do these ideas get started?) that the herb prospered only in homes where women called the shots. We assume many a fine rosemary specimen bit the dust as a result.

Rosemary's flavor is not a light one. Combine it with substantial winter foods: delectable roasts (especially lamb), squashes, beans, rich stews, heavy soups, creamy sauces, and homemade bread. It has become traditional on focaccia. Because the leaves are like tiny spears, chop or crush them before you add them to foods.

In summer, pick a whole branch of rosemary and lay it on your barbecue coals and/or on top of your food, so the flavored smoke permeates it. (You can try this with any herb, but rosemary's tough leaves stand up to it well, and you won't have to worry about the effect being too subtle.) You can also skewer meat on its woody stems to add an inner flavor to barbecue.

Rue (Ruta graveolens)

Rue, a member of the citrus family, is an evergreen perennial native to the Balkans and southeastern Europe, somewhat woody near the bottom and growing up to 3 feet tall and wide. The divided leaves are both fernlike and slightly succulent; each powdery-coated leaflet has a spoon or club shape.

From late spring until fall, rue bears clusters of bright yellow, five-petaled, ½-inch-diameter flowers with a dimpled green center, followed by an ornamental five-lobed seed capsule. Poor rue has been described as emitting "a powerful, disagreeable odour." We would more charitably describe the smell as "interesting."

Ruta graveolens.

How to grow

There's a myth that this perennial will thrive if you steal it from a neighbor. We don't recommend that, but if you do commit a little botanical larceny, be sure to wear gloves. Some people react to the herb's touch as they would to poison ivy.

Better than inviting a criminal record, start rue seeds indoors in late winter. Transplant seedlings to a sunny spot with average, well-drained, neutral to slightly alkaline soil, spacing them about 18 inches apart. You can propagate more rue from cuttings or division. Rue is hardy from Zones 4 to 11.

Rue was once a staple of knot gardens. Plant it as an edging, or as contrast to greener (or yellower) or bolder-leafed herbs and ornamentals. The long-lasting flowers are stunning with blues and purples, such as those of salvias.

Cultivars and related plants

Despite rue's limited uses, breeders have liked it enough to select strains with even bluer foliage ('Jackman Blue', 'Blue Curl') and variegated foliage ('Harlequin', 'Variegata'). Another species, fringed rue *(Ruta chalepensis)* has larger flowers and tear-dropped shaped leaves; it is hardy in Zones 6 to 8.

At least two plants have similar common names. Goat's rue *(Galega officinalis),* a member of the pea family, has bright green, lance-shaped leaves and purple flowers, and is hardy in Zones 3 to 9. It was once fed to cows to increase milk and used to make cheese. Syrian rue *(Peganum harmala),* a perennial hardy in Zones 7 to 10, is the source of a red dye used in Persian rugs.

Lore and usage

Rue may set you free — if you don't rue the day you planted it. The genus and common names came from the Greek word *"reuo,"* meaning "to set free." It may refer to rue's reputed abilities for healing, or more likely, for breaking the spell of witches. Hearing that it would prevent eyestrain, painters and sculptors of ancient Rome ate vast amounts.

Used to sprinkle on holy water, rue became the "herb of grace," symbolizing repentance. Judges brought sprigs of it into courtrooms to ward off "gaol fever" (jail fever) carried by prisoners; and during the plague, thieves who stole from corpses included "vinegar of the four thieves" in a brew devised to prevent contagion.

Today, the word on ingesting rue is **don't.** It can cause powerful cramps, hallucinations, and twitching. More commonly, ingestion and even external contact can cause phototoxicity — ultrasensitivity to the sun — leading to severe burns and blisters.

Saffron (Crocus sativus)

Most of us know crocus as a harbinger of spring, so we can be a bit disoriented the first time we see one blooming in fall. The saffron crocus, a native primarily of the Mediterranean region, blooms in September and has 2-inch, rich lilac-colored flowers with darker veins and throats. The long, bright orange-red stigma may poke out of the blooms when they close at night.

Dreaming of raising enough of this expensive flavoring to make tons of paella? Better knock down your house and a couple of neighbors' homes so you'll have enough room. The "threads" of saffron are the stigmas from the heart of this fall-blooming crocus. Each flower has only three, so it takes some 60,000 blossoms (and a lot of hand-picking) to make a pound of this golden spice.

Crocus sativus.

How to grow

Give your crocuses light, gritty soil of average fertility. They prefer full sun, but will bloom with five hours of sun daily. Crocuses grow from corms (a modified bulb) and should be planted in spring or early summer. If you can't buy corms until fall, get them into the ground posthaste: They're putting out shoots and are ready to roll. Set the corms 3 to 4 inches deep and 6 inches apart. You can give them a nutritional boost with a little rock phosphate. Plants do best in Zones 7 to 9; they dislike both cold, wet climates and hot, humid ones.

Plant crocuses where you can gaze down on them, along a path or toward the front of a bed, in your herb garden among creeping thymes, or in the crevices of a rock garden. They're also wonderful in a lawn where grass grows sparsely, such as under the drip line of a tree.

If you collect the stigmas to make bouillabaisse or risotto Milanese, handle them gingerly, dry with utmost care, and keep them in a stoppered glass vial in a cool place.

Cultivars and related plants

You may see plants advertised as autumn crocuses (or meadow saffron) that are really the bulb of another genus, *Colchicum autumnale*. These have bigger flowers and are never bothered by pests because they're poisonous — you definitely don't want to munch any part of them. They contain a toxic alka-loid, colchicine, which was once used to treat rheumatism and gout. Modern plant breeders have harnessed colchicine to manipulate the chromosome count of plants, producing triploid flowers with thicker, damage-resistant petals.

Two other herbs are often stand-ins for saffron: calendula, which was described earlier in this chapter, and safflower *(Carthamus tinctorius).* Safflower, an annual with yellow-orange thistlelike flowers, has been used so often to adulterate saffron that it's also called bastard saffron. Its flowers give food a more reddish tinge than true saffron.

Lore and usage

The Greeks, Chinese, and Egyptians have used saffron as a dye since ancient times. The Romans were wild about its perfume, sprinkling saffron water on theater benches, flinging the leaves about their banquet halls, and cramming them into pillows.

Culpeper recommended saffron for strengthening the heart and for menstrual depression, but warned that a large dose could lead to drowsiness or, even more alarming, "convulsive laughter, which ended in death." In the 19th and 20th centuries, it was sometimes mixed with brandy to treat measles. Modern studies link its active ingredient, crocetin, to reduced risks of cardiovascular disease. But for most of us, it would be a lot cheaper to invest in a top-of-the-line treadmill.

Sage (Salvia officinalis)

Sage is a hardy subshrub (woody at the bottom, with softer new growth above) native to the northern Mediterranean. Where happy, it will grow 3 feet tall and wide. The elongated oval leaves grow up to 3 inches long, pebbly in appearance and sandpapery to the touch; their hue is grayer in dry climates, greener in humid ones. Sage's late spring racemes of blue-violet flowers would be reward enough for growing this herb.

How to grow

You can start the species from seeds if you're willing to wait several years for your first harvest, but we recommend buying a plant or two.

Give sage full sun and organically rich, slightly acid, well-draining soil. Prune plants regularly to keep them from becoming leggy (you can use stem cut-tings to produce new plants). In winter, poor drainage is invariably fatal (with protection, common sage thrives in Zones 4 to 19). Sages that are three or four years old are less vigorous, but even one old stalwart plant usually pro-vides more than enough of this strong-flavored herb for a family.

Because of its high oil content, sage can be tricky to preserve. Make sure it's completely dry before you store your harvest.

Cultivars and related plants

If you tire of gray-green leaves you can buy sage cultivars with foliage that is golden, purple, or the popular 'Tricolor' that combines green, white, and pinkish purple and is said to withstand humidity and heat better than its parent. 'Berggarten' has larger leaves, and 'Icterina' is variegated green and gold.

Of some 900 *Salvia* species, at least 899 of them are worth growing, especially if you live in a hot, dry climate and love their range of purple, magenta, and red flowers. Unfortunately, far too many of them are hardy only through Zone 8, at best.

Here are some of the sages with culinary or medicinal uses, or pungent leaves worth growing for the same reason you might grow scented geraniums:

- **Greek sage** *(S. fruticosa)*. Although inferior to common sage, Greek sage is often used in commercial spice products. More upright (to 4 feet) and less spreading, it often has compound, lobed leaves, and blooms earlier and heavier with pink to mauve flowers. Zones 8 to 11.

- **Cleveland, or blue, sage** *(S. clevelandii)*. This California native stays under 2 feet tall with white, blue, or lilac flowers. It has toothed, wrinkled leaves that you can use like common sage. Zones 9 to 11.

- **Lyreleaf sage** *(S. lyrata)*. Lyreleaf is native to woods in the northern and central United States, and earned the nickname "cancer weed" because of its traditional use as a cancer cure. Two feet tall with violet flowers, its most attractive feature is the dandelion-shaped leaves with maroon markings, sometimes turning solid maroon in dry conditions. Zones 5 to 10.

- **Painted sage** *(S. viridis)*. One of the few annual (sometimes biennial) salvias, painted sage is native to Europe, Africa, and western Asia. Sometimes confusingly called annual clary, it is grown for lovely purple or pink bracts that are striking in arrangements, both fresh and dry.

- **Peruvian sage** *(S. discolor)*. This plant is hardy only in Zones 9 and 10, but has great charm in a hanging basket, with woolly white stems and leaves setting off indigo blue flowers.

- **Pineapple sage** *(S. elegans)*. The pineapple sage is soft-stemmed with edible red flowers; its leaves add tropical fruit to the usual sage scent. It can reach 6 feet in Zones 8 to 11 where it is hardy. 'Scarlet Pineapple' has especially fine blossoms.

> ✔ **Spanish sage** *(S. lavandulifolia)*. This is similar to common sage except in one regard: Spanish sage has leaves that are smaller and clustered at the bottom of the plant, so the flowers appear on bare stems. Its flavor is described as stronger than that of common sage; in Spain, it's a diabetes treatment. Hardy in Zones to 10.

On a final note: Sagebrush is not a sage; it is more closely related to the artemisias, like southernwood and wormwood, and is not edible. Also unrelated is Russian sage *(Perovskia atriplicifolia),* a popular perennial with late-blooming purple flowers. The leaves are fragrant enough to try in potpourri, however.

Lore and usage

We're not old sages, but take our advice: 'Tis a wise and well-seasoned gardener who plants this herb, although not necessarily an immortal one. The genus name *Salvia* comes from the same Latin word as "salvation," and while the Romans and Greeks thought it enhanced memory (like rosemary), it was the Arabs who concluded that it could bestow immortality. This led to aphorisms like "Why should a man die who grows sage in his garden?" As far as we know, there is not a single surviving male or female from that period.

Herbalist John Gerard said sage was good for senses, memory, and sinews, especially "shakey trembling of the members." Later, the French thought it would assuage grief, and in some places sowed graves with its seeds. In 19th-century America, herbalists touted sage tea for squelching sexual desire and hence, venereal disease.

In truth, sage might enhance your sex appeal, but as an antiperspirant. You can try applying an infusion externally or drinking some sage tea (if you can wait, because it's not effective for two hours). Because sage contains both astringents and antiseptics, it's often recommended for oral hygiene (just rub a fresh leaf over tooth and gum), as a mouthwash to prevent gum disease and bad breath, or as a gargle for sore throats.

As for aromatic appeal, the smell of Mom's sage-and-crouton mix says "Thanksgiving" as strongly as balsam and pine needles speak of Christmas. This herb dances with poultry like Rogers with Astaire. Rub it on duck, goose, or turkey before roasting for a light touch, or mix it in a marinade. Toss it on a grill with Cornish game hens. Not too proud to change partners, sage also does wonders for pork and meatloaf. Pair it with any cheesy dish — quiche, toasted sandwiches, macaroni — and snip it into hearty stews, bread dough, or corn muffins. The flowers are slightly sweeter than the leaves and are excellent in salads.

Savory, summer and winter (Satureja hortensis; S. montana)

With a name like savory, it's got to be good (our apologies to the jam and jelly people). But savory means tasty and well-seasoned, and for a long time this herb was the "big gun" for European cooks. (People from ancient cultures seemed to try herbs for every ache and ailment under the sun before they considered throwing them into the stewpot. But when you have an average life expectancy of 25 as they did, it stands to reason that haute cuisine might take a back seat.)

Summer and winter savory (both mint-family members) have needlelike leaves up to 1-inch long, erect stems, and whorls of edible blossoms summer through fall.

Summer savory, *S. hortensis,* has the more delicate aroma and flavor of the two herbs. It is a rather slumping annual, growing to 18 inches, and has abundant but tiny pale pink flowers that hunker down in the leaf axils. The gray green, downy leaves often turn purple in fall.

Winter savory, *S. montana,* is a semi-evergreen perennial or subshrub, growing only about a foot tall. The white to pale purple flowers, which often have purple spots on their lower lips, bloom on spikes. The leaves are dark green and glossy, and have a more peppery flavor than the annual species.

Satureja hortensis.

How to grow

You can start either type of savory from fresh seeds, sown indoors or out. Like most perennials, winter savory is slow to get moving, so we recommend you opt to buy plants. Space either species about a foot apart in well-drained, neutral to slightly acid soil of average fertility. Summer savory wilts quickly in droughts, so be sure its soil is rich in moisture-retaining organic matter.

Summer savory bolts quickly — flowers and sets seeds prematurely — in hot weather. Plant it where you can harvest it regularly while it lasts.

Prune winter savory often to keep it producing tender new foliage. Winter savory prunes so well it's often used as a formal edging or in knot gardens. It can be short-lived (although hardy in Zones 6 to 9), so take cuttings or make divisions during its second or third year so you won't be without plants.

Cultivars and related plants

Look for creeping savory *(S. spicigera),* a prostrate subshrub still sold under the name *S. reptans,* if you have a rock garden or need an herbal ground cover. Creeping savory has white flowers and is hardy in Zones 7 to 9.

Once classified in the savory genus are the calamints *(Calamintha* spp.), which are more minty in flavor. Lesser calamint *(C. nepeta)* is an erect perennial that grows 18 inches tall and has toothed green leaves and masses of ¼-inch mauve to pink flowers. Showy calamint *(C. grandiflora)* can reach 2 feet when it produces its 6-inch flower spikes. It has bigger leaves, to 2 inches long, and the hot pink flowers are more than an inch across. Even more of a knockout is 'Variegata', with pale green and white leaves and magenta flowers that never seem to quit. All are hardy in Zones 5 to 9.

Lore and usage

Because of savory's fragrance, it was widely planted near beehives to flavor honey. The Romans took the opposite tack and used savory as a flavoring for vinegar. In 17th-century England, winter savory was dried and crumbled for breading meat and fish — still a fine idea. Both species were among the first herbs brought to America by the early settlers.

The genus name comes from "satyr," the goatlike woodland deity whose name is synonymous with men who are, well, a bit goatish. But while summer savory was supposed to increase sexual appetite, winter savory was more like a cold shower. Culpeper thought it could even cure deafness, but Dioscorides and Galen were probably more on target when they said it was "heating and drying."

Traditionally used for colds and other respiratory problems, winter savory does have some mild antibacterial and carminative, or gas-squelching, properties, as do many of the culinary herbal superstars. That works out well because this herb, which combines the tastes of mint and thyme, has a particular affinity for beans of all types — dried beans such as lentils and favas, bean soups, bean salads, and peas.

Scented geranium (Pelargonium spp.)

Scented geraniums, also called pelargoniums, are perennial natives of South Africa. Every scented geranium is different and not even subtly so. Some have leaves as big as the palm of your hand, sharply lobed and rough as a two-day beard. Leaves of others aren't much bigger than a quarter, scalloped, and downy as a peach.

Many scented geraniums squat coyly at just about 6 inches, whereas others shoot up quickly to a couple feet or more, and twice as wide. The differences in their scents can be subtle, and even require a certain amount of imagination. These herbs, like an expensive wine or a symphony, need no excuses for being other than pure sensuous pleasure. Sample and savor.

Pelargonium.

How to grow

Scented geraniums' natural habitat has trained them to expect little in the way of water or fertilizer. Give them light soil amended with organic matter; diluted feeding of organic fertilizer monthly during the growing season; and enough water to keep them from wilting. What they must have is plenty of sun, so don't buy more than your south-facing windows or grow lights can accommodate in winter. Keeping them in pots that fit a bit tight helps restrain their growth.

Don't be afraid to prune scented geraniums back — a little careful cutting will give you a bushier plant. Scented geranium cuttings can root in damp sand year-round, so this is a good way to give yourself some insurance plants or to share with friends.

Scented geraniums are hardy only in Zones 10 and 11, but do reasonably well indoors in winter. Stems of older plants become woody.

Cultivars and related plants

One of our favorite mail-order sources lists more than 50 scented geraniums. The names often clue you to their scent — but not to their size. If your space is limited, watch for words like "vigorous" and "robust."

A few that have done well: *Pelargonium* 'Clorinda', with a sweet cedar fragrance and bright rose flowers; *P. crispum,* or lemon geranium; *P. crispum* 'Variegatum', a lemon-scented cultivar with cream-and-white leaves; *P.* 'Graveolens', or rose geranium; apple geranium, *P. odoratissimum;* and *P.* 'Royal Oak', which has pink flowers and oaklike leaves that smell like balsam.

'Old-Fashioned Rose' smells just like its name, and the lemon-shaded edges and pleating on the leaves of 'Lady Plymouth' are irresistible. And 'Cody's Nutmeg' not only wafts a spicy scent when you stroke its mint-green leaves, but also always seems to have a few airy white flowers. And of course, you'll have to get 'Coconut' for a hanging basket . . . and the list goes on.

Lore and usage

Scented geraniums were first introduced to England in 1690, and popularized about a century later in a five-volume publication by a fellow appropriately named Robert Sweet. After you try a few, you'll be hooked. The first time we sauntered into a well-stocked garden center for just one or two of these scent-sationals, we were lucky to leave with our bank account in the black.

Sorrel (Rumex spp.)

There are some 200 species in this genus, many of which are called either sorrel or dock — or in one confusing instance, sorrel dock. Oxalic acid gives all of them a slightly sour taste, but the two species most commonly used for cooking are garden sorrel *(Rumex acetosa)* and French sorrel *(R. scutatus)*.

Sorrel forms clumps of lance-shaped, wavy-edged leaves that look a bit like spinach. The mid-to-late-summer flowers are whorled densely around spikes and are star-shaped, first greenish and then flushed with purple or rust, followed by dark brown achenes, or fruits. The reddish brown taproot, up to a foot long, is yellow inside. Garden, or common, sorrel has stems up to 3 feet tall from clumps of 5- to 8-inch leaves, whereas French sorrel tends to form mats, 6 to 20 inches tall and twice as wide, with thick, broad leaves only 1 to 2 inches long.

Rumex.

How to grow

Sorrels are easy to start from seed, indoors or out. Space plants 8 inches apart in the garden in deeply dug soil (to accommodate the plants' long taproots) that is rich in organic matter. Sorrels tolerate partial shade but not drought; most plants are not long-lived but are root hardy (garden sorrel, Zones 5 to 9, French sorrel, Zones 3 to 10).

Pinch off flower heads to keep new foliage coming and to prevent self-sowing. (Not only do plants seed generously, their deep taproots can be difficult to dislodge if you decide to say "so long" to sorrel.) Try it in a deep container. We like it as the "top-knot" of a strawberry jar.

Cultivars and related plants

Two garden cultivars of French sorrel, 'Blonde de Lyon' and 'Nobel', have especially succulent leaves and are perfect for salads. A new selection, 'Profusion', is considered seedless, which will keep you from growing sorrel where you don't want it; 'Silver Shield' has gray-green foliage.

Curled, or yellow, dock *(Rumex crispus)* is a giant, as tall as 5 feet tall with wavy, foot-long leaves. Although edible, its historic use is for making salves to treat skin problems.

Sheep sorrel *(R. acetosella)* also has tasty leaves and especially attractive seed pods. Naturalized in North American meadows, it has been used for fevers, inflammation, diarrhea, and by Native Americans as a cancer treatment.

Lore and usage

In 1720, John Evelyn wrote that "Sorrel sharpens the appetite, assuages heat, cools the liver and strengthens the heart . . . and in the making of sallets imparts a grateful quickness to the rest as supplying the want of oranges and lemons." The nutrition and taste made not only salads, "but men themselves pleasant and agreeable." We suspect that you, too, know someone who could benefit from sorrel.

Sorrel also was used for venereal disease (usually described more circumspectly as "purifying the blood") and for skin ailments, particularly nettle stings. Popular as a laxative, it contains tannins that also prevent diarrhea; because it is rich in vitamin C, sorrel was often used to prevent and treat scurvy. Both species have been called cuckoo's meate and cuckoo's bread because it was thought that birds ate them in order to have a clearer song. Birds do like to eat sorrel seeds.

The French started the custom of sorrel soup and then added the herb to ragout and other stews. It's also popular in fish sauces and pâté. You can cook the leaves like spinach, or use them fresh in salads. Not only are they high in vitamin C, they contain vitamin A, calcium, phosphate, potassium, and magnesium.

Southernwood *(Artemisia abrotanum)*

It may sound like the national herb of the Confederacy, but southernwood gets its common name from the fact that it's native to southern Europe, unlike its more northerly counterpart, wormwood *(Artemisia absinthium)*.

Members of the aster clan, most artemisias have insignificant flowers and are grown for their aromatic, delicate, divided foliage. Southernwood is a woody perennial that grows to 3 to 4 feet and about as wide, with finely divided gray-green leaves up to 2 inches long. You can barely discern individual leaves for all their threadlike lobes, which are gray underneath and somewhat hairy, especially on new growth. The almost invisible late summer flowers are dingy yellow on panicles 4 to 12 inches long.

How to grow

Start southernwood from a plant or a cutting — semihard stems root easily — spacing plants at least 2 feet apart. As long as they have good drainage, artemisias adapt well to any soil. They don't like wet winters or humid summers, but tolerate light shade and drought. Prune southernwood — hardy in Zone 5 (with winter protection) to Zone 10 — in spring to keep it from looking weedy.

Cultivars and related plants

You can read more about other members of this genus just ahead, under the entries for tarragon and wormwood. But wait! There are still more artemisias.

✔ **Mugwort** *(Artemisia vulgaris)*. This artemisia was used in both medicine and food — and was a beer flavoring before hops came along. Said to repel evil and poisons, it was planted along the roads of Rome for weary soldiers to stick in their shoes. The plant is not attractive, however, and is invasive.

- **Seashore artemisia** *(A. stelleriana).* If you need seaside plants, consider *A. stelleriana,* an evergreen East Coast native that forms silver clumps on sand dunes. Usually available as 'Silver Brocade' (a.k.a. 'Boughton Silver'), it grows up to 6 inches tall and is hardy in Zones 3 to 7.

- **Silvermound** *(A. schmidtiana* 'Silver Mound'). Silvermound forms a silky, sensuous hump. Cold hardy in Zones 3 to 7, it often "melts" and loses its form in the South. 'Silverado' is less shapely but holds up to heat. 'Powis Castle' is another clump former, with feathery leaves of silver gray, hardy in Zones 4 to 9.

- **Sweet Annie** *(A. annua).* This annual, a staple of dried bouquets and wreaths, can zoom up to 6 feet in a warm summer, and spread 3 feet wide. Mature plants look like feathery little conifers with their fine, divided green leaves, wider at the bottom than at the top. In summer it's speckled with clusters of tiny yellow flowers. Its warm autumn fragrance will work wonders for any room (we know firsthand that it even over-powers the smell of wet dog fur and high school football uniforms).

- **White mugwort** *(A. lactiflora).* Need a big bruiser for the back of the border? White mugwort (also known as ghostplant) is your boy. It's named for its flowers; the lobed and compound leaves are green, form-ing a rosette that shoots up stems 4 to 6 feet tall, with 1- to 2-foot feath-ery panicles of flowers from late summer to fall. Hardy in Zones 5 to 8.

- **White sage** *(A. ludoviciana).* This plant has silver foliage but differs from other artemisias in that its 2-to-4-inch leaves form daisy-shaped whorls. Deciduous and soft-stemmed (rather than woody), it grows 2 to 4 feet tall; its gray flowers bloom in summer. Because of underground roots, popular cultivars 'Silver King' and 'Silver Queen' often pop up where not wanted. Hardy in Zone 4.

Because we're sure you're wondering, the sagebrushes that perfume the hills of our West and turn into the tumbling tumbleweed used to be artemisias, but have now been reclassified by those wacky botanists and are called *Seriphidium.*

Lore and usage

Commonly known as old man — a tip of the hat to its gray foliage — southernwood was also called lad's love and boy's love. Young men put a sprig in a bouquet to symbolize fidelity to their sweetie, and the herb was said to be an aphrodisiac. (Oddly enough, the genus name *Artemisia* alludes to Artemis, the Greek goddess of chastity.)

Young men also burned southernwood, mixed the ashes with oil, and rubbed the solution on their chins to stimulate beard growth. (Old men tried it on their pate.) Burning southernwood was a popular activity because it was also thought to drive away snakes.

The French called the herb *garderobe* — which sounds like a web address for horticultural duds — because it was a good moth repellent. Remember that bees don't like it either when choosing a spot for it in the garden. Like rue, southernwood was used to protect judges and other respectable people from prisoners' infectious diseases, and like costmary, it was poked in lapels and tussie-mussies to keep church-goers from nodding off.

The medicinal value of artemisias — even for their longtime use against parasites — is hotly debated. Southernwood does have antiseptic properties, so consider mixing it with oatmeal for a facial mask. Most species dry well for potpourri and crafts; semi-woody types such as southernwood make good bases for wreaths.

Sweet cicely (Myrrhis odorata)

Talk about an identity crisis. Here's an herb that tastes like licorice and looks like a fern, and found its way into kitchens as anise, great chervil, sweet chervil, cow chervil, sweet bracken, and sweet fern.

This perennial from Europe grows as tall as 4 feet, and its thick stems are hollow and slightly hairy, whereas the leaves are white and downy underneath. It looks for all the world like a big, bright green fern. In late spring or early summer, clusters of white flowers appear, similar to flowers of Queen-Anne's lace. Similar to others in the carrot clan, sweet cicely has a long taproot.

Myrrhis odorata.

How to grow

Sweet cicely thrives in woodland conditions. That means plants need not only some shade but deep, humus-rich, moisture-retentive soil like you might find in a forest. Even then, sweet cicely is rarely happy in the Deep South because it can't take the heat.

If you saved your own seeds, refrigerate them for two or three months before sowing or sow them in the fall. Space plants 3 feet apart. Don't let plants dry out, and remove flower heads to prevent self-sowing — sweet cicely, which is hardy in Zones 5 to 8, naturalizes easily.

Cultivars and related plants

Myrrhis odorata is the only species in its genus, but a genus of plants native to North American woods, *Osmorhiza* spp., is also called sweet cicely. Like *M. odorata,* these herbs have aromatic, segmented leaves; their flower clusters are white or yellow-green. Native Americans used them to treat respiratory ailments, skin irritations, and indigestion. Their roots were so attractive to livestock that plants were used to lure horses and other animals into pens.

Lore and usage

Although a roadside weed in England, sweet cicely also found its way into gardens, as garden guru Gertrude Jekyll admired it. "For its beauty," she wrote, it "deserves to be in every garden; it is charming, with its finely cut, pale green leaves and really handsome flowers."

Maude Grieve's *A Modern Herbal* says that sweet cicely roots were soaked in wine to treat consumption, and an ointment of sweet cicely was applied to "cure green wounds, stinking ulcers and ease the pain of gout." The roots were said to increase the lust and strength of "old people that are dull and without courage" and served as "a valuable tonic for girls from 15 to 18 years of age." Having some experience in this matter, we find it hard to imagine that anyone ever needed to increase the lust of high-school-age maidens. . . .

The flavor of sweet cicely is usually compared to lovage combined with anise. You can cook the root like other root vegetables, and eat the seeds out of hand. (Like anise, they help to freshen your breath.) Add the seeds and/or chopped leaves to fruit salad or stewed fruits or baked goods.

Sweet woodruff (Galium odoratum)

If you think of a ruff as a collar (like those big, starched things the Elizabethans wore), you'll remember that this perennial holds its lance-shaped leaves in whorls 1 to 2 inches across, marching up its stem. Creeping along the ground on horizontal stems, sweet woodruff rarely reaches more than 8 or 9 inches tall. From late spring to midsummer it produces clouds of fragrant, white, star-shaped flowers.

Galium odoratum.

How to grow

Even nursery professionals have trouble getting sweet woodruff seeds to germinate. If you don't have a friend who will share a few plants with you, we recommend you purchase plants to get started with this herb.

This woodland native wants a bit of shade and humus-rich soil that doesn't dry out. Sweet woodruff, a tough groundcover, spreads on its own and is hardy in Zones 5 to 8. To increase your stand more quickly, divide plants in spring (make sure each division has a piece of the crown with some root attached) or propagate from stem cuttings.

Cultivars and related plants

Lady's bedstraw is a sun-loving cousin to sweet woodruff; goosegrass *(Galium aparine)* is an annual member of the family. Also known as cleavers and sticky Willie, this herb grows to 4 feet and has been used in a variety of folk medicines for treating everything from glandular fever and hepatitis to skin inflammations and psoriasis.

Lore and usage

This delicate herb's claim to fame is as the flavoring agent in May wine. The Germans drink the concoction, called *Maibowle,* on May 1 to celebrate the coming of spring. The honey-and-vanilla-scented herb smoothes the rough edges of the immature grapes. The French name translates as musk of the woods, but most people say it smells less musky and more like new-mown hay. The aroma is barely detectable until the foliage dries.

Sweet woodruff's fragrance is produced by a chemical called coumarin, which is used in perfumery for its own sake as well as to "fix" other scents. Pharmacists of old used the herb to mask other, less pleasant smells. An ingredient in high-quality snuff, sweet woodruff was also stuffed in mattresses like its cousin, lady's bedstraw.

Note: Coumarin is an anti-coagulant, so if you take blood thinners, do not use sweet woodruff or drink May wine. A chemical similar to coumarin is an ingredient in rat poison; death results from internal hemorrhaging.

Once thought to be good for the kidneys and liver, sweet woodruff has been found to cause liver damage in laboratory animals, and large amounts can trigger dizziness and vomiting. You can employ it in a *Maibowle,* however, by steeping a couple sprigs in white wine for a day or two. (Most people use an inexpensive Rhine wine; it won't improve your best Pouilly-Fuissé one whit.)

Tansy (Tanacetum vulgare)

A perennial native to Europe, tansy has arching stems that form a mound of finely divided, fernlike leaves; plants reach 2 to 3 feet tall, about 18 inches wide. Also called golden buttons for its 4-inch, flat-topped clusters of ½-inch yellow knobs that appear from late summer through fall, tansy looks quite like its cousin feverfew, especially *Tanacetum parthenium* 'Golden Ball'. The entire plant smells of camphor.

How to grow

Tansy is one of those herbs that are easier to grow than to control because it spreads by underground rhizomes. You should have no problem starting it from seed or from divisions from a neighbor who has way too much. Give tansy a home in a naturalized or contained area — plants are unparticular about soil but need good drainage and plenty of sun — where you can enjoy its graceful form and cheerful flowers. One gardener we know grows this tough customer, hardy in Zones 4 to 8, as a low hedge between her lawn and drive and disciplines it with her lawn mower.

Cultivars and related plants

If you want to grow tansy for the long-lasting flowers, try a cultivar called 'Goldsticks', which has larger blooms on its long stems that are easy to cut and arrange. If it's pretty foliage you're after, then try one (or all) of these three: *T. vulgare* var. *crispum,* or curly tansy, a compact cultivar that has larger, light green fernlike leaves; 'Isla Gold', which has near-gold foliage; and 'Silver Lace', with variegated leaves.

Lore and usage

The name of this herb comes from a Greek word *athanaton,* meaning "without death" or "immortal." Not only do the cut flowers last almost forever, but tansy was said to be "capital for preserving dead bodies from corruption." Laid in coffins, it apparently kept the deceased from attracting flies until the funeral service was over. It was also rubbed into meat to repel flies and other insects.

Tansy was once an ingredient in cakes and puddings eaten at Easter, when it was thought to counteract any ill effects of a Lenten diet. Culpeper recommended tansy for wives who wished to become pregnant: "Let those women that desire children love this herb; it is their best companion, their husbands excepted. . . ."

This herb is now considered far too strong and potentially toxic to be used in home remedies. If you're not pregnant, it's probably safe in small amounts as a seasoning. One popular destination is egg dishes; chopped leaves will add peppery zip to stuffing, salad dressings, and spreads. A little goes a long way.

Tarragon, French (Artemisia dracunculus var. sativa)

Tarragon, a perennial from central and eastern Europe, doesn't look a thing like most other artemisias because its 1- to 3-inch, bluish green leaves aren't divided, but look more like blades of grass. It grows up to 2 feet tall with somewhat lax stems. Tiny yellow-green flowers rarely open and are almost always sterile.

In the 17th century, some people believed tarragon came from flax seeds that had been inserted in a radish or an onion. This was not a sci-fi propagation theory, but probably stemmed from the fact that flavorful French, or culinary, tarragon cannot be reliably propagated from seeds.

Artemisia dracunculus var. sativa.

How to grow

Always buy tarragon as a plant, either at a local market where you can do a scratch and sniff, or from a mail-order supplier you trust. Seeds are invariably those of Russian tarragon *(A. dracunculus* var. *inodora [*formerly *dracunculoides]);* it grows to 5 feet and has 6-inch pale green leaves that are about as tasty as lawn grass.

One plant will be enough. Give it organically rich, well-worked soil that drains well and full sun (perhaps a little afternoon shade in hot regions). Periodic light pruning is a good idea, as is a loose mulch during the winter months. Divide your plant every two or three years to keep its long fibrous roots from tangling and committing suicide. These fierce roots inspired the plant's name, from the French word *estragon,* meaning "little dragon." French tarragon is hardy in Zones 3 to 9.

Cultivars and related plants

Kin to tarragon by taste is the Mexican mint marigold *(Tagetes lucida),* a relative of our garden marigold. Also known as Mexican tarragon, this yellow-flowered herb is upright and slender, with lance-shaped leaves nearly identical to tarragon's. It's hardy only in Zones 8 to 11 and is usually grown as an annual, especially by gardeners in the Deep South where high summer temperatures can keep tarragon plants from doing well.

Lore and usage

Tarragon was said to cure bites and stings of mad dogs and "venomous beasts." The Greeks used it for toothaches (nibble a leaf and you'll feel a numbing sensation); and because it was supposed to prevent fatigue, travelers in the Middle Ages put it in their shoes.

Herbalist John Gerard reduced tarragon to an herbal shrug, which he said was "not to be eaten alone in sallades, but joyned with other herbs . . . neither do we know what other use this herbe hath." What other use, indeed? No béarnaise or *sauce tartare* is complete without this herb, which is also a standard ingredient in the herb mix known as *fines herbes* and among the most popular herbs for herbal vinegar.

Thyme (Thymus spp.)

Botanists estimate there are 350 species of thyme — all evergreen perennials and subshrubs in the mint family — plus scores of subspecies and cultivars. Most cooks grow common or English thyme *(Thymus vulgaris),* although there are several "chemotypes" with different flavors, from the high-thymol 'Narrowleaf French' to others — the flavors of which have been compared with tar.

As a rule, common thyme grows 12 to 18 inches tall, spreading as it ages. The base is woody and the branches upright with gray-green, oval or slightly lance-shaped leaves up to a half inch long. Bees are passionate about the small tubular pink or lilac flowers that cluster in early to mid-summer.

Because of its shrubby shape, common thyme can be used as a low hedge. Other thymes, known collectively as "creeping thymes," make ideal ground covers, are elegant in pots or window boxes, and are charming tucked between rocks or stepping stones.

How to grow

Thymes, which are generally hardy in Zones 5 to 8, are so easy to propagate from cuttings or divisions that few gardeners start from seed (although that's easy, too). Space plants 6 to 8 inches apart in light soil that has been enriched with organic matter. Harvesting thyme with abandon will keep new growth coming. Plants get sparse and woody in the center after two or three years, so renew your plants by dividing, layering, or taking cuttings from the old ones.

Cultivars and related plants

After you get hooked on thymes, you may have to pull out all your other herbs to make room for them. You can choose them for variations in taste, such as lemon thyme *(Thymus x citriodora)* and *T. vulgaris* 'Orange Balsam'. Others smell and taste of caraway *(T. herba-barona)* or lavender *(T. thracicus).* Herb specialists offer dozens of possibilities, including mint thyme, nutmeg thyme, coconut thyme, and more, and it's here that names get muddled. When you visit a nursery, crush a leaf to smell what you're getting.

A popular creeping thyme is *T. praecox* subsp. *arcticus.* As you might guess from the name, it is more cold hardy than the species — Zones 4 to 9. 'Elfin', 'Minimus', and 'Minor', cultivars of the creeping species *T. serpyllum* vie for the honor of dinkiest thyme. Also hardy down to Zone 4, they stay under 4 inches tall and have leaves the size of pinheads. (If you plan to cook with creeping thymes — and we don't recommend that you do — plant them so they'll hang over the side of a container; otherwise, harvesting will be murder on your knees and back.)

If it's foliage color you want, you can choose lemon thyme's gold-leafed cultivar, 'Aureus', or silver thyme, *T. vulgaris* 'Argenteus', which lights up an herb bed with its white-edged leaf and looks beautiful in a hanging basket. Flowers? Look for *T. serpyllum* var. *coccineus,* commonly known as creeping red thyme, which is loaded with magenta flowers and hardy from Zones 4 to 9. Also lovely is the more subtle effect of *T. praecox* subsp. *arcticus* 'Alba' (sometimes called 'White Moss') for the tiny white flowers that cover the bright green leaves. It's hardy in Zones 3 to 10. And don't overlook woolly thyme, *T. pseudolanuginosus,* a prostrate species with hairy stems and woolly gray-green leaves that's hardy in Zones 6 to 9.

Lore and usage

The next time you're harvesting thyme for the *bouquet garni,* pick a sprig to hide under your pillow. It will either dispel melancholy or prevent nightmares. Maybe both.

There are two explanations for thyme's name as well. It may mean "courage" because it was an invigorating tonic. (During the Crusades, ladies who fancied a particular knight presented him with a scarf embroidered with a sprig of thyme.) More prosaically, the name may stem from a word meaning "to fumigate," as it often was burned to drive off insects and assorted vermin.

Thyme contains a powerful antiseptic, thymol, which was popular for treating wounds until World War I. It is still found in mouthwashes and other commercial products. Europeans use it for respiratory ailments; and it seems to ease the spasms of coughs. Try sipping thyme tea, making a thyme syrup, or making a "tent" with a towel and inhale its steam.

The antiseptic properties make it a good ingredient for a face lotion, and as an antispasmodic it may relieve menstrual cramps or an upset stomach. As John Parkinson noted, "To set down the particular uses whereunto Time is applied, were to weary both the writer and the reader. . . ." Not wishing to weary you, dear reader, we'll add only that most of us know thyme as a friend in the kitchen, where it was first used as a preservative rather than a flavoring.

Valerian (Valeriana officinalis)

Valerian is a hardy perennial growing to 5 feet tall. The stems, produced from a rosette of foliage in the second year, are hollow and grooved, branching with rows of toothed, dark green leaves set along the stems like rungs of a ladder. Both the leaves and stems emit the odd, signature valerian aroma when touched.

One of our all-time favorite *Saturday Night Live* skits is the faux commercial for a product that is both a dessert topping and a floor wax. Valerian's smell is a bit like that. Often sold as garden heliotrope with catalog copy that extols its sweet scent, its roots and the pills made from them smell exactly like an adolescent's dirty gym socks.

The herb's tiny white or pink flowers are arranged in flat clusters and appear from mid spring until late summer. So what do they smell like? You got it — sort of like sweet gym socks. True fans compare the aroma to vanilla.

How to grow

It's possible to start valerian from seeds, but because they don't stay viable for long, it's easier to begin with plants spaced 18 inches apart. Valerian, which is hardy in Zones 4 to 9, grows best in organically rich, moist, slightly acid soil, either in sun or partial shade. Plants sometimes self-sow; you many want to remove spent blooms. Divide large plants in spring every three years or so to keep them healthy; reset the rhizome divisions if you want to increase the size of your valerian patch.

If you want to harvest valerian roots, do so in their second fall. Their strong scent becomes stronger as the root dries, and valerian tea is bitter. We prefer to admire the plant in the garden and buy stress-reducing valerian capsules when book deadlines loom.

Cultivars and related plants

Don't let the common name garden heliotrope confuse this plant with true heliotrope *(Heliotropium arborescens)*. A 2-foot-tall annual with deep green, puckered leaves, it has deep purple blue flowers that most people think smell like cherry pie.

Red valerian *(Centranthus ruber),* which is also called Jupiter's beard, is a short-lived perennial that grows in dry, chalky soil, most famously on England's white cliffs of Dover. The tubular, spurred flowers are most commonly red, but there are pink and white flowered types as well. Hardy in Zones 5 to 8.

Lore and usage

Cats are said to like the scent of valerian as much as catnip. It's also irresistible to rats: The Pied Piper of Hamelin allegedly owed his success not to musical prowess but to having tucked sprigs of valerian in his pockets.

Valerian is the Valium of the herb world, calming the agitated and helping insomniacs nod off with no "hangover" the next morning. In the 14th century, it was written that you could stop men from fighting by giving them juice of valerian. During World War II, some Londoners reputedly took it to ease their jitters during air raids. It's been used to cure nervous disorders, cramps, and vertigo, to stop seizures, to reduce pain, to treat venomous bites, and to heal wounds. No wonder the herb is also known as "all heal."

Valerian extracts are almost never found in home kitchens, but they are used commercially to flavor ice cream, baked goods, condiments, soft drinks, liqueurs, and tobacco. Considering our comments about dirty gym socks, we won't mention product names.

Violet (Viola odorata)

A perennial from southern and western Europe, the sweet violet (also known as the English violet, garden violet, and common violet) grows to 6 or 7 inches tall and a foot wide in a mound of kidney- or heart-shaped leaves that rise out of a tuft of roots. The 3/4-inch flowers have five petals and are usually purple but occasionally pink or white. The plant's runners root at their tips.

*Viola
odorata.*

How to grow

You can start violets from seeds gathered in fall — if you can catch them. The
fall flowers, which are nearly petal-less, can spit seeds several feet (the familiar spring flowers are sterile). Violet seeds need exposure to cold, so leave
them where they land or stratify them before sowing.

It's far easier to begin with divisions, either in fall or early spring. Space
plants 18 inches apart, and give them organically rich soil and partial shade,
especially in warm regions. Violets grow best in cool weather; red spider mite
often plagues plants where conditions are hot and dry. They are hardy in
Zones 5 to 9.

Cultivars and related plants

There are some 500 species of violet, many of them charming North
American natives such as the birds-foot-violet *(Viola pedata)* but not widely
available for sale to gardeners. In the 19th century, a highly fragrant double
form called Parma violets was sold for nosegays, but it, too, is difficult to find.

V. odorata 'Alba', which has white flowers, is the violet you're most likely
to find at the garden center. 'Queen Charlotte' has dark blue flowers; the
blooms of 'Royal Robe' are deep violet and wonderfully fragrant. However,
most of today's "violets" are rigorously cultivated pansies.

Heartsease or Johnny jump-up *(V. tricolor)* is an annual or short-lived
perennial (hardy in Zones 4 to 8) beloved for its little "face" of dark purple,
lavender, and yellow. It's used medicinally, like the common violet, as an
expectorant, and as a wash for itching, acne, and other skin problems.

Lore and usage

Even under the most trying circumstances, we've never considered turning
our beloved into a cow. But that's supposedly what the Roman god Jupiter

did to his side dish, Io, when wife Juno caught wind of her. As solace, he gave Io violets to munch, and her name evolved into the name for this shy spring-blooming plant. The chemical that gives violets their intense brief volley of fragrance is called ionine.

The Greeks thought the violet would moderate anger, whereas Roman naturalist Pliny suggested that a garland of violets would prevent hangovers from wine. (No word on whether this worked for wine made from violets, which was popular at the time.) The Celts soaked violets in goat's milk to create a beauty treatment. Violets have often been used as a sleep aid (one approach called for soaking one's feet in violet water before going to bed), and violet syrup was a tasty treatment for myriad ailments, including inflamed eyes, pleurisy, jaundice, epilepsy, and headaches.

Violets were Napoleon's annual anniversary gift to his wife Josephine. (He supposedly announced, when banished to Elba, "I will return with the violets in the spring.") Violet nosegays were all the rage early in the 20th century, when young women were warned about smelling them with too much abandon. Some people believe the scent is so strong that the nose shuts down from sensory overload after a few seconds.

You can toss violet flowers into salads and fruity drinks, candy them for desserts, make syrup for jelly and sorbet, or freeze them in ice cubes. Violet water, like rose water, adds subtle flavor to fruit salads and baked goods. Herb expert Jim Duke maintains that violet tea may help prevent varicose veins because it contains a compound called rutin that helps strengthen the walls of blood vessels.

Watercress (Nasturtium officinale)

There's not nearly enough overlap between herb gardening and water gardening. Those who like to do both should be grateful for watercress, which also happens to be tasty and nutritious.

A perennial member of the mustard family, watercress is native from Europe and southwest Asia, where it is found growing wild in slow-moving water. Plants creep along for a way, and then stick up 12-inch stems. The dark glossy leaves are compound, with oval or heart-shaped leaflets; the small, white, four-petaled flowers, which are borne in flat-topped clusters, bloom from late spring through summer.

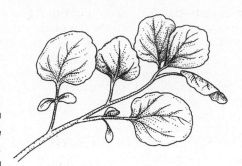

Nasturtium officinale.

How to grow

Watercress, which is hardy in Zones 6 to 9, is unusual even among water plants for preferring moving rather than still water. It's at home in a cleared area along a natural stream bank (be sure the water isn't polluted). If you've built your own back yard pond, grow it in a container placed where the pond's waterfall or fountain creates some gentle turbulence. You can start seeds indoors in flats. Easier and quicker, buy watercress at the supermarket, take cuttings, and root them in wet soil.

No river running through it? You can also grow watercress by submerging clay pots in large tubs of water. To make the plants believe they're in running water, run a hose into the tub for several hours at least four times a week.

Cultivars and related plants

In England, gardeners can choose among all sorts of named watercresses (usually named for towns), but American gardeners must make do with the species or with 'Broad Leaf', an improved cultivar with larger leaves.

Cresses grown on dry land are also members of the mustard family and taste like watercress, but they're members of other genera. They include garden cress *(Lepidium sativum);* curly cress, or cresson *(L. sativum* 'Crispum'); and upland, or winter cress *(Barbarea verna)*. You can have cress continuously from spring to fall by sowing a crop every two weeks, and through the winter by sprouting seeds indoors.

Lore and usage

Watercress has been used since ancient times to prevent scurvy, and as early as the fifth century B.C. it was thought to make children stronger. The Greeks considered it brain food, which meant it was something of an insult to be told to "eat cress."

According to the Roman Pliny, the genus name comes from the Latin *nasus tortus,* which means "writhing nose," an allusion to the plant's peppery qualities. We don't know whether or not watercress's slightly shocking flavor has anything to do with the plant's being recommended for stimulating hair to grow, but we prefer to tuck it in salads, soups, sandwiches, and stir fries, where we can take advantage of its nip and the vitamin C it contains.

Wormwood (Artemisia absinthium)

A hardy Mediterranean perennial averaging 3 feet tall and 2 feet wide, wormwood has with a woody base and forms a sprawling mound of silver green. Its pungent leaves are deeply divided and covered with silky hairs. In summer, plants produce upright panicles of small yellow and gray flowers.

*Artemisia
absinthium.*

How to grow

Similar to other artemisias, wormwood looks delicate but grows tough (it's hardy in Zones 4 to 9). You can start the seeds indoors and then transplant them, keeping in mind their slow but inevitable spread. Or propagate new plants from divisions or cuttings.

You may want to site wormwood away from other plants, especially expensive specimens. Absinthin, one of the compounds that gives the herb its bitter taste, is toxic to some other plants, stunting them or killing them outright.

Cultivars and related plants

A popular cultivar is 'Lambrook Silver', whose foliage is both more gray-green and more deeply divided. It is less hardy than the species, however, thriving in Zones 5 to 9. For information about other artemisias, see the entries for southernwood, sweet Annie, and tarragon.

Lore and usage

Wormwood is sometimes called absinthe. It was the primary ingredient in the addictive liqueur by that name that became notorious in 19th-century France. Immortalized in a painting by Edgar Degas, it was banned in 1915 after being linked to convulsions, madness, and death. Drinking absinthe reputedly caused the deaths of both painter Toulouse-Lautrec and the poet Verlaine.

Also an ingredient in vermouth, wormwood was called "wermuth" — ironically, "preserver of the mind" — because it was thought to stimulate the brain. Absinthium, meaning "without sweetness," was a more appropriate name for this bitter herb. Its strong scent made it popular as a strewing herb and insect repellent, and it sometimes was used a substitute for hops in beer making.

Wormwood contains large amounts of thujone (also found in sage and tansy), which may work in the brain in the same manner as THC, the active substance in marijuana. Use it only externally, in a compress to relieve pain and kill germs. It contains antiseptics and also seems to act as an anesthetic and anti-inflammatory. The camphorous scent may help drive moths from your closet.

Yarrow (Achillea millefolium)

A perennial in the daisy family, yarrow is native to Europe and western Asia. It grows upright to 3 feet tall and bears leaves up to 6 inches long that are so feathery they look like they belong in a hatband. The white flowers — occasionally pink — appear in 3-inch flat clusters in late summer.

How to grow

How to control may be a better question than how to grow. Yarrow has naturalized throughout North America — in old farm fields and along roadsides — and it may romp all over your garden if not there already. Impressively drought tolerant and hardy in Zones 3 to 9, yarrow will be happy and healthy if it has sun and enough soil in which to sink its roots. Seeds germinate quickly, or you can begin with divisions or purchased plants.

To keep the flowers coming, deadhead your plants; and if you really need more yarrow, divide. Dividing, which is the only way to propagate yarrow cultivars, will also make your plants more vigorous.

Cultivars and related plants

There's a whole world of yarrows beyond the somewhat muddy white flower color of the species. Better yet, many cultivars are also less invasive than the species. Possibilities include the pink-to-cherry 'Cerise Queen', bigger and whiter 'White Beauty', reddish-orange 'Paprika', and mixes such as 'Summer

Pastel Beauty'. You can also find lavender, red, cream, rose, salmon, and purple cultivars.

Popular evergreen yarrows that form clumps instead of mats (so they tend to be less invasive) are the huge fernleaf yarrow (*Achillea filipendula* 'Cloth of Gold'), 5 feet tall with golden yellow flowers, and *A.* 'Moonshine', 2 feet tall with pale yellow flowers. Most cultivars are hardy in Zones 3 to 8.

Woolly yarrow *(A. tomentosa)* has fuzzy leaves; try the bright yellow-flowering dwarf cultivar 'Aurea'. Avid cooks might want to experiment with mace yarrow *(A. ageratum),* which grows only 6 or 8 inches tall. It has silvery leaves that smell like the spice called mace, which comes from the membrane of nutmeg seeds. Both of these yarrows are hardy in Zones 3 to 9.

For cut flowers you want sneezewort *(A. ptarmica),* once used for headaches and toothaches, as well as for sneezes. Its popular cultivar 'The Pearl', grown for its double white flowers, is hardy in Zones 3 to 10.

Lore and usage

Names such as devil's nettle, devil's plaything, and bad man's plaything (which sounds like the name of an X-rated movie) might scare anyone away from this herb, which was favored for incantations in days of yore. But yarrow was actually more famous as an herbal bandage, earning it the sobriquets soldier's woundwort, knight's milfoil, and carpenter's weed (which you understand if your do-it-yourself skills are as lacking as ours).

The most famous story about yarrow holds that Achilles used it to treat the wounds of his soldiers in the Trojan War. (Apparently, it was no good for his famously flawed heel.) Popular for stopping nosebleeds, it was also used to trigger nosebleeds as a means of relieving headache pressure. If a young maiden's nose bled when she stuffed yarrow in her nostril, it meant she was beloved (at least until her sweetie caught a glimpse of this behavior). Seems much more seemly to slip yarrow under your pillow (another tradition) for a vision of your dreamboat.

Modern researchers can't decide if Achilles was right. The chemistry of yarrow plants varies immensely. But some scientific evidence that the herb contains blood-clotting and anti-inflammatory compounds — plus anecdotal accounts from friends— would prompt us to try a yarrow poultice if we had an accident in the garden.

Index

• M •